THE
PENDLE WITCH
FOURTH CENTENARY
HANDBOOK

HISTORY AND ARCHAEOLOGY
FACT AND FICTION

1612 – 2012

JOHN A CLAYTON

ISBN 978-0-9553821-9-2

Cover design by Barrowford Press
www.barrowfordpress.co.uk

Printed and bound in Great Britain by 4edge Ltd, Hockley, Essex.

FOR SYLVIA

CONTENTS

THE FOREST OF PENDLE:

LOCATION AND AREA REFERRED TO

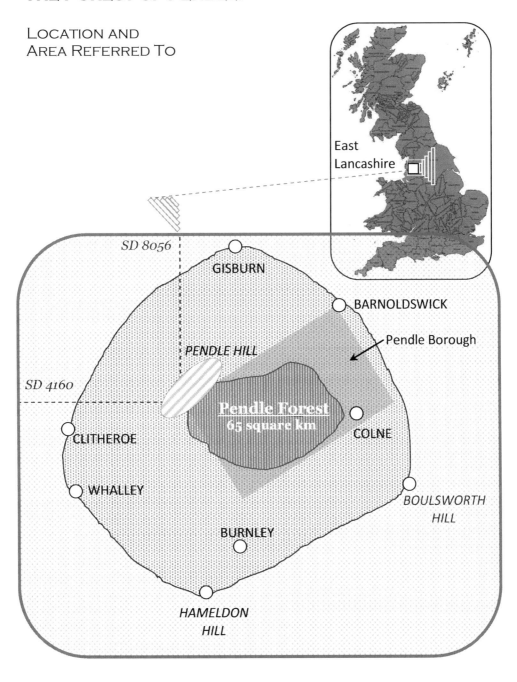

OTHER TITLES BY THE SAME AUTHOR

Higher Barrowford
ISBN 978-0-9553821-8-5 2009

Central Barrowford
ISBN 978-0-9553821-7-8 2009

Lower Barrowford
ISBN 978-0-9553821-5-4 2009

Admergill with Blacko and Brogden
The History of an Ancient Pennine Estate
ISBN 978-0-9553821-6-1 2009

Cotton and Cold Blood*
The True Story of a Victorian Barrowford Murder
ISBN 978-0-9553821-4-7 2008

The Lancashire Witch Conspiracy (1ST and 2nd editions)*
A History of Pendle Forest and the
Lancashire Witch Trials
ISBN 978-0-9553821-2-3 2007

Rolling Out the Days (editor)
From a Barrowford childhood to wartime Burma
ISBN 978-0-9553821-3-0 2007

Valley of the Drawn Sword*
An Early History of Burnley, Pendle and West Craven
ISBN 978-0-9553821-0-9 2006

The Other Pendle Witches*
The Pendle Witch Trials of 1634
ISBN 978-0-9570043-2-0 2012

Annals and Stories of Barrowford*
(Republication of Blakey, J. 1929)
ISBN 978-0-9570043-1-3 2012

* Also available on Kindle© format

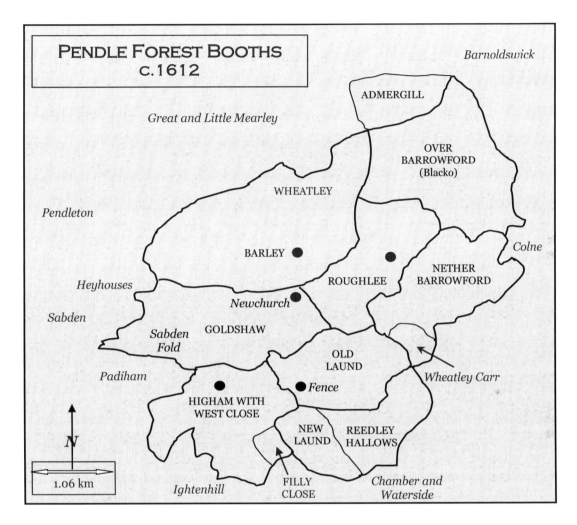

The forest booths were areas that once formed part of the cattle-breeding vaccaries - the principal agricultural system of the post-Norman Forest (or Chase) of Pendle.

From the early sixteenth century the inhabitants of Goldshaw, Barley, Wheatley, Roughlee and Old Laund became parishioners of St. Mary's in Newchurch-in-Pendle. However, Over and Nether Barrowford were within the Colne parish of St. Bartholomew's while the southern forest areas of Reedley Hallows, Filly Close, New Laund and Wheatley Carr were classed as extra-parochial - this meant that the inhabitants remained within the old chapelry of Clitheroe and were required to marry there.

PREFACE

It is now four years since the publication of the first and second editions of *The Lancashire Witch Conspiracy*. [1] It had not been intended to update the book at this time but circumstances have conspired to lead into new research on the subject. Over the period November 2010 to May 2011 I was conscripted into acting as advisor/researcher to a new BBC television production (*The Pendle Witch Child*) relating to the Pendle Forest 1612 witch trials and, during this period, new evidence came to light.

With this in mind there was the consideration as to whether it would be better to publish a third edition of the *Lancashire Witch Conspiracy* or to start afresh with a new approach. It has to be said that the large amount of information contained within the *LWC* does not make for light reading; rather, the content was designed to take the form of a reference book.

It seems prudent, then, to leave the *LWC* to stand on its own and to publish this new book in a format that (hopefully) the more casual reader will find easily digestible. The earlier book should prove valuable as a cross-reference not only with this present publication but with other texts available on the subject (see Bibliography).

The misconception proffered by some is that the evening skies over Pendle are filled with the swooping, cackling and screeching of black-clad witches on broomsticks with their attendant black cats and pointed hats. This portrayal of the witches stems from the writings of Medieval historians and Early Modern social observers (Shakespeare included) whose opinions, over time, transmuted into the archetypal Victorian romantic version of the witch that we see today. The truth, of course, is far more fascinating than this and will reward those who care to look deeper into the lives of our forebears.

Image of the fictional witch taken from an early nineteenth century print-block

Research is the enemy of half-truth and assumption and it is through a study of the available records that we are able to at least form an educated opinion on the traditions that we have before us. Any researcher with an eye to the events of the Pendle witch trials has but a single starting point and that is the invaluable record, *The Wonderful Discoverie of Witches in the Countie of Lancashire*, left to us by Thomas Potts.[2] Potts was clerk to the court at Lancaster when the Pendle witches were tried and it is his subsequent account of the trials, published in 1613, that supply us with the basis of the witch story - in fact, without Potts' account there would probably be no witch story, neither would we see a broomstick-bound hag portrayed on the side of local buses or flying across the sign of the local inn.

It is fair to say that Potts' account is that rare weapon within the historian's armoury - a contemporary account of the common man and woman. There is the consideration that Potts wrote the account for a specific purpose of impressing his masters and gain promotion within the judicial system but, that said, he provides us with a stepping-stone from which we can move on to other invaluable local records.

Cross-reference between such resources as local court records, land ownership deeds, hearth tax, communicant and poor relief lists puts meat on the bones of the characters within Potts' *Discoverie* and allows for a wider picture to be built up. It also provides evidence that corroborates much of the information relating to the people who were involved in the trials. It is only by comparison with contemporary events elsewhere that we can form as clear a picture as possible.

Many of the local historians who have taken an interest in the witches have gone on to employ available resources to formulate valuable insights into the lives of our predecessors; we now know far more about the economy, agriculture, disease, population, politics and religion of the people who created the Pendle Forest that we know and love.

In Potts' work we have a rare and valuable record that, if treated with an awareness of the pro-authority bias therein, provides priceless facts and clues for the local historian. We hear the voices of the poor and it would be to the great detriment of our local culture if we were to ignore it.

The bones of the 1612 witch trials story, then, can be put forward with a reasonable degree of accuracy. What is more difficult to get to grips with is the simple question - why were the authorities at the time so ready to accuse a number of Forest people of witchcraft and why were they so keen to see them wiped from the face of the earth - what brought things to a head in 1612? If we can go some way to answering these questions then we will better understand one of the most notorious events of its type within world history - events that happened on our own doorstep.

We will never change the popular perception of the historical witch in its present archetypal form, even though this is the product of pure fiction. Perhaps the best that we can hope for is that people absorb the real facts of the story as far as we know them. The witches bring valuable tourist revenue to the area and in turn this leads to employment for local people.

Knaresborough has its Old Mother Shipton and Nottingham has Robin Hood. Why should we not capitalise on our own world-famous legend? To my mind the answer is that we should make the most of a fascinating story that played out upon the stage of our villages, hills and dales - with the caveat that the fictional context of tradition is tempered as far as possible by the facts.

It is the local historian's job to sweep aside the hyperbole and theatrical diabolism attached to the story and to ensure, as far as possible, that the facts speak for themselves. Owing to a lack of clear description within Potts' text, when it comes to the actual landscape occupied by the characters we are on sandy ground. Where, for instance, was Malkin Tower, or the Chattox residence at West Close?

We can now, perhaps, get closer to answering these questions than at any other time. Through an intimate knowledge of the district relating to the witch story, along with the employment of landscape archaeology and an interpretation of known facts, it is hoped to furnish within the following text both answers and strong possibilities. Further to this, it is central to the true story that the events of 1612 cannot be taken in isolation. As in all things, history colours the present and the cast of characters were playing out roles that had been written for them many years before. Even from the Roman period there are parallels within the Christian practises of the icon, the religious relic and the worship of saints. By the time these had been filtered through the Anglo Saxon culture, and the heavy hand of the post-Norman church, the scene was set for a garbled version of historical religious intent to be played out on the stage of Pendle Forest.

We will see that a number of factors affected the situation; poor crop yields meant high food prices and population increase resulted in social pressures. The supply of land became an issue and, when coupled with the previous fifty years of religious upheaval, attitudes to the landless poor changed for the worse. The atmosphere of political mistrust and religious persecution formed a backdrop to the trials within which certain individuals were to play a pivotal role - on both sides of the judicial divide.

The aim of the following text is to provide a picture of the witch story that is as accurate and up to date as possible. New suggestions are made as to the location of the elusive Malkin Tower and the Chattox dwelling and, after four hundred years of legend and half-truth, it is hoped that we are now beginning to approach the truth.

THE WITCH STORY ~ INTRODUCTION

The story of the 1612 Pendle witch trials is a complex tale of social tensions, interfamilial accusation and fantastic statement; this being the case, it will be useful to include here a condensed account of the events. In 1861 Chapman and Hall published *Witch Stories*, an account of the Pendle witches written by E. Lynn Linton. Here the author sums up the series of events of 1612:

THE WITCHES OF PENDLE

In Pendle Forest, a wild tract of land on the borders of Yorkshire, lived an old woman about the age of fourscore, who had been a witch for many years, and had brought up her own children, and instructed her grandchildren, to be witches. *"She was a generall agent for the Deuill in all these partes;"* her name was Elizabeth Southernes, usually called Mother Demdike; the date of her arraignment 1612. She was the first tried of this celebrated "coven," twenty of whom stood before Sir James Altham and Sir Edward Bromley, charged with all the crimes lying in sorcery, magic, and witchcraft.

Old Mother Demdike died in prison before her trial, but on her being taken before the magistrate who convicted them all, Roger Nowell, Esq., she made such a confession as effectually insured her due share of execration, and hedged in the consciences of all who had assailed her from any possible pangs of self-reproach or doubt.

About twenty years ago, she said, she was returning home from begging, when, near a stone pit in Newchurch-in-Pendle, she met a spirit or devil in the shape of a boy, with one half of his coat brown and the other half black, who said to her, if she would give him her soul, she should have all that she might desire. After a little further talk, during which he told her that his name was Tibb, he vanished away. For five or six years Mother Demdike never asked any kind of help or harm of Tibb, who always came to her at *"daylight gate"* (twilight); but one Sabbath morning, she having her little child on her knee, and being in a light slumber, Tibb came to her in the likeness of a brown dog, and forced himself on her knee, trying to get blood from under her left arm. Mother Demdike awoke sore troubled and amazed, and strove to say, *"Jesus, save my child,"* but could not, neither could she say, *"Jesus, save myself."* In a short time the brown dog vanished away, and she was *"almost starke madde for the space of eight weekes."*

She and Tibb had never done much harm, she said; not even to Richard Baldwin, of Wheathead, for all that he had put them off his land, and taken her daughter's day's work at his mill without fee or reward, and when she, led by her grandchild Alison (for she was quite blind), went to ask for pay, gave them only

11

hard words and insolence for their pains, saying, *"Get off my ground, witches and whores - I will burn the one, and hang the other,"* and bidding them begone. She confessed though, after a little pressing, that at that moment Tibb called out to her, *"Revenge thee of him!"* to whom she answered, *"Revenge thou either of him or his!"* on which he vanished away, and she saw him no more. She would not say what was the vengeance done, or if any. But if she was silent, and not prone to confession, there were others, and those of her own blood, not so reticent.

Elizabeth Device her daughter, and Alison and James and Jennet Device, her grandchildren, testified against her and each other in a wonderful manner, and filled up all the blanks in the most masterly and graphic style. Alison said that her grandmother had seduced her to the service of the devil, by giving her a great black dog as her imp or spirit, with which dog she had lamed one John Lawe, a petty chapman (or pedlar), as he was going through Colne Field with his pack at his back. Alison wanted to buy pins of him, but John Lawe refused to loosen his pack or sell them to her; so Alison in a rage called for her black dog, to see if revenge could not do what fair words had failed in. When the black dog came he said, *"What wouldst thou have me to do with yonder man?"* To whom she answered, *"What canst thou do at him?"* and the dog answered again, *"I can lame him."* *"Lame him,"* says Alison Device; and before the pedlar went forty yards he fell lame.

When questioned, he, on his side, said, that as he was going through Colne Field he met a big black dog with very fearful fiery eyes, great teeth, and a terrible countenance, which looked at him steadily then passed away; and immediately after he was bewitched into lameness and deformity. And this took place after having met Alison Device and refused to sell her any pins. Then Alison fell to weeping and praying, beseeching God and that worshipful company to pardon her sins. She said further that her grandmother had bewitched John Nutter's cow to death at Bull Hole in Newchurch, and Richard Baldwin's daughter on account of the quarrel before reported, saying that she would pray for Baldwin, *"both still and loud,"* and that she was always after some matter of devilry and enchantment, if not for the bad of others then for the good of herself.

Alison once got a piggin full of blue milk by begging, and when she came to look into it, she found a quarter of a pound of butter there, which was not there before, and which she verily believed old Mother Demdike had procured by her enchantments. Then Alison turned against the rival Hecate, Anne Whittle, *alias* Chattox, between whom and her family raged a deadly feud with Mother Demdike and her family; accusing her of having bewitched her father, John Device, to death, because he had neglected to pay her the yearly tax of an aghendole (eight pounds) of oatmeal, which he had covenanted to give her on consideration that she would not harm him. For they had been robbed, these poor people, of a quarter of a peck of cut oatmeal and linens worth some twenty shillings, and they had found a coif and band belonging to them on Anne Whittle's daughter; so John

Device was afraid that old Chattox would do them some grievous injury by her sorceries if they cried out about it, therefore made that covenant for the aghendole of meal, the non-payment of which for one year set Chattox free from her side of the bargain and cost John's life.

She said, too, that Chattox had bewitched sundry persons and cattle, killing John Nutter's cow because he, John Nutter, had kicked over her canfull of milk, misliking her devilish way of placing two sticks across it; and slaying Anne Nutter because she laughed and mocked at her; slaying John Moor's child, of Higham, too by a picture of clay—with other misdeeds to be hereafter verified and substantiated. So Alison Device was hanged, weeping bitterly, and very penitent.

James Device, her brother, testified to meeting a brown dog coming from his grandmother's house at Malkin Tower about a month ago, and to hearing a noise as of a number of children shrieking and crying, *"near daylight gate."* Another time he heard a foul yelling as of a multitude of cats, and soon after this there came into his bed chamber a thing like a cat or a hare, and coloured black, which lay heavily on him for about an hour. He said that his sister Alison had bewitched Bulcock's child, and that old Mother Chattox had dug up three skulls, and taken out eight teeth, four of which she kept for herself and gave four to Mother Demdike; and that Demdike had made a picture of clay of Anne Nutter, of Newchurch, and had burned it, by which the said Anne had been bewitched to death.

Also she had bewitched to death one Henry Mitton, of Roughlee, because he would not give her a penny; with other iniquities of the same sort. He said that his mother, Elizabeth Device, had a spirit like a brown dog called Ball, and that they all met at Malking Tower; all the witches of Pendle—and they were not a few— going out in their own shapes, and finding foals of different colours ready for their riding when they got outside. He then confessed, for his own part, that his grandmother Demdike told him not to eat the communion bread one day when he went to church, but to give it to the first thing he met on the road on his way homewards. He did not obey her, but ate the bread as a good Christian should; and on the way he met with a thing like a hare which asked him for the bread; but he said he had not got it; whereupon the hare got very angry and threatened to tear him in pieces, but James *"sained"* (crossed) himself, and the devil vanished.

This, repeated in various forms, was about the pith of what James Device confessed, his confession not including any remarkable betrayal of himself, or admission of any practical and positive evil. His young sister Jennet, a little lassie of nine, supplied the deficiencies. She had evidently been suborned and gave evidence enough to have hanged half Lancashire. She said that James had sold himself to the devil, and that his spirit was a black dog called Dandy, by whom he had bewitched many people to death; and then she said that she had seen the witches' meetings, but had taken no part in them; and that on Good Friday, at

Malkin Tower, they had all dined off a roasted wether (sheep) which James had stolen from Swyers, of Barley; and that John Bulcock, of Mosse End, in Newchurch, turned the spit. She said that her mother Elizabeth had taught her two prayers, the one to get drink and the other to cure the bewitched. The one to get drink was a very short one, simply—*"Crucifixus, hoc signum vitam eternam, Amen;"* but this would bring good drink into the house in a very strange manner.

The other, the prayer to cure the bewitched, was longer:—

Vpon Good Friday, I will fast while I may,
Vntill I heare them knell,
Our Lord's owne Bell, Lord in his messe
With his twelve Apostles good,

What hath he in his hand?
Ligh in Leath wand:
What hath he in his other hand?
Heaven's doore key.
Open, open, Heaven doore keyes,
Steck, steck, hell doore.
Let Crizum child
Go to it Mother mild.

What is yonder that casts a light so farrandly?
Mine owne deare Sone that's nail'd to the Tree,
He is nail'd sore by the heart and hand,
And holy harne Panne.

Well is that man
That Fryday spell can,
His Childe to learne
A Crosse of Blewe, and another of Red,
As good Lord was to the Roode.

Gabriel laid him downe to sleepe
Vpon the grounde of holy weepe;
Good Lord came walking by,
Sleep'st thou, wak'st thou, Gabriel?

No, Lord, I am sted with stick and stake,
That I can neither sleepe nor wake:
Rise up, Gabriel, and goe with me,
The stick nor the stake shall never deere thee,
Sweete Jesus our Lorde. Amen.

On such conclusive testimony as this, and for such fearful crimes, James Device was condemned *"as dangerous and malicious a witch as ever lived in these parts of Lancashire, of his time, and spotted with as much Innocent bloud as euer any witch of his yeares."* Poor lad!

O Barbarous and inhumane Monster, beyond example; so farre from sensible vnderstanding of thy owne miserie as to bring thy owne naturall children into mischiefe and bondage, and thyselfe to be a witnesse vpone the gallowes, to see thy owne children, by thy deuillish instructions, hatcht vp in villanie and witchcraft, to suffer with thee, euen in the beginning of their time, a shamefull and untimely Death!

These are the words which Thomas Potts addresses to Elizabeth Device, widow of John the bewitched, daughter to old Demdike the *"rankest hag that ever troubled daylight,"* and mother of Alison and James the confessing witches; mother, also, of young Jennet of nine, their accuser and hers, by whose testimony she was mainly condemned. Elizabeth was charged with having bewitched sundry people to death, by means and aid of her spirit, the brown dog Ball, spoken of by James; also she had gone to the Sabbath held at Malking Tower, where they had assembled to consult how they could get old Mother Demdike, their leader, out of prison, by killing her gaoler and blowing up the castle, and where they had beef and bacon and roasted mutton—the mutton that same wether of Christopher Swyers' of Barley, which James had stolen and killed; with other things as damnable and insignificant. So Elizabeth Device, *"this odious witch, who was branded with a preposterous marke in Nature even from her Birth, which was her left Eye standing lower than the other, the one looking down the other looking up,"* was condemned to die because she was poor and ugly, and had a little lying jade for a daughter, who made up fine stories for the gentlefolks.

Anne Whittle, *alias* Chattox, of West Close, was next in influence, power, and age to Mother Demdike, and she began her confession by saying that old Demdike had originally seduced her by giving her the devil in the shape and proportion of a man, who got her, body and soul, and sucked on her left ribs, and was called Fancie. Afterwards she had another spirit like a spotted bitch, called Tibbe, who gave them all to eat and to drink, and said they should have gold and silver as much as they wanted. But they never got the gold and silver at all, and what they ate and drank did not satisfy them.

This Anne Whittle, alias Chattox, was a very old withered, spent, decrepid creature, her Sight almost gone; A dangerous Witch of very long continuance; always opposite to old Demdike; For whom the one fauoured the other hated deadly: and how they curse and accuse one another in their Examinations may appear. In her Witchcraft always more ready to doe mischiefe to men's goods than themselves; Her lippes ever chattering and talking; but no man knew what. She lived in the Forrest of Pendle amongst this wicked Company of dangerous

Witches. Yet in her Examination and Confession she dealt always very plainely and truely; for vpon a speciall occasion, being oftentimes examined in open Court, she was neuer found to vary, but always to agree in one and the selfe same thing. I place her in order next to that wicked Firebrand of mischiefe, old Demdike, because from these two sprung all the rest in order; and even the Children and Friendes of these two notorious Witches.

Nothing special or very graphic was elicited about old Chattox. She had certainly bewitched to death sundry of the neighbourhood, lately deceased; but then they all did that; and her devil, Fancie, came to her in various shapes— sometimes like a bear, gaping as though he would worry her, which was not a pleasant manner of fulfilling his contract—but generally as a man, in whom she took great delight. She confessed to a charm for blessing forespoken drink; which she had chanted for John Moore's wife, she said, whose beer had been spoilt by Mother Demdike or some of her crew:—

Three Biters hast thou bitten,
The Hart, ill Eye, ill Tonge;
Three Bitter shall be thy boote,
Father, Sonne, and Holy Ghost,
a God's Name

Five Paternosters, five Avies,
and a Creede,
For worship of five woundes of our Lord.

Of course there was no help or hope for old Chattox if she said such wicked things as these. The righteous justice of England must be satisfied, and Anne Whittle was hung—one of the twelve who sorrowed the sunlight in Lancaster on that bloody assize.

Her daughter, Ann Redfearne, was then taken, accused of making pictures (dolls) of clay and other maleficent arts; and she, too, was hanged; and then well-born, well-bred, but unfortunate Alice Nutter—a gentlewoman of fortune living at Rough Lee, whose relatives were anxious for her death that they might come into some property—Alice Nutter, whom one would have thought far removed from any such possibility, was accused by young Jennet of complicity and companionship, and put upon her trial with but a faint chance of escape behind her. For Elizabeth Device swore that she had joined with her and old Demdike in bewitching the man Mitton, because of that twopence so fatally refused; and young Jennet swore that she was one of the party who went on many-coloured foals to the great witch meeting at Malking Tower; and so poor Alice Nutter, of Rough Lee, the well-born, well-bred gentlewoman, was hanged with the rest of that ragged crew; and her relations stood in her place, quite satisfied with their dexterity.

Then there was Katherine Hewitt, *alias* Mouldheels, accused by James Device, who seemed to think that if he had to be hanged for nothing he would be hanged in brave company, and, by sharing with as many as could be found, lessen the obloquy he could not escape; and John Bulcock, who turned the spit, and Jane his mother, for the same crimes and on the same testimony; for the added crime, too, of helping in the bewitching of Mistress Dean, of Newfield Edge, about which nefarious deed other hands were also busy; and Margaret Pearson, delated by Chattox as entertaining a man spirit cloven-footed, with whom she went by a loophole into Dodgson's stable in Padiham, and sat all night on his mare until it died.

She was also accused by Jennet Booth, of Padiham, who went into her house and begged some milk for her child; Margaret good-naturedly gave her some, and boiled it in a pan, but all her reward was that Jennet accused her of witchcraft, for there was, said she, a toad at the bottom of the pan when the milk was boiled, which Margaret took up with a pair of tongs and carried out of the house. Of course the toad was an imp, and Jennet Booth was quite right to repay an act of neighbourly generosity by accusation and slander. Margaret got off with standing in the pillory in open market, at four market towns on four market days, bearing a paper on her head setting forth her offence written in great letters, about which there could be no mistake; after which she was to confess, and afterwards be taken to prison, where she was to lie for a year, and then be only released when good and responsible sureties would come forward to answer for her good behaviour.

And there was Isabel Roby, of St. Helens, who bewitched Peter Chadwick for jilting her, and in the spirit pinched and buffeted Jane Williams, so that she fell sick with the impression of a thumb and four fingers on her thigh; and Jennet Preston, of Gisburn, who had attended the Good Friday meeting and who was afterwards hung at York for the murder of Thomas Lister of Westby Hall—for Master Thomas in his last illness had been for ever crying out that Jennet Preston was *"lying heavy upon him"*, and when she was brought to see the body it gushed out fresh blood when she touched it, which settled all doubts, if there had been any. So the famous trial of the Pendle Witches came to an end; and of the twenty who were accused twelve were hanged while the rest escaped only for the present, many of them meeting with their doom a few years afterwards.

———————

Let us press on, then, to Part One with a look at the long period within which events began to move toward the major Pendle Forest witch trials of 1612. This is followed in Part Two with the latest evidence relating to the 1612 story: Part Three will cover the homes and places frequented by Demdike and Chattox.

PART ONE

SETTING THE SCENE

Beneath the collective of so-called *Lancashire* Witches arraigned at Lancaster Castle in August 1612 were a number of people from the Pendle, Colne and Padiham districts of East Lancashire and it is with these unfortunates, the *Pendle* witches, that we are concerned. Before meeting the cast of the main story it will serve us well to look at the long build-up of events through the fifteenth and sixteenth centuries that were to conspire in a vortex of suspicion and social upheaval that would eventually reach its peak in the first half of the seventeenth century.

Carried out by religious zealots, and members of the minor gentry in search of bettering their social and political standing, the witch-hunts of our Early Modern past were protracted and often brutal. Little wonder, then, that the Pendle witches (who formed the great majority of those accused in the Lancashire Witch Trials) still hold a strong influence over the Pendle Forest psyche. The local historian can carry out very little research without bumping up against the legend of the witches.

The story of the Pendle witches has been told on countless occasions, with a varying degree of accuracy, but Frank Hird (*Lancashire Stories - 1911)* described the nub of the legend:

In the early part of the seventeenth century the inhabitants of the Forest of Pendle, with few exceptions, must have been miserably poor and ignorant, since they had little communication with the outside world. Superstition (and folk medicine) exist in the district to this day. When James I was on the throne it held absolute domination over the simple minds of the inhabitants. And no belief was stronger than that in witchcraft. Upon this belief two old women, called Elizabeth Southern and Anne Whittle, but better known in the chronicles of witchcraft as Old Demdike and Old Chattox, had played for many years with great success. Both these women were old, and both pretended to possess supernatural powers, and were therefore bitterly opposed to one another. Each woman had her following amongst the credulous peasantry, and in their anxiety to outvie one another each represented herself as more death-dealing, destructive and powerful than her neighbour, and the one who could show the most damage done to man or beast (whether real or not was quite immaterial) was more likely to get a larger custom for her charms and philtres, and horrible incantations.

The author was correct in that *folk medicine exists in the district to this day* (1911). In fact the same generic treatments for both human and animal ailments were being used by doctors and veterinary surgeons right up to the Second World War. In many cases the vet would feel that convincing his customers of the efficacy of the treatment of their livestock was as important as the outcome of the treatment itself. In cases where the treatment or prevention of infection was paramount, mixtures containing things such as turpentine, brimstone and iodine would be applied simultaneously to a wound and the resultant outpouring of thick purple smoke would convince the farmer that his animal was receiving the best possible treatment.

What was the difference, then, between this 'scientific' approach and the pungent concoctions of herbs, natural chemicals and antibiotic salves applied to animal wounds by the healers/wise people/sooth sayers/conjurers/witches?

There is little doubt, where contemporary records of rural witchcraft are concerned, that the ordinary members of society held a strong belief in the powers of the supernatural. To a certain extent this tenet ruled the lives of the farmer, the weaver, the dairymaid and the labourer and it is fair to say that it held more relevance to their daily lives than did the official church.

Fair enough, the church blessed new fields in order to engender fertility, the priest and vicar blessed the harvest crops, saw to the spiritual needs of the newborn and the dead and performed the ritual of marriage. They also acted as unofficial greaves within society - where disputes flared up they were expected to sooth the troubled waters. The church incumbents acted as valuable go-betweens when the gentry had need to communicate with the commoners and they were often called upon in times of crisis to organise the local muster of militia.

The village church bells provided a modicum of solace to the tired, cold and mud-covered ploughman toiling on his marginal acre somewhere on the outer town fields. The tolling bells marked Saint's days, national celebrations and warnings. Sanctus and Angelus bells were constant reminders to the parishioners scattered far and wide that they were expected to unify with their neighbours in worship.
However, the church did not fulfil all the needs of the community. During the disastrous national famines and plagues of the fourteenth century the people were informed by their priests that the disease and crop failures were a visitation from God - sent to punish their sins. However, the man and woman in the street became all too aware that the clergy were as likely to be struck down by the Black Death as were the shepherd and the weaver.

To the modern mindset it is unthinkable that whole families of the poorer class could be accused of manifold diabolical murders and be snatched from their humble dwellings without a shred of hard evidence. However, seventeenth century culture did not conform to that of the modern era and so we see that rambling disarticulated testimony of old women and children sufficed for them to be thrown into the dungeons of the Well Tower at Lancaster Castle. From here there was to be the single outcome of mass execution. The following is an outline of the salient events within the Pendle witch story:

CALENDAR OF EVENTS - FROM PENDLE TO PURGATORY

 18TH MARCH 1612

Malkin Tower: *"Reight Gran me old lass - I'll be off to t'badlands o' Trowdin fer a bit o' beggin'- I'll si'thee when I si'thee."*

. . . . Demdike's granddaughter, Alison Device, sets off from Malkin Tower on a begging spree to Trawden Forest and in so doing it can be said that she set in motion a train of events that would reverberate through the forest for centuries to come.

Alison meets John Lawe in Colne Field Lane and asks him for a few pins. Lawe, described as a 'pedlar' would later say that he refused to open his pack but his son, Abraham, contradicts this by stating that his father actually gave Alison the pins.

Whatever the case may be the official line is that John Lawe took the huff at being pestered and cursed by Alison and, suffering what appears to have been a stroke, collapsed in Colne Field. He was taken into what was probably the Greyhound Inn in Market Street (demolished around 1790) where Alison, obviously shaken at the events, looked in on him before continuing on her way.

 21ST MARCH

Halifax: Abraham Lawe receives a letter, possibly from Sir Thomas Gerard of Ashton, informing him of his father's condition.

 29TH MARCH

Abraham Lawe goes to Colne and is informed by the local people that his father had been the victim of Alison Device who, being the granddaughter of the infamous witch, Old Demdike, must have used witchcraft to strike him down.

Lawe goes to Malkin Tower and, finding Alison, takes her to Colne to confront her with his sick father – Alison is contrite and confesses.

30TH MARCH

Magistrate Roger Nowell, of Read Hall, examines both Alison Device and Abraham Lawe at Read. After she admits to having a familiar, in the shape of a black dog, Nowell decides that there is sufficient evidence to hold Alison.

 2ND APRIL

Demdike and Chattox are examined at Ashlar House in Fence by Nowell. Also present are John Nutter, Margaret Crook (née Nutter) and James Robinson. Accusations of witchcraft fly thick and fast and more local people are brought into the fray.

 4TH APRIL

Anne Whittle (Old Chattox), Demdike, Anne Redfearn and Alison Device are packed off to the Well Tower at Lancaster Castle to await trial in the coming August.

 6TH APRIL

Jennet Preston is tried at York Assizes after being accused by Thomas Lister (of Westby Hall, Gisburn) of killing a child of the Dodgeson family in the Gisburn area. She is acquitted.

 10TH APRIL

Good Friday: Roger Nowell hears from his constable, Henry Hargreaves, that some twenty witches held a 'diabolical' meeting at Malkin Tower.

 27TH APRIL

Roger Nowell and his fellow Justice, Nicholas Bannister of Altham, are again at Ashlar House, this time to examine the Device family of Elizabeth, James and Jennet. Another bout of apparent confession, recrimination and accusation breaks out – James and Jennet are only too happy to chat with the nice magistrates about their party at Malkin.

The fate of many of those they insist were in attendance at the Good Friday gathering is now sealed.

 MAY

Elizabeth Southern dies in the dungeon of the Well Tower at Lancaster Jail while on remand. She was, therefore, never convicted of witchcraft.

27TH JULY

Jennet Preston is again tried at York, this time on a charge of having bewitched to death Thomas Lister senior of Westby. Roger Nowell has sent the relevant witness statements relating to the Good Friday Malkin meeting to York Assizes. Jennet is said to have enlisted the help of others to kill Lister and his brother - she is found guilty and sentenced to death by the same judges who would later try the Pendle accused.

 18TH AUGUST

Elizabeth and James Device, along with Anne Whittle, are found guilty at the Lancaster Assizes. Anne Whittle's daughter, Anne Redfearn, is found not guilty of murdering Robert Nutter of Greenhead.

 19TH AUGUST

Anne Redfearn is tried for the murder of Christopher Nutter of Greenhead and this time is found guilty. Alison Device, Margaret Pearson, John and Jane Bulcock, Isabell Roby, Alice Nutter and Katherine Hewitt are all found guilty.

 20TH AUGUST

The condemned are executed at a public hanging on Gallows Hill in Lancaster.

- ❖ **Anne Whittle**: (Old Chattox) of West Close in Pendle

- ❖ **Ann Redfearn**: of West Close: daughter of Anne Whittle

Elizabeth Southern: (Old Demdike) of Malkin Tower - died in prison in May before the August hearing

- ❖ **Elizabeth Device**: of Malkin Tower: daughter of Elizabeth Southern

- ❖ **James Device**: of Malkin Tower: son of Elizabeth Device

- ❖ **Alizon Device**: of Malkin Tower: daughter of Elizabeth Device

- ❖ **Alice Nutter**: of Damhead, Roughlee

- ❖ **Katherine Hewitt**: wife of John Hewitt, a clothier of Colne

- ❖ **Jane Bulcock**: of Moss End Farm

- ❖ **John Bulcock**: of Moss End Farm (son of Jane Bulcock)

- ❖ **Isobel Robey**: of Windle, St. Helens

PROTECTIVE CHARMS

At the time of the Black Death (1348-1350) the skills of the village healers were called upon as never before to bring comfort to the dying and to take measures to protect those not yet infected. Those who survived occupied a changed society where the power of the church, and the iron grip long exercised by the villagers' feudal masters, was viewed in a much more realistic (if pessimistic) manner.

To the Medieval mind, the countryside was an entity of ultimate power; there were still sacred places within the landscape and hidden forces beyond the control of man could enforce a famine as savage as any Biblical disaster. Lightning and devastating floods could appear from nowhere, disease lurked around every corner and plagues of insects and blight could wipe out entire crops within hours.

From their mother's knee the country folk were immersed within a fantastic world of the supernatural and these beliefs in elements and entities (both wicked and spiritual) were enforced by a commonality of cultural belief throughout each person's lifetime.

Many landscape features, such as hollows, cloughs and crags, were home to supernatural beings. Fairies, Boggarts, Goblins, Pixies and Elves were just a few of the entities ready and willing to cause mischief (and worse) to the unwitting forest dweller. Further to this, the nights were usually as black as pitch. No distant town streetlights illuminated the darkness and even the best lantern light was all but useless to those hardy (or foolish) souls who had need to venture out after dusk.

It is difficult for us to imagine the fantasies that would play out within the imaginations of those who did travel during the night-time. The sounds emanating from the tangible blackness would have been completely different to those commonly encountered by the country person during the daytime. The wind, soft or strong, would carry the eerie ghost cries of the screech owl. Foxes, badgers, otters, stoats, wild cats and all manner of nocturnal animals would add to the melee of strange sounds while the soft whoosh of a flitting bat, inches from the face, would feel like the caress of the long-dead. The splash of a jumping fish in the mill pond, or a duck noisily taking flight from the river heralded the awakening of those who had drowned.

The cattle left out in the fields overnight were in great danger from many unseen nasties. Prior to the fifteenth century attack from wolves was an all-too-real danger and cattle were 'strangled' by these wild beasts on a regular basis. [3] Not-so-real, but still firmly believed to be the cause of many unexplained cattle deaths, was the attack of the hedgehog. This innocent little creature was thought to drink the milk from the udders of cattle, as they lay in the field, until they ran dry and died. Consequently the hedgehog was considered a dangerous pest with a bounty of a few coppers paid for each dead specimen handed in to the local constable.

The night air became an entity not to be ingested if it could possibly be avoided - dangerous miasmas and vapours swirled unseen but deadly. The moon would provide welcome light under certain weather conditions and at particular stages of the lunar month - however, even this was dangerous as moonlight was considered to be the cause of many cases of madness and melancholy. Moonlight also served to illuminate the diabolical witch gatherings that took place in secret corners of the Forest - gatherings that God-fearing people should never have to witness!

So, it is little wonder that the night was considered to have been the realm of witches, thieves and murderers; decent people did not venture out if they could help it. Given the amount of danger stalking the night-time countryside it is no surprise to find that people employed the services of the local wise person in order to combat the unseen forces. One of the most popular methods of protecting the house and its occupants, the barn and its livestock, the fields and their crops was the written 'charm.'

Ordinary people – farmers, labourers, housewives, weavers, blacksmiths and butchers – relied on the services of the local 'cunning folk' to offer protection and this was usually supplied in a form of a written spell. Each district had its own cunning person, wise person, blesser, healer, charmer, soothsayer, conjurer or prophet and these people were more than willing to supply whatever service the populace might require. These people, generally, worked in opposition to the witch and specialised in the removal of any spells and curses thought to have been cast by the latter.

During the sixteenth century travelling practitioners began to tour the villages and farms offering their quack medicines and formulaic charms in exchange for money or food. These travellers would set up their stalls at markets and fairs and were, in some respects, the forerunners of the gypsy fortune tellers who would offer their own lucky charms in the form of heather, ceramic Cornish pixies and other trinkets.

In 1680 John Brinley wrote in *A Discovery of the Impostures of Witches and Astrologers* (London 1680) that *'Ignorant and Narrow-sould'* people regularly consulted cunning people and witches and that *'these sort of abused people have as many followers as the greatest Divines.'* Brinley went on to state that the cunning folk *'do evil that good may come of it, that is use Charms, Spells and Incantations (all of which are no force without the Cooperation of the Devil) to remove Distempers, and do certain Feats in some measure useful to mankind yet of pernicious consequence to themselves.'* The author here was expressing the strongly held official view that any form of magic, white or otherwise, could only be carried out by the aid of the Devil and the practice of providing (or using) charms in any form was an act against God.

However, the prosecution of cunning folk was rare as they provided a service and they were popular. Further, those found to be employing their services were seldom punished other than by the church where they were usually required to perform some minor penance – there was little, then, to dissuade the populace from practising their beliefs.

The use of charms was far more prevalent than the small number of extant examples might suggest. The occurrence of livestock disease, human disease and ailments and the vagaries of the weather in a strictly agrarian community meant that every single person was affected in some form or another and it is little wonder that some of them had recourse to the only protection they knew of – magic. Thus we see that, dependent upon their particular purpose, holed witch stones, horse shoes, human shoes, dead cats, crosses of wood and iron, horse shoes, witch bottles and written charms were placed in the fabric of barns and cottages or hidden in fireplaces and fields.

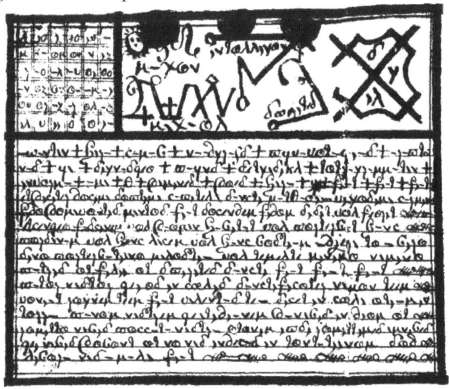

The Healey Charm

During the demolition of an old barn at Healey (Rossendale) in 1876 workmen discovered a small wooden box beneath one of the roof timbers. The box was found to contain a charm written in cipher and was almost identical to another example found at Daubers Farm in Foulridge. Deciphering of this document was reasonably easy due to the fact that an earlier example (which made a total of three identical documents) had been found in a barn roof at West Bradford near Clitheroe. This particular charm had been sent to the British Museum in 1825 for inspection by Richard Garnett, their expert in script, who gave his opinion on the contents.[4]

The Daubers Charm

The table in the top-left corner is a magic square dedicated to the sun and this is a common feature of this type of charm. Within the square are various numbers expressed by letters formed from the Greek alphabet; any six sums in this square taken in a straight line make the number III, and together these make up a total of 666, this being the number of the Biblical *'Beast'* (Rev. xiii. I8). In line with this square are the symbols of the sun and moon and under them the word *'Machen'* meaning *'strife or contention.'* Below this is a symbol consisting of a Jerusalem cross and the sign of Jupiter under which is the word *'Michael.'* In the centre is a symbol to which no meaning can be attached and above it is the word *'Intelligence.'* The other figure, on which is *'sigil,'* is the seal of the sun.

The text in the charm begins with two lines of gibberish in Greek characters and end with the word *'tetragrammaton'* and following this we find Latin script roughly translating as:

I love God, the Lord God, the Hour, Christ, let it be done, let it be done; let it be done as it is said in the xvii. Chapter of St. Matthew and at the twentieth verse. By faith ye may remove mountains. Let it be according to your faith. If there is or shall be however a bewitcher or a demon dwelling in, or in the habit of disturbing, this person, this place, or this thing, I exorcise it to depart without any disturbance, trouble or the least tumult, in the name of the Father, and of the Son, and of the Holy Ghost. The Lord's Prayer follows.

Written on the reverse of the charm are the words; *'Agla en Tetragrammaton.'* The four letters in the *'Agla'* form the initial letters of a cabalistic word meaning; *'Thou o Lord, art mighty forever.'* Tetragrammaton means *'four letters'* and represents the Hebrew word for Jehovah. Another almost identical charm was reputedly found around 1900 under a brass plate on a tombstone in a Lancashire churchyard.

Photograph courtesy of John Tattersall

The Coldweather House Charm

In 2003 Mr. J Tattersall, the owner of Coldweather House, Nelson (Borough of Pendle) discovered a document while renovating the front door to the property. The paper had been placed between two panels of the door and was folded and secured by means of an unimpressed red wax seal.

Having read *The Lancashire Witch Conspiracy,* Mr. Tattersall was kind enough to inform me of the document to see if any sense could be made of it. Fortunately there was a precedent; being aware of the other, almost identical charms, an attempt at translation could be made. We see that the types of diagram employed by the writer of the Coldweather example differ from those of the others, however, the same basic design principal still applies in that we see a magic square in the upper-left corner which is dedicated to the sun and containing numbers represented by Greek letters. In the centre is placed a six-pointed figure carrying a crucifix at each station. Again, this is a popular figure and appears in published accounts of witchcraft in the seventeenth century.

The same wording appears here as in the Healey, Daubers and West Bradford examples while to the right there is a circular jumble which appear to be letters representing numbers arranged in threes and these possibly add up to the sum of 666. The body text also appears to be identical to the daubers charm, the number of lines differs but there are an equal number of character sets. This, then, is an exorcism and charm written to a well known local formula – it is, however, by a different hand to the other extant charms from the district.

Further questions to be asked of the Coldweather document are – at what date was it written and who wrote it? To address the first question it is necessary to identify the type of material that the charm is written on. In general the writing medium within Europe to the end of the seventeenth century was vellum and this is clearly not the Coldweather document material. Although paper had been available for centuries it did not become the standard writing medium until the later eighteenth century.

Initially paper was made from pulped rags and available only in limited quantities but advances in technology during the period 1770 to 1844 meant that it became readily available. By the middle of the nineteenth century wood pulp was being used to create paper by mechanical means and this saw a massive increase in volume and standardised paper sizes. Wood paper, however, tended to be more acidic than rag paper and, unless it was chemically treated, deteriorated rapidly.
Where the Coldweather document has been torn by opening the wax seal the paper appears to have a rag pulp fabric overlain by a finer skin. The paper lacks the grain usually evident in wood pulp and the generally unfired and unfoxed condition of the parchment also indicates the lower acidity of rag as opposed to wood.

The black ink used in the document has faded to brown in places and this is strongly indicative of the iron gall inks which were commonly used through to the twentieth century. The materials used in the document, then, tell us only that we can expect it to date to a period following the building of the property and prior to the general adoption of wood pulp paper: this provides a very rough dating of 1775 to 1844.

Fortunately the Coldweather House charm carries the signature, or at least the name, of one John Robertshaw; research of the Robertshaw name shows that a John Robertshaw lived at Coldweather House. John was born at Yeomans Farm in Briercliffe, on the eastern outskirts of Burnley, in 1732 to a family who had occupied that property from the middle of the seventeenth century at least.

By the early 1760s John Robertshaw had left Briercliffe and set up home at Old House, Little Marsden, with his wife Jennet. Here they had a number of children: Ambrose born 1763, Susan born 1765, John born 1768, Robert born 1772 and possibly others. On 27th June 1776 John purchased the neighbouring property of Coldweather Farm House from Joshua Smith for the sum of £875 and in the following May he paid a further £20 '*in part for the land.*'

When John died on 11th January 1803 he was described as being from Coldweather House as was his wife, Jennet, who died on 6th June 1810 at the age of 71: they were both buried at Colne parish church. Almost one year after John's demise his son, Ambrose, died at the age of 41. If we take it that John Robertshaw was the person who commissioned the Coldweather charm then the question arises as to whether the deaths of father and son within a year of each other might have a bearing on the matter.

Were both John and Ambrose suffering from some ongoing affliction that the doctors of the time could not cure? If so it is not difficult to imagine that John would have resorted to any possible means of protection from whatever he considered might have been the cause of his family's ailments – in other words the charm could be seen as a type of supernatural insurance policy.

Certainly John would have been steeped within the local folklore of witchcraft, magic, charms, spells and suspicion. He was born into an isolated world in 1732 and his father would have been born only a generation or so following the execution of the Pendle Witches in 1612. He also had ancestors in the Sagar family of Catlow Hall who had married into the gentry family of Towneley and this branch happened to inherit the estate of the Nutters of Waterside in Reedley. In turn this Nutter family had inherited the estate of witch Alice Nutter of Roughlee.[5]

Furthermore, Walter Bennett showed in his *History of Burnley* that in the 1633 Pendle witch episode a woman named Alice Higgin, of Coldweather, was accused of being a witch and sent to London for examination. These traditions would certainly have remained within the Sagar and Robertshaw families of Coldweather and could have had a bearing on the mindset of John Robertshaw when he thought fit to protect his house and family by means of a charm.

Even as the twentieth century bore down on its predecessor there were recorded incidents of farmers in Briercliffe and Pendle who maintained a strong belief in witchcraft and this was almost two hundred years after John Robertshaw had been born.

The date of the paper that the charm is written on can be placed broadly between 1750 and 1850 and the excellent preservation of the document suggests a later, rather than earlier, date. Further, the building extension within which the charm was located was not erected until around 1775-1785. Expert analysis of a similar example by Richard Garnett states that it is likely to be of a later date than 1785. An apparent health crisis hit the Coldweather household in the period 1803 to 1804 when both father and son died (a possible reason for placing the charm at the entrance to the property) and this narrows the date to the period 1785 - 1803.

The wise person would construct a charm for a specific purpose, such as to protect the occupants of a house from witchcraft or as an exorcism for those considered to have been the victims of witch spells. Writing in the *Folklore* publication (Vol.31. No. 2 - 1920) William Weeks, of Clitheroe, noted the popularity of witch charms within the Pendle district as late as the end of the nineteenth century:

CHARMS AGAINST WITCHES AND EVIL SPIRITS

The charm No. II., from the Common-place Book of William Sykes of Marsden, occurs in a publication of the Percy Society (1849) and it is there given as follows:-

A Night Spell to Catch Thieves: The charm will drive away any evil spirits that haunt houses, or any other place; and having it about you no thief can harm you, but if he comes to rob a garden, orchard or a house, he cannot go till the sun riseth: having in every corner of the house this sentence written on true virgin parchment. *'Omnes Spiritus laudet Dominus Mosem habe. Prophetas exerget Deus, dissipari inter inimicos.'* But if for a garden, or orchard, it must be placed at the four corners thereof; and if to keep one from being robbed on the road, to have it always about him, and to fear God.

I have a charm containing a similar formula which I obtained between twenty and thirty years ago from an old farmer in Pendle Forest. This district obtained considerable notoriety in the seventeenth century in connection with the trial of Mistress Alice Nutter and others for Witchcraft, and belief in witchcraft still lingers there, or did till quite recently, among the older inhabitants.

The old farmer, to whom I referred, was a firm believer in witches, and averred that he had seen some, and that they could make themselves larger and smaller at will. He had about twenty charms of various kinds written on pieces of paper, by which he set very great store. I managed to get two of them, and the one to which I wish to refer is written on a very small piece of paper in an illiterate hand. It is endorsed *'For the House'* and was intended to be placed over the door to protect the house and its inmates. On the front is written,*'Omnes Spiritu laudet domnum mason habent dusot propheates exergrat disipentur inimicus.'* The last three words seem intended for the opening words of Psalm lxviii. *'Exergat Deus, et Dissipentur inimici ejus.'*

Amongst the other charms which this old farmer had was one labelled *'For the Field.'* It was similar to the last one described, but had these words added, *'Let all the cattle in this field prosper'* and there was the following direction for its use appended, *'Put in a gap.'*

These charms were not intended in Pendle Forest as mere curiosities. The old farmer, a short time before my interview with him, was consulted by a neighbour with reference to a cow that was seriously ill. The good man, instead of consulting a book on veterinary science, had recourse to his collection of charms. Selecting the one labelled *'For the house'* he proceeded to the shippon where the cow was and placed the potent paper over the door. This was believed to have produced the desired effect as the animal speedily recovered.

This document was found in a Sabden cottage but does not conform to the formulaic examples described earlier: it could be one of the examples described by William Weeks.

William Weeks tells us that around the end of the eighteenth century the use of charms was common practice within the Pendle district. Who, then, were the people supplying these documents? In answer to this it might be that we have the answer to the puzzle of the Coldweather charm.

A few miles to the east, across the moors from Coldweather House, lies the West Yorkshire village of Haworth (famous for the Bronte sisters). Here, in 1776 a man named John Kay had a son, also named John. Young John grew up in Haworth and, following his marriage, took his new wife, Rebecca, to live on Acton Street in the village. John (or Jack as he was better known) and Rebecca had a son Thomas and, while Rebecca was busy bringing up the lad, Jack took to studying the paranormal.

Jack purchased an English translation of a volume of Greek astrology and began to formulate a method of writing charms for people. He soon found that his skills were widely sought after and his time was taken up in writing charms, supplying love potions, counteracting witch spells, holding séances, making up medicinal draughts and tinctures and telling fortunes. As time passed Jack's fame spread near and far and the village saw many people, local and strangers alike, wandering its steep, cobbled streets in search of '*Old Jack Kay, The Wise Man of Haworth.*'

It is not surprising that Jack Kay was much in demand: the people of Haworth were largely home-based wool combers working for the local merchants. The sanitation in Haworth was notoriously poor and effluent from dung heaps, cess pits and the overcrowded graveyard spilled down the village, tainting the water supply and infecting the cellar dwellings of the wool workers. Things became so bad that the high mortality rate caused the government to publish a report on the matter. In 1850 the inspector in charge of the inquiry, Benjamin Babbage, stated that the age at death in Haworth, between 1838 and 1849, averaged out at 25.8 years. In fact 41.6 per cent of people in Haworth died before the age of six and this compared poorly even with the most deprived areas of London.[7]

The working people, then, were struggling against an extremely unhealthy environment and when they fell sick there would be little money to pay for doctor's fees. Jack Kay, no doubt, would have done his best to provide whatever help he could. Rev. Patrick Bronte moved with his family to Haworth in April 1820 and he saw the misery inflicted by disease upon his flock, in fact much of his day would have been taken up by visiting the sick and burying the dead.

Patrick, of course, was usually at loggerheads with Jack Kay and matters were not helped when a woman called at the vicarage one day asking for '*the wisest man in Haworth.*' Because the Reverend was the wisest man she knew the maid duly directed the woman into Rev. Bronte's study where she was met with a frosty reception. Following a long lecture on the evils of dabbling in the occult the unfortunate truth seeker left the vicarage with a flea in her ear! In the end Rev. Bronte officiated at the burial of Jack Kay following his death in 1847.

For many years Jack had travelled the district selling his wares at the markets of Burnley, Bradford and Colne, and it very likely that it was at the latter place where John Robertshaw could have purchased his Coldweather charm. He would have been fully aware of the reputation of Jack Kay and when he saw him at Colne market he would have had the opportunity to purchase a charm to protect the house and to rid it of any malign presence. Jack would then have cobbled together his document of gobbledegook over the following week, written the customer's name on the top and taken it for collection to the next market.

We will never know the exact reason why John Robertshaw thought that he needed the charm/exorcism. Whatever the case may be it is certain that the Coldweather House document is a rare example of contemporary evidence for a belief system that seems alien to the modern mind. Although the charm/exorcism conforms to a formulaic design it is, nevertheless, a unique example of its type and as such it is of importance to the history of the local area.

Coldweather House

This building is John Robertshaw's later 18th century extension of the earlier Coldweather Farm (c. 1650) to the rear.

Until the end of the 20th century the two buildings were joined internally.

LAND AND POPULATION

The half-century or so leading up to the witch trials of 1612 was a period where the seeds of disquiet were being sown throughout the land. Of course, the Reformation under Henry VIII was an obvious source of social uncertainty but other forces were also at play. Eventually we would see the resultant chaos when the pressures of religious fanaticism and political upheaval surfaced in the execution of the Pendle witches and a bloody civil war.

The sixteenth century, then, saw a dramatic change in the political and religious atmosphere within Britain. Suspicion amongst the highest authorities served to divert many subjects of the Crown from following a way of life that they had trusted and served for many generations. Those within the old establishment who were not willing to adapt to the new order of Henry Tudor became victims of a state that they had formerly served faithfully and without question.

The higher strata of society who continued to openly practice the 'old' religion of Rome were commonly punished by means of heavy fines and confiscation of their lands and property. Further, those who were steadfastly unwilling to conform to the new Protestant doctrines, despite their having endured near ruin, could pay the ultimate price of martyrdom or, at the very least, be banished from their homes, land and country.

In the Pendle Forest district the *status quo* of authority was thrown into a state of flux where the formerly powerful (Catholic) families, such as the Towneleys of Burnley, saw their status slip away to be replaced by ambitious rising stars among the yeomanry and minor gentry. The Protestant movement engendered a new breed of religious fundamentalism and people such as Richard Baldwin, a miller and yeoman of Lower Wheathead Farm (now in Blacko), became stewards of the new Church and oversaw the adherence of local society to the Protestant doctrines.

Baldwin and his fellow stewards had little sympathy for those less fortunate than themselves and were not slow to use their contacts with the higher authority of the law to maintain a society that would function within the parameters of God's will - as they themselves saw it. Little wonder, then, that Baldwin is recorded as having thrown Elizabeth Southern, and her granddaughter, off his land calling them *'witches and whores.'*

In other words, those who were unemployed while being able bodied should starve; there was no quarter given to the fact that there was little or no work for them to do. The old and the truly destitute were to be given a subsistence level of alms provided that these wretches acknowledged the will of God as outlined by the Puritanical doctrine.

Richard Baldwin had the ear of the Pendle Forest authorities in the form of Reedley magistrate Roger Nowell and he was not unwilling to report any perceived misdemeanour within his domain of the Pendle Forest to his superior.[8] Those of the forest people who did not attend church on the Sabbath were presented before the local courts to be fined; people were prosecuted for swearing, working, gambling, dancing, sporting and even tending their gardens on the Sabbath.

Enjoying life was strictly forbidden and the likes of Baldwin wandered the borough with a keen weather eye for such blasphemous activities. Baldwin had land, he had property, he acted as a form of tax collector for the Queen by working his corn mill and he was an official within the Queen's church. He would have had little time for those beneath him on the ladder of society.

In many respects the growing social tensions of the sixteenth and early seventeenth centuries had arisen through events that took place in 1507 when some 7,250 acres of land within Pendle Forest were granted to the existing farm tenants on very favourable terms. A new security of tenure came into being and this meant that farmers were willing to enclose large tracts of formerly waste land. As the sixteenth century progressed the increase in agricultural land meant that the offspring of the new farm copyholders were able to establish new farms to take advantage of the situation.

Further to the addition of new farms there was also an increase in landowners who were quick to recognise the wealth to be had from renting out their copyholds to sub-tenants (on very profitable terms) and from the woollen trade. The farms began to incorporate 'shops' for conversion of raw wool into finished cloth pieces and this meant more work for those who did not own land.

As the sixteenth century progressed the population within the Forest of Pendle increased: in 1563 there were approximately 640 people in the Forest while records for the year 1650 show around 1,620 inhabitants. This situation was grist to the mill for the woollen merchants who were prospering from the increase in supply of both land and labour.

A period of high inflation ensued and this was to affect the economy through the later part of the sixteenth century and into the following century. This meant that the terms upon which the farmers held their copyhold contracts became highly advantageous. Because the agreements of 1507 had not stipulated any increase in farm rents in relation to economic conditions then over time the landowners were able to sell their goods in line with rising prices while at the same time paying a low fixed rent for their lands. They were also in a position to increase the rents of their sub-tenants while suppressing the wages of their cloth workers to sub-inflation levels - happy days for the yeoman and merchant!

Increased pressure on land saw more small farms sprouting within marginal areas as the offspring of existing farmers continued to split their parent's farms. By around the turn of the century, say 1580-1610, this had become unsustainable which meant that some of the sons and daughters of existing farmers had to leave the land and find work either on other farms or in the local towns. These formerly land-secure people were now joining the landless whose parents and grandparents had never managed to benefit from securing land tenancies. There was a situation where many districts began to see an increase in people without permanent work and without even a small plot of land from which they could feed themselves and their families.

Given the scarcity of land it is little wonder that there was an upsurge in the number of desperate people who were willing to fence off small plots of poor land and erect huts to house their families. These squats were tolerated by the Clitheroe overlords (the *'Lords of the Forest or Chase of Pendle'* to whom all copyhold fees eventually came) provided that rent was paid.

The new smallholdings became established but it was often the case that the tenant had little security; it was common for the leases of the poorer sub-tenant to cover a period of less than one year and one day. Beyond this length of time lease transactions were required to be entered in the halmote court rolls.[9]

It is possible that we see this situation arise within the Pendle trials of 1612 where Elizabeth Southern (Malkin Tower) and Ann Whittle (West Close) appear to have been living in dwellings with a small area of attached land (certainly enough to run chickens in Whittle's case).

A common preconception is that Demdike and Chattox lived in tiny hovels; however we do not know the particulars of the tenure involved here but it is stated in Potts that the families had occupied their dwellings for a long period prior to 1612 and this suggests a security of tenure of some kind - even ownership. Perhaps these dwellings had initially been created as squats, farm worker's cottages, woollen worker's dwellings, disused water mills or converted grain malting kilns (see Part Three).

CORN AND CRISIS

Another socio-economic factor to be taken into account in a largely agrarian society is the incidence of famine. Where weather and blight conspired to limit crop returns (including grass for livestock) there was often a direct correlation between corn yields, death rates and social instability.[10]

During the first part of the Early Modern period (around 1550-1650) the population within the whole district of Pendle Forest numbered around 400 families. The common perception of this era is of an agrarian economy where the land provided for everyone's needs and life was uncomplicated; however, the historian is always aware that the lives of our ancestors were never untouched by outside forces and use can be made of a number of statistics to illustrate this. Baptisms, marriages and burials can be cross-referenced against corn crop production and the consequential price of wheat. Mortality rates, probate incidence, Acts of Parliament, parish records – all of these sources allow for an insight into the periods of severe shortage when life was truly difficult for the poorer people.

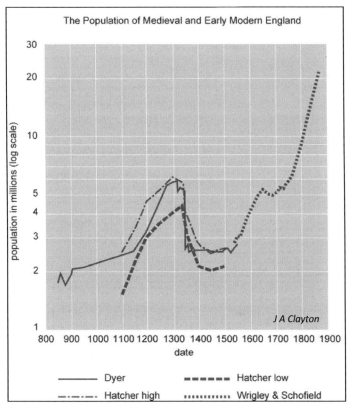

Four sets of statistics were entered into a database and converted into the chart (left). This represents the national population totals of Medieval and Early Modern England. Although each product does not agree exactly the general trends are sympathetic.[11]

Most of the 14th century saw protracted crop failure and plague epidemics while the 15th century was a period of stabilisation.

The 16th century produced population expansion that lasted to around the middle of the 17th century.

The deadly enemies of Medieval and Early Modern societies were the unholy trinity of War, Disease and Famine. To a certain extent wars were never unexpected within the local populace as preparations were always necessary before the event. The threat of disease was ever-present but the one crisis that could not be predicted was next year's corn crop; failure of this vital food source hit communities hard. Facilities did not exist to enable the long-term storage of grain and the poorest within the community were susceptible to any fluctuation within the annual crops.

It is not clear as to exactly how much the fourteenth century plague outbreaks affected the population within Pendle Forest, being a relatively sparsely populated backwater its inhabitants do not appear to have suffered the high mortality rates of nearby Preston and Manchester. It is thought that famine could have played a more important role in premature fatality within the forest areas; for example, a seven-year period in the late fourteenth century saw major crop failures locally.[12]

In the mid-twentieth century the statistician, William Farr, carried out an analysis of the national crisis years of crop failure and concluded that each century could expect seven years of famine. Because certain famines affected the following year's grain supply the result was an average of ten famine years per century. [13]

This table shows the average corn crop quality during the first part of the Early Modern period. The figure against each year represents the percentage yield of a 'normal' year. Here (in bold) can be seen definite years of crisis.

1575	-10	1585	-10	**1595**	**-30**	1605	20	1615	-5
1576	**-12**	**1586**	**-44**	**1596**	**-85**	1606	11	1616	-3
1577	-5	1587	20	**1597**	**-65**	1607	8	1617	-12
1578	13	1588	26	1598	2	**1608**	**-38**	1618	15
1579	12	1589	-2	1599	12	1609	8	1619	22
1580	0	1590	9	1600	0	1610	10	1620	38
1581	20	1591	28	1601	12	1611	-1	1621	20
1582	28	1592	32	1602	14	1612	-9	1622	25
1583	26	1593	12	1603	22	**1613**	**-23**	1623	12
1584	-10	1594	20	1604	15	1614	3	1624	10

Here we can see that crop yields within the whole period were less than ideal but certain years were far worse than others. The period 1595, 1596 and 1597, for instance, marks a definite period of crisis that did not really improve until 1601 when we see a better six-year period. However, by 1611 crops yields were declining again with 1612 returning the worst yield within the next twelve years (the 1613 figure reflects the yield from the previous year).

Here, then, the question arises as to the social impact on local communities; while the wealthy might maintain a standard of living through the crisis years of famine how did the common people fare? Obviously the supply of corn (wheat and rye in particular) affected the supply and price of the bread on the poor person's table but what impact did this really have?

Farr undertook a study of the duties payable on wheat, along with national parish and manorial records, in order to establish a cross-match between the seasonal wages of the farm worker and the price of wheat. To quantify the actual wheat price in terms of wages he translated the outcome into the indicator of pints of wheat (as shown in the table below).

PROPORTION OF AGRICULTURAL WAGES TO THE PRICE OF CORN: (*THE LEAGUE* 1844)			
Period	Weekly Summer Pay (ex. harvest time)	Wheat per Quarter	Wages in pints of wheat
1495	2s:0d	6s:3d	163
1514	2s:0d	8s:8d	118
1545	2s:6d	18s:8d	68
1593	2s:6d	20s:0d	64
1610	3s:6d	34s:1d	52
1725	5s:0d	35s:4d	72
1750	5s:0d	29s:2d	122
1763	7s:0d	33s:1d	108
1770	7s:4d	41s:4d	92
1793	8s:5d	46s:9d	94
1824	8s:7d	64s:0d	68
1829	11s:0d	62s:1d	85
1833	11s:5d	55s:9d	104

1601	3.5
1602	3.6
1603	3.7
1604	3.9
1605	3.6
1606	3.6
1607	5.4
1608	5
1609	4
1610	4.1
1611	5.3
1612	5
1613	5.3
1614	4.6
1615	4.8
1616	5
1617	5.2
1618	5.3
1619	3.7
1620	4
1621	5
1622	5.8
1623	5.5
1624	6
1625	5.4

The table above sharply illustrates the inversion of rising prices through the sixteenth century against a reduction in the value of money. The year 1610 saw the lowest amount of wheat that could be purchased despite a 50 per cent rise in wages from the end of the previous century.

The table (left) represents the latter half of a 50 year sample (1575 - 1625) relating to the cost of a 4lb loaf of bread in pence. It can be concluded that the weekly average costs over the 50 year sample (from 1575) are 4d per four-pound wheat loaf and 317d per quarter of wheat.

39

When comparing prices directly it is perhaps surprising that wheat price and bread price are not incremental; this suggests that prices rose and fell independently in relation to other forces not yet accounted for. One possible explanation here is the control of authority exercised over the profits made by merchants within the grain business. An Act of Edward Tudor stated that *'whosoever should buy corn with intent to sell it again, should be reputed an unlawful engrosser.'* For a third offence the miscreant could be imprisoned for life and have all his possessions confiscated. As far as possible the middle-man between the farmer and the consumer was to have limited rights – these 'kidders' were required to hold a licence showing their probity and fitness for the job. Other factors at play were the volume and price of wheat imports, incidence of war and forward selling by grain merchants.

LOCAL CRISIS EVENTS

Having looked at national events it is time to assess the local situation where the incidence of births, marriages and deaths can be compared to the fluctuations in crop yields, inflation and bread prices.

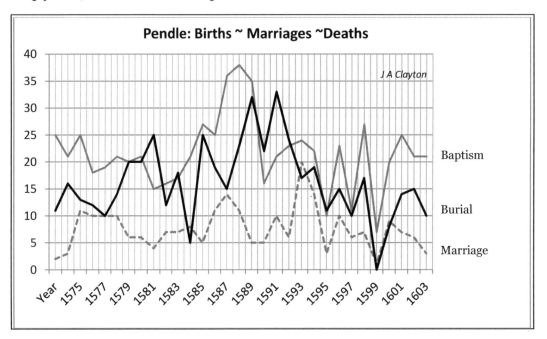

The statistics above show a doubling of the birth rate in the decade 1580 to 1589 while the following two years saw this plunge in direct proportion to marriage rates (as might be expected). The period of crop crisis 1595-96-97 saw all rates peak and trough alarmingly. Death rates fell to a low in 1599 and this is possibly a reflection of the fact that from 1589 to 1591 a large number of burials occurred i.e. the majority within the most vulnerable groups had already died.

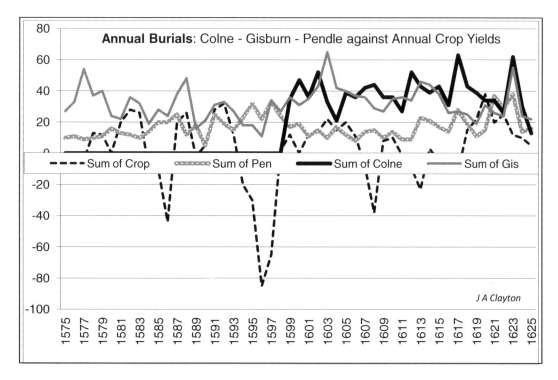

The table above has been created through the use of four data sets relating to Gisburn, Colne and Pendle mortality rates as against crop yields (in annual percentage).

These statistics show that the Colne and Pendle death rates correspond with the decrease in crop yields – rates peak in relation to falling yield. However, the Gisburn district trends run opposite to these trends in as much as deaths often rise when crop yields rise and vice-versa. A possible explanation for this lies in the fact that the Yorkshire parish of Gisburn was a 'closed' parish owned and administered by two large local landowners with restricted farm tenure.[14] This meant that a tight control was exercised upon those allowed tenure of the farms. Furthermore this area tended towards an agricultural 'commune' where farming enterprises helped each other. Grain was stored in bulk within purpose-built lathes and this might well have helped to ensure a relatively constant supply of grain to the Gisburn district community in times of dearth.

Pendle and Colne, on the other hand, consisted of many smaller farming tenancies who were sub-tenants of the copy holding over-tenants who were, in turn, tenants of the Clitheroe overlords. This meant that the individual farmer was more isolated when crops failed.

Many other statistics can be employed within the assessment of the socio-economic state of the Early Modern Pendle Forest. The adoption of mortality rates in relation to corn availability does not provide the whole picture by any means. Other factors to take into account when assessing the social and demographic trends within parish records are the effects of the money supply, price of wheat, national and international politics, religion, number of gentry estates, topographical issues relating to land quality, incidence and quality of roads, water supply for the provision of power to industry, local credit supply etc.[15]

Disease, wars and economic difficulties were all instrumental in influencing vital statistics. Furthermore, birth rates and marriage rates have their own statistical story to tell, especially in assessment of the family unit. However, the adoption of mortality rates has been useful to illustrate that the price and availability of corn had a definite influence on the common people both locally and nationally. Those in towns fared differently to the agricultural areas; bread was more accessible but disease was more prevalent. Certain districts (as in the 'closed' parish of Gisburn) appear to have survived corn crisis years better than their 'open' parish neighbours.

To sum up the relationship between crop yields, inflation and pressure upon the poorer members of Pendle it can be said that the salient year of 1612, where society turned inward on certain of its poorer members, sits within a difficult period. Inflation through the previous century had lowered the real value of wages and, despite a 50 per cent increase over the past decade, the year 1610 marked the beginning of a protracted period where bread prices remained between 25 per cent and 50 per cent above the previous fifty-year average.

However, it must be remembered that exchange within agricultural communities would help to negate the effects of high bread prices in that the labouring class often had the opportunity to be paid partly in produce. A study by Carole Shames (*Economic History: No.3* 1988) suggests that no more than 50 to 60 per cent of the income of Early Modern workers in England was 'dietary expenditure.' This might suggest that high prices in times of crisis would affect spending on other necessities such as clothing - there are recorded instances within Pendle where people were excused from church attendance because they had no suitable clothes to wear.

The final decade of the sixteenth century, then, was disastrous in terms of crop yields and this could well have been the period in which a tangible change occurred in the attitudes of local society towards its needy. From 1611 to 1617 crops again failed thus adding pressure to domestic income. Not surprisingly this was also a period where the steady increase in population (from 1520) was running down - by 1640 the upward trend had reversed, albeit temporarily.

While the massive fluctuation in crop yields, high inflation and wheat prices cannot be held as the single cause of the 1612 witch hunt within Pendle Forest it is clear that they were contributory factors and cannot be ignored.

THE POOR

Population increase during the sixteenth century affected the supply of housing, land and food. Many breadwinners were forced to leave their village, town, parish or county and travel in search of work: unfortunately the itinerant poor often found that things were just as bad elsewhere and a great number consequently fell by the wayside.

It is true that alms were provided by the church, state and charities to those considered most in need but this hardly scratched the surface of the problem. The official Poor Relief provided by the parish was raised by means of a tax on landowners and property holders and had worked reasonably well because the better-off paid the tax (albeit grudgingly). However, the great insurgence into towns and villages of people in search of work hardened the hearts of the taxpayers who began to view the landless multitude as a public nuisance.

The early Poor Relief laws were aimed largely at beggars and vagabonds within local communities – in 1349 the *Ordinance of Labourers* prohibited private individuals from giving relief to *'sturdy beggars'* as the able-bodied were known. The 1388 *Statute of Cambridge* was intended to further restrict the movement of labouring workers and beggars by making each hundred responsible for its own poor. In 1494 the *Vagabonds and Beggars Act* stated that '*Vagabonds, idle and suspected persons shall be set in stocks.*'

Taking this further the *Statute of Legal Settlement* allowed for the branding of a sturdy beggar or alternatively they could be forced into slavery for a period of two years or for life if the person absconded. An early sixteenth century record relating to the status of *Rogues and Beggars* showed the prevalent attitude to the wandering worker at that time – regardless of the level of wages earned the following trades were classed as undesirable:

> *Proctors of Spittle houses - Patent Gatherers - Collectors of Gaols, Prisons or Hospitals - Fencers - Bearwards - Common Players of Interludes - Minstrels Wandering Abroade - Glassemen - Saylers - Soulders - Schollers - and all other idle persons which goe about begging.*

In an attempt to address this situation a 1547 Act of Parliament gave each parish the power to repatriate any pauper who did not belong to that parish. As a consequence a great number of people were driven over the parish boundary at the painful end of the constable's whip - the idea being that they would be repatriated into the parish from where they originally came. In some cases, where families had settled and were claiming rights to parish relief without good cause, the courts were able to elicit a *Resettlement Order* which meant that (in theory) the original parish from whence the paupers had come was legally liable to pay for their resettlement. In many cases, however, these fees went unpaid resulting in each parish paying a fortune in court costs - money that would have been better spent on feeding the poor itinerants in the first place!

In 1601 a further *Act for the Relief of the Poor* was passed and this was effectively the beginning of the modern rating system whereby the tenant of a property was assessed on the value of his holding and expected to pay into the poor relief of his parish accordingly. If any person were to default on this relief payment then the local Justice of the Peace had the power to fine them or seize their goods. Under this Act individual parishes were obliged to provide for the aged and the infirm, to bring up unprotected children in habits of industry, and to provide work for those who were capable but lacking their usual trade.

Certain members of the elite appear to have been of the opinion that it was acceptable for the poor to live hand-in-hand with serious malnourishment, cold, damp, disease and death; furthermore the destitute were expected to conform to the social niceties of 'civilised' standards. Even in the late seventeenth century, when it might have been expected that the previous *Acts for the Relief of the Poor* would have begun to improve matters, there were still disturbing incidents on record. In 1665 an appeal was made to the Justices of the Peace in relation to an unpaid Poor Relief application. Robert Sheppard and his wife Isabel, of Great Marsden (Nelson) had asked for payment because their advanced ages meant that they were incapable of work and had no income. The overseers, who were usually property owners and therefore liable to contribute towards the poor, had refused this application and so the couple were reduced to selling their clothing in order to buy food. The Justices of the Peace eventually ordered the overseers of Great Marsden to carry out their duties.[16]

A surviving overseer's account book of 1688 shows that a total of £0: 33s: 8d from three charities and £0: 4s: 5d from the poor rate of the township of Great Marsden was distributed among thirty-four paupers there. The sums per head varied from 6d to 3s; amongst the recipients were: Old Jenny - Whackersall - Delphes wife - Black John - Nan with two childer - Old Martha Darnesley and a woman in Journey House End.

It is likely that an application for parish relief was only made by a person who had fallen upon hard times after the patience and generosity of their neighbours had worn thin. It is difficult to say exactly how long a community would sustain their begging poor with good grace as this would probably depend upon the economic climate of the time and the particular circumstances of the individual alms-seeker. In the case of the Pendle Witch trials the only clear instance of protracted begging is that of the extended Malkin Tower family of Elizabeth Southern. The (limited) available record shows that this family regularly travelled throughout the Pendle and Trawden Forest areas in search of alms; a few coppers, blue milk and oatmeal seeming to be the usual aid.

Taking into account Elizabeth Southern's age of around seventy years it is likely that long experience provided at least a modicum of advantage in her trade – it is apparent that this advantage was her perceived ability to heal the farmer's sick cattle, cure sour ale and supply various potions for the needs of her fellow countrymen.

If her reputation was such that people were frightened of refusing her requests for alms then all well-and-good; this would have been a distinct advantage in the begging trade. It would also prove to be useful when local people were in need of a healer; the old ways were still prevalent in these parts of the forest and the competition amongst wise folk for the business would be stiff. It would follow, therefore, that the person with the strongest publicity machine might expect to get the job of healing the majority of sick livestock - in turn the few coppers, or farm produce received in payment would fill the bellies of the hungry family for another day or two.

Shortage of land, rapid growth in population and crop failures led to an unsustainable increase in those who were reliant on handouts to survive. This engendered a change in the attitude of the local populace towards the poor. Generally, up to middle of the sixteenth century the landless beggars were tolerated within society - *'there but for the grace of God go I.'* In fact those who travelled the countryside in search of a piggin (a wooden bucket) of blue milk, or a peck or two of oats, were looked upon as a useful source of casual labour available as and when the farmer might require them.

However, hard times in the latter part of the sixteenth century saw a corresponding boom in those reduced to begging and the old-timers of the locality now found themselves in competition for alms and temporary work with others who had moved in from outside the parish. This was especially the case within the urban district of Colne whereas the rural forest area appears to have been the stamping ground of alms-seekers such as the family of Elizabeth Southern who were tolerated to live only on the periphery of the farming society in their squats and hovels.

However, having seen that growing numbers of alms seekers would have been a contributory factor in the witch trials of 1612 a comparison with other northern counties shows that they did not experience a particular increase in levels of witchcraft. Other factors need to be considered in relation to the Forest of Pendle.

THE CHURCH

WHALLEY ABBEY

Following the Norman invasion of 1066 the new overlords erected the squat, square-towered churches that we are all familiar with to this day. The Norman baronage of the Honor of Clitheroe, and the Abbey of Whalley, were the two influences that led to the later unified development of the Pendle Forest area.

Long before the founding of Whalley Abbey a Saxon church there had been dedicated to All Saints and was known as *The White Church under the Leigh;* this would have been a wooden structure, later to be replaced by a stone building. The rectors, or deans, were the lords of the town and, as they were allowed to marry, the succession of their position was hereditary. The office of dean was looked upon as that of a dignitary, rather than a purely ecclesiastical position, he was inferior only to the feudal overlords and, therefore, enjoyed a privileged existence. Members of the local gentry enjoyed the status provided by this position, not least among them being the Towneley family of Burnley.

The earl of Lincoln laid the foundation stone for the new abbey at Whalley on the morning of St. Barnabas day (12th of June) 1308. The abbey prospered over the centuries; many grants of land (and in some cases whole townships) saw their power continually increase. The more land that they controlled and the more tithes they could extract from the parishes; these were payments of a tenth part of the profits derived from the crops, livestock and labour of the inhabitants. In 1296 the tithe income to the abbey from Burnley parish alone was £47.[17]

During the mid-1530s a natural reaction of the Catholic gentry to Henry VIII's *Dissolution of the Monasteries* was to rebel; they organised an armed uprising in an attempt to persuade the king to reverse his policies and restore the dissolved monasteries to their former owners. Robert Aske placed himself at the head of the rebellion (known as *The Pilgrimage of Grace)* and was soon joined by church dignitaries, the gentry and many of the labouring classes who all rallied to his standard of *The Five Wounds of Christ.* The whole of the county of Yorkshire was to be counted amongst Aske's number and this soon spread into Lancashire under the guidance of important local Catholics. Amongst these were Nicholas Tempest of Bashall and Sir Stephen Hamerton of Craven who had mustered a force of some four-hundred men.

The *Pilgrimage of Grace* peeved Henry VIII and he naturally viewed the insurrection as an act of treachery. Abbot John Paslew had the dubious honour of being the very last abbot of Whalley - he had been implicated in the uprising and this was enough for Henry to have him executed. Opinion is divided as to the site of Paslew's execution, folklore has it that he was executed at either the Abbey, or in Imps Field at Whalley or at his former home in Wiswell. The strongest argument seems to be that Paslew was hanged at Lancaster following his trial.

The king ordered the forfeiture of the abbey's possessions and the transfer of some of the monks who remained within the area to other monasteries. The abbey remained the property of the king until June 6th, 1553 when the abbey site, along with the manor of Whalley, were sold to members of the local gentry. John Braddyl and Richard Assheton purchased the site for the sum of £2,132: 3s: 9d. Braddyl then built himself a new manor house at nearby Portfield while the Assheton family moved into the Abbot's House.

For a century following the Dissolution the structure of the abbey buildings would still have rivaled the ruins at Fountains and Furness. Unfortunately, having survived the Civil War, the abbey was systematically dismantled during the reign of Charles II. The owner at that time paid groups of workmen to remove and carry off the stonework – they were paid to destroy the abbey fabric by the yard. A number of our parish churches claim to have parts of the abbey buildings within their own structure and many gentry houses of the district also show architectural details relating to the abbey. It is said that much of the ornamental stonework from the windows and door arches was dumped into the river on the abbey site.

The Lining-out of the Foundation of the Abbey Church, Whalley

Whalley Abbey ruins

It is difficult to overestimate the role that Whalley Abbey played in the overall function of the thirty townships within its jurisdiction. Prior to the Dissolution the 180 square miles that made up the parish had no bishop, nor did it have a cathedral and therefore the abbey found itself central to the economic and spiritual lives of the tens of thousands of people within its extended environs.

The abbey was a major landowner, employer and provider of alms to the poor of the district. The two *compotus* (accounts) lists for Whalley Abbey compiled in 1478 and 1521 show that the income from the parish was drawn from the chapelries of Clitheroe, Downham, Burnley, Colne, Altham and Haslingden along with Blackburn, Eccles and Rochdale.

The abbey was not slow to capitalise on its equity and expanded its land holdings, it also spent copiously on entertaining the many people who had need to visit the abbey in either spiritual or commercial capacities. Building works, at the abbey and in the parishes, were an ongoing source of employment, an example of which can be seen in the extension of Saint Peter's church in Burnley. Between 1521 and 1533 local masons were employed to enlarge the north aisle of the church, the head of this project being the Sellers family, of Whalley, who were attached permanently to the abbey building and maintenance team.

Within a few months of Abbott Paslew's execution for high treason (March 1537) the whole abbey system had been virtually disbanded. The destruction of the Whalley estate was carried out with clinical precision and the monks were unceremoniously ejected from their ecclesiastic home and sent on their way.

It is an ill-wind that blows nobody good, however, and the period following the destruction of Whalley Abbey can certainly be described as good for certain members of local society - the gentry. Locally important families such as Bradyll, Nowell, Assheton and Towneley were to benefit from the old abbey estates in no small way.

The destruction of the central economic authority was to usher in a change for certain people within the Pendle Forest communities; the former abbey lands changed hands and therefore many tenants found themselves with new masters to please. Whereby the authority of the abbey would have dealt with minor problems relating to its economic estates the local halmote courts at Colne, Higham and Ightenhill were now having to address an increasing number of small grievances.

The loss of a cohesive spiritual authority was to have an even more profound effect upon the ordinary forest folk; as the care of the poor became a localised responsibility the local taxpayers began to resent the fact that they were required to pay for the upkeep of their neighbours. When the abbey oversaw the alms relief it was a case of *'out of sight, out of mind'* but the new relief brought home to people the fact that they were actually paying for the poor.

The 'old' doctrines had not disappeared under the new Protestant sovereigns, far from it in fact; many of the forest clergy continued with their 'traditional' Catholic-based services following the Reformation, paying only lip-service to the new ways. This can be partly explained by the fact that the Catholic form of worship was only slowly subjugated by the later Protestant forms - Henry VIII had set the ball rolling when he nationalised religion but the full-blown Protestant Reformation did not really take effect until the reigns of Edward VI (1547-53) and Elizabeth I (1558-1603).

It also has to be remembered that the generation born before the Reformation had been raised within a strong Catholic culture, as had their priests. It would be impossible for strongly held beliefs to be subjugated within a single generation and it is no surprise, therefore, that pockets of Catholic 'resistance' existed at the time of the 1612 witch trials amongst certain gentry families and the ordinary people.

Other gentry families fully embraced the Protestant faith (often for political reasons only) and prospered while their Catholic counterparts suffered confiscation of land, property and money– and sometimes their lives.[18]

The lack of ecclesiastical leadership led to a number of clerics with definite Catholic leanings being attached to the livings within Whalley Parish; not least of these was one George Dobson; the parish church at Whalley attained the services of Dobson in 1558 and he was to serve there for the next thirty three years. Dobson had an unfortunate trait in that he would only recognise the pro-Catholic worshippers amongst his congregation, a small clique formed and this, of course, upset the other parishioners. An extract from a letter sent to the bishop of Chester describes Dobson in the following terms:

He is a common drunkard, and such an ale-knight as the like is not in our parish, and in the night when most men be abed at rest then is he in the ale-house with a company like unto himself, but not one of them can match him in ale-house tricks, for he will, when he cannot discern black from blue, dance with a full cup on his heade, surpassing all the rest.

This, at least, was the description of Dobson as his Protestant congregation saw him – a strong traditionalist (if not fully Catholic) cleric who was accused of promulgating the old doctrines and thus keeping the 'magic' suspicions of the forest folk alive.

Other clerics were reported as being downright incompetent - of one incumbent at Saint Mary's, Newchurch-in-Pendle, it was said that he refused to marry people and that he spent most of his time frolicking with the landlady of the Fence Gate ale house! This was not an entirely local phenomenon; nationally there are many recorded instances whereby Puritan clergy described the whole of Lancashire as a spiritually barren area - the inference being that many pockets of Catholicism not only survived in the area but that they were positively thriving.

During the sixteenth century the Forest clergy at St. Mary's were largely an itinerant group who would serve the parish for two or three years before they were moved on. Very few settled for long within the parish; this meant that they would not have known their flock very well or have had the time to engender their respect.

St. Mary's Newchurch

One of the longest serving incumbents was Thomas Hird who served St. Mary's through the difficult aftermath of the Dissolution between 1537 and 1562. This 25-year period of service was only ever surpassed by one other incumbent in the form of Thomas Varley, a man from a local farming family who served from 1569 to 1607. We then see a Christopher Nuttall (Nutter) serving from 1607 to 1608 followed by John Town from 1610 to 1611. The next recorded incumbent does not appear until 1620 when he served for one year. This raises the interesting point that a gap existed within the clergy serving the Pendle Forest at the very time that the witch accusations were coming to the fore.

St. Mary's interior 1916

Although it is probable that locum clergy would attend the church the question is raised as to whether a lack of spiritual guidance within the Forest was relevant to the 1612 outbreak? Would a settled clergyman have recognised the rumblings of discontent and acted to quell them - thus preventing the executions of 1612? We will probably never know the answer to this but nevertheless the question remains.

50

The generation to which Old Demdike and Old Chattox belonged grew up in the ruins of a once-proud abbey system. Their parents before them lived through the Dissolution and would have been loyal to the old faith; these people would see the enforced change in the religious practices of the nation and this would certainly have coloured their views and the views of their children.

Henry VIII had instigated *Catholicism Without the Pope* and this was enthusiastically taken up by his son, Edward VI (1547-53), in his general *Protestantisation*. During the reign of the pro-Catholic Mary Tudor (1553-58) many new Catholic clergy were either ordained or converted to the faith. However, the pendulum swung back again when Elizabeth I (1558-1603) ascended the throne and quickly re-established the Protestant doctrines of her father. Many refused to conform to the new ways and, of those who did, a great number continued to encourage Catholic practice within their own parishes. Elizabeth's many Protestant Acts were to become collectively known as the *Penal Period* and during this time the penalties for refusal to adopt the new ways became increasingly severe. In 1571, 1581 and 1585 Acts were passed to make it an offence of high treason to call the queen a heretic, to be reconciled to the Catholic church or to be a Catholic priest (or harbour such) within Elizabeth's realm.

This had the effect of sending the Catholic faith underground. Many secret places of worship existed locally and even today a small number of examples can be found within farm outbuildings where ordinary people would hear Mass. The Catholic gentry were able to hide their priests and chapels within their large mansions and halls.

Elizabeth's reign saw the halls of academia purged of their former Catholic influence and this left a vacuum when the acquisition of Catholic learning was forced abroad. In 1568 a Lancastrian named Cardinal William Allen, who was the son of Jane Lister of Westby near Gisburn, founded a college at Douai in the Low Countries. This new academic centre produced an English New Testament in 1582 and an Old Testament in 1609-10. The Douai institution ran alongside the English College in Rome as the power-house of the Catholic mission to England.

Many of the sons of Catholic gentry, usually the younger sons who would not inherit the family estates, were sent to Douai to train as priests in which role they would return to England and secretly provide for the spiritual needs of those who upheld the old faith. A local product of this system was Robert Nutter, the son of Ellis Nutter of Waterside and New Laund within the Forest of Pendle. Robert accompanied his brother John to the Douai college and was ordained at Rheims in December 1581 – within a fortnight of this Robert, who assumed the surname of Rowley (after the area near to his home in Reedley) was sent on the English mission where he concentrated on the areas of the South Midlands, London and the South Coast.

Unfortunately for the English missionaries Elizabeth's government had a highly effective spy network that were adept at quickly apprehending the illegal priests. A surviving record of this network shows that Robert was an excellent missionary and this led to his being quickly caught in Oxford early in 1584; he was imprisoned in the Tower of London and tortured. While this was going on his brother John, also recently apprehended, was executed in February 1584. The case against Robert appears to have collapsed because he was put on a ship in January 1585 and, along with a number of other captured missionaries, was banished abroad under the threat of death if they were to attempt to return to England.

Before the year was out Robert was once again throwing himself upon English shores and was arrested even before he had reached dry land. The threat of execution was not carried out, instead he was subjected to a number of prison sentences culminating in a long stay at Wisbech Gaol where he enlisted as a Jesuit in the Saint Dominic's Order of Preachers. His second attempt to escape from Wisbech succeeded and by early 1600 Robert was making his way back to his native Pendle Forest.

Probably because the government agents expected him to return home Robert Nutter was arrested in Lancashire in May 1600 and was imprisoned in Lancaster Castle and executed in July of that year for being a priest under the Act of 1585. This was intended to have been a deterrent to the Catholic people of Lancashire. Ellis Nutter, the nephew of Robert and John, was ordained as a priest in 1601 and went on to train at the English College in Rome for the English mission.

Another member of the Pendle Nutter family, John Nutter of Newchurch-in-Pendle (Goldshaw) could also boast of an important member of the church. John Nutter entered Brasenose College in 1575 where, in that same year, he took the degree of B.D; he became a royal chaplain and was characterised by Queen Elizabeth as a *'Golden Ass.'* He was probably the curate of Eccles in 1563, was rector of Haighton, in Liverpool, in 1577 and of Bebington in 1579. Nutter had appointments in Chester Cathedral and became dean there in 1589. He was also the rector of Sefton, in Liverpool, and it was here that he was buried in 1602 following his sudden death.[19]

It is clear, then, that the religious and social upheaval that was apparent throughout Elizabeth Southern's life would have had a profound effect upon the way that she, and her contemporaries, would have related to their environment. The church authority, at least within Pendle, had become lax and it would be natural for the older generation to employ many of the 'old' ways learned at their mother's knee. Thus we see that many of the 'spells' employed by the accused in the 1612 witch trials were actually garbled Catholic prayers.

THE ROLE OF THE GENTRY

GUNPOWDER PLOT

Each year, on the fifth of November, we fill the skies with thousands of pounds-worth of fireworks and a good time is had by all. However, it is fair to say that the majority of revellers on Bonfire Night will never have given a thought to the fact that, without the Gunpowder Plot of 1605, the Pendle witch trials might never have taken place. On the Good Friday of 1612, shortly after Elizabeth Southern had been arrested and imprisoned, it became apparent that a meeting had been held at Southern's home of Malkin Tower. According to statements taken from Southern's grandchildren, by magistrate Roger Nowell of Read Hall, the purpose of the meeting was to use gunpowder to blow up Lancaster Castle, kill the warders and release the prisoners.

The fanciful statements taken by Nowell do not reflect the reality of the situation at Malkin Tower. It is highly probable, as we shall see later, that the meeting was no more than a gathering of friends, family and neighbours with the intention of discussing the worrying situation of Elizabeth Southern's arrest. However, to Nowell this was an ideal opportunity to up the ante from accusing a few simple peasants of witchcraft to foiling a major diabolical crime against the state, and by definition, the king. King James I had been lucky to escape with his life when the Gunpowder Plot had been prevented and in 1612 his lucky escape still haunted him. How grateful, then, would he have been to learn that one of his magistrates, in a northern backwater of his realm, had actually foiled another attempt on his authority by the use of gunpowder?

As the son of the Catholic Mary, Queen of Scots, James I was expected to be much less severe against the Catholics than Elizabeth had been, in fact the Catholic hierarchy had petitioned in order to gain his favour for some time before he ascended to the throne upon the death of Elizabeth I in 1603. Some Catholics even believed that he might lift the persecution, and allow them to worship freely; the new king, however, was under pressure from many members of the House of Commons who were strongly anti-Catholic. He also became less sympathetic towards Catholics following the discovery of a series of minor Catholic plots against him. The *'Bye Plot'* of 1603 was a conspiracy to kidnap the king and force him to repeal anti-Catholic legislation whilst the *'Main Plot'* was an alleged plan by Catholic clergy and nobles to remove the king and replace him with his cousin, the Catholic Arabella Stuart.

James' wife, Anne of Denmark, converted to Catholicism and this was one of a number of factors that led many Catholics to hope for toleration under his rule. These final hopes were dashed when it became clear that James was not going to honour his pre-reign promises to the Catholics, in fact he denied ever making them and the persecution under him was going to be worse than under Elizabeth. James now made clear his utter detestation of papists, he stated that *'the bishops must see to the severe and exact punishment of every Catholic.'* He also made a new proclamation on February 22nd 1604 ordering all priests out of the realm; recusancy fines were tightened and became payable immediately with arrears.

At James' request a Bill was introduced into the House of Commons on April 24th to classify all Catholics as excommunicates, an idea which had been presented to, and rejected by, Elizabeth as being too severe. Tesimond describes the effect of this bill:

In consequence, they were no longer able to make their wills or dispose of their goods. The effect of this law was to make them outlaws and exiles; and like such they were treated. There was no longer any obligation to pay them their debts or rents for land held from them. They could not now go to law or have the laws protection. They could seek no remedy for ills and injuries received. In a word, they were considered and treated as professed enemies of the state.

The Catholics saw this as a disaster as it was thought that it would lead to their utter ruin. It was also the final straw for a group of dissident Catholic gentry who had been gathering together across the country for some time, thoroughly disillusioned with the treatment that they and their fellows had received for many years the matter came swiftly to a head. The leader of this group, Catesby, almost immediately after the passing of the Act, sent for his cousin Thomas Wintour and revealed the Gunpowder Plot to him at a meeting with Jack Wright at his house in Lambeth. Catesby felt that *'the nature of the disease required so sharp a remedy'* and that the Plot was a morally justifiable act of self-defence against the oppressive rule of a tyrant.

However, Catesby saw the Plot as an act of last resort and was determined to leave no stone unturned in his quest to remedy the situation by peaceful means and without bloodshed. To this end, he sent Thomas Wintour to Flanders to meet with the Constable of Spain, who was on his way to England to conclude the peace negotiations between Spain and England. He was to *'inform the Constable of the condition of the Catholics here in England, entreating him to solicit his Majesty at his coming hither that the penal laws may be recalled, and we admitted into the ranks of his other subjects.'* This, of course, was to no avail and so Catesby and his co-conspirators went ahead with their plans to blow up the Houses of Parliament and the king along with them.

Guy Fawkes had been recruited into the plot on the strength of his experiences in the Low Countries where, as a munitions expert, he had worked with gunpowder; he was therefore entrusted with the task of obtaining the powder and placing it within the House of Commons cellars. During October of 1605 Fawkes rented a storage room beneath the intended target and placed there some thirty-six kegs of powder. These were covered by bundles of faggots and on Wednesday 30th October Fawkes inspected the cellar again to satisfy himself that the gunpowder was still in place and had not been disturbed.

In the meantime a letter, known as the Monteagle Letter, warning of the intended danger had found its way into the hands of the authorities and a search of the cellars was carried out on Sunday 3rd November; it is possible, even likely, that the powder was found by the authorities at this stage but, wishing to catch the plotters red-handed, this was kept quiet. A few of

the leading conspirators met in London and agreed that the authorities were still unaware of their actions. However, all except Fawkes made plans for a speedy exit from London. Fawkes had agreed to watch the cellar alone; having already been given the task of firing the powder his orders were to embark for Flanders as soon as the charge was fired and spread the news of the explosion on the continent.

On the following Monday afternoon, the Lord Chamberlain, Thomas Howard, Earl of Suffolk, searched the Parliament buildings accompanied by Monteagle and John Whyniard. In the cellar they came upon an unusually large pile of billets and faggots, and saw Guy Fawkes whom they described as *'a very bad and desperate fellow.'* They asked who owned the pile, and Fawkes replied that it was Thomas Percy's in whose employment he worked. They reported these details to the king describing Fawkes as a man *'who seemed to be shrewd enough, but up to no good.'* They again searched the cellar, a little before midnight the following night, this time led by Sir Thomas Knyvett. Fawkes had gone forth to warn Percy that same day, but returned to his post before nightfall. Once again the pile of billets and faggots was searched; the powder was discovered, and this time Fawkes was arrested. On his person they discovered a watch, slowmatches and touchwood. Fawkes later declared that if he had been in the cellar when Knyvett entered it he would have *'blown him up, house, himself, and all.'*

When the House of Commons briefly assembled on the morning following the arrest of Guy Fawkes the Clerk, Ralph Ewens, added a note to the official records:

'This last night the Upper House of Parliament was searched by Sir Tho. Knevett; and one Johnson (Johnson was the assumed name of Guy Fawkes), *servant to Mr. Tho. Percy, was there apprehended; who had placed Thirty-six Barrels of Gunpowder in the vaulte under the House, with a purpose to blow King, and the whole Company, when they should there assemble. Afterwards divers other Gentlemen were discovered to be of the Plot.'*

Thirteen of the main conspirators were eventually apprehended, most of them being tortured and executed – many other known Catholic sympathisers were also arrested and questioned in the aftermath of the plot. Effectively the Gunpowder Plot increased the hostility of the nation to the Catholics and the penal laws were again enforced. Catholics who had begun to attend Church were now required to take the sacrament, churchwardens and constables were fined if they did not prosecute recusants (those who failed to attend church) and were rewarded for their success when they did so. New fines were inflicted on those who kept Catholic servants and recusants were forbidden to come within ten miles of London. They were forbidden to practice as attorneys or physicians; they could not be executors of a will, nor guardians of children, they might not be married except in the Church of England, their books could be destroyed and their houses visited by the magistrates in search of arms. It is said that courtiers bought from the king the shameful privilege of seizing land and property belonging to the wealthier Catholics.

In our own area Nicholas Bannister, of Altham, was a trusted agent of the crown whose remit was to strip local Catholics of a large percentage of their property.[20]
Life under James I, then, was no more a bed of roses for the Catholics than it had been for the past sixty-five years. In the few years leading up to the Witch Trials the social environment was uneasy, the government, and therefore their underling gentry, could well be described as being skittish. The Catholic gentry went about their business with more than the occasional glance over their shoulder whilst the Protestant gentry, within the limits of their own particular powerbase, took pains to court the king. A Puritan attitude was beneficial here, anyone with social aspirations was constantly seen in church and heard to preach the Protestant doctrine loud and clear; behind the scenes, however, there was much disagreement among the high Puritan clergy as to what exactly constituted the official spiritual line.

One thing was for certain, if gentry families such as the Listers of Westby, and the Nowells of Read, were to enjoy the continuing favour of the king they had to respond in kind; furthermore, any deed or service they provided to benefit the crown had to gain the ear of Westminster – publicity was the name of the game. It was of little use to industriously serve the king from a Lancashire backwater if he was unaware that you were doing so – the thing that was required here was a sound network of fellow civil servants stretching from the depths of the Forest down to London. The local gentry were not shy in this department and what better way to catch the king's eye than to be seen to foil a dastardly attempt on His Majesty's authority by a socially disingenuous group of demon-worshipping terrorists ensconced within the diabolical Malkin Tower? Armed to the teeth with barrels of gunpowder this treacherous band were all-but ready to blow the Castle at Lancaster sky high until our brave local Justices, employing all their available wit, intelligence and supreme loyalty to the Crown, stepped in and foiled the new Gunpowder Plot at the last minute.

On Good Friday 1612 Roger Nowell was able to provide written evidence that a diabolical meeting of witches had taken place at Malkin Tower and that the main purpose of this meeting of some twenty witches was to blow up the prison at Lancaster Castle, in so doing they would kill the governor and release their colleagues incarcerated there. No matter that this group were actually families of poor elderly people and children who, in the cases of Ann Whittle and Elizabeth Southern, had survived in a harsh and unforgiving environment for over seventy winters. In later life at least, these matriarchs were without the aid of men-folk and had reared their children and grandchildren to the best of their ability; in reality these people had probably harmed not a single person. No matter either that Nowell's 'evidence' was based upon the disjointed testimony of a child and the twisted words of a naive young man. These facts were of no consequence to certain social-climbing landowners ensconced within their halls and mansions.

When the opportunity of being seen to foil another Gunpowder Plot presented itself Roger Nowell was not about to let the truth stand in the way of excellent propaganda. The Northern Circuit of Westminster Judges in the coming August was to be attended by James Altham and his colleague, Justice Edward Bromley. Roger Nowell knew these judges well, he knew their methods and was able to gather his 'evidence' for the witch trials in such a manner that would impress them at the coming August Assizes. The first cog within a larger wheel of injustice was set in place.

Magistrate Roger Nowell, then, was a member of the new Protestant gentry whose collective conscience required salving. They were the offspring of former Catholic landowners and, like all reformers, had a chip on their shoulders; they were constantly seeking new ways to impress their superiors and it is apparent that the lives of those less well off than themselves were considered to be nothing other than game-pieces to be played with as and when the opportunity arose.
A parallel interest arises her in that one Sir Thomas Knyvet was the man who actually discovered the Gunpowder Plot and saved the day. Now it just so happens that Sir Thomas Knyvet, Baron of Eskrick and privy Councillor, was the very man who commissioned Thomas Potts to write his account *(The Wonderfull Discoverie of Witches)* of the 1612 witch trials.

Knyvet realised the accounts relating to the Pendle witch trials, containing as they did direct references to a gunpowder plot of sorts, would make interesting reading for the king and this would remind his sovereign just how efficient Knyvet had been back in 1605. Potts, who was clerk of the court at the Lancaster trials, was an effective conduit through which Knyvet could gain the ear of the king.

There was indeed good reason for Knyvet to wish to impress James I. As a keeper of the Jewel House, under Elizabeth I, Knyvet held a certain amount of respect but this was never a high-flying position. Following the Gunpowder Plot he became a favourite of king James and was appointed Warden of the Mint, he was also made a knight and privy councillor, was guardian to James' daughter Mary and, in 1607, was made Baron of Escrick.

Unfortunately for Knyvet his skills in handling money were somewhat limited and thousands of pounds of royal funds were lost. He held on to his position by exaggerating the threat to James' person from the Catholics and promoting himself as Keeper of the King's Person. The publishing of the *Wonderfull Discoverie of Witches* in 1613 was timed so as to revive Knyvet's fortunes within the royal court.

Within the Gunpowder Plot story we see a sub-text of Catholic intrigue played out against the insecurities of not only those charged with keeping the Crown authority on an even keel in difficult times, but also those people at the very top within society - the king's court.

Under the authority of Roger Nowell, then, we see that the frail and the old, men, women and children, mothers and sons were rounded up from their cottages, manipulated into providing unbelievable testimony regarding a new Gunpowder Plot, and thrown into the dungeons of Lancaster Jail. It was perfectly clear to the authorities that the unspeakable conditions within the jail often led to the deaths of prisoners long before their trials had even begun. And so it proved with Elizabeth Southern who died in her new dungeon home only a few weeks following her incarceration.

The Pendle witches were ordinary people who happened to belong to a sub-culture whose priorities were to stave off malnutrition and keep a fire burning in the hearth. They were not concerned with the niceties of society - the social machinations of the gentry did not concern them. These diverse sub-cultures had managed to avoid any meaningful interaction for a long time but they had now collided head-on. There was to be, of course, only one loser.

What chance were the likes of Elizabeth Southern and Anne Whittle ever going to stand when faced with the full might of an insecure, self-serving, socially aspirational and suspicious society?

THE LOCAL GENTRY

LISTERS OF WESTBY

In the March of 1612 the Pendle Witch round-up was gathering pace. There was, however, a precedent for these events and this is where a gentry family, some three-miles to the east of the Pendle Forest (over the old Yorkshire border) was causing a stir. The Listers of Westby Hall, an estate just outside the village of Gisburn, had been through trying times. Although the family were certainly not alone in experiencing the pressures caused by the past fifty-years of religious strife the Listers took their inter-family tensions to a new height. The resultant injustice here saw an innocent woman dragged to the gallows; this is the story of Jennet Preston of Gisburn.

Ribblesdale Lower Hall (Gisburn Park) 1914

The name of Lister is synonymous with the Gisburn area of West Craven – the family was first mentioned at Gisburn in 1312 and eventually the title of Lord Ribblesdale applied to this branch of the family, a name that has long been connected with the village through the extensive Ribblesdale estates and Gisburn Park.

A potted history of the family is that, in the early fourteenth century, a John Lister of West Derby married Isabel de Bolton who was the widow of Roger de Clitheroe. Isabel was the daughter and co-heiress of John de Bolton, of Bolton-by-Bowland and Middop, bowbearer of the Forest of Bowland and was descended from Leofric, king of Mercia and his wife, Lady Godiva of Coventry, who also had two sons, the youngest of whom was Hereward the Wake. The eldest son was Algar who succeeded Leofric to the throne. Clitheroe was part of Mercia at that time.

The Listers of Gisburn therefore hold a direct kinship with the Mercian royal family and the coronet on top of their coat of arms is the heraldic emblem of this connection - this can be seen in the Ribblesdale chapel in Gisburn parish church. The marriage of Isabel de Bolton and John Lister brought the areas of Middop, Rimington, Gisburn and Clitheroe into the Lister family. Adelaide Lister, sister of the fourth Baron Ribblesdale, was the last of the Gisburn Listers and died in 1943.

The seat of the Listers was originally at the fortified manor house of Arnoldsbiggin, on the edge of the villages of Gisburn and Rimington, but in 1520 Thomas Lister married Effamia de Westbye, of neighbouring Westby Hall, and this brought Westby into Lister hands. Arnoldsbiggin was demolished in the 1730s to provide stone for the refurbishment of Ribblesdale Lower Hall (Gisburn Park), this being the property to which the Lister family were to move.

Jennet Preston was *'of Gisborne in Craven in the Countie of Yorke'* and it is likely that she was born Jennet Balderston as, in 1587, a woman of this name married William Preston at Gisburn Parish Church. William was possibly of the Preston family of Giggleswick where, in 1572, Roger Preston and Agnes Lund had a child Alice baptised. Jennet was a servant of Thomas Lister, the head of the Lister household and in his *Lancashire Witch Craze* Jonathan Lumby makes a strong case for Thomas Lister and Jennet Preston having grown up together in the Gisburn area - they had possibly been lifelong friends.[21]

According to the church records Jennet Preston would have been aged thirty eight years when Thomas Lister died in 1607.

Lumby shows that Thomas Lister probably collapsed and died at the marriage of his sixteen year-old son, Thomas Lister junior, at Bracewell Church. Thomas senior lay dying and cried out for Jennet in front of the assembled wedding guests and this would be highly embarrassing for his wife, Jane and son, Thomas. Having earlier tried and failed to have Jennet Preston prosecuted for the killing of a child of the Dodgeson family (probably from the Gisburn locality) Lister junior eventually found an unlikely ally in James Device, grandson of Elizabeth Southern of Malkin Tower.

Jennet Preston was said to have taken against the young Lister following his failed attempt to prosecute her for practising witchcraft and James Device stated that she had attended a meeting of witches at Malkin Tower on Good Friday, 10th April 1612 – this was four days after Jennet's acquittal at York. One of the purposes of this 'diabolical' meeting was, according to James Device, for Jennet Preston to enlist the aid of her neighbours in Pendle to bring about *'the utter ruin and overthrow of the name and the blood of this gentleman* (Thomas Lister).' In other words, according to the evidence of the young Device, Jennet planned to murder Thomas Lister junior and, just for good measure, his uncle Leonard Lister (1575-1618) of Cowgill on the outskirts of Gisburn.

Having his witnesses in place and his case prepared young Lister enlisted the aid of his father-in-law, magistrate Thomas Heber of the neighbouring village of Marton, and had Jennet indicted at the July 1612 York Assizes where she was summarily convicted and executed on the Knavesmire (the present site of York racecourse). Many friends, family and neighbours of Jennet vociferously protested her innocence, probably because they knew the real story of her good relationship with Thomas Lister and the jealous acts of his young son following his father's death.

Jennet was first accused of witchcraft in 1607 and this would reinforce the new mind-set of suspicion amongst the local, inter-related gentry that would simmer until coming to a head in Pendle some five years later. Further to this, the judges Altham and Bromley, who were to try the Pendle witch cases at Lancaster later in the year of 1612, were the judges at the trial of Jennet Preston and this created a legal framework within which Roger Nowell could operate. Nowell would have had plenty of time to assess the Westby case and set out his methods of interrogation accordingly. By the time of the August Assizes of 1612 Nowell's case for the prosecution was finely honed so as to press all the right buttons with Altham and Bromley.

STARKIE OF HUNTROYD

Roger Nowell married Katherine Murton in 1551 and he was the son of Roger Nowell and Florence Starkie. At the time of this marriage Florence was the widow of Laurence Starkie of Huntroyd Hall, in Simonstone. One of the Starkie offspring of this marriage, Nicholas, inherited Cleworth Hall in Lancashire and it was here that a celebrated case of supposed witchcraft occurred when Starkie's two children began to have fits in 1595. Not long afterwards Starkie's three other children began to suffer the same symptoms followed by a maid and an elderly relation. In line with the mindset of the day the symptoms of these people were immediately assigned to possession by the devil whereas today the case would be viewed as nothing more than adoptive hysteria.

To cut a long story short, Starkie hired a professional wise man in the shape of one Edmund Hartley, his remit being to effect a cure upon the affected people within the Starkie household. It is probable that Hartley was a close relative of John Hartley of Liverpool, clerk and servant to John Nutter (dean of Chester). The Starkies owned estates in Haighton (Liverpool) where John Hartley was based – no doubt John Hartley, or dean Nutter, were able to recommend Edmund Hartley to the Starkies as being 'the man for the job' – with consequences!

Through the use of herbs, potions and psychology Hartley regained some degree of control over the mass hysteria within Starkie's domain. Things quietened down for about one year but Hartley began to demand increased payment for his services. The children began to grow wilder and related that Hartley had kissed them and laid on their beds – Freudian tales of furry devils began to emerge and this proved to be too much for Starkie who accused Hartley of employing the use of witchcraft. He was therefore arraigned at the Lancaster Assizes of 1597 and sentenced to death.

The first attempt at hanging failed when the rope snapped and Hartley hit the ground standing; stupefied and amazed at his survival he decided that he must have been guilty after all and didn't think twice about saying so - gibbering and obviously in shock Hartley proclaimed his guilt loudly and clearly! At this point he was strung up again, this time with more success.

The salient point of this story is that Nowell, who was closely related to the Starkies, would have followed these events closely; by 1612 the Starkies had removed to the family seat of Huntroyd. The fact that this estate was almost adjacent to Nowell's home at Read, and that Nowell was related to Starkie, would have ensured that he could draw upon Starkie's experience as prosecutor during Hartley's witchcraft trial. In fact this whole peculiar episode within the everyday life of the gentry could be said to have been the trial-run (no pun intended) for the major events that were to unfold in 1612.

Lawrence Starkie's son, John Starkie, was to be involved in the second Pendle witch hunt of 1633 when he, and fellow magistrate Richard Shuttleworth, examined Edmund Robinson at Gawthorpe Hall.

Huntroyd Hall

ROGER NOWELL OF READ

Not being the most stable of characters James I appears to have become somewhat obsessed by the 'science of demons' and to this end he published a treatise on witchcraft in 1597 entitled *'Daemonologie, in Forme of a Dialogue, Divided into Three Books,'* this was reprinted in London as *'Daemonologie'* when he gained the English crown in 1603. This unfortunate work was to become the reference text for all those in authority who were charged to uphold the law in James' kingdom. Not least of these proponents of the king's views on the subject of witchcraft were the circuit judges, Justices of the Peace and the Puritan gentry – the very people who were central to the prosecution of the Pendle Witch Trials.

When, in his official capacity as magistrate, Roger Nowell of Read Hall began to receive official complaints of witchcraft on his patch there was a weight of bias upon his shoulders; whether he realised it or not he was just as much a victim of the paranoid atmosphere of the times as was the lowliest forest dweller - unfortunately it was to be the latter who would 'carry the can' for this state of affairs.

Read Hall from an engraving of c.1750

Roger Nowell was also related to Alexander Nowell (1507-1602) who was dean of Saint Paul's throughout the reign of Elizabeth I, despite the fact that she detested him! Alexander Nowell has been credited with the invention of bottled ale; when on a fishing trip he decanted a jug of beer into a bottle and placed it in a net in the river at Read Bridge to keep cool. Having forgotten to take one of the bottles home with him he noticed on his return a week or so later that the beer had fermented slightly within the bottle and this gave it a pleasant aerated quality. He worked out that the fermentation process could be carried on once beer had been sealed in a container and passed the knowledge on to a friend in the brewing trade. Alexander's brother, Lawrence, became the dean of Lichfield and another brother, Robert, became a prominent lawyer and held the post of Queen's Attorney of the Court of Wards; Queen Elizabeth's minister, Lord Burghley, was an executor of Robert's will.

Roger Nowell could also boast as second cousins John Wolton, Bishop of Exeter and Dr. William Whittaker, Regius Professor of Divinity at Cambridge and a relative of T. D. Whitaker the historian. The Nowells were also closely related to the local gentry families of Towneley, Sherburne of Stoneyhurst and Bradyll of Portfield and Whalley.

Nowell's son, Christopher (who was one of ten children), married Eleanor Shuttleworth of Gawthorpe Hall; her family employed Robert Nutter of Greenhead who was supposedly bewitched to death by Old Chattox. Another son, Roger, followed his father into the magistracy.

It is often claimed that Roger Nowell had cause to prosecute Alice Nutter of Roughlee in the 1612 trials because of a contentious land dispute between the two families of Nowell and Nutter. There does not appear to be any direct evidence for this but confusion may have arisen from the fact that another Nutter family had land dealings with Nowell in Pendle Forest.

Roger Nowell, in common with most gentry of the time, was not averse to claiming or re-claiming lands and property wherever possible – in the years following the 1612 trials he was constantly at odds with his son Roger over his Read and Simonstone land holdings; Roger junior took his father to court in a bid to prove that he did not owe suite to him in respect of Nowell senior's manorial rights.

Having built up their fortunes under Elizabeth I the Nowell family were keen to be seen to serve the new king, to this end Roger signed the Loyal Address of the Lancashire Gentry, a document welcoming James I to the throne. Nowell's standing within the extended area of Lancashire was considerable and it did him no harm to be seen to actively pursue the king's enemies within his own area of control. The imposition of religious uniformity throughout the Forest of Pendle, and the wider parish of Whalley, served as an example to people that the laws of the Protestant church were to be obeyed.

We have, then, at least a flavour of the man who instigated the Pendle Witch trials.

TOWNELEY OF CARR HALL

The Towneleys were a powerful landowning family with their roots firmly set in the Medieval period. The main family seat became the Towneley Hall, at Burnley while offshoots of the family set up estates at various other sites; chief among these being Barnseat, to the east of Colne, and Carr Hall, in the Pendle Forest booth of Wheatley Carr.

In 1544 Lawrence Towneley, of Barnside, erected a new water corn mill on the riverside at Wheatley Carr and around 1580 Henry Towneley, son of Lawrence, erected Carr Hall on a site to the north of the mill. This new building was orientated north-south and was later absorbed into a rebuild of the hall as the entrance hall and main kitchen.

The rear of Carr Hall during demolition in 1954.

The central bay was the chapel, oriented on the line of the original hall where James Device was ushered out by Anne Towneley

Photograph courtesy of R J Hayhurst

Our interest lies in the fact that Demdike's grandson, James Device, was going about his usual routine at the end of February, 1610, when his business took him by way of Carr Hall. James left the trackway running from Laund Farm down to the ford across the Calder and arrived at the rear of the hall where the outbuildings were situated. He entered the kitchen in the hope that one of the staff would feel sorry for him and give him a stale bun or two. However, this was not James' first visit to the Hall and when Anne Towneley, mistress of the Hall, came into the kitchen she remembered him all too well.

Mistress Towneley shouted at James, accusing *'him and his mother'* of having stolen some of her turves (peat fuel for the fire) and bade him begone. As he *'went forth of the door the said Mistress Townley gave him a knock between the shoulders.'* A day or two later a black dog met him, and reminding him of the insult put upon him by Mrs. Towneley, directed him to make a clay image like Mrs. Towneley and he would help him to destroy her. Bidding James to call him Dandy, the spirit disappeared. The next morning he made an image of clay of Mrs. Towneley and dried it the same night by the fire. Every day he crumbled away a piece of this image and at the end of a week it was all gone - two days later Mrs. Towneley died.

In his statement to Roger Nowell James said that he had been accused of stealing turves but this sounds to be a strange thing to have done as turves had very little value and he would have only managed to carry two or three for any distance; these would not have burned for long enough to make the effort worthwhile! However, there is a strong possibility that James would have taken a hand-barrow on his travels. We hear accounts within Potts' record that even when one or other of the accused was some distance from home they still welcomed gifts in the form of heavy piggins of milk.

A full piggin would have weighed more than an elderly woman could have carried for any distance, it would also be difficult to carry due to the fact that this type of bucket only had one handle. The likelihood is, then, that a barrow would have been taken on begging expeditions and it appears that James Device, and his mother, Elizabeth, had called at Carr Hall previously and filled their barrow from the turf house at the back of the hall. It is likely that they were seen by one of the staff who, not wishing to confront the pair, had reported the theft to Mistress Towneley. It would have presented a comical scene as James Device and his mother legged it up the hill with a fully laden barrow - him wild-eyed, puffing and blowing and stealing constant furtive glances to the rear in case they were being pursued. Elizabeth, meanwhile, would have hoisted her skirts clear of the heavy boots that she always wore when foraging and set off in full sail, cursing ill-fit-to-burst!

SHUTTLEWORTH OF GAWTHORPE

Gawthorpe Hall stands by the Calder at the southern foot of Pendle Forest. The name of Shuttleworth has become synonymous with Gawthorpe, there having been tenants of that name there since at least 1389. Gawthorpe Hall stands on the site of an early tower of four stories and walls eight feet in thickness - possibly a watch-tower related to the neighbouring king's manor at Ightenhill or a Pele tower to warn of Scots marauders.

Over the centuries the Shuttleworths married well and accumulated wealth and lands; during the 1520s they acquired the area of West Close in Pendle and went on to enclose parcels of Ightenhill and Padiham. By 1588 Hugh Shuttleworth, of Gawthorpe, was wealthy enough to have been lending money to the Crown; by 1600 the Shuttleworths had joined the Towneleys as the two most influential families in the district. Sir Richard's daughter, Eleanor Shuttleworth, married Roger Nowell's son, Christopher.

The Hall as we now see it was begun in 1600 and the roofing level had been reached by June 1602. By 1605 the Hall accounts show that there were ten male servants and four female servants.[22]

Sir Richard Shuttleworth figures in our account of the Pendle witches as he was a Justice of the Peace on the Cheshire circuit. Early in 1593 Robert Nutter, of Greenhead, was the retainer of Sir Richard and he accompanied his master to Cheshire early in 1593. Robert had fallen out with Anne Redfearn at her home in West Close around May-time of 1592 and he had fallen ill by June. He obviously did not recover from this illness as he was dead by the 2nd of February (Candlemas) 1593 - Anne Redfearn's mother, Old Chattox, carried the blame for his death. Having died in Cheshire it is likely that his cousin, John Nutter, who was dean of Chester at that time, would have buried Robert there as Robert does not appear to have been buried locally.

Christopher Nutter, Robert's father had initially scolded his son for believing he was bewitched but he too became ill and by late September of the same year he too was dead - this was blamed upon Anne Redfearn. This ties in exactly with the record of Christopher Nutter who was buried at Burnley in late September 1593. In her reply to the accusations of witchcraft Chattox said that Robert Nutter had been to her house at nearby West Close and made a pass at Anne Redfearn; when she scorned his advances Nutter rode off in high dudgeon saying that *'If ever the ground came to him she would never dwell upon his land.'*

Gawthorpe Hall

Sir Thomas Gerard of Bryn

Sir Thomas Gerard hardly warrants a mention within the Pendle witch story but, as we shall see, he had a definite role to play. In fact, Gerard was possibly instrumental in setting the whole thing in motion. It is very probable that Gerard was enlisted by Roger Nowell to act as an aide in the witch hunt. His uncle, Gilbert Gerard, was the Queen's Attorney at law and, as such, prosecuted a major witch trial in 1566 - Gilbert also owned farms and land in Pendle Forest.

On the 19th August 1612 Isabell Roby was found guilty at the Lancaster Assizes of witchcraft and sentenced to death. Although not from the Pendle area she is of interest to the local case as she stood shoulder-to-shoulder with the Pendle accused and died with them on the scaffold.

Isabell Roby was accused of being a dangerous witch within her home area of Windle, near Saint Helens (Liverpool), and her case was brought by Sir Thomas Gerard of Bryn whose family seat was The Brynne, near Ashton-in-Makerfield. Sir Thomas's father was a notorious Catholic recusant who had been involved in subterfuge against the Crown; he eventually conformed (at least in public) and held on to the majority of his estate which, in turn, he passed on to his son Sir Thomas. Thomas's younger brother was one John Gerard who, as a leading Catholic missionary, played a major role in the Gunpowder Plot for which he was imprisoned – Gerard did not take kindly to this and so he escaped to France.

There is no doubt that there was a strong network between the owners of many Liverpool estates and our local forest gentry. Sir Thomas Gerard married the sister of Sir Richard Houghton, of Houghton Tower, and this brought him into the powerful families of Lister, Towneley, Nowell and Asshton. Not least of the links between the two areas was John Nutter of Newchurch-in-Pendle, dean of Chester and parson of Sefton, whose sponsor was the earl of Sefton. Nutter's right-hand-man was clerk John Hartley, also of Liverpool and close relative of the Pendle Forest Hartley families. Along with properties within Liverpool dean Nutter had rights to lands adjoining the estates of Sir Thomas Gerard in Wigan and Ashton.

The prosecution of Isabell Roby, at the same time as the Pendle Witches were being arraigned, would almost certainly have been as a consequence of her nemesis, Sir Thomas Gerard, being close to the major players of 1612 i.e. Roger Nowell, the Towneleys, Thomas Lister, Nicholas Bannister and Sir Richard Shuttleworth *et al*. Gerard would very quickly have heard through the old (underground) Catholic grapevine of the feeding-frenzy that was happening within Pendle Forest; reputations were to be enhanced by arresting a few poor wretches and offering them up to the seat of idiocy occupied by the Sovereign. If his mates in Pendle were finding witches then Thomas Gerard was not going to be left out – unfortunately for one Isabell Roby.

There is no greater, or more intense, a proponent of a subject than a recent convert intent on proving themselves and so it was with the newly-Protestant Sir Thomas Gerard who went out of his way to court the king; he was almost the first to purchase one of the new baronetcies, at a cost of £1,000, in May 1611 and he quickly made a show of his new-found loyalty to the king in that year by being the first baronet to fund the Protestant movement in Ulster. Gerard now needed to prove himself as worthy of his role as a Justice of the Peace and what could be better than to put a nice juicy witchcraft case under his belt? The evidence against Isabell Roby was that anyone who happened to disagree with her fell ill and died. Despite the testimony of a prosecution witness, who firmly stated that Roby was not a witch, she was found guilty and sentenced to death.

Hearing lurid stories of the unrest within Pendle Forest, Gerard lost no time in contacting his gentry family in Pendle with the intention of offering his services. Meanwhile he saw in the accusations against Isobell Roby the opportunity to bag a witch on his own patch and it is no coincidence that Roby stood accused at the same trials as her Pendle Forest counterparts.

RICHARD ASSHETON OF DOWNHAM

In 1567 Richard Assheton purchased part of, *'all the desmesne of Whalley and the lands called Whalley Park, and all the capital house and site of the said monastery of Whalley...'*

By the 1580s Richard Assheton has acquired the manor of Downham and his two sons were Richard (died 1597) and Nicholas (1590-1625).[24] In 1592 Richard junior married Isabell, the daughter of William Hancock of Downham and Kirkby (West Yorkshire); William inherited Pendle Hall in Lower Higham (West Close) and the property went to his widow who granted it to trustees in 1649 for the sum of £500.

Downham Manor House

The Hancocks were a gentry family who had owned lands in West Close at least back to fifteenth century, a Hen Cock (Hancock) Hall still exists there today. The Asshetons were also closely related to Sir Thomas Gerard, the Towneleys, the Listers, the Haydocks of Burnley, Roger Nowell and the Starkies of Huntroyd.

In a statement taken from her at Lancaster Jail, Old Chattox said that Demdike had admitted to her that she had killed one Richard Assheton, of Downham. This throw-away line is curious in that it is difficult to see why Demdike would have known Richard Assheton, let alone have motivation to bewitch him to death.

However, as we have seen, Assheton's brother-in-law was a major landowner in West Close where Chattox lived - this at least brings Assheton into the proximity of Demdike's realm. Further, the Asshetons owned land at Billington and other areas around Whalley and in this capacity they might just have been landlords of Demdike's family (see later under Elizabeth Southern).

SOUTHWORTH OF SAMLESBURY

The name of Southworth is synonymous with Samlesbury Hall, in Blackburn. The family can be traced to at least the twelfth century - when they received land at Southworth near Winwick, Lancashire, the family changed their name from de Croft to Southworth.

The family had two houses: the Lower Hall set by the Ribble, to the north of Samlesbury, and the Upper Hall which is now located on the A677. The original Lower Hall is thought to have been destroyed by the Scots in 1322 and around this time Gilbert de Southworth married Alice D'Ewyas thus gaining the Samlesbury manor. Gilbert built the Upper Hall and this site was the home of the main Southworth families from 1330 until it was sold in 1789. The Southworths stayed true to the Catholic faith and suffered numerous fines, and imprisonment, for recusancy.

In 1547 Sir John Southworth married Mary Assheton at Middleton, Lancashire. Mary was the daughter of Sir Richard Assheton, whose offspring took the seat of Downham manor - son Richard being supposedly bewitched to death by Demdike. Sir John's son, also John, married Jane Sherburne, daughter of Sir Richard of Stoneyhurst. Jane was a Protestant and this upset Sir John deeply - he even refused to pass by the Lower Hall where his son and daughter-in-law lived.

Samlesbury Hall: *Rev. A. Lambert*

In 1612 Jane's husband, John died and this provided an opportunity for the Southworth family to settle old scores. Christopher Southworth, a priest secretly attached to Samlesbury Hall, enlisted a fourteen year-old girl, Grace Sowerbutts, to accuse widow Jane of witchcraft. Grace also accused her aunt and grandmother of acting with Jane to cause Grace to sicken and waste away. Christopher Southworth, as a priest, had knowledge of the machinations of witchcraft and put Grace to describing all manner of dastardly deeds carried out by those she accused.

Grace stated in evidence that the three women had drawn her by the hair on her head and laid her on a hay mow, also that they appeared to her in their own likeness and sometimes in the form of a black dog. She declared that by their black arts she had been induced to join their sisterhood and they were met from time to time by *'four black things'* going upright, yet not like men in the face, who conveyed them across the River Ribble, where they danced and had intimate knowledge of them. The prisoners were also charged with bewitching a child of Thomas Walshmons by placing a nail in its navel; and after its burial they took up the corpse, when they ate part of the flesh and made an ointment by boiling the bones.

The main prosecutor of the trial of the Samlesbury women, on Wednesday the 19th August, was Robert Holden who happened to be the son-in-law of Roger Nowell's magistrate colleague, Nicholas Bannister of Altham. Justice Bromley was also a magistrate on the case and he knew the Southworth family.

Yew Tree Farm: reputed home of Grace Sowerbutts

Bromley was well aware of the very strong Catholic leanings within the family and he was suspicious of the case presented by Grace Sowerbutts. A number of witnesses from the Samlesbury area stood up and testified that Jane Southworth's father-in-law often accused her of being a witch and they were firmly of the opinion that this was because she attended the Anglican church. Bromley decided to re-examine Grace and she eventually admitted that the whole thing was a fabrication dreamed up by Christopher Southworth - the three accused women were duly freed.

During the early part of 1612 the authorities were clamping down on non-attendance at church and it was made clear that recusants would be prosecuted. This was yet another of the pressures that would lead to the arrest of the Pendle accused and it is probable that Justice Robert Holden was very aware of this. Given that the Southworths were flaunting their Catholicism on his patch. Holden would have seen an opportunity to flush out the Samlesbury priests and so he brought the case of the Samlesbury 'witches' to trial.

Although the case did not directly relate to the subject of his pamphlet Potts took great pains to include it. He delighted in describing how the justices had used great discretion and judgement in uncovering Catholic subterfuge and dismissing the case against innocent Protestants. This showed the prosecution to have been of a wise and kindly disposition and, therefore, it made the Pendle witch trials look all the more dastardly - those from Pendle who were convicted were tried by a fair system and must have deserved their fate. Further, a Catholic plot had been uncovered Potts ensured that the justices were bathed in glory.

Priest's 'hiding holes' found at Samlesbury

The Hall also contained an intricate web of subterranean tunnels which connected to an internal fireplace [25]

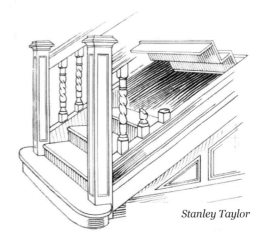

Stanley Taylor

THOMAS POTTS

In the year 1613, a few months following the Witch Trials of the previous August at Lancaster Assizes, Thomas Potts published his first-hand account of the proceedings under the title of *The Wonderfull Discoverie of Witches in the Countie of Lancaster*. *Potts* was the Associate Clerk on the Northern Circuit during the autumn sessions; he was also possibly the Clerk of Arraigns on the summer circuit of 1612. In this capacity he was responsible for drafting indictments and producing examinations and witness statements to the court as required.

Potts did not fare badly from his publication; under royal patronage in 1615 he was granted the keepership of Skalme Park where the favourite hounds of the king were trained. In 1618 he was granted the *'office of collecting forfeitures on the laws concerning sewers, for twenty-one years.'* Having the remit to appoint collectors under his keepership Potts could now consider himself as a minor patron, not too bad a position for a lowly clerk who had no university training.

Potts' account of the trials, then, can be viewed to a certain extent as propaganda with the intent of exalting the wisdom of all those in authority concerned with the removal of so many diabolical witches from the country – not to mention the fact that they had probably foiled another instance of the Gunpowder Plot!

Potts is at pains to explain that he provided us with a true and honest account of the trial proceedings, an account taken straight from the records at Lancaster Castle and therefore irrefutable. Unfortunately this cannot be substantiated and we have to look at Potts' motives for his publication. He wishes for the reader to stand in awe of the successful legal machinations so expertly carried out by His Majesty's northern authorities and Westminster judges. We are lucky on the one hand that Thomas Potts reported his version of events in that frenzied year of 1612, without his *Discoverie* we might well have never heard of the Pendle Witches – on the other hand the evidence provided to us almost four-hundred years ago must be examined not only with sympathy for the mindset of the day but also with the evidence furnished to us by both common sense and the hard facts of surviving written record.

If we were to remove the statements of the accused from the context of a witchcraft trial, and strip them of their fanciful Faustian embroidery, the many instances of diabolical happenings quoted within the Pendle Witch Trials would be rendered both normal and totally insignificant. However, this does not detract from the fact that we have a rare contemporary (if biased) record of Pendle Forest folk within the Early Modern period. It is of great value to our local history.

THE GENTRY VERSUS ALISON DEVICE

March 1612: this is the point where the social unease and religious unrest of the past half-century began to come to a head. A couple of years earlier, in February 1610, Anne Towneley, of Carr Hall, had a run-in with Demdike's grandson, James Device, and shortly afterwards she died. Convinced that she had been bewitched by Device, Anne's husband, Henry Towneley, found himself in somewhat of a tricky situation. If the master of Carr Hall were to voice his fears publicly then he would have little choice other than to back up his accusation through the law.

He knew that this would mean a protracted court case and in the end it would mean standing in court, with no firm evidence, in opposition to a daft young man who made his living from begging, interspersed by the odd labouring job. This would not do much for Towneley's reputation.

However, Towneley would have informed Roger Nowell of his suspicions and these would be duly noted alongside the accusations of Thomas Lister junior of Westby Hall. In 1607 Lister had accused Jennet Preston of having murdered his father by witchcraft and the Pendle gentry were well aware of this. In the October of 1569 Henry Towneley had passed the lease of his Carr Mill to Thomas Lister senior which shows the close business and social ties existing between members of the gentry throughout the extended district.

Beside the complaints of members of the gentry there were also an increasing number of concerns being voiced by the yeomanry of the area who were convinced that their families had been subjected to the evils of the Demdike and Chattox clans. Sir Richard Shuttleworth was well aware that he had lost his steward (Robert Nutter) and that the word on the street was that both Robert, and his father, had been bewitched by Shuttleworth's tenants. Ellena, the daughter of Richard Baldwin, of Wheathead, was buried at Colne on September 8th 1610 and Baldwin was convinced that Demdike had caused her death. There is no doubt that Baldwin would have informed Nowell at the first opportunity and so the tally of the fatally bewitched began to rise.

Further to this, we also see friction between the sub-tenants of the Pendle lands and the gentry landowners. Early in the reign of James I the Crown decided to contest the land tenure of the forest area and this caused a great deal of anguish and upheaval amongst the small landowners and tenants. The king's bare-faced cheek was rewarded by a compromised settlement whereby the tenants made a one-off payment to the Crown.

Things quietened down for a while but by 1611 the king was up to his old tricks. He commissioned another enquiry as to the 'doubtful' land-holdings and new lands taken from wastes. The crown commissioners appointed to oversee the new legalised robbery were Sir Richard Mollyneux and Sir Ralph Asshton, to whom John Nutter of Greenhead was servant.

The commissioners stated that they would only recognise copyholds if they were purchased from the king for £0: 9s: 4d per acre (twenty-eight years rent at four pence per acre). A carrot was offered here in as much as any tenant wishing to pay this sum was offered extra waste land but the ordinary people were understandably unhappy with this state of affairs.

The gentry, however, were quick to spot an opportunity to acquire yet more land and this put them at variance with their smaller neighbours. Again, the crown won the case and the copyholders of the Manor of Ightenhill paid a settlement of £2,141: 10s: 10d – this ensured that the remaining waste lands were divided amongst them at a rental of six pence per acre. However, this incident would have caused much unrest and ill feeling on behalf of the poorer classes against the local gentry.

The steward's deputies were despatched into the forest with their customary heavy-handed approach and demanded equal payment regardless of whether the inhabitants were struggling or prospering. It is perfectly reasonable, then, to assume that the poor would oppose the government authorities on the new tenancy order; to what extent, however, did the rich landowners see an opportunity to evict the smallholders adjoining their own lands and thus gain them for themselves?

———————————

Roger Nowell was all too aware that the friction between the landowners and tenants was running high and he had been unwilling to risk inflaming matters further by arresting a couple of poor old women from the depths of the Forest. However, he was also aware that the 'chattering classes' we becoming restless with his hands-off approach to what they saw as a major threat to their security. Into this volatile situation stepped Sir Thomas Gerard. Nowell spotted an opportunity to set the witch ball rolling by drafting in a man from outside of the area who would be known within Pendle only to those of the same class.

By the latter part of 1611, then, Roger Nowell had his ally, Gerard, in place and ready to act. What they now required was a well-defined case of witchcraft so that Nowell could be seen to exercise his authority with a firm hand and, hopefully, put an end to the festering discontent amongst the community. Things were taken out of Nowell's hands somewhat when, in the February of 1612, a Bill of Complaint was presented to the Lord Chancellor by a Roger Rigbye, gentleman, of Ditton;

'*Against Roger Nowell of Reade, gentleman and son of Roger Nowell, and others, for alleged fraud and unlawful retention of documents relating to the office of Clerk of the Peace...*'.

Roger Nowell junior had followed his father into the halls of justice and this record suggests impropriety on Nowell junior's part. His father would have seen an opportunity to kill two birds with one stone here - by prosecuting a high profile case within his district Roger Nowell senior would have hoped to throw a smoke-screen over the accusations being levelled against his son.

On the 19th March 1612, a few weeks following the accusation against his son, Roger Nowell hears of an event that had occurred in Colne the previous day. Henry Hargreaves, the Pendle constable, had been instructed to keep his ear to the ground and report anything that might be of use to his master in the form of witchcraft. Of course, the *actuality* of young Alison Device's meeting with the chapman John Lawe, on what is now Keighley Road, Colne was never reported.

The official story goes that Alison had asked Lawe for a few of the copper pins (value – 1d per 100) used in most households for dressmaking - and in witch households for sticking into clay effigies of the enemy! Lawe took umbrage at Alison's request and set off toward Colne market place. However, Alison's large black dog followed the chapman and began to snarl and threaten him. At this point Lawe fell to the ground suffering the effects of a stroke and Alison dragged her dog away. A few concerned townsfolk carried the stricken Lawe to the Greyhound Inn (later the site of Burtons the Tailors) while Alison and her dog watched from a safe distance. Obviously shaken at the unexpected events, Alison eventually went to the inn and peered around the door at Lawe as he lay on a bench.

Seeing Alison the customers at the inn recognised her and, being certain of what had happened, informed Lawe that he had been bewitched by the granddaughter of the most infamous witch in the district. And so an innocent meeting on the road to Trawden Forest lit the fuse beneath the most notorious witch hunt in English history.

Roger Nowell acted swiftly. He sent word to Sir Thomas Gerard that there now appeared to be enough evidence on which they could take action. Arriving at Read, Nowell briefed Gerard on the recent events at Colne and the ball began to roll. Gerard made enquiries and found that John Lawe had a son, Abraham Lawe, a cloth-dyer living in the Yorkshire wool town of Halifax.

Gerard wrote a letter to Abraham Lawe informing him of his father's illness and suggested that he make the journey to Colne. On the 21st March Abraham received the letter and had arrived in Colne within the week. Having arrived in Lancashire, Abraham was briefed by Roger Nowell and Thomas Gerard as to the situation with his father and the wider implications of the events. It was made clear that should Abraham wish to take his father's bewitching further he would receive every encouragement from the law.

It would, of course, be an ideal situation for Nowell where an out-of-towner prosecutes the local witch thus ensuring that Nowell's dealings in the matter were open and above-board and, just as importantly, appeared to have been carried out at arm's length.

We get the impression from Potts' account of the Colne Field incident that John Lawe was a Yorkshire man and that there would, by inference, have been little contact between him and the people of Pendle Forest. In other words, John Lawe was from other parts and his less than warm welcome to Colne made the facts all the more diabolical when presented to the trial jury.

As with many statements within Potts' work, however, things are not what they might seem to be. While there were indeed Lawe families in Halifax, to which

Abraham probably belonged, it is worth considering that there was a strong Lawe family connection to the Pendle and Burnley district. They also farmed on the Braddyll estates around Whalley, and were thus well known to Roger Nowell - others lived in Wiswell and Padiham. The Halifax family of one Richard Lawe, who could well have been of the same family and generation as Abraham, had dealings with the Towneleys and the Listers both of whom had extended estates within the Halifax districts.

Further, and perhaps more interestingly, we have seen that Henry Hargreaves was the constable of Pendle Forest and, therefore, Roger Nowell's right-hand man. On the 24th October 1602 the Colne marriage index shows *Henric Hargreaves* marrying *Elizabetha Lawe*. If this was the marriage of constable Hargreaves then it would have been a simple matter for Nowell to coerce his man into involving his family – this raises the possibility that the Lawe family had indeed become entangled within Roger Nowell's judicial net.

Furthermore, a tantalising deed of land settlement in Barrowford also takes us along this line of enquiry. The deed shows that in the nineteenth century, some two-hundred years after the 1612 trials, a member of the Lawe family of Halifax owned lands at Whittycroft in Over Barrowford.

The document states that William Lawe, gent of Halifax, settled land at Higherford on his attorney, James Wigglesworth of Halifax.[23] Another, related deed shows William Lawe's son, William Lawe of Hebden Bridge, surrendering the Whittycroft land to Thomas Grimshaw of Barrowford. Whittycroft is the area of Higherford between Blacko and Barrowford that once belonged to the Bannister estate of Park Hill (Barrowford) and the Robinson estate of Stone Edge in Blacko (this would later pass to the Towneleys of Barnside through marriage).

The possibility here is that the Lawe family inherited this land from a family member in the Pendle and Colne locality; they might also have purchased the land at some time. However, if the Lawes were indeed a Halifax family it is difficult to see why they would purchase the Whittycroft plot of land. In fact, as it was part of a long established family farm whose owners were far more interested in acquiring land rather than selling, it is equally difficult to imagine them purchasing this land under any circumstances.

Is it possible, then, that Abraham Lawe was approached by Roger Nowell with a deal brokered between himself, the Towneleys and the Braddylls whereby Lawe would be given a plot of land in return for his pressing charges against young Alison Device? It is worth remembering that the Braddyll's of Whalley were landlords of the Lawe family there and also closely related by marriage to Roger Nowell and the Robinsons who owned Whittycoft.

Another matter of particular interest arises here. It was not unusual for the travelling Catholic priest to disguise himself as a chapman as this allowed for free movement between districts without attracting undue attention from the authorities. The museum at the Stoneyhurst Catholic College has an example of a chapman's carrying case which, instead of pins etc. was designed to hold a priest's vestments and chalice. Given the fact that the Lawes from the Whalley area were strongly Catholic families it is very possible that chapman John Lawe was actually an undercover priest. If this was indeed the case then we see the real reason why he was so anxious not to open his pack at Alison's request - having been struck down at Colne when Alison's dog chased him, his disguise would have been discovered. Hearing of this situation it would then be possible for Nowell and Gerard to bribe Lawe and is son into acting against Alison; they would keep quiet about his secret if he agreed to appear for the prosecution.

Whatever the actual truth of the matter might be one thing is certain. Roger Nowell played a master stroke in his prosecution against Alison Device. He took the lame John Lawe to the Lancaster trial and sat him in plain view of the Jury. Potts describes the pitiful site of Lawe, all but lame apart from one eye and one arm and unable to travel (just how he survived the long jolting carriage journey from Colne to Lancaster is not mentioned).

When John Lawe took the stand his performance sealed the fate of the Device family and the judge called upon Sir Thomas Gerard, and his brother-in-law, Sir Richard Houghton, to provide for him. This is somewhat odd and can perhaps be seen as testimony to the involvement of Gerard in the Lawe case. Further, it also shows that members of the gentry from far and wide had gathered to hear the titillating accounts of diabolical murder and mayhem caused by the poor wretches now standing trial for their lives. As we shall see with an earlier case in Chelmsford, the gathering of the gentry at the spectacle of an important witch trial took the form of ghoulish theatre and reflected the fascination with executions where the public would flock to the gallows fields in their thousands.

Englands Grievance Discovered: 1655

No doubt the Sirs Gerard and Houghton would have been amid illustrious company in the court gallery by the Towneleys, Listers, Asshetons, Shuttleworths, Braddylls *et al*; and equally as sure would be the fact that, following the trials, they would all congregate in one of Lancaster's town inns to toast their success - even while the limp bodies of the condemned twisted slowly on the ropes of Gallows Hill.

PART ONE ~ CONCLUSION

Many factors can be seen to have contributed to the Pendle witch trials of 1612. This was a difficult period of political and religious transition between the old feudal ways of the Medieval period and the faltering dawn of a burgeoning new industrial era.

Piled upon the social pressures induced by forced change, we also see the festering discontent engendered by generations who had never had the chance to acquire precious land. Even those who had managed to gain marginal smallholdings often found themselves being ejected from their livelihoods by the encroaching enclosures of the large landowners.

These landowning merchants were rapidly rising within the minor gentry class and were becoming not only increasingly wealthy but also increasingly isolated from the common men and women of their locality.

Keenly aware that their old Catholic doctrines were now a threat to their very existence the gentry found that it was necessary to court favour with their Protestant superiors in authority. Further to this, many of the gentry acted as Justices of the Peace in which capacity they regularly came up against the charges of witchcraft prevalent among the communities of Western Europe at that time.

Thrown into this melting-pot of social, political and religious unrest were the many years of crop failure and famine that occurred throughout the sixteenth, and early seventeenth centuries. This, coupled with the adverse effects of rising inflation, meant that the poor were in crisis. At the time of the witch trials bread prices were at an all-time high and many people found themselves having to beg to survive.

However, rather than ensuring that at least a small percentage of their increasing wealth and land found its way to helping the destitute (Poor Relief taxation apart) the landowners found it more prudent to sit in judgement. It was far easier to hang the troublesome beggars of the parish than it would have been to set up a viable welfare system to help the poor to help themselves.

In particular, those of the poor who made nuisance of themselves were a political tool to be manipulated within a framework of religious insecurity among the gentry.

It is significant that the actual arrests, and subsequent trials, of the Pendle accused followed an incident initially involving 'outsiders.' Abraham Lawe and Sir Thomas Gerard were from outside the Pendle Forest and instigated proceedings against the witches within the community.

No one among those who subsequently complained of bewitchment was prepared to stand up and be the first to officially accuse those they held responsible. This was ultimately down to string-pulling by the gentry - once Abraham Lawe (with the possible encouragement of Sir Thomas Gerard) set the ball rolling it became increasingly unstoppable as more and more accusers came out of the woodwork.

Notes Relating
to
Part One

1: Clayton, J. *The Lancashire Witch Conspiracy* (2nd ed.) Barrowford Press (2007) ISBN 978-0-9553821-2-3

2: Potts, T. *The Wonderful Discoverie of Witches in the Countie of Lancaster* (1613) Chetham Society (1845). Also published by:
Stuttard, A. Carnegie Publishing Ltd, Lancaster (2003)

3: Late Medieval records relating to the Pendle Forest vaccaries list regular losses of cattle through the attack of wolves by 'strangulation' - see:

Brigg, M. *The Early History of the Forest of Pendle.* Pendle Heritage Centre. (1989)

4: The charm was examined by an expert at the request of Wingspan Productions (London) in 2011. The earlier translation does not appear to have been a verbatim account, rather an impression of the intention of the writer who, it must be remembered, was not fluent in either Greek or Latin.

5: Unpublished paper on the Sagar families of Catlow held in the local studies department of Nelson Library

6: Campbell, M. *Curious Tales of Old West Yorkshire.* Sigma Leisure (1999)

7: O'Neill, J. *The World of the Brontës.* Carlton Books Ltd. London (1997)

8: Extract from Clitheroe Court Rolls - showing that Richard Baldwin and Henry Nutter, both yeomen, mixed with the minor gentry families of Nowell and Starkie:-

June 1600: *Ellize Robinson of Gouldshaiebooth, yeoman, to Mr. John Nutter, Dean of Chester by John Nutter his servant)...... to the use of Anne, the second daughter of Ellize Robinson, for her referrment in marriage. Witnessed by: Roger Nowell, Edmund Starkie, Roger Nowell, Henry Nutter and* **Rychard Bawdine**......

9: The Halmote records were recorded as court rolls some of which were published by William Farrar as *TheCourt Rolls for the Honour of Clitheroe.* Volumes 1, 2, 3 (1912)

10: Burke, P. *History and Social Theory* (2nd ed.) Polity Press. Cambridge. (2005)

11: Wrigley, E. A and Schofield, R.S (1981) *The Population History of England, 1541-1871; A Reconstruction.* Reprinted Cambridge (1989).

12: Saltmarsh, J. (1940) *Paper to the Cambridge Historical Society* . . . 'The death rate of the single year of 1349, stupendous though it was, cannot explain the creeping paralysis of more than a century. Weight must be allowed to other political factors such as the Hundred Years War and its aftermath. Abroad, foreign factors were partly responsible for a contraction in English foreign trade. We lost the French Dominions and there was heavy taxation.'

13: Farr, W. *The Influence of Scarcities and of the High Prices of Wheat on the Mortality of the People of England.* (Paper, June 1846) Journal of the Statistical Society of London, Vol. 9, No. 2. Via Galenet

14: Kenyon, D. *The Origins of Lancashire.* Manchester University Press. (1991)

15: Smith, R. (Occasional paper) *Blackburnshire - A Study of Early Lancashire History.* Leicester University Press. (1961)

16: Bennett, W. *The History of Marsden and Nelson.* Nelson Corporation. (1957)

17: Whitaker, T.D. *The History of the Parish of Whalley,* (1st ed. - 1801)

18: Mullett, M. and Warren, L. *Martyrs of the Diocese of Lancaster.*Rome (1987)

19: Snape, A. W. *English Martyrs – Whalley,* SP (2000)

20: *Farrar Papers,* Manchester Central Library

21: Lumby, J. *The Lancashire Witch Craze,* Carnegie Publishing. (1995)

22: Conroy, M. P. *Backcloth to Gawthorpe* (1971)

23: Farrar, W. *The Court Rolls for the Honour of Clitheroe.* (1912)

24: Nicholas Assheton, the seventeenth century diarist, wrote an account of his life at Downham, copies of which are available in many local libraries

25: Eaton, R. *Stories of Samlesbury* (1927-1929-1931-1937)

PART TWO

THE WITCH CAST

EARLY WITCHCRAFT & RELIGION

Beliefs trigger aggression only when they fit with other anxieties and conditions; often, they lie dormant in the mind, the contents of which are very far from being a set of coherent arguments. This is one reason why witch-hunting was characteristically episodic, striking particular areas at moments of crisis, and leaving others untouched. From the outset, demonology teased the imagination. Its intellectual problematic, too, circled around the issue of the nature of the imaginative faculty, the realm of illusion and the power of the senses, all questions central to the nature of art itself.[1]

Here we see cross-reference between the 'demonology' so beloved by the dramatists of the sixteenth and seventeenth centuries, and the idea of the witch stories developing as art - where the diabolical became theatrical titillation. The ensuing fictional depiction of the witch follows the archetypical broomstick-borne hag and this colours our view to this day.

Unfortunately, early fictional accounts have affected the Pendle witch story to the extent that what few hard facts we are able to uncover are often clouded by misconception. An example of this is the ubiquitous *'witches Sabbath'* where all manner of fantastic and diabolical events are played out against the backdrop of a faux Christian holy day. Steaming haunches of meat miraculously appear on ropes from the sky while manic witches cavort naked in every blasphemous act imaginable. Flaming devils fly above the scene, keeping a close eye on their flock, while infants are torn limb-from-limb and their flesh roasted on spits.

The Sabbath 1608: from the Compendium Maleficarum

The Pendle witch trials of 1612 contain very few references to the devil within the statements of the accused. The closest we come to seeing a Black Sabbath is the Good Friday meeting at Malkin Tower.

Even here it is patently obvious that the fanciful notions of the younger members of the Demdike clan were encouraged by the examining magistrates. We have a mention of a sheep being turned on a spit and the naming of demonic familiars to confirm the youngsters within the black arts. Further, those present at Malkin Tower were said to have promised to meet on Romleys (Rombalds) Moor (near Kildwick, West Yorkshire) widely famed for its witch connections and as they departed the meeting they all left on horses of different colours and disappeared. These statements are plainly contrived so as to turn a simple meeting of concerned friends and relatives into at least a semblance of the Black Sabbath.

And so we see the influence of fantasy and fiction at play within the witch trials - the prosecution knew very well that they only needed to trot out the standard version of diabolical events to convince the jury that they were sitting in judgement upon a very dangerous group of devil worshippers. This mindset can be seen again in 1633 when young Edmund Robinson, of Pendle, concocted a fantastic story, based on the generic Black Sabbath, where he iterated the long held traditions of the district and accused a large number of local people of having been witches. The fact that the case progressed to trial shows that the Forest people were titillated by the diabolical happenings and were only too willing to believe any idiot who might enliven their humdrum day.

The modern idea of the witch in history has been manufactured by the imaginations of a long string of writers, playwrights and novelists but the question needs to be asked as to where to place the witches of 1612? Were they true proponents of the Wiccan beliefs or practisers of black magic, were they cunning folk or merely chancers? Furthermore, to what extent did orthodox religion play its part in the beliefs and attitudes of the Early Modern 'witch?'

The very word *religion* is difficult to quantify when applied to a specific time and place within the past. There is an extensive range of phenomena that fall under the rubric of religion, including myth, ritual, taboo, symbolism, morality, altered states of consciousness, and belief in non-corporeal beings.[2] Realised benefits of practised religion include improved health, survivorship, economic opportunities, sense of community, psychological well-being, assistance during crises, mating opportunities, and fertility. In contrast to these benefits the organised state religion came to be seen as a controlling method of subjugation of the masses by an unelected elite. However, the longevity of the major religions can be said to be evidence for their doctrines having been weighted towards the benefits accrued by their followers.

Shamanism is widely believed to be the earliest form of religion and was present in all religions of the world at some time in their prehistoric hunting and gathering past. Shamanism is largely a focus on healing and this engendered a lower rate of morbidity and mortality in society.[3]

Belief in non-corporeal beings is the most commonly held definition of religion. Specific beliefs and rites vary across cultures but it is the enduring framework of religious *ritual* that actualises these symbols and defines the sacred within a community. Ritual is primarily a form of communication whose components are exaggerated formality, sequencing, invariability and repetition all of which facilitate communication by eliciting arousal, directing attention, enhancing memory and improving associations.

The overlap between religion and ritual, then, can be seen within the actions of ceremony, belief complex, cultic practice, ethical demands and symbolism. Sacred things are defined by emotional charging rather than by intrinsic properties. Their existence depends on shared creation and evocation of emotionally charged symbols.

So, by the time that our European ancestors had arrived permanently in Britain (perhaps 6,000 BC) they followed established religious practice; archaeology tells us that ritualistic practises (especially treatment of the dead) defined each European culture and that around 2,000 BC there appears to have been an increase in cross-cultural belief. Cremation replaced burial, and then vice versa, while types of grave goods and burial containers became increasingly universal.

During the British Roman period, before the acceptance of Christianity, those who followed the new religion were persecuted mercilessly. This meant that Christian burials became highly secretive with great importance being attached to accompanying ritual. Relics of those who had played vital roles in spreading the Gospel were taken following their deaths; fingers, hair, eyes, bone fragments and blood-stained clothing were placed within highly stylised reliquary containers and these were imbued with great spiritual significance to the following generations of Christians. Thus we see encoded within the symbolism of the relic a power to express values of widely collective significance - a focus of spiritual belief and a tool with which to carry the Divine message far and wide.

The power of the relic did not diminish over time; the Medieval period saw what amounted to an international trade in religious artefacts. Those wealthy enough to acquire such things were able to boast that they owned genuine pieces of Christian history - the king of France, for instance, thought that he had in his possession the original crown of thorns worn by Christ at the crucifixion.

The post-Reformation Catholic martyrs were prosecuted under the state law of treason and this meant that they were usually hanged, drawn and quartered. Huge crowds would gather at these barbaric spectacles in the hope of gaining a memento. The easiest prize to obtain from these executions was a handkerchief dipped in the blood of the martyr. Following the eventual death of the condemned their bodies were parboiled in a huge vat to preserve the flesh, the body parts were then hung on spikes around the city as a deterrent to other would-be 'traitors.'

During the boiling process the braver souvenir hunters in the crowd would remove the ears, eyes, hair, toes, fingers and any other part they could get their hands on. These grisly ecofacts were then sold off as they were much sought-after as symbols of spirituality, aids for healing the sick and souvenirs of men, some of whose number would eventually become saints.

IN 1850 The Wesleyan-Methodist Magazine ran an article in which it was said that:[4]

Witchcraft was founded in a universal belief in a middle class of spiritual beings, who had power over the elements and over human affairs, and whose agency might be sought by offerings, or commanded by charms. This was especially strong among the early Teutonic nations of Western Europe; and it was a further article of their popular belief, that woman-kind was more easily brought into connexion with this spiritual world than the other sex.

Priestesses were the favourite agencies of the deities in the ages of Saxon Paganism; they knew the effects of the charms; the qualities, noxious or beneficial, of herbs or animals, or other articles, and how to secure them; for these were supposed to be given immediately by spiritual beings, when under the power of their invocations. Hence the Teutonic women became prophetesses, foretellers of future events, warners of danger, healers of wounds and diseases, conciliators of love, sometimes averters of calamities, at other times workers of vengeance; and, as in those wild an passionate ages the latter feeling too frequently prevailed, women who had resource to such expedients, and who were often of the highest rank, became naturally objects of dread.

The Christian Gospel, in its first introduction, destroyed the Gods of the old creed, but it left a belief in this middle class of spirits, and in their power, merely inculcating the doctrine that they were spirits of evil - fallen angels who were condemned to wander the earth, jealous of the happiness of mankind and ever seeking to work them harm. As the influence of Christianity advanced, people were taught that they were demons. Many were outwardly Christians, who in secret addressed their invocations to the spirits in whom they had been accustomed to place their trust. Even Christian Priests and Monks were not free from many superstitious practises which were condemned by the church as relics of heathendom.

Witchcraft seems to have been very common among our Anglo Saxon forefathers; and, as in the time of their Paganism, it appears to have been exercised mostly by women in the better classes of society. The old worship naturally remained longest in the wilder and more thinly populated parts of the country and these became known as the peculiar haunts of the evil spirits.

Among the Anglo Saxons witchcraft seems not to have been a crime against the law, except where it was joined with some offence against the person. Immediately after the Norman Conquest we find that the practice of witchcraft was in general confined to women of a lower grade. But accidental circumstances, and the interference of a higher intelligence for temporary objects, came repeatedly to raise to new importance superstitions which might otherwise have died gradually away.

In the eleventh and twelfth centuries a general intellectual movement came throughout Europe, to alarm the Church of the middle ages; and it conjured up spectres on every side, in the shape of a host of heresies. Proscribed sects, in ages when it was death to differ with the Established Church, naturally courted concealment and held their assemblies in the strictest privacy, often seeking to avoid observation by meeting in wild and solitary places. This secrecy easily gave rise to malicious reports; and the Church, in its hatred of heresies, spread and encourages the belief that these secret meetings were the scenes of impious worship and horrible vices.

Popes and Church Councils culled everything that was impious and disgusting, to father upon these Church reformers of the middle ages; and they proceeded at once to identify them with the popular witches. Then it is that we first hear of the secret assemblies - diabolical Sabbaths; it is then too that we first hear of the witches riding on besoms and having the powers to transform themselves. The invocation of spirits was judged to be an act of heresy, and the ecclesiastical power now claimed the jurisdiction over sorcerers.

Thus did the crime of witchcraft take a new development; and the Church, by changing it from a mere relic of heathendom, to an actual heresy, gave it an importance in the eyes of the world which it had not possessed before. It was this time, probably, that the notion first arose of the witches or sorcerers selling themselves to Satan.

So the grand religious festivals of our Pagan forefathers became eventually village wakes; and so again their most secret ceremonial went through a series of degradations, until it made its final stormy exit in the great witchcraft madness of the seventeenth century. Thus in literature, the grand mytho-historic witchcraft stories of the earliest ages became the romances of chivalry of a subsequent period, and gradually degenerated into popular ballads and cheap books, until at last they disappeared into the nursery.

As the cases of witchcraft became multiplied, the motives of the criminals became diminished, until they drew ridicule on themselves, and gave a shock to common sense. The absurdity of supposing that one-half of the world should have entered into a league with Satan, with no other apparent object of result than to live a life of privation to end in an ignominious death, became too apparent to last. Judges and juries refused to convict, and there were no longer either prosecutors or objects for prosecution. And thus the supposed witchcraft defined by the authorities lost its importance and ceased to exist.

And so we see that beneath the veneer of established religion there have always been those who were more comfortable on the periphery. Perhaps it is somewhat of a generalisation to say that the more isolated people were within the landscape then the more ignorant they would be in the teachings of their church. It is clear that the Pendle Forest had always been a spiritual backwater where Christian missionaries of the Saxon period visited only rarely. Even into the established era of the Abbey at Whalley there only existed a small chapel of ease within Pendle - a shelter of sorts where travelling priests from Whalley could hold their services, perhaps once a week.

Having seen the culture of their birthright disintegrate before their eyes the likes of Demdike and Chattox would have set little store in the sermons of the Reformation. Sure, they would have attended St. Mary's church on occasion, if only to avoid being fined for non-attendance. However, survival in a harsh world required more than pious words and there was money and vitals to be had from healing people and animals, and begging.

A strong tradition lingered in the Forest, filtering through from much earlier times the Pagan legends of demons, spirits, imps, boggarts and devils died hard hereabouts. Large natural hollows, streams, caves, rocky outcrops and ancient standing stones were all imbued with a natural magic - they formed a link with the underworld and were, therefore, very potent places to those who had been taught to recognise them. Demdike, then, was of a sub-culture whose roots were lost within the mists of time.

It is fair to say that even Demdike, as the supposedly most skilled of all the Pendle witches, would have had no more than a low-level working knowledge of the craft she was to die for. Rather, she appears to have acquired her 'diabolism' later in life - perhaps at a time when her need for income became most pressing. If she had not been exposed to the arts of witchcraft during her early years then she would certainly have come across the practice, living as she did in Pendle. Her apparent position at the head of a 'dangerous brood of witches' within the Forest might have been as a result of her mentors dying off leaving Demdike, as an elder within society, to assume their crown.

Within the statements of the accused lip-service was being paid to the customs of old when ancient religious symbolism was employed - Chattox removed a scalp (skull) from St. Mary's graveyard and gave a couple of the teeth to Demdike. This does not mean that Chattox set about a grave with a shovel and spade; St. Mary's graveyard at that time had reached capacity and it became necessary to remove the bodies of earlier burials in order to make room for new ones. This meant that the bones of the disinterred were thrown into a heap in a corner of the graveyard or placed within a charnel house. It was for this reason that church sextons employed 'whippers out' whose job it was to keep stray dogs from legging it up the road, chomping on the prize of a thighbone.

Other examples of symbolism are seen when Chattox's daughter formed a cross from two sticks and placed it over a can of milk to protect it - unfortunately this did not work as farmer Nutter kicked the can over. Clay 'pictures' were a favourite method of causing injury or death; pins could be stuck into the dolls or they could be crumbled slowly away thus causing a lingering death for those unfortunates in whose image the doll was made. Demdike requested of her grandson that he bring her a communion wafer from church; the fact that this had been blessed by the curate gave it special powers; holy water and communion wine were also in demand by witches.

Taking the accounts of 'diabolical witchery' published by scholars leading up to the seventeenth century a single thread is apparent above all others and that is the presence of the devil. William Perkins was the leading Puritan writer of his age and a friend of William Whittaker, who was in turn a relative of Roger Nowell. In 1608 Perkins published his *Discourse of the Damned Art of Witches* in which he wrote:

> The ground of all witchcraft is a league or covenant made between the witch and the devil, wherein they do mutually bind themselves together the one unto the other. For his part (the devil) promises to be ready to his vassals command, to appear at any time in the likewise of any creature, to consult with him, to aid and help him.

The feature of actual consort directly with the devil is notably absent in most cases of English witchcraft trials and the Pendle trials were no exception. This did not deter the redoubtable prosecution, however, as enough 'evidence' of the old Catholic practices was apparent in the spells and incantations that the accused admitted to using. Further to this, Nowell would be well aware of the writings of Perkins and was at pains to ensure that the accused of the Pendle Trials were given every opportunity to brag about their own personal demons or *familiars*.

To the forest folk, many of the small animals around them served the purpose of familiars - hares, cats and dogs being among their favourites. This is no surprise as we see again the adoption of ancient belief; animals and birds (especially the raven) were considered within Pagan times to have been earthbound representatives of the underworld. In other words, they were the conduit through which humans could converse with the spirit world. The adoption of animals as familiars, and their endowment with spiritual powers, is as old as the hills and in the case of the Pendle Forest would have filtered down the generations from time immemorial.

Many of the Pendle accused appear to have owned up, or even boasted about having the companionship of a familiar and this was grist to Nowell's mill – the presence of a malevolent familiar firmly linked the accused to the devil. At least this would be the case by the time that the jury heard the evidence. On the subject of familiars, a Chetham Society publication notes that:

> Bernard, who is learned in the nomenclature of familiar spirits, gives, in his *Guide to Grand Jurymen*, 1630, the following list of the names of the more celebrated familiars of English witches:
>
> *Mephistophiles, Lucifer, Little Lord, Fimodes, David, Jude, Little Robin, Smacke, Litefoote, Nonsuch, Lunch, Makeshift, Swash, Pluck, Blue, Catch, White, Callico, Hardname, Tibb, Hiff, Ball, Puss, Rutterkin, Dicke, Prettie, Grissil, Tobattacco and Jacke.*

The apparent readiness of the Pendle accused to admit to having familiars suggests that they were actually a necessary accessory, a powerful familiar would lend weight to their claim to be able to heal and protect themselves and their fellows or, when conditions dictated, to bring harm to others. Interestingly, whenever a familiar appears in the confessions (in relation to the charge of murder by witchcraft) the accused admit that their familiars were responsible for actually carrying out the foul deed and it was, therefore, out of their own hands. The familiars had taken it upon themselves to harm or kill the victim whilst the accused stood by – *"Good heavens, now look what you have done you naughty little familiar."*

Chattox had her *Fancy*, Demdike had her *Tibb*, James Device had his *Dandy* and Elizabeth Device had her *Ball*. These were common names for the familiar found throughout the land and all appear to have been taken at random from some 'witches manual'. It is difficult at a distance of some four hundred years to understand the mindset of these individuals in this respect. To what extent did they actually believe in their animal familiars and just how much of this phenomenon was silly superstition? Certainly, these people were born-and-bred into an age of superstition and belief in the power of nature. A constant exposure to such tales and beliefs, learned at their mother's knee, could well have implanted a strong notion within a person's psyche to such an extent that they believed that hares conversed with them. The familiar, then, was a virtual interface between the reality of the witch and the perceived powers of the underworld.

Further to this we know that the wise people were expert herbalists and had no shortage of materials to work with in God's great garden. Within reach of everyone were common plants whose effects upon the human body were both powerful and dangerous. The soporific effects of flora such as valerian, St. John's wort, hen-bane, 'magic mushrooms' and birch leaves meant that they would have been seen as basic stock within the armoury of the healer. The experience and skill of the practitioner would be necessary when medicines, salves and potions containing the more dangerous plants (such as belladonna) were administered - in the wrong hands these would have been deadly.

Given the fact that mind-altering drugs were freely available at the time exactly what part would these have played in the many instances of apparent fantasy reported by the accused? This is strongly reminiscent of the shaman who would medicate himself in order to enter the shadowy land between reality and the underworld. From this perceived contact with the spirits the shaman would bring back prophesies and stories of fantastic imagery - this would then be translated in artistic representation, such as can be seen in early cave paintings. Shamanism played a vital part in Pagan religious commonality from the earliest of times and is still practised in parts of the world.

The shaman was highly respected within his community; not only did he have the power to heal, to predict, to engender fertility but he could also cause harm where necessary. Thus the notion of flight, speaking animals, the ability to harm or to heal - these are relics of a ritual memory passed down to the Early Modern witches - only to be absorbed into popular culture where the ancient religious tradition became no more than a source of fun.

The Incantation

Plate from 'The Lancashire Witches' by William Harrison Ainsworth (1849)

This romantic novel, above all, propagated the model of the Pendle witches as we often see them portrayed today

91

Elizabeth Southern Alias Demdike

The appellation of *Demdike* translates as *'Demon Woman,'* the obvious connotation of the name thus suggests that the recipient of the title was feared and loathed within the community. Certainly there had to be a reason for acquisition of the name and in earlier times it was applied to strong women within a more matriarchal society – an excellent case in point here being the name of the famous early British queen, Boudicca. Here we have the proto-Celtic word *boudiko* meaning *victorious* and the addition of the *dicca* (*dike*) suffix thus giving us *Victorious Woman.*

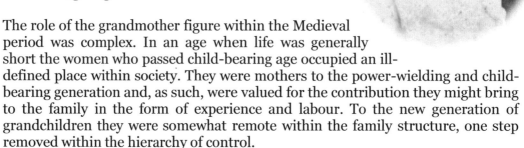

The role of the grandmother figure within the Medieval period was complex. In an age when life was generally short the women who passed child-bearing age occupied an ill-defined place within society. They were mothers to the power-wielding and child-bearing generation and, as such, were valued for the contribution they might bring to the family in the form of experience and labour. To the new generation of grandchildren they were somewhat remote within the family structure, one step removed within the hierarchy of control.

In *Professions for Women* (1931) the novelist, Virginia Woolf, touched on the complexity of interfamilial relationships by referring to the mother figure as *The Angel in the House.* This appears to have been a reaction to the writing of generations of novelists whose ideas of the family imbued the mother with a celestial status. The permanent abandonment of self in favour of the needs of others showed the mother to be *'immensely charming . . . utterly unselfish . . . she excelled in the difficult arts of family life. She sacrificed herself daily.'*

To Woolf, however, this represented a set of social shackles from which it was imperative to break free - as can be seen in the following passage:[5]

You who come of a younger and happier generation may not have heard of her - you may not know what I mean by *The Angel in the House.* . . In those days - the last of Queen Victoria - every house had its Angel. And when I came to write I encountered her with the very first words. The shadow of her wings fell on my page; . . . I did my best to kill her . . . in self-defence. Had I not killed her she would have killed me. . . She died hard. . . But it was a real experience; it was an experience that was bound to befall all women writers at that time. Killing the *Angel in the House* was part of the occupation of a woman writer.

The modern outlook, then, steered away from the role of the woman purely as a dedicated wife and mother; emancipation and independence entered the lexicon of the early twentieth century. In Woolf's *Angel* we see the concept of the mother as an elevated entity within the family and it is interesting to contrast this with the attitudes shown towards the elderly women in the 1612 trials. Potts had it that Demdike was *'a very old woman . . . a sink of villainy . . . from whom no man near her was safe'* and he was not slow to ascribe the *Demon Woman* appellation to her whenever possible. She was considered to be the very antithesis of *The Angel in the House.*

Nor did Chattox escape the charms of Thomas Potts; she was, he said, *'a very old, withered, spent, and decrepit creature, her sight almost gone, her lips ever chattering and walking, saying no man knows what.'* Again, age and age-related disability are enough to consign a person to care of the devil - no matter what that person might have achieved during their lifetime. The character and temperament of the old woman was irrelevant so long as she fulfilled the criteria of witchcraft where age and physical fragility proved her to be an obvious candidate as a leading agent of the devil within her district.

This was certainly the attitude of the authorities, the gentry and probably the strata of yeomen beneath them as illustrated by Richard Baldwin's outburst when Demdike and granddaughter Alison appeared in his field in front of Wheathead. To Baldwin the matter was clear and simple, the females of the Demdike family were *'witches and whores.'* It would, however, be interesting to know how the ordinary people within the community treated their elderly; how were Demdike and her ilk treated as they went about their everyday business? It is probably fair to say that the younger women in Pendle had a respect for Demdike and Chattox but, unless they required their specific midwifery or herbalist skills, they would probably keep out of their way.

To the men of the local villages and farms the Demdike brood were probably a nuisance; when they appeared with an empty piggin it was usually prudent to give them at least a token of milk, butter or oatmeal in order to ensure a quiet life. However, wherever men gathered, at the market or the alehouse etc., the subject of Old Demdike and Chattox would arise and it is sure that the opinions vented among the gathering were less than complimentary.

Today it is difficult to comprehend the values attached to the family system of the Early Modern period but one thing is certain, by and large the women of that time were not afraid to stand up for their family. There is apparent within the Clitheroe court rolls where numerous records refer to women being fined for violent affray upon their fellow foresters. Oddly, the incidence of violence by women usually involved an attack upon men - as the following court records show:

1541: Mark Nutter's wife, Margaret, was put in the stocks for making a violent affray upon Edmund Robinson.

1546: In defence - John Ingham, of Padiham, made a violent affray upon Isabell and Alice Crook and drew blood.

Having passed the age of seventy, Elizabeth Southern could have been expected to fulfil a role as aide to her daughter and son-in-law. She was evidently unmarried at this time - either because she had remained a spinster or she was a widow. However, we see clearly within Potts that she was no shrinking violet within the family, nor within the community. When her daughter had trouble collecting a days' pay from Richard Baldwin she enlisted Demdike's help in confronting him. She was also still active within her animal healing duties despite the fact that she had lost her sight. Granddaughter, Alison Device, stated at her trial that her grandmother was the only person who could have cured the striken chapman, John Lawe, had she not died before the trial. This implies a great deal of respect was assigned to Demdike by all of her family.

The reasons for the Demdike appellation, then, are manifold; we can see that an elderly woman, with a strongly independent character, would have made the men within the neighbourhood somewhat uncomfortable; especially those in authority and with a more Puritan leaning. The strong matriarch would, therefore, have been the target of derision from certain members of the community, not least the lay and church authorities. Perhaps Demdike grew increasingly cantankerous with age, after all she would have lived an extremely hard life despite which she successfully (and possibly single-handedly) raised at least two children, and helped to raise at least three grandchildren (a fourth, Henry, had died at the age of four). On top of this she also lost her sight at some stage in later life, probably as a result of cataracts.

On the other side of the coin, Demdike may have earned her title through the somewhat grudging respect of the community as it is apparent that she was called upon by neighbouring farmers to cure their ailing livestock. She may well have been an outstanding herbalist and healer and have acted as the local midwife in her younger days. She certainly appears to have been the longest serving person within her craft of all the Pendle accused and might, therefore, have worn the Demdike tag as a badge of honour.

However. . . there is also a strong possibility that nobody in the Forest of Pendle actually called Elizabeth Southern *Old Demdike*, nor Anne Whittle *Old Chattox*. In their so-called confessions the accused bandy the names around like confetti, Demdike this and Chattox that; closer inspection, however, shows a definite interpolation of the name within the prosecution statements and this must have been a deliberate policy on behalf of either Potts or the examining magistrate, or both. The wording within these statements relates an odd mixture of first person and third person thus giving the impression that the words were directly attributable to the examinate. Reading the *Wonderfull Discoverie* in this light it becomes apparent that the only person who could be proved to have actually employed the Demdike title was Thomas Potts, this he did as voraciously and as often as he possibly could.

There is not a single instance within the Assize Court prosecution documents where there is proof that anyone other than the magistrates, and Potts, addressed the elders of the accused as Demdike and Chattox. Words were constantly put into the mouths of the accused, ideas were floated before them and these were quickly adapted to their culture and, in turn, translated by the prosecution into evil malpractice. This was shamelessly designed to horrify the Assize judges (not that they needed much persuasion to hang a few wretches here and there), the jury and the Crown authorities.

The evidence against Elizabeth Southern was never put before the Lancaster court owing to her having died in custody. We will probably never know what information the bulk of her statements contained but Potts was at pains to furnish at least some of the information. He also used Demdike's reputation as an indictment of all the accused, despite the fact she was never convicted. The following is Potts' description of Demdike within the *Wonderfull Discoverie* preamble:

Therefore I pray you give me leave, (with your patience and favour,) before I proceed to the Indictment, Arraignment, and Tryall of such as were Prisoners in the Castle, to lay open the life and death of this damnable and malicious Witch, of so long continuance of whom our whole business hath such dependence, that without the particular Declaration and Record of her Evidence, with the circumstaunces, wee shall never bring any thing to good perfection: for from this Sincke of villanie and mischiefe, have all the rest proceeded; as you shall have them in order.

Shee was a very old woman, about the age of Foure-score yeares, and had been a Witch for fiftie yeares. Shee dwelt in the Forrest of Pendle, a vast place, fitte for her profession: What shee committed in her time, no man knowes. Thus lives shee securely for many yeares, brought up her owne Children, instructed her Graund-children, and tooke great care and pains to bring them to be Witches. Shee was a generall agent for the Deuill in all these partes: no man escaped her, or her Furies, that ever gave them any occassion of offence, or denyed them any thing they stood need of: And certaine it is, no man neere them, was secure or free from danger ......the common opinion of the Kinges subjects for the losses of their Children, Friendes, Goodes, and Cattle, (as there could not be so greate Fire without some Smoake) ......

In the end, Roger Nowell esquire, one of his Maiesties Justices in these partes, a very religious honest Gentleman, Painefull in the service of his Countrey: whose fame for this great service to his Countrey, shall live after him, tooke upon him to enter into the particular examinations of these suspected persons: And to the honour of God, and the great comforte of all his Countrey, made such a discovery of them in order, as the like hath not been heard of ......

And that, as far as it goes, is the opinion of authority. No quarter was given for the fact that the prosecution knew little of the circumstances in which the supposed acts of witchcraft were carried out. Nor did Potts, Nowell and the judges have any idea of the true nature of those that they accused and this relegates Potts' description of Demdike to the level of the dramatists who, as we have seen, were keen to propound the popular fictional notion of the witch in stark contrast to the reality.

IN SEARCH OF ELIZABETH SOUTHERN

THEORY I: ELIZABETH BLACKBURN

Despite her reputation as the most notorious of the Pendle witches Elizabeth Southern is the most enigmatic of them all. As will be seen, it is difficult to ascribe a definite background to her eventful life. It is possible, however, to take the best available evidence and employ this in a manner that makes sense. In the following Southern will be adjoined to a family of good background and this might seem surprising given her ignominious end. In defence of this it must be said that circumstances change over the lifetime of a person and in the Early Modern period the line between security and poverty could be a very fine one indeed.

W illiam Harrison Ainsworth provided us with the romantic novel *The Lancashire Witches; A Romance of Pendle Forest* in 1849 and the book went on to be a best seller, even outdoing Ainsworth's rival, Charles Dickens, at the time. Ainsworth travelled to Pendle when he was researching the book, staying with a relative at Whalley and also with the vicar of Newchurch-in-Pendle. The vicar introduced the author to many of the local characters and the folklore he gleaned from the Forest folk formed the basis of his novel.

One of the more interesting stories the locals told to Ainsworth was that Elizabeth Southern was the daughter of an Elizabeth (Bess) Blackburn who had been sent from her home as a child to *'live with two peasants in Barrowford.'* Bess Blackburn grew up and had a child which turned out to be Elizabeth Southern. Now, as in many of the folk tales bandied around there is often a grain of truth disguised behind a good deal of supposition and added dramatic effect. Further to this it seemed a good idea to at least check the Blackburn connection to see if any sense could be made out of it - the results turned out to be interesting to say the least.

Before we move on to Demdike's possible family roots it is necessary to have a look at the background of her daughter, Elizabeth, as this adds fuel to the debate. The Demdike family have long been a source of mystery to writers on the subject, her age, and the ages of her offspring, varying depending on the opinion of the author. Fortunately, while researching the *Lancashire Witch Conspiracy*, the truth came to light when it was noticed that the St. Mary's (Newchurch) records contained entries for baptisms, marriages and deaths in the name of Denis and Dennis.

There are a total of five entries within the registers for the surname of Denis and a single one for Dennis. This surname was extremely uncommon within our area, occurring nowhere else within the whole of the extended forest area, other than at Newchurch, over the 180 year period covered by the early registers. By the sixteenth century church officials were writing names phonetically in a mixture of Latin and English and the name of *Denis* was actually the name of *Devis* which in turn was *Davis/Davies*. These were further confused by later transcribers as the letter N often resembled the letter V.[6] In the case of Newchurch St. Mary's the same incumbent, one Thomas Varley, served from 1569 to 1607 and therefore he would cover the whole of the Denis family records – this run of records can be seen to relate directly to the family of Elizabeth Southern - the first relevant entries being her daughter and son:

- ❖ 1590: John Dennis* married **Elizabeth Ingham**
- ❖ 1590: **Christopher Holgate** married Isob. Robinson
- ❖ 1590: Jacobus (James) Denis (baptism)
- ❖ 1593: Alicea (Alison) Denis (baptism)
- ❖ 1595: Henry Denis# (baptism)
- ❖ 1599: Henry Denis# (burial)_
- ❖ 1600: Jenneta Denis (baptism)
- ❖ 1600: John Denis* (burial)_

Here we see that the daughter, Elizabeth, had the surname of Ingham when she married John Device in 1590. We also see that this was possibly a shotgun wedding as son James was born in the same year. The very next entry in the registers to that of Elizabeth's marriage shows her brother, Christopher Holgate, marrying Isobell Robinson of Barley.

Alizon Device was actually baptised Alicea while a fourth child, Henry, died at the age of four - this son was previously unknown. It had been widely assumed that the lawless Device family would not have been baptised but these records prove the sceptics wrong.

The name of Elizabeth Device is firmly fixed within the psyche of anyone with an interest in the Pendle Witch legend, a legend that we have, in fact, been exposed to for generations. It can be difficult to assimilate new evidence into the firmly established folklore because there is often a counter-balance somewhere along the line. And so it is with the Southern/Device confederacy long held to have been the lynchpin within the story of 1612.

Having seen that Elizabeth Device carried the surname of Ingham prior to her marriage to John Dennis (Device) it becomes apparent, as in all genealogy research, that the extended family is becoming ever more complicated. For instance, what was the marital status of Elizabeth Ingham at the time of her marriage? Was she born an Ingham or had she married an Ingham and been widowed in the interim? If she was indeed born with the Ingham surname why was her mother apparently called Southern? As we proceed with the life of Elizabeth Southern we have now a vital new piece of evidence to work with - the Ingham name of her daughter.

In relation to Elizabeth Southern's origins how much credence can we give to the Blackburn connection? Ainsworth has it that Southern was the granddaughter of a *'freebooter called Blackburn'* who eventually settled at Malkin Tower. There are almost no references to the Southern name, and very few to that of Blackburn, within the Pendle Forest but a relatively large number of these within the Whalley area. This is interesting when we look at Ainsworth's account of Demdike's supposed grandfather, the marauder Blackburn, who supposedly came from the Whalley area into the forest.

The Clitheroe Court Rolls, and land and property surrenders held at the Preston Records Office, show numerous records relating to the extended Blackburn family, all of whom were tenant farmers of the Braddyll estate at Billington, on the outskirts of Whalley. Two of the principal tenants were William Blackburn (of Billington) and George Blackburn (of Dinckley).

On the 18th April, 1541, an Elizabeth Blackburn was baptised at Whalley and her subsequent offspring carry exactly the same Christian names as do the children of brothers William and George Blackburn. This baptism could very well be confirmation of the folklore that Demdike was a daughter of the Blackburn family from Whalley - instead of Elizabeth Blackburn coming to Barrowford and giving birth to Elizabeth Southern we see her giving birth to Elizabeth Device. If we do indeed have the baptism of Elizabeth Southern then she would have been aged around seventy one when she died in Lancaster Jail in 1612.

Having seen the folklore related by Ainsworth, following his visit to the forest in the mid-1800s, the available recorded evidence appears to reinforce the argument that he picked up the local knowledge that Demdike had been named Blackburn. Furthermore, she then moved into Pandle Forest from the Whalley area.

William Blackburn married Jennet Singleton in 1568 and it is proposed that this William was the brother of Elizabeth Southern; the two were baptised within six years of each other. A perusal of the names given by William Blackburn and his wife, Jennet (Singleton), to their children shows exactly the same Christian names as those given by Southern's daughter, Elizabeth Device, to her children and by Demdike's son, Christopher Holgate, to his offspring.

William also names a child Elizabeth, after his proposed sister, or mother (after whom Southern was possibly named). Southern's children appear, then, to have named their children after their Blackburn cousins. Christopher Holgate also named a son George, this appears to have been after his mother's proposed father, George Blackburn - it is notable that the name George was very rarely used in the Forest at that time.

Demdike's daughter carried the surname of Ingham at the time of her marriage to John Device in 1590. In the sixteenth century, branches of the Ingham family were located from Whalley through to Colne but there were definite concentrations of the family on the periphery of the forest area at Read and Padiham. Within the forest itself the main Ingham families were to be found to the south of West Close where an Inghams Farm exists to this day.

The question remains as to why Elizabeth Blackburn moved into Pendle from the Whalley district and a simple answer would be that she married a man named Ingham from Pendle or Burnley who then moved his new wife into his home. This explains why Elizabeth was called Ingham upon her marriage; but what of Demdike's son, Christopher Holgate - where does he come into the equation?

We know that he was married in 1590 and so we can estimate that he would be born around 1565, when Demdike was aged twenty three or twenty four. A number of permutations are apparent within the Blackburn/Ingham/Holgate/Southern complex of names and these will be explored further.

ELIZABETH SOUTHERN ~ BLACKBURN FAMILY (PROPOSED)

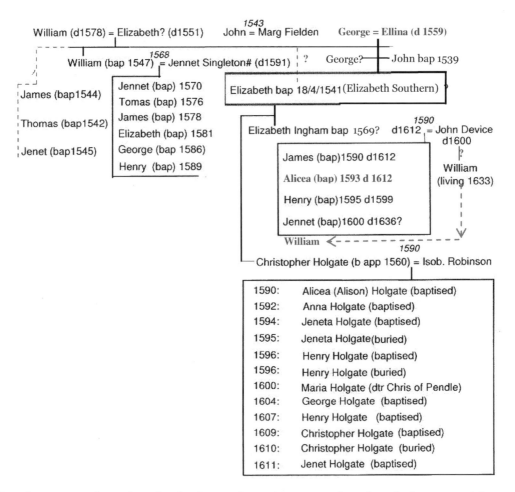

If the above genealogy for Elizabeth Southern is correct then her father was either George or William Blackburn; she had brothers William, James, Thomas, John (and possibly George) along with a sister Jenet. Demdike's daughter Christened her children with exactly the same names (Thomas being an exception) as Demdike's brother, or cousin, William. In turn, Demdike's son christened his children with exactly the same names as his nephews, nieces, uncles and cousins - with the addition of George. This was a rare Christian name at the time and possibly indicates that George was Christopher Holgate's grandfather (Demdike's father) as opposed to William.

Another explanation for the surnames of her offspring is that Elizabeth Blackburn never married an Ingham, rather she had her illegitimate son and daughter by an Ingham and a Holgate and gave the children their father's names. Whatever combination of relationships are considered there is an outstanding factor in why was Demdike known as Southern in 1612?

THEORY 2: ELIZABETH SOUTHERN

We are informed by Potts that, at the time of the 1612 trials, Demdike's surname was Southern/Southernes/Sowthernes/Suthern. This was a rare surname within Pendle but slightly more common in the Whalley district; in 1316 Robert de Southerne re-granted Great Mitton Hall to Thomas de Southerne. Sons of Robert were Thomas and Adam. Later in the reign of Edward II (1307-27), Isobell Southerne, heiress to Sir John Southerne, married Walter de Hawksworth of Hawksworth near Otley thus bringing the Mitton property to that family.

In 1616 '*John Braddill of Portfield in Whalley esquire, and Richard Sowthen of Whalley, gentleman*' surrendered lands. Richard Sowthen/Southern was actually the servant, or right-hand-man, of John Bradyll and in this capacity he knew Bradyll's many tenants around the Whalley area. Richard Towneley esquire granted to Sowthen lands at Barneside and Monkroyd (Laneshawbridge), Foulridge, Carry Heyes (Colne) and Low Massey in Little Marsden (Brierfield), Colne, Wrightington and Goosenargh.

Apart from Elizabeth Southern there are few other examples of the name in local records, a rare phonetic match can be seen when a Jenneta Southan was buried on the 3rd January 1619 at Whalley. A perusal of the incidence of Southern families in the sixteenth century shows that, nationally, there are a few scattered examples but a significant cluster of people carrying the name appears in the area of Holme in Lincolnshire.

It has to be said that the Southern families mentioned above were of the lower gentry and this is typical of the restrictive information found within the available records. As a rule it was only the people dealing in land, or paying taxes, who showed up in the contemporary sources and this could well have been the case with Elizabeth Southern who would not have been recorded in land transactions. Because the relevant church records (Newchurch-in-Pendle, Clitheroe, Colne, Burnley, Padiham, Whalley) are not available for the time in which she could have been expected to marry we are very much in the dark as to her full background.

Perhaps there were a number of Southern families living within the Pendle district and they do not show up because of their lowly status. On the other hand, running with the idea that Elizabeth Southern originated in the Whalley area, is it possible that she was the illegitimate child of a Southern mother or father who was the sent into the Forest as a child to disguise the scandal of the birth? This would certainly not have been a rare event as church and legal records show a high percentage of illegitimacy at that time - where the father did not wish to be involved he would pay a type of maintenance to the mother on the understanding that the child was given the mother's surname. Conversely, the child would be given the father's name as an *alias* and would often be entitled to membership of the father's family and would often inherit his land and property along with any half-siblings.

THEORY 3: BY A NAME SHE'S KNOWN - BUT IT'S NOT HER OWN

It is also worth considering the fact that the names within written records often took a dynamic form; the clerks of the day would write phonetically in coarse forms of Latin and English. Thus a surname could be rendered almost unrecognisable, as we have seen in the transition of Davies to Dennis. Furthermore, Thomas Potts was a Liverpool man who had settled in London - as such he would not be conversant with the Pendle Forest dialect. Also, the magistrates who took the statements of the accused also wrote phonetically and this led to mistakes - such as we see in Isobell Holgate becoming Elizabeth Howgate via the pen of Roger Nowell.

The Southern surname itself is subject to a number of variations in Potts and this probably reflects the number of different people who had a hand in the transcriptions - the oral statement of the accused was written by one or more of the magistrates and then this was written in Potts' record, to be re-written in haste the following year, further editing was carried out by yet another party and then the result was printed as the *Wonderfulle Discoverie*.

On the 19th March 1610 an Isabell Suttherd was buried at Newchurch-in-Pendle and, in 1637, the Colne baptism records show, *Johannes fili Johanis Sowthard de Trawden illegi 17th December*. Sutherd and Sowthard are both corruptions of Southworth and this is another illustration of the mutation of names. If the letter D is replaced with N we have a creditable spelling Suthern, Sowthern - an obvious candidate for the Southern appellation. As a matter of interest, local folklore of the nineteenth century had it that another of the Pendle accused, Alice Nutter of Roughlee, *'came originally out of Trawden Forest.'* We now know that this is incorrect but a grain of truth within the story might just relate instead to Elizabeth Southern and this could place her within the Sowthard family of Trawden.

It is interesting that a phonetically similar name crops up in historic witchcraft accounts over a wide area. In 1488 Ursula Southel was born in the Knaresborough area of West Yorkshire. She married a Toby Shipton in 1512 and died in 1561 at the age of seventy three. Old Mother Shipton, as Ursula became known, went on to become a famous seer - her prophesies are now legendary, although their provenance is somewhat suspect.

A renowned Norwegian witch, Mor Saether, lived from 1793 to 1851 and a woman from St. Osyth, in the county of Essex, accused of bewitching at least four people was found guilty and remanded to prison. As of August 2, 1582, she was still imprisoned at Colchester Jail, along with her co-accused, Ellen Southern.

In 1566 Old Mother Waterhouse of Hatfield Peverel, Chelmsford, stood trial for witchcraft and admitted to having had a familiar, in the form of a cat, who willed her to call him *Sathan* - this is an early French word meaning Satan which entered the Middle English language. Examples of the use of Sathan in literature are numerous; *'Christ's victorie over Sathan's tyrannie'* was the title of a book written

in 1615. Jeantin, in his *'Manuel de la Meuse'* of 1860, has it that, *The appellation SATHAN is, at once, geological, cosmogonical and Hebraic.* Phillip Stubbes, who published in 1583 his *'Anatomie of Abuses,'* said that . . . *for there is a great Lord present amongst them, as superintendent and Lord over their pastimes and sportes, namely Sathan, prince of hel.* In the early Scottish dialect the word *Sathan* means *evil.*

Given the close phonetic proximity of the names *Sathan* and *Southern* the possibility arises as to whether Elizabeth Southern was either assigned the surname of Sathan by her fellow Foresters; or was she given her name when Roger Nowell wrote up the case for the prosecution? It would be fair comment to say that this is a long-shot but a consideration arises whereby the odds become somewhat shortened: it just so happens that the Chelmsford witch trials of 1566 were very similar to the Pendle trials that would follow almost fifty years later - a forerunner in fact. We saw earlier that Sir Thomas Gerard, of Bryn, was instrumental in bringing a witch from his own district of St. Helens to the 1612 Pendle trials - and that he was quite possibly instrumental in starting the prosecution ball rolling by enlisting Abraham Lawe into the cause.

Chelmsford took the form of a show trial; this was the first witchcraft trial to be held following Queen Elizabeth's *Act Against Conjurations, Enchantments and Witchcrafts* of 1562. A number of celebrity lawyers and big-wigs attended the trial and, lo-and-behold, we find that the Queen's Attorney overseeing the prosecution was none other than Sir Thomas Gerard's uncle, Sir Gilbert Gerard. Gilbert Gerard (1523-1593) was appointed Attorney-General in 1559 and became Master of the Rolls in 1581.[7] He was also a close friend of Roger Nowell's family.[8]

To further illustrate the connection that the Gerard family had with the Pendle Forest we also find that the area of Brierfield, now known as Quaker Bridge, encompassed the farms and lands within area including Chamber In Pendle (and the Chamber fulling mill), Hawks Hole and the lands of Reedley Hallows. At the 1568 halmote court of Ightenhill the above, plus three other farms, were granted to Gilbert Gerard and his wife Anne (née Radcliffe).

It is almost certain, then, that Sir Thomas Gerard would have known every detail of the famous trial at which his uncle presided; the gory details would have been the chief dinner-table conversation for many years. In fact Sir Thomas would have been steeped in the legend of the Chelmsford events and would have brought his knowledge to bear on the Pendle trials. Central to the Chelmsford trial was the cat familiar, Sathan, and Gerard would have introduced this concept to Roger Nowell. The Old French word *Sathan* was topically applied as a description of evil i.e. to the workings of demons and the devil. It is interesting to note that the earlier period of the Anglo Saxons also had similar words where we find:

Soðan = sooth as in soothsayer - truth - wise (Old English)
Séoðan = troubled in mind - disturbed (Old English)
Sōðian = soothsayer - bear witness to the truth (North German)
Suðon = pretext of *Séoðan* (Old English)
Seith = type of witchcraft practised by the pre-Christian Norse people (Old Norse)
Siðen = closely related to *Seith* (Old Norse)
Seiðr = a potent and malevolent form of magic practised by females - includes shape-changing, flight and spell-casting (Old Norse ?)

Having seen that some of the most famous witches of the pre-modern era carry the similar names of Ursula *Southel*, Mor *Saether* and Elizabeth *Southern* it seems prudent to ask the question as to whether those considered to have been potent witches were given their appellations in relevance to their calling at the time? Certainly, within the above examples it can be seen that *Southel, Saether* and *Southern* could well be Anglicised versions of Old French or Old English descriptions applied to a witch, a soothsayer, a wise woman or an unfortunate considered to have been mentally infirm. Alternatively, did their surnames originate within the mists of time where soothsayers acquired a surname that would be passed through subsequent generations - in other words, the arts of the wise person were passed down and we see in Southel, Saether and Southern a 'trade' name equivalent to Smith, Cartwright and Cowman?

The word *Sathan* sits within the descriptive framework of its Anglo Saxon relations and it is clear that, if they so wished, the people of the sixteenth and seventeenth centuries had a useful lexicon with which they could describe those within the community who did not fit well with the Puritan standards of the day.

Elizabeth Southern, then, might have carried a typical name assigned by others or inherited through a line of wise people. That name was not necessarily *Southern* - it could have been *Soðan* or *Suðon* etc. Alternatively, Roger Nowell would have known of the witchcraft context in which *Sathan*, the cat familiar, had appeared. By applying this to his prisoner (the leader and most dangerous of the Pendle witch brood) he knew very well that he would gain an element of advantage when the case came before a jury - likewise he probably assigned the name of Demdike just for good measure.

THEORY 4: BEST EVIDENCE

The trial prosecution assigned to Elizabeth Southern the highest profile of all the Pendle accused and there is no doubt that she was the most enigmatic of the group. Nothing within her statements appears to hint that she was from outside of the North West district. Southern does not appear to have had a long-standing family anchor within the Pendle locality - she is not referred to in any relationship context outside of her immediate family. Further to this, clues exist to suggest that she might have moved into the Forest sometime in the latter half of the sixteenth century.

We have seen that local folklore had Southern (or her mother Bess Blackburn) coming to Pendle from the Whalley area; further to this there is a viable Blackburn family tree within which Elizabeth Blackburn fits. If this had indeed been the case then the reason for the enmity between Demdike and Chattox would become clear - Demdike arrived on Chattox's patch and began to make a name for herself in the area. Chattox, having been the matriarchal wise woman of the district did not take kindly to the pushy newcomer and so the pair were destined to be forever at loggerheads.

Taking it that Southern was born in Whalley we know that at some stage she arrived in Pendle. The fact that she was baptised in Whalley suggests that her mother was not sent away to have the child and so she was probably born in wedlock. He daughter was an Ingham at marriage and her son a Holgate; the main possibilities here, then, are that Elizabeth Blackburn:

- . . . married an Ingham and had daughter Elizabeth. A record exists for an Elizabeth Blackburn marrying Thomas Ingham at Whalley in 1563 (he died in 1573). No record yet found for daughter Elizabeth from this marriage.

- . . . had an illegitimate child with an Ingham. Burnley St. Peter's church records show an Elizabeth Ingham baptised in July 1569, father Richard Ingham, mother unknown. This is a distinct possibility and could have brought Elizabeth Blackburn into the southern Forest.

- . . . married an Ingham, had Elizabeth and illegitimate son, Christopher, by a Holgate.

- . . . married a Holgate, had son Christopher and illegitimate daughter, Elizabeth, by an Ingham.

- . . . never married and was known in the Forest as Southern, or given that name by Roger Nowell. Son and daughter both illegitimate.

- . . . married an Ingham, had Elizabeth, was widowed, had Christopher illegitimately then married a Southern.

- . . . never was a Blackburn - born as Southern, Ingham or Holgate.

And so on! Given the lack of church records with which to define the life of Elizabeth Southern the best we can do is to take the best available evidence. A study of land and property transactions during the sixteenth and seventeenth centuries provides a basis for the location of particular families within Pendle at that time. Although this approach is not perfect it does nevertheless allow for a general placing of families within a specific district of the Forest. Thus, for instance, we find that the Nutters were clustered around Roughlee, Goldshaw, Old and New Laund and Sabden Fold. The Robinsons were generally located on farms at Thorneyholme (Roughlee), Barley, Wheatley Lane and Old Laund while the Hartleys and Hargreaves families were 'scattered'.

When the records relating to the Holgate and Ingham families are studied it is clear that, in general, they occupied different areas of the Forest. The Inghams were mainly farmers of lands to the south of Higham (West Close, Hunterholme, Filly Close, Ightenhill) and woollen merchants in Burnley and Padiham while the Holgates farmed at Barley (the Black Moss area and Under Pendle). In Part Three the site of Malkin Tower will be discussed and here it will be suggested that the Holgates of Barley played a major part in Elizabeth Southern's life. It is suggested that she first came to the Burnley/West Close area where she had her daughter Elizabeth, possibly by Richard Ingham in 1569, and later moved across the Pendle ridgeway to the Holgate lands in Barley.

To date, then, based upon the best evidence currently available the proposal is that Elizabeth Southern was born in the Whalley area around 1541, came to the Burnley/Padiham/southern Pendle district at about the age of 25, had a daughter by her Ingham husband, or an acquaintance named Ingham. Ingham maintained the mother and child but he died, Elizabeth then had a son with her Holgate husband or an acquaintance named Holgate. Mother, daughter and baby son then moved over to Barley where the Holgates farmed. The family were maintained in a cottage at 'Mank Ing' (see Part Three) by Holgate but he died. Daughter Elizabeth took up with an older man named John Device, her mother lived with her while brother Christopher worked on the nearby Holgate farm. John Device died in 1600 and his widow had an illegitimate daughter, Jennet, by a local man named Seller.

The Remaining Witch Cast

Elizabeth Device

Elizabeth Ingham married John Device at Newchurch-in-Pendle in the year 1590. When she stood trial for her life, in August of 1612, she would have been around forty years of age. Elizabeth's trial followed immediately after that of Old Chattox and she is described by Potts as having been;

Branded with a preposterous mark in nature, even from her birth, which was her left eye standing lower than the other, the one looking down, the other looking up, so strangely deformed, as the best who were present in that honourable assembly and great audience did affirm, they had not often seen the like.'

There has to be some doubt here as to the true extent of Elizabeth Device's affliction. The description enthusiastically proffered by Potts certainly paints the poor woman in a demonic light but the reality was exaggerated. It is probable that Elizabeth either fell and banged her head as a child or received a trauma to the skull during child birth. Both of these could have resulted in the misalignment, to some degree or other, of an eye socket. Whatever the cause of Elizabeth's appearance might have been it certainly was not the result of some Satanic mark, as Potts subliminally suggests.

When Elizabeth's daughter, Jennet, was put before the court to give evidence against her mother, the latter broke out into such a storm of curses and reproaches that the child *'with weeping tears cried out to my Lord the judge, and told him she was not able to speak in the presence of her mother.'* Nothing would silence Elizabeth Device, and the learned judge, seeing in her curses and threats nothing but an attempt to terrify the child into withdrawing the statements she had already made to Roger Nowell, ordered her removal from the court. Jennet was then placed upon a table in the presence of the whole court, and there gave evidence that her mother was a witch, and that she had frequently seen her familiar spirit, which was called Ball, in the shape of a brown dog - Jennet's (half) brother, James Device, told practically the same story.

On the 9th January 1591 James Baldwin of Colne made a will;

I James Bawden of Colne in the county of Lancaster glover sick in body but whole in mind do ordain and make this my last will: the residue of my part of goods I will shall be equally divided to the said John Bawden, James Bawden, Annyse now wife of the said Lawrence Botheman, **Elizabeth Davye** alias Bawden and **Jennet Davye** alias Bawden supposed to be the bastard daughters of me the said James Bawden. I make executors Elizabeth my wife and John Walker of Colne desiring Christopher Bawden of the Weethead to see this my last will and testament be fulfilled as my trust is in him. . . .

James Baldwin, then, had two illegitimate daughters by a woman named Davye (Davies) thus showing a link between the Baldwins and the Device family. We have seen that Elizabeth Device carried out a day's work at the mill run by Richard Baldwin's family but he refused her payment. Elizabeth enlisted her mother to approach Baldwin at his home at Wheathead but as they approached the farm Baldwin intercepted them. Calling them *'witches and whores'* he chased Demdike and Elizabeth off his land. Demdike told Baldwin what she thought of him and then promptly fell into a hedge, this was followed by much muttering and cursing.

Why did Richard Baldwin hit the roof when the women approached with what appears to have been a perfectly reasonable request? The plain answer is that we do not know for certain but we must consider the fact that Elizabeth Device could well have been related to the Baldwin family through her husband, John Device. If so, the fact that the Demdike family were related to his own family through the illegitimate offspring of his (probable) brother James Baldwin, of Colne, would have been enough to grossly offend the high Protestant morals of Richard Baldwin. The un-Godly family of *'witches and whores,'* as he unkindly named Demdike and Elizabeth Device, would have been a constant thorn in his side. The fact that his neighbours, and moreover, his fellow church congregation, would have known of the relationship would have been enough to cause him a serious bout of apoplexy.

Elizabeth Device, then, appears to have been rather unfortunate in both her physical appearance and in her unwitting relationship to a local Puritan worthy by the name of Richard Baldwin. The fact that Elizabeth enlisted the aid of her aged and blind mother to approach Richard Baldwin on her behalf raises a couple of points. Elizabeth Device was unwilling to ask Baldwin for her dues – was this because of the old enmity between the families? Or was Elizabeth of a shy disposition because of her disfigurement; was she educationally challenged to such an extent that she was incapable of communication upon this level?

With regard to this latter possibility Potts stated that Roger Nowell could not extract any kind of submission from Elizabeth during their initial interview. Her stubborn refusal to either incriminate herself, or make any kind of statement, showed that either she was aware of the dangerous situation in which her family found themselves or she was incapable of communicating with Nowell. If she was inclined to shrink from social contact, as the Baldwin episode might suggest, Elizabeth would probably have become sullen and uncooperative when confronted with Nowell's authority. According to Potts, it was only when Elizabeth realised that her own son and daughter (James and Jennet) had accused her of causing death by witchcraft did she finally confess to being a witch.

However, the story does not add up here; when Elizabeth stood before the Lancaster Assizes she maintained her innocence by pleading not guilty. Nowell then pulled his masterstroke by calling Jennet Device to testify against not only her own mother but the whole shebang of the gathered accused. Potts fained surprise at the appearance of Jennet, calling her '*This unexpected witness*' - here he gives the impression that God Himself had sent the child trotting along to the court in order to carry out His work in rooting out the ubiquitous devil from amongst the poor Foresters. Quite naturally, when confronted by her own child making accusations that would lead to her death, Elizabeth went berserk.

Potts says that she screamed and cursed and so frightened the child that Elizabeth had to be physically removed from the courtroom. This has been used by many writers upon the subject as proof that Elizabeth was mentally unstable but the circumstances were such that even a well-balanced character might snap when confronted with such a gross miscarriage of justice - as this so patently was.

Potts also made the telling statement that Elizabeth denied having made any confession as she was dragged from the court – there is here a strong suggestion of there having been an interpolation of facts by either the prosecution or, later, the writing up of the case by Potts.

The very next entry in the church records to that of the marriage for John Dennis and Elizabeth Ingham shows the marriage of Christopher Holgate and Isabell Robinson.

CHRISTOPHER HOLGATE

Christopher Holgate was described in the prosecution evidence as being the uncle to the Device children and, if we take it that Elizabeth Device was the true child of Elizabeth Southern, (rather than the adopted daughter or step-daughter), he would in all likelihood have been the son of Elizabeth Southern.

Whether he was the full or half-brother to Elizabeth Device is not clear at this stage. The Newchurch marriage record of 1590 shows Elizabeth Southern's daughter getting married and she could well have married in a double wedding with her brother, Christopher; the two couples were certainly married within a short period of each other.

As with Elizabeth and John Dennis the marriage of Christopher Holgate coincides with the baptism of their first child – Alicea Holgate was baptised at Newchurch in 1590. Moreover, the other Holgate children were given exactly the same names as the offspring of Elizabeth and John Dennis.

The following are all Newchurch-in-Pendle entries relating to the family of Christopher and Isabell Holgate, unless otherwise stated:

    1590: Alicea (Alison) Holgate (baptised)~

1592: Anna Holgate (baptised)
1594: Jenneta Holgate (baptised)_
1595: Jenneta Holgate (buried)_
1596: Henry Holgate (baptised)__
1596: Henry Holgate (buried)__
1600: Maria Holgate (dtr Chris of Pendle, baptised Padiham)
1604: George Holgate (baptised)
1607: Henry Holgate (baptised) _ _
1609: Christopher Holgate (baptised) **
1610: Christopher Holgate (buried) **
1611: Jennet Holgate (baptised)

THE NEXT GENERATION
1626: Henry Holgate (baptised, son of Henry)
1632: James Holgate (baptised, son of Henry or George)
1632: Anna Holgate (baptised, daughter of Henry or George)^
1636: Isabel Holgate (baptised, daughter of Henry or George)
1636: Isabel Holgate (buried, possible wife of Christopher)
1637: Alice Holgate married Thurstan Garstang~
1640: John Holgate (baptised)*
1645: Ellena Holgate (baptised)
1647: Isabella Holgate (baptised)
1655: James Holgate (baptised)
1664: Henry Holgate (burial) _ _ _
1664: John Holgate (burial)*
1673: Anna Holgate (burial)^

So... who were the Holgates by whom Demdike apparently had a son? In 1443 a Richard Holgate was one of the free tenants of Pendleton, by the time of the New Hold within Pendle Forest the family appear as two definite branches, one in the Colne/Foulridge area and the other in the Pendle Forest itself. In 1507 William Holgate was fined at the Ightenhill halmote for digging turfs on a pasture called The Flash (meaning land subject to flooding) in the Goldshaw area, this land was tenanted by James Hargreaves and Robert Bulcock. By 1513 it becomes clear that the Holgates were tenants in their own right as Henry Hartley of Pendle surrendered a farm of twenty two acres and other premises in Barley that Richard Holgate had delivered to him. This was possibly Mancknowles Ing and will have a significant bearing on our story in Part Three.

Two years later a farm at Wheatley Hay Booth, Barley (£0: 8s: 11d rental), reverted to king on the death of William Holgate, his son and heir was Richard Holgate and Richard's younger brother, Thomas Holgate, sought admittance to the property. This was obviously the cause of some ill-feeling within the family as another record of 1515 shows that Margaret Holgate, the widow of William, and her son Thomas complained against Richard Holgate for illegally entering their farm at Hay Booth.

In 1523 it is apparent that Richard Holgate had the lifetime tenancy of another farm at Hay Booth, this was no doubt an inheritance from his father and possibly the reason why his mother wished the other property to be tenanted by her younger son. In this instance John Hargreaves complained that Roger Hartley, Thomas Varley and Robert Varley were occupying the farm illegally as Richard Holgate had granted him the tenancy on contract. The three defendants were the feoffes of Richard Holgate and were, therefore, holding the property on his behalf. Richard Holgate found surety for his tenancy by John Smith and Miles Nutter (father-in-law of Alice Nutter).

The township of Barley included the four original farming operations that were carved out from the Forest area, these were Barley Booth, Wheatley Booth, Hay Booth and Whitehough. This region is formed within a strip of high land running from Stang Top in the east, through the Black Moss area and onwards to the slopes of Pendle Hill above the village of Barley.

We see a further land transaction involving the Holgates when, in 1524, John, Richard and Robert Bulcock, along with Thomas Varley, surrendered a farm and other buildings in Hay Booth (£0:8s: 11d rental) to the use of Richard Holgate. Richard again found surety for his tenancy by John Smith and Miles Nutter - he was obviously friendly with these, the two wealthiest men in Roughlee.

Christopher Holgate was described by Jennet Device as being her uncle *'of Pendle'* in order to distinguish him from a Christopher Holgate who lived in Colne at that time. This latter branch, also closely related to the Holgates of Foulridge, were the largest group of the Holgate family within the area. Christopher of Pendle married Isabell Robinson of the Barley family who farmed at Barley, Black Moss, Foothouse Gate and Whitehough.

Christopher Holgate, and his wife, were amongst the few named persons at the Good Friday gathering to escape with their lives; for some reason they were never prosecuted but lack of evidence against them is not the first reason for this that springs to mind. Most of those who were executed at Lancaster lost their lives on the basis of an almost farcical prosecution case. One possibility for the Holgate's escape is that they had a number of dependent children – in the twenty years following their marriage (1590) the Holgates had produced nine children. Alternatively, the Holgates were not accused of anything other than attending Malkin Tower of Good Friday and their contacts within the local yeomanry would ensure that they were not prosecuted. Three of Christopher Holgate's children died in infancy and he was now also to lose his mother, sister, nephew and niece at a single stroke.

Demdike's son, then, married into the Robinson family of Barley and this begs the question as to why her daughter, Elizabeth Device, allegedly brought about the deaths of both John and James Robinson of Barley? According to the statement of James Device his mother, Elizabeth, had killed John Robinson for having accused her of having a child by a man named Sellers. As we shall see, it is in fact true that Jennet was the illegitimate daughter of a man named Sellers. It also appears that the Robinson brothers were related to Richard Baldwin of Wheathead as the former pledged for the dower of a female member of the Baldwin family. The Robinsons were of the same strata in society as Richard Baldwin and it appears from their attitude to the illegitimate birth of Jennet that they shared his Puritan leanings. It is also possible that Elizabeth was related to the Robinsons via her husband and the Baldwins - another example of the social complexity and tensions of the period.

In the latter part of the nineteenth century members of the Holgate family ran Barley Green Mill while others, who were merchants, a banker and a solicitor from the Burnley district, were in possession of Under Pendle Farm at Barley and it is probable that they had been tenants here for a long period. In fact this could well have been the farm on which Christopher Holgate lived when his mother occupied Malkin Tower.

An ancestor of Roger Nowell, Robert Nowell of Read Hall, left a will in the 1570s in which he provided for the distribution of woollen cloth to the poorer people of the Whalley and Pendle districts. In the list of those receiving this beneficence was one Elizabeth Holgate and we will never know if this was, in fact, Christopher Holgate's mother, Old Demdike.

JOHN DEVICE

John Device was probably a good few years older than his wife, Elizabeth - it appears from accounts of the 1633 Pendle trials that he already had a son named William Device as he was then described as half-brother to Jennet Device.

John was said to have paid an annual contribution of one aghendole of oatmeal to Chattox – an aghendole was originally the term used for a 'hand out' ('dole' is still used in this context) where 'aghen' and 'hanck' share the same root for 'hand' or 'in hand.' The aghendole equivalent in weight today would be around eight and-a-half pounds. Alison Device said that the reason for John Device providing this contribution to Chattox was to gain protection for his family, property and goods against the powers of Chattox. Again this hints at John having been elderly, perhaps too frail to resist the Whittle/Redfearn family. The first year that John Device missed paying the contribution he fell ill and blamed Chattox for having bewitched him, he died in 1600.

To accept this story at face value we must also accept that Demdike, as John's mother-in-law, stood idly back and allowed her rival to blackmail her family without retaliation. According to Potts' accounts Demdike had been practising her craft for many more years than Chattox (this was not actually true) and must have seen herself as being at least the equal of her great rival. We have no explanation for this, nor do her family's statements shed any light on this curious incident; why would the family of the supposedly most omnipotent witch in the whole area pay for protection from another witch who was subordinate in power? There is surely more to this than meets the eye; a possible explanation for the mystery springs to mind and that centres upon Chattox's daughter, Bessie Whittle, sister to Anne Redfearn.

Bessie was said by Alison Device to have broken into the *'fire house'* at Malkin Tower from where she stole a quantity of clothing and food. Following the theft Bessie had the audacity to turn up at church wearing Alison's best bonnet. This could well furnish us with the character of Bessie Whittle, a burglar and bare-faced (but not bare-headed) with it! If Bessie Whittle was something of a bruiser, besides being a thief, did John Device pay Chattox in order for her daughter to leave them alone, rather than risk an all-out war between the different factions within the Forest?

Certainly, the method of settling these types of dispute within the Forest was often the use of open conflict; many records of physical assault survive from this period when the law was seen as a last resort. It was not uncommon for families, armed with muskets and staves, to confront each other over some perceived wrong doing by their rivals – many instances of this type stemmed from a petty land dispute.

JENNET DEVICE

The girl of eleven, Jennet Device, was instrumental in the conviction of many of the accused in 1612 but what exactly was her 'evidence' proffered so triumphantly to the court by Roger Nowell? The following takes up Potts as he describes the events immediately following Elizabeth Device's courtroom outburst against her daughter:

> The Examination and Euidence of Iennet Device, Daughter of the said Elizabeth Device, late Wife of Iohn Device, of the Forrest of Pendle, in the Countie of Lancaster. Against Elizabeth Device her Mother, Prisoner at the Barre vpon her Arraignement and Triall. viz
>
> In the end, when no meanes would serue, his Lordship commanded the Prisoner (Elizabeth Device) to be taken away, and the Maide (Jennet Device) to bee set vpon the Table in the presence of the whole Court, who

deliuered her euidence in that Honorable assembly, to the Gentlemen of the Iurie of life and death, as followeth. viz.

Iennet Deuice, Daughter of Elizabeth Deuice, late Wife of Iohn Deuice, of the Forrest of Pendle aforesaid Widdow, confesseth and saith, that her said Mother is a Witch, and that this shee knoweth to be true; for, that shee had seene her Spirit sundrie times come vnto her said Mother in her owne house, called Malking-Tower, in the likenesse of a browne Dogge, which shee called Ball; and at one time amongst others, the said Ball did aske this Examinates Mother what she would haue him to doe: and this Examinates Mother answered, that she would haue the said Ball to helpe her to kill Iohn Robinson of Barley, alias Swyer: by helpe of which said Ball, the said Swyer was killed by witch-craft accordingly; and that this Examinates Mother hath continued a Witch for these three or foure yeares last past. And further, this Examinate confesseth, that about a yeare after, this Examinates Mother called for the said Ball, who appeared as aforesaid, asking this Examinates Mother what shee would haue done, who said, that shee would haue him to kill Iames Robinson, alias Swyer, of Barlow (Barley) aforesaid, Brother to the said Iohn: whereunto Ball answered, hee would doe it; and about three weekes after, the said Iames dyed.

And this Examinate also saith, that one other time shee was present, when her said Mother did call for the Ball, Her Spirit. who appeared in manner as aforesaid, and asked this Examinates Mother what she would haue him to doe, whereunto this Examinates Mother then said shee would haue him to kill one Mitton of the Rough Lee, whereupon the said Ball said, he would doe it, and so vanished away, and about three weekes after, the said Mitton likewise dyed.

The flow of content here is obviously contrived; the pronounced hand of biased-intent shines through when we recall that the statement is that of an eleven year-old child. The description accorded to the word of Jennet in relation to the spirit, Ball, follows through the story and is standardised throughout – far too standardised in fact! That the accused were prone to imbue their animals with extraordinary powers was a fundamental tenet within the writings of Medieval witchcraft observers; we see this in the Chelmsford trials and again it is wheeled out in the Pendle cases.

Elizabeth Device may well have returned home from her day in the forest with a piggin of blue-milk and a scant copper or two; she might have been the subject of derision by her neighbours during the day. In this case it would be little wonder that she would return home in a mood of despondency, with little good-will to extend to her fellow man. Sitting by the fire she might have stroked her brown pet dog, Ball, for solace and muttered of the constant ills done to her and how sweet any revenge would be if this were possible.

It is not clear whether the multitude of dogs cropping up within the statements of the accused actually belonged to them (as pets) or if the dogs were semi-strays wandering the neighbourhood and visiting people on a regular basis in search of scraps. This is entirely possible as it would be unlikely that dogs were kept solely as pets by the poor, they would have to earn their living by catching rabbits, hares and game from the surrounding moors. The suggestion in Jennet's 'evidence' points to the dog, Ball, having appeared at various intervals throughout the story, this lends weight to the animal having had some kind of relationship with the Device family. Whatever the case might have been, Jennet was repeating the conversations overheard within her family over a period of many years.

A small percentage of the people who had been perceived to insult her family would become ill or die and this was then automatically assigned to the mutterings of Jennet's mother or grandmother. Elizabeth Device would not deny the rumour that she had 'killed' someone by using her powers; this was useful ammunition with which to arm herself against the outside world. Jennet was stating as fact that she knew her mother had been a witch for some three or four years but this did not seem to strike anyone as having been questionable at the time. Certainly the judges did not take the view that Jennet, being only around six or seven when Elizabeth apparently became a witch, was not capable of presenting admissible evidence in what amounted to a murder trial.

JENNET DEVICE ALIAS SELLER

Elizabeth Device was said to have given her reason for killing John Robinson of Barley as revenge for him having accused her '*of having an illegitimate child by one Sellers.*' Elizabeth's youngest child, Jennet, is usually taken to be the child she was accused of having by Seller and this is the most acceptable explanation because Elizabeth's husband, John Device, had died in the same year that Jennet was born. The argument has been made for John having been senior in years to Elizabeth and it has been suggested that this is one reason why she might have 'played away.'

It is worth remembering here that Richard Baldwin called Demdike and Elizabeth Device *Witches and whores* - can we take it, therefore, that Elizabeth Device was the '*whore*' and Demdike the '*witch*'? This would point towards Elizabeth having had a tryst with a man named Seller, possibly whilst her husband was still living. It is just possible in the natural scheme of things that, if John died early in the year 1600, Elizabeth could have taken up with Mr Seller following John's death and still produced a child within the same year – she would have had to be quick though!

The Seller surname was well established within the Whalley area where they were neighbours of the Blackburns but the name grew thinner on the ground as it approached the Forest. That is not to say that there were no Sellers hereabouts as, by the early seventeenth century, they were farming at Barley and Goldshaw.

As a final note on the Seller/Jennet Device mystery there is a very interesting entry in the Newchurch burial records where we find:

JENNET SELLER ALIAS DEVIS: SEPULT (INTERPOLATED ENTRY):
22ND DECEMBER 1635 [9]

In all probability this is the burial of Jennet Device. It would appear that Jennet (quite understandably) changed her name to that of her father following the execution of the rest of her family. There is also a strong hint here that Jennet would have gone to live with her father although there is also the possibility that she changed her name and went to live with her uncle, Christopher Holgate. Whatever the case may have been it is clear that Jennet lived out the rest of her post-trial days in the forest. In the 1633 Pendle Witch case, as we shall see later, Jennet was implicated when young Edmund Robinson accused her, along with her half-brother, William Device, of being a witch. Robinson said that he often saw Jennet Device walking through a close of land by his father's house in Wheatley Lane and, knowing who she was, this frightened him.

Jennet Device, then, died in the winter of 1635, aged 35 years, and was buried at St. Mary's. The curate was Robert Hill and amongst the small group of mourners on that December day would have been Jennet's Holgate relatives along with her Seller family. The following churchwardens at the time were John Robinson, Laurence Robinson, James Ridehalgh and Thomas Varley; this latter was a friend of the Holgates and the curate who officiated at the marriage of Jennet's mother and John Device.

What did the curate say as Jennet was buried? What was said amongst that sad, graveside gathering of the events some twenty-three years earlier when Jennet played a major part in the deaths of her family? At least Jennet was afforded a Christian burial which was more than those who were executed in August 1612 were afforded.

JAMES DEVICE

James Device would have been around twenty-two years old when he was hanged as a witch. Demdike's grandson not only confessed to his own participation in the craft, but testified against his mother, his grandmother and his sister Alison. His evidence was given in the matter-of-fact way which distinguishes that of all those who made confessions, they all speak as if witchcraft were an ordinary every-day reality where evil spirits went about the countryside in various disguises.

James Device declared that on a certain Shrove Tuesday, his grandmother bade him go to church to receive the sacrament. He was not to eat the bread but to bring it away with him, and hand it to *'such a Thing'* as he should meet on his way homeward - however, he disobeyed and ate the wafer. On his way home, when about fifty metres from the church, he was met by a *'Thing in the shape of a hare'* which asked him if he had brought the bread according to his grandmother's directions. He answered that he had not, whereupon the Thing threatened to tear him to pieces; at this point James said that he called upon the name of God at which time the Thing disappeared.

A few days later a *'thing in the shape of a brown dog'* met him near the new church in Pendle (St. Mary's had been consecrated in 1544 and was still known as the New Kirk). The Thing asked him for his soul, promising him in return that he should be avenged on his enemies. To this James made answer that *'his soul was not his to give but was his Saviour Jesus Christ's, yet as much as was his to give he was contented to yield to the spirit.'* Within two or three days of this meeting, James went to Carr Hall, where Mrs. Towneley, after charging him and his mother with having stolen some of her peat turves, bade him begone. As he went *'forth of the door the said Mistress Townley gave him a knock between the shoulders.'*

A day or two later a black dog met him, and reminding him of the insult put upon him by Mrs. Towneley, directed him to make a clay picture in her image and he would help him to destroy her. Bidding James to call him Dandy, the spirit disappeared. The next morning he made a clay image of Mrs. Towneley, and dried it the same night by the fire. Every day he crumbled away a piece of this image and at the end of a week it was all gone - two days later Mrs. Towneley died.

In the following Lent, one John Duckworth of Laund promised James an old shirt, but when he went to get the gift, Duckworth refused to give it to him, and he was driven away. As he was going out of the house, the spirit Dandy appeared to him, and said *'Thou didst touch the said Duckworth.'* James denied this but the spirit answered, *'Thou didst touch him and therefore I haye power of him. . .'* whereupon James expressed his wish to the spirit that Duckworth might be killed - within a week he was dead.

The 'confessions' made by the Pendle accused were, in all probability, given under the promise that if they told the truth their lives would be spared. There is no record of any of the Lancashire witches being put to the torture, although this horrible means of extorting confessions was resorted to in other parts of the country. In actual fact the use of torture was completely unnecessary given the fact that it was a simple matter for the examining magistrates to falsify and manipulate the staements of the accused.

Thomas Potts' description of James Device's appearance when he was brought to trial, gives rise to a widely held assumption that in his case, at any rate, torture had been employed although great stress was laid, both in Potts' account and in the judge's summing-up, of the fact that the confessions were voluntary. Of James Device Potts says;

> This wicked and miserable Wretch, whether by practise, or meanes, to bring himself to some untimely death and thereby to avoid his Tryall by his Countery, and just judgement of the law; or ashamed to bee openly charged with so many devilish practises, and so much innocent blood as hee had spilt; or by reason of his imprisonment so long time before his Trial (which was with more favour, comisaration and reliefe than hee deserved) I know not: But being brought forward to the Barre, to receive his Tryal before this worthie judge, and so Honourable and Worshipfulle an assembly of justices for this service, was so insensible, weake and unable in all thinges as he could neither speake, heare, or stand, but was holden up when hee was brought to the place of his arraignement to receive his trial!

Here, yet again, we hear the voice of the prosecution echoing its bias and propaganda down the centuries. James Device had to be dragged to his trial from the stinking dungeons, his home for the past few months, and held up between two jailers. It is almost certain that the young man was suffering from 'Jail Fever' (typhoid), which killed many incarcerated prisoners, guilty and innocent alike. This disease was probably the cause of Demdike's demise in the previous May. However, never one to pass over an opportunity to exact the maximum drama from a situation Potts accused James Device of making himself ill deliberately in order to escape justice. Worse than this, the wretch had the gall to be ill when all the fine judges and gentlemen of the north had assembled to watch him be tried for his life and if he were to miss his trial then this would be a huge inconvenience for them all.

It is clear from the Potts accounts that anyone accused of witchcraft would need to present a clean, blemish-free profile to the court otherwise they would be pilloried on the sharp end of derision and suspicion before being hanged. An eye that was offset (Elizabeth Device), signs of Parkinsons disease and old age (Chattox), cataracts and old age (Demdike), illness (James Device) and senile dementia (Alice Nutter) - all of these were grist to the mill of the prosecution and were gleefully put forward as proof positive of the person's guilt.

The fact that James Device was insensible in court led to some early writers on the subject describing him as stupid or backward. Described as a labourer James would certainly have been as ill-educated as most of the lower strata of the Forest community. There is no evidence, however, to indicate that he was anything other than a naive country lad steeped in the lore and culture of an isolated rural community. Having said that, in addition to testifying against his mother, and his sister Alison, he and his sister Jennet were instrumental in sending three innocent women to their deaths - Katherine Hewitt, Anne Redfearn and Alice Nutter.

ALICEA (ALISON) DEVICE

THE CONFESSIONE of Alizon Device, Prisoner at the Barre: published and declared at the time of her Arraignement and Triall in open Court: She saith, That about two yeares agone, her Grand-mother, called Elizabeth Sothernes, alias Dembdike, did (sundry times in going or walking together, as they went begging) perswade and aduise this Examinate to let a Diuell or a Familiar appeare to her, and that shee, this Examinate would let him suck at some part of her; and she might haue and doe what shee would. And so not long after these perswasions, this Examinate being walking towards the Rough-Lee, in a Close of one Iohn Robinsons, there appeared vnto her a thing like vnto a Blacke Dogge: speaking vnto her, this Examinate, and desiring her to giue him her Soule, and he would giue her power to doe any thing shee would: whereupon this Examinate being therewithall inticed, and setting her downe; the said Blacke-Dogge did with his mouth (as this Examinate then thought) sucke at her breast, a little below her Paps, which place did remain blew halfe a yeare next after: which said Blacke-Dogge did not appeare to this Examinate, vntill the eighteenth day of March last: at which time this Examinate met with a Pedler on the high-way, called Colne-field, neere vnto Colne. . .

Christened as Alicea Device, but named throughout Potts' account as Alison, Demdike's eldest daughter would have been around eighteen in 1612. It is fair to say that Alison's statement given to Roger Nowell at Read Hall (following the John Lawe incident at Colne Field) set in motion a series of events that became unstoppable. When he saw how easily the young woman could be cajoled into dragging others into the fray Nowell realised that he had hit the jackpot.

On the 29th March, 1612, Abraham Lawe arrived in Pendle with the specific intention of bringing Alison to see his father, probably for him to officially identify her and to see what she had to say. Having ridden over to Malkin Tower, Lawe found Alison and the pair made their way back to Colne where she was confronted with the lame chapman. John Lawe proceeded to accuse Alison, in front of a number of people, of bewitching him; according to the Lawe's statements Alison readily accepted that she had done wrong and begged for his forgiveness. There must have been something about Alison that touched John Lawe as, supposedly believing as he did that she had lamed him, he publicly forgave her. This did not appease Lawe junior, however, as the very next day saw him taking the matter to the authorities; by lunchtime he was knocking on the door of Roger Nowell at Read Hall.

Taking the fantastic and the downright impossible out the statements of Alison Device we are left with the definite impression of a poor girl, no better nor worse than her fellow Forest dwellers, going about her daily business, seizing any small opportunity that might have come her way. Equally, we have in John Lawe a traveller said to have been mundanely following his daily routine; however, in the witch story things are rarely what they seem to be.

As we have seen, it is very possible that Roger Nowell enslisted his friend, Sir Thomas Gerard, to help to quell the social unrest within the Forest. Gerard's uncle, Gilbert Gerard, had married Anne, the heiress of the wealthy Radcliffe family who owned large tracts of land and property within Pendle at that time. Nowell and Gerard probably arranged for Abraham Lawe to visit them at Read Hall on the 30th March. Somewhere within this initial event of the witch story is a hidden sub-text - possibly John Lawe was a travelling priest and was enlisted by the prosecution in return for their silence or were the Lawes friends of the prosecuting gentry and, as outsiders, were better placed to set the ball rolling?

It is difficult to ascertain the true depth of guilt that the Device family admitted to at this early stage, the lurid and flowery statements credited to them could have been added to at a later date. Nowell would take his lead not only from Sir Thomas Gerard but also from Thomas Lister's strident persecution of Jennet Preston; certainly by the time of the Good Friday meeting at Malkin Tower the genie was well and truly out of the bottle. The 'statements' accredited to the accused were admitting to every heinous crime under the sun, accusing their own families of the most diabolical murders, accusing their neighbours of the same, owning up to having been attacked by exploding hares, having seen flying horses, owned dogs that spoke English - and that was all before lunch!

History shows us that John Lawe was to be the real catalyst in the series of events of that spring of 1612. His role did not finish there, however, as Roger Nowell had plans for him to appear at the Assizes three months later in a dramatic finale. Lawe was to be Nowell's star witnesses against Alison Device and when he was wheeled in to court his afflictions were proudly displayed to the packed courtroom. With half of his body (apparently) awry, and his speech slurred, Lawe would have made a pitiable sight. Alison was dramatically brought forward into the sight of Lawe at which she is said to have thrown herself to her knees in contrition. The statements of both Abraham and John Lawe were read to the court and we see that the son was adamant that Alison had demanded pins of his father whereby John said that she had offered to buy them. Abraham's statement also contained the following line: '*And this Examinate seeing his said Father so tormented with the said Alizon and with one other olde woman, whome this Examinates Father did not know as it seemed.*' (See *Final Conclusion* at the end for more on this).

According to Abraham Lawe his father was in a continuous state of bewitchment, Alison and an old woman who John Lawe had never met tormented him. Reading between the lines of Abraham Lawe's statement two things become apparent: firstly, he is adamant that Alison *demanded* pins of John Lawe, thus enhancing the prosecution view that Alison was an aggressor. Secondly, we see the sudden appearance of *'one other old woman'* although there had been no mention of this before the trial. All previous statements had it that Alison was alone when she met John Lawe but Abraham's statement says that she was accompanied by an old woman - this would have been a reference to Demdike and it is probable that this was played down in order for Alison to take the blame.

Abraham's statement also said that ever since his father had been struck down, some three months previously, he had been unable to travel; it is confusing, then, to see that John Lawe was not only able to make the long and arduous journey, from either Halifax or Colne, to Lancaster, but he had also attended the whole of the court proceedings from the very start - he was also able to appear in court where he gave a dramatic performance.

Another incident occurred which Alison's brother, James, seems only too willing to relate to Roger Nowell on his visit to Read Hall on the 30th March. Here, an irate Henry Bulcock, of Whitehough in Barley, appeared at Malkin Tower and demanded that Alison recant the 'spell' that she had cast over his daughter. Yet again we see a contrite Alison falling to her knees and begging for forgiveness after having been accused of bewitching someone. These regular reports of Alison grovelling on her knees were perhaps designed by the prosecution to illustrate the abject depths to which Alison had sunk; showing the perpetrator to be aghast at the crimes they have committed serves to illustrate the enormity of that crime - in other words, even Alison the witch admitted that her crimes were heinous!

Alison was not actually accused in court of bewitching the Bulcock child, this was her brother's testimony, but we have to wonder whether Henry Bulcock, as a probable friend of Alison's uncle, Christopher Holgate, had refused to provide a prosecution statement. There is reason to assume at least an element of truth in James's story, the question is why would Alison bewitch a child? As Alison walked home along the dusty track from Roughlee to Barley did young Elizabeth Bulcock, as Henry the yeoman's daughter, look down on the somewhat unkempt figure and point the finger of derision *'Oy, witch, where's yer broomstick then?'* or words to that effect? Little wonder, then, that Alison might have reacted to the taunts of a child who did not know what it was like to have to beg for a living. In an attempt to gain respect Alison might have taken the line that if she was indeed a witch then she would cast a spell on young Elizabeth if she didn't shut up!

Her pleas for forgiveness hint at the fact that Alison was only too willing to accept the fact that she was in the habit of bewitching people but was equally surprised when there were consequences. In other words, she was not convinced that her own powers of witchcraft had been as dangerous as they now appeared to be! On the other hand when she asks for forgiveness she is admitting her guilt and here we see the distinct signature of Roger Nowell.

In respect of the Device children it is worth remembering that the majority of the Forest people of that time, especially the youngsters, were extremely naive in comparison to the young people of today. Alison, James and Jennet Device were born into an age where things had changed little since their Iron Age forefathers had lived in the Forest area. Only the strongest survived and this can be seen in the high death-rates amongst infants; often every other child within a family would die. The Device children had no official education but they were extremely well aware of their surroundings. They lived according to the seasons, their food was unadulterated by poisons, their spring water was as pure as it was possible to be and they could name every bird and animal around them. They knew the names of all the plants and the medicinal uses of each herb and flower, each forest tree was known to them. Their nights were as black as pitch and a billion bright stars, each constellation of which they could name, lit the ceiling of their world.

The flip-side of the coin was that they were keenly aware of their place within society, this meant that they were frightened of authority and this was the main reason why they appear to have been so willing to accommodate Roger Nowell in his quest for information on the diabolical goings on in the forest. That is not to say that the youngsters were stupid, no doubt they would have been quick to learn, they had to be when they were living largely off their wits – it would be very interesting to see exactly how much information that Nowell and company would have gleaned from them if the cards had been fully laid on the magisterial bench. If the accused had been made fully aware of the consequences of their accusations and 'confessions' just how informative would they have been? If they had known that families were to be executed because of their naive fantasies how far along the road to Gallows Hill would the 1612 case have progressed?

ALICE NUTTER OF ROUGHLEE

Alice Nutter is, perhaps, the most unlikely character to be arraigned at Lancaster; she played a smaller part within the 1612 drama than any other of her co-accused. The prosecution case hinged upon Jennet Device's statement that Alice had been one of those who attended the Good Friday meeting. Jennet actually picked Alice out from the crowd of accused people in the courtroom, when asked by the judge if she recognised Alice Nutter she went over and took her by the hand.

As a ruse to prove that Jennet did indeed recognise Alice the judge asked imperiously if she knew a Joan A'style; when Jennet replied in the negative the smug prosecution would nod to each other, what a clever judge they had! In actual fact the question was absolutely pointless, the southern judges might have heard of Joan A'style being used as a metaphor for Mrs. Bloggs but Jennet would not have heard this in her life. Were the judge to have enquired whether Jennet knew Bess O' Bob's (Robert's daughter, Elizabeth) or Alice O' Dick O' Miles (as Alice was known) he might have received a different answer.

It is clear from their 'statements' that neither James nor Jennet could be relied upon to provide the exact truth of the matter. Potts had this to say with regard to Alice Nutter;

THE ARRAIGNMENT and Triall of Alice Nutter, of the Forrest of Pendle, in the Countie of Lancaster:

The two degrees of persons which chiefly practise Witch-craft, are such, as are in great miserie and pouertie, for such the Deuill allures to follow him, by promising great riches, and worldly commoditie; Others, though rich, yet burne in a desperate desire of Reuenge. But to attempt this woman in that sort, the Diuel had small meanes: For it is certaine she was a rich woman; had a great estate, and children of good hope: in the common opinion of the world, of good temper, free from envy or malice; yet whether by the meanes of the rest of the Witches, or some vnfortunate occasion, shee was drawne to fall to this wicked course of life, I know not: but hither shee is now come to receiue her Triall, both for Murder, and many other vilde and damnable practises.

It is very certaine she was of the Grand-counsell at Malking-Tower vpon Good-Friday, and was there present, which was a very great argument to condemne her. This Alice Nutter, Prisoner in the Castle at Lancaster: Being brought to the Barre before the Great Seat of Justice; was there according to the former order and course Indicted and Arraigned, for that she felloniously had practised, exercised, and vsed her diuellish and wicked Arts, called Witchcrafts, Inchantments, Charmes and Sorceries, in and vpon Henry Mitton: and him the said Henry Mitton, by force of the same Witchcrafts, felloniously did kill and murther. Contra formam Statuti, &c. Et Contra Pacem, &c.

To the prosecution the fact that Alice Nutter was said to have been at the Malkin Tower gathering was a positive indictment of her guilt, despite her previously good character. Just to make sure, the prosecution also threw in, almost as an aside, that she also conspired with her friends at Malkin Tower to kill Henry Mitton, of Roughlee. These ridiculous charges, despite Alice's not guilty plea, were enough to convict and execute her. Alice was described as being 'a rich woman with a great estate and children of good hope' and this was designed to mark her out from the rest of the accused. Potts used Alice's position of higher status to show how much more damnable was a witch who had fallen from high - the further the fall the more evil was the woman.

Alice had married Richard Nutter (son of Miles) by 1561 and her new family was of a relatively high standing within the Roughlee area. They had held the same property from at least 1527 through to 1609 when Alice's son Miles was paying rent for it. At the time of the 1612 trials Alice Nutter would have been around seventy years old. Alice would no doubt have known Demdike well, they were roughly the same age and from much the same background – the two were from yeoman families, with Catholic leanings, and could well have been related. This is suggested because Alice, her daughter Elizabeth and her sister-in law (John Nutter's wife who later became Jane Bulcock and was hanged alongside Alice) attended the Good Friday family meeting at Malkin Tower.

Young Jennet referred to Alice in her statement as *Dick O' Miles wife* and it appears that Alice was much younger than her husband, Richard Nutter, and that their marriage had been arranged by her father.[10] Alice had been widowed in her mid-forties and was left with five children to bring up; Miles (the eldest at nineteen), John, James, Richard and Elizabeth. Even though the family owned land Alice would have struggled to keep things on the straight-and-narrow.

Who, then, was Alice, wife of Dick O' Miles? The Whitaker family had been in the Padiham area since the thirteenth century and eventually split into three main branches; the Whitakers of Holme-in-Cliviger, the Whitakers of Broadclough and the family of Simonstone. Attached to this latter branch was Gyles Whitaker of Huncoat, he had been constable of Huncoat four times, greave of Huncoat in 1556 and was of sufficient importance to have been only one of two men to have appeared on the Muster Roll. Alice was one of Gyles Whitaker's five children, the others being the eldest, James, John, Agnes and Joan.

There is no surprise in the fact that the Roughlee Nutters and the Huncoat Whitakers were related; although some five miles in distance the Simonstone Whitakers were continually trading lands within Pendle Forest. In this capacity they rubbed shoulders with almost all of the landowners hereabouts and when Gyles saw an opportunity to marry his daughter, Alice, off to the ageing Richard Nutter, of Roughlee, he jumped at the chance. Just what Alice might have thought about the matter is another story! There appear to be parallels here between Alice and Demdike's lives where they both found themselves widowed in middle age with young children to support.

One of the most commonly held beliefs in the Pendle Witch legend is that Alice Nutter found herself being prosecuted because she had been in an acrimonious land boundary dispute with magistrate Roger Nowell. Unfortunately this piece of folklore does not hold water. It is true that Roger Nowell and the Simonstone Whitakers were often at contretemps with each other over lands in the Read area – also, Nowell was involved in an acrimonious dispute with the powerful Radcliffe family over lands at Sabden – however, the Nowell-Nutter dispute was a garbled version of the facts.

The boundary dispute of legend almost certainly has its root in the fact that Alice's father-in-law had been an executor of the will of the father of her 'victim,' Henry

Mitton. Henry's father had over forty acres in Roughlee during the sixteenth century but by the early 1600s his son had inherited only six acres. Henry blamed Alice Nutter's husband for this and so we see the foundation of the story: Henry Mitton's family farm bordered onto that of the Nutters and Henry was adamant that he had been defrauded of much of his rightful estate. There was, then, good reason in Henry's mind to accuse Alice of practising witchcraft and, when he found himself on his deathbed in 1610, he no-doubt proclaimed to all-and-sundry that he had been bewitched by Alice Nutter: and so her fate was sealed.

Another 'fictional fact' is that Alice Nutter lived at Roughlee Old Hall but research by local historian Gladys Whitaker shows that Alice never actually lived at the Hall - her home was very likely to have been at Crowtrees in Roughlee, some half a mile to the west of the Hall. Nor did she have the riches and estates that Potts would have us believe; it is fair to say that she was wealthier than her companions in the Well Tower dungeon at Lancaster but any real wealth would have stayed with her Whitaker family outside of the Forest.

It is an integral part of the Alice Nutter legend that her family refused to speak up for her and actively allowed her to be prosecuted in order to gain her estates. It is said that her son, Miles, lived a remorseful life following his mother's demise and in the end he died a lingering, painful death. It is also said that when Miles heard of the Malkin family troubles he enlisted young Jennet to accuse his mother and bring her into the melee. There is a small problem with this because the Nutter estate, under the stewardship of Miles, had actually halved in size and consisted solely of a farmstead at Roughlee.

Miles had inherited the lion's share of the Nutter properties from his father in any case; the only benefit to Alice's children on her death would have been a small share of a small estate, was this worth bumping off their mother for? What we do have in this story is the idea that Jennet Device was open to bribery when it came to placing people in the dock. This is of interest as we have seen that Roger Nowell could well have coerced Jennet into making fantastic statements relating to the Malkin Tower gathering.

Being a Seller in a household of Devices might just have caused Jennet to feel isolated within the family; just how close she might have been to the rest of her Malkin kin is open to conjecture. Did she resent her mother, brothers and grandmother? If so it is not impossible that Jennet might gladly have seized the opportunity to drop the rest of the family in the proverbial when the opportunity arose!

It is clear from Potts' writings that Alice Nutter was decidedly taciturn when being interviewed. She would not make a statement or defend herself in any manner; if she had made any attempt at explanation it is likely that Potts would have reported the content with glee. We have the image of an upright, proud, well-dressed yeoman's wife standing before a courtroom full of accusers, all ready and willing to send her to her Maker.

One might at least have expected Alice, who would probably have had the education to enable her to speak out for herself, to say something in her own defence. Surely she would have been horrified that the family name was being dragged through the gutter?

Another popular theory is that Alice refused to speak in order to protect her Catholic friends and family, although this does not really hold water. She was not before the jury on recusancy charges and could easily have denied that she helped to kill her neighbour, Henry Mitton. A single explanation for her recalcitrance stands out above all the rest and that is that the unfortunate Alice Nutter may have suffered from an age-related dementia. Any one of a number of diseases within this category would cause Alice to lose her short-term memory; if this is indeed the case then the poor woman would have stood before the court in a complete state of bewilderment.

This would also have appertained when she had stood before Roger Nowell's bench some weeks previously. She would not be aware of where she was and why she was there; she would know, however, who she was and where she was from and could have unwittingly fooled her accusers into thinking that she was of sound mind.

Still we have the nagging question as to why her family did not appear to raise a defence for Alice; why did Miles Nutter not take the witness stand and speak up voraciously for his mother? Perhaps he did not have the opportunity to do so - or did he actually stand up for his mother only to have his testimony left out of Potts' accounts - we will probably never know.

The following genealogies are based on the work of Gladys Whittaker in her *Roughlee Hall, Fact and Fiction:*

THE WHITAKER FAMILY OF HUNCOAT

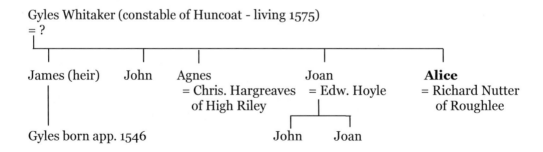

Gyles Whitaker (constable of Huncoat - living 1575)
= ?

James (heir)   John   Agnes   Joan   **Alice**
                        = Chris. Hargreaves   = Edw. Hoyle   = Richard Nutter
                          of High Riley   of Roughlee

Gyles born app. 1546   John   Joan

THE NUTTER FAMILY OF ROUGHLEE

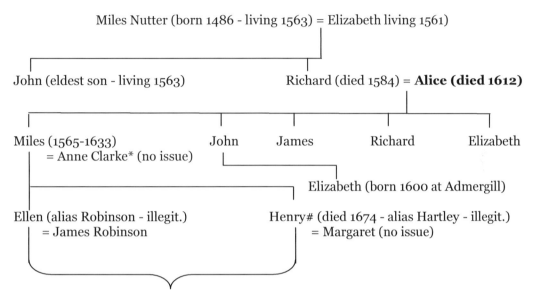

Miles Nutter (born 1486 - living 1563) = Elizabeth living 1561)

John (eldest son - living 1563)   Richard (died 1584) = **Alice (died 1612)**

Miles (1565-1633)   John   James   Richard   Elizabeth
   = Anne Clarke* (no issue)

Elizabeth (born 1600 at Admergill)

Ellen (alias Robinson - illegit.)   Henry# (died 1674 - alias Hartley - illegit.)
   = James Robinson   = Margaret (no issue)

Henry and Ellen Inherited Nutter properties on the death of Miles in 1633

#Henry Nutter Hartley's share eventually passed to the Nutter family of Waterside

*Anne was falsely accused of witchcraft in 1633 – see Clayton, J. *The Other Pendle Witches* ISBN 978-0-9570043-2-0 Barrowford Press 2012

ANNE WHITTLE ALIAS CHATTOX

Old Chattox was described as being around eighty years of age and from West Close, below the village of Higham. Chattox's real name was Anne Whittle and her daughter, Anne Redfearn, was the wife of Thomas Redfearn by whom she had at least one child, a daughter named Marie. Chattox's other daughter, Elizabeth, was commonly known as Bessie Whittle. The Newchurch-in-Pendle, Burnley and Padiham parish records show a distinct paucity of the Whittle surname, in fact there is but a single relevant entry and that is where a Jenneta Whyttle was buried at Newchurch in 1576. Given the extreme rarity of the name locally the assignment of this person to the family of Anne Whittle would not be a serious offence.

In 1563 there is evidence that the Whittle family were small tenant farmers in Pendle as Edmund Stevenson surrendered a parcel of land (around two acres) to Christopher Whittles. Along with this parcel Stevenson also granted Whittles a;

> *'Turbary in Red Mosse, Goldshaw, sufficient for a fire to be spent and burnt on said parcel to the use of Christopher Whittles and his assigns for 29 years at £0: 7s: 4d per year.'*

Turbary was the right of Forest tenants to dig peat turves for their own use, providing they kept to a single fire per dwelling house. This suggests that Whittles had a house on the parcel of land. Edmund Stevenson had farmed land at East Delph, adjacent to Bull Hole Farm in Newchurch, for a number of years and another land record shows him letting a close of the Bull Hole Farm estate to Christopher Whittles. The turf-fields were part of the moss below Newchurch village on which Higher Moss, Moss Nook and *possibly* the Bulcock property of Moss End were situated. Bull Hole was the farm belonging to John Nutter whose cow Old Demdike was accused of killing.

Christopher Whittle found himself in front of the magistrates in 1567 when he and James Moor, of Higham, were each fined 20d for making an affray together. This is interesting as Chattox was said by Alison Device to have bewitched the family of John Moor sometime around 1610 - this illustrates the depth of feeling when Forest folk were at loggerheads - Chattox, for one, certainly did not forget a grudge. Alison's statement related that;

And further, this Examinate (Alison Device) saith, That about two yeares agoe, she, this Examinate, hath heard, That the said Anne Whittle, alias Chattox, was suspected for bewitching the drinke of John Moore of Higham Gentleman: and not long after, shee this Examinate heard the said Chattox say, that she would meet with the said John Moore, or his. Whereupon a child of the said Iohn Moores, called Iohn, fell sick, and languished about halfe a yeare, and then died: during which languishing, this Examinate saw the said Chattox sitting in her owne garden, and a picture of Clay like vnto a child in her Apron; which this Examinate espying, the said Anne Chattox would haue hidde with her Apron: and this Examinate declaring the same to her mother, her mother thought it was the picture of the said John Moores childe.

And she this Examinate further saith, That about six or seuen yeares agoe, the said Chattox did fall out with one Hugh Moore of Pendle, as aforesaid, about certaine cattell of the said Moores, which the said Moore did charge the said Chattox to haue bewitched: for which the said Chattox did curse and worry the said Moore, and said she would be Reuenged of the said Moore: whereupon the said Moore presently fell sicke, and languished about halfe a yeare, and then died. Which Moore vpon his death-bed said, that the said Chattox had bewitched him to death.

Anne Whittle was gleefully described by Potts as having been a shambling old crone of about eighty years, she muttered and mumbled to herself, *'her lips continually moving and walking but saying no man knows what.'* His description is aimed at consolidating the opinion of his readership into the general belief that a dangerous hag had been removed from society. There was no empathy with this elderly woman who found herself before the Lancaster court – just a certainty that she deserved to die. Taken from Potts' account the following is the statement accorded to Old Chattox:

THE CONFESSION AND EXAMINATION of Anne Whittle alias Chattox, being Prisoner at Lancaster; taken the 19 day of May, First, the sayd Anne Whittle, alias Chattox, sayth, that about foureteene yeares past she entered, through the wicked perswasions and counsell of Elizabeth Southerns, alias Demdike, and was seduced to condescend & agree to become subiect vnto that diuelish abhominable profession of Witchcraft: Soone after which, the Deuill appeared vnto her in the liknes of a Man, about midnight, at the house of the sayd Demdike: and therevpon the sayd Demdike and shee, went foorth of the said house vnto him; wherevpon the said wicked Spirit mooued this Examinate, that she would become his Subiect, and giue her Soule vnto him: the which at first, she refused to assent vnto; but after, by the great perswasions made by the sayd Demdike, shee yeelded to be at his commaundement and appoyntment: wherevpon the sayd wicked Spirit then sayd vnto her, that hee must haue one part of her body for him to sucke vpon; the which shee denyed then to graunt vnto him; and withall asked him, what part of her body hee would haue for that vse; who said, hee would haue a place of her right side neere to her ribbes, for him to sucke vpon: whereunto shee assented.

And she further sayth, that at the same time, there was a thing in the likenes of a spotted Bitch, that came with the sayd Spirit vnto the sayd Demdike, which then did speake vnto her in this Examinates hearing, and sayd, that she should haue Gould, Siluer, and worldly Wealth, at her will.

And at the same time she saith, there was victuals, viz. Flesh, Butter, Cheese, Bread, and Drinke, and bidde them eate enough. And after their eating, the Deuill called Fancie, and the other Spirit calling himselfe Tibbe, carried the remnant away: And she sayeth, that although they did eate, they were neuer the fuller, nor better for the same; and that at their said Banquet, the said Spirits gaue them light to see what they did, although they neyther had fire nor Candle light; and that they were both shee Spirites, and Diuels.

And being further examined how many sundry Person haue been bewitched to death, and by whom they were so bewitched: She sayth, that one Robert Nuter, late of the Greene-head in Pendle, was bewitched by this Examinate, the said Demdike, and Widdow Lomshawe, (late of Burneley) now deceased. And she further sayth, that the said Demdike shewed her, that she had bewitched to death, Richard Ashton, Sonne of Richard Ashton of Downeham Esquire.

This statement was made by a woman described by Potts as having been the equivalent of a gibbering idiot. On the one hand her *'lips were walking and saying no man knows what'* and on the other hand she is providing detailed and lucid statements - and here is the rub. Anne Whittle's statement is a contrived mish-mash of the perceived events that took place at witch meetings. We saw earlier that the Samlesbury case was based on the ideas of the Sabbath picked up by priest, Christopher Southworth, during his religious training and Whittle's so-called statement compares directly to Southworth's ideas.

A number of model 'controls' were used by the prosecutors in witch trials and these became the standard tool with which to condemn the accused. Common sense and scepticism of the powers held by the 'witch' had no place in Early Modern justice and so it proved in the Pendle trials. The notion of a familiar sucking at some part of the witch's body was basic to the national prosecution handbook, as were the ideas that a witch could imbibe of vast amounts of food and drink and never be satisfied. Perhaps the clinching 'control' necessary to ensure that the accused were convicted was the giving of the soul to the devil in exchange for some favour or worldly riches. There was no way back for the accused once this heinous crime had been committed - they were beyond earthly redemption and therefore had to be removed from the face of the earth.

And so we have to discard the vast majority of the 'evidence' within Potts' *Wonderfull Discoverie*. Statements describing familiars (dogs, foals and exploding hares), the appearance of butter from blue milk, opulent banquets, transference of the soul, zoomorphic transmutation - all of these fanciful notions were ascribed to the Pendle group and, by-and-large, they were all the fictional work of the prosecution. Statements were prepared by the magistrates and jailers according to a standard formula propounded by king James I, dramatists and the earlier Chelmsford trials; a few 'facts' related by the accused were then interpolated and this gave the statement an air of authenticity.

In light of the blatant miscarriage of justice carried out at Lancaster, in the August of 1612, it would be tempting to assume that the people standing trial for their lives were simply an innocent group of poor Forest folk caught up in a whirlwind of political and social intrigue. It has to be said, however, that when the lurid fiction is stripped from the 'statements' we are left with a viable view of Demdike and Chattox *et al*. The true basis of the story is that certain members of their society were all too willing to accept that a female sub-group within the Pendle Forest region were willing to cause the deaths of their enemies by bewitchment.

Almost all of those supposedly bewitched to death were men and this is highly significant for two reasons. Within the primogenitary nature of land and property inheritance it was the eldest son who was first in line to his father's estate. Younger sons and female offspring were usually placed down the pecking order, although women inherited where there was no male heir. In general, then, women were liable to be ejected from the family estate upon the death of the father - unless the male heir/heirs were to meet with an untimely demise! Such was the case when Chattox was enlisted to kill the heir to the Greenhead estate of the Nutter family (see below).

Another reason for the likes of Demdike and Chattox wishing to cause the deaths of their Forest neighbours was where they had been slighted. We see this in the case of Richard Baldwin, of Wheathead, who insulted the Demdike family and refused to pay their wages - a consequence of this being that Baldwin's daughter died. Henry Mitton, of Roughlee, was 'killed' by Demdike and Alice Nutter for refusing to give them alms (although there is far more to this story than we will ever know). Chattox bewitched members of her immediate neighbours, the Moor family, because they accused her of bewitching their cattle and their drink. James Device supposedly killed members of the Hargreaves family (probably because they would have thrown him off their property) and Anne Towneley, for the same reason.

And so we see that, to the modern mind, the accused would not have been ideal neighbours as they were sullen, devious, dishonest, ignorant, foul-mouthed and lawless. It is fair to say that it is not for us to judge our predecessors by modern standards; however, within the context of the period the indictment of the Pendle group indicates the low esteem in which they were held by their community. Even though the prosecution fabricated great swathes of the evidence against them there is the fact that, as Thomas Potts had it, *'the common opinion of the Kinges subjects for the losses of their Children, Friendes, Goodes, and Cattle is that there could not be so great Fire without some Smoake.'*

A scene more awash with pathos than that of Anne Whittle's courtroom appearance can hardly be imagined; when her daughter, Anne Redfearn, was being sentenced in court Old Chattox fell upon her knees and wept loud and long. She said that she fully admitted her guilt but that her daughter was entirely innocent; the protective mother pleaded with the judges to spare the life of her daughter but her entreaties fell upon deaf-ears – she might as well have asked for the moon.

The main reason for the demise of Anne Whittle and her daughter was the enmity between this West Close family and their neighbours, the Nutters of Greenhead. Anne Redfearn appears to have been the victim of a spoilt younger son of the yeomanry who, not able to have his own way when asking for sexual favours from a married woman, threw his toys out of the pram. Robert Nutter, son of Christopher, worked as Richard Shuttleworth's right-hand man and as such he would be in constant contact with the Shuttleworth tenants of West Close. This position obviously gave young Nutter delusions of grandeur as he was of the opinion that he was entitled to treat the lesser tenants as he wished.

CHATTOX ~ THE NUTTERS AND THE COUSINS

Robert Nutter, and his father Christopher Nutter of Greenhead, were central to the prosecution case against Chattox and Anne Redfearn. The prosecution in this case used the statement of Christopher's son, John, whereby he said that around *'eighteene or nineteene yeares agoe'* he had been travelling home from Burnley when his brother Robert, who had been complaining of being unwell, stated that he had been bewitched by Chattox and her daughter.

Christopher Nutter married his second cousin, Ellen Nutter, in 1557 and she was buried at Burnley in 1587. His son, Robert Nutter, married Marie, the daughter of Richard Grimshaw of Clayton, and they had three daughters, Eleanor, Elizabeth and Margaret. Robert's sister, Margaret Nutter, married a local famer, John Crook of Fence, at Newchurch in 1590 - Margaret made the following statement:

> This Examinate, sworne & examined vpon her oath, sayth, That about eighteene or nineteene yeares agoe, this Examinates brother, called Robert Nutter, about Whitsontide the same yeare, meeting with the said Anne Redferne, vpon some speeches betweene them they fell out, as this Examinats said brother told this Examinat: and within some weeke, or fort-night, then next after, this Examinats said brother fell sicke, and so languished vntill about Candlemas then next after, and then died. In which time of his sicknesse, he did a hundred times at the least say, That the said Anne Redferne and her associates had bewitched him to death.
>
> And this Examinate further saith, That this Examinates Father, called Christopher Nutter, about Maudlintide next after following fell sicke, and so languished, vntill Michaelmas then next after, and then died: during

which time of his sicknesse, hee did sundry times say, That hee was bewitched; but named no bodie that should doe the same.

Robert Nutter was the retainer of Sir Richard Shuttleworth (JP) of Gawthorpe Hall and in this capacity he had accompanied his master on the Cheshire Justice circuit early in 1593. Robert had fallen out with Anne Redfearn at her home in West Close around May of 1592 and he had fallen ill by June. He obviously did not recover from this illness as he was dead by the 2nd of February (Candlemas) 1593. Having died in Cheshire it is likely that his cousin, John Nutter, who was dean of Chester at that time, would have buried Robert there as Robert does not appear to have been buried locally. Christopher Nutter had become ill shortly after his son Robert (by the 22nd of July - Maudlintide - according to Anne Redfearn) and by the 29th September (Michaelmas) he was dead. This ties in exactly with the record of Christopher Nutter who was buried at Burnley on the 27th of September 1593.

In her reply to this Chattox said that Robert Nutter had been to her house at nearby West Close where he made a pass at Anne Redfearn; when she scorned his advances Nutter rode off in high dudgeon saying that *'If ever the ground came to him she would never dwell upon his land.'* This would have been a source of enmity between the two families but things appeared to get worse as the prosecution reported:

> This Examinate (Chattox) further sayth, that Elizabeth Nutter, wife to old Robert Nutter, did request this Examinate, and Loomeshaws wife of Burley, and one Iane Boothman, of the same, who are now both dead, (which time of request, was before that Robert Nutter desired the company of Redfearns wife) to get young Robert Nutter his death, if they could; all being togeather then at that time, to that end, that if Robert were dead, then the Women their Coosens might haue the Land.

Old Robert Nutter's wife, Elizabeth (née Robinson), had once asked Chattox and two other women to kill young Robert, so that *'the women their Coosens might have the land.'* Anne Redfearn's husband, Thomas, managed to persuade them not to carry out this act and all the thanks he received for this act of humanity was that Lomashaye's Wife became intent on killing him! Nicholas Baldwin, the schoolmaster at Colne Grammar School, dissuaded her from this and, to show his gratitude, Thomas Redfearn rewarded him with a capon.

If it were possible to find the truth behind the accusation against Elizabeth Nutter there might be much light shed upon the reason for the enmity between the Nutters and the Chattox family – indeed, there might be an explanation relating to some of the reasons contributing to the cause of the 1612 Pendle Witch round-up.

The records of the Early Modern period show a definite thirst for land and property among the Forest people and this is understandable when it is realised that there was a very fine line between subsistence and abject poverty. Those with no land struggled, those people with small areas of land scraped by while the tenants of larger holdings had the opportunity to expand and prosper. An example of this is where the Chattox family appear to have lived on a smallholding upon the lands owned by the Gawthorpe estate. The Nutters were tenants of the estate and their Greenhead property would have stretched to at least one hundred acres with a house of high-status; the family also had other farms and it is clear that they were prospering. It is no surprise, given this state of affairs, that there was a great deal of inter-family rivalry, chicanery and manoeuvring where land and property were concerned.

'So that the Women their coosens would have the land.' This statement can be taken to have different meanings – beside Chattox the women involved in the plot were Elizabeth Nutter, Lomashaye's wife and Jane Boothman. If we take this trio as being *'the women'* then it could be said that their cousins would inherit and therefore these three women were related. Alternatively the women could be taken to be the cousins of *'them,'* the connotation being that they were the cousins of the Nutters; it has to be remembered that the term 'cousins' was generally used to describe a kinship between families and not necessarily in the strict capacity that we now use the term.

There are few records pertaining to Jane Boothman other than a baptism and a burial at Burnley: *'Thomas base begotten sonne of Jane Boothman baptised 12th August 1571'* and *'A child of Jane Boothman's buried 8th December 1581'* and a burial at Newchurch *'Jane Boothman sepult 1602.'* *Lomashaye's Wife* is a reference to the Lomeshaye estate owned by the Hargreaves family and situated between Barrowford and Reedley Hallows; the estate ran to three farms and a cottage. In 1548 William and Elizabeth Hargreaves, and their son John, were at Rigby Farm, one of the estate properties. Chattox stated (in 1612) that Lomashaye's Wife had recently died and we find that the following fits our bill perfectly; the wife of John Hargreaves, *alias Lomatchey,* was buried at Burnley on the 5th March 1611.

There are two separate Newchurch records for the marriage of John Hargreaves; one of 1582 tells us that a John Hargreaves married Ellena Robinson and a slightly later entry of 1584 shows a John Hargreaves marrying Margaret Robinson. Lomashaye's Wife, then, was a Robinson and Old Robert Nutter's wife was also a Robinson. There is every probability, then, that Lomashaye's Wife was sister to Old Robert Nutter's wife, Elizabeth Robinson - in turn these two women would probably have been sisters to Jane Boothman (née Robinson?).

Now that we have the Robinson/Nutter family connection things begin to fall into place. Another of those willing to give evidence against the Chattox family was a

James Robinson who said that in 1593, at the time of young Robert Nutter's death in Cheshire, he (James) was living with Old Robert Nutter at Greenhead. James Robinson, then, would appear to have been Old Robert's step-son, by his wife Elizabeth (Robinson) - James was stated in a court roll record to have been Old Robert's 'second son.'

We know this from a land surrender of 1570 which also goes on to provide the additional information on Greenhead family.[11] If Old Robert's eldest son, Christopher Nutter, had no issue at the time of his death then his younger brother, James, was to inherit the Greenhead estates. If James had no children then the issue of his younger brother, Robert, were to inherit - Robert was not married at this time (1570) as the phrase *'if he were to marry'* is used. In a further land surrender a few years later it is stated that Robert had married an Alice (possibly née Hartley).

THE NUTTER FAMILY OF GREENHEAD

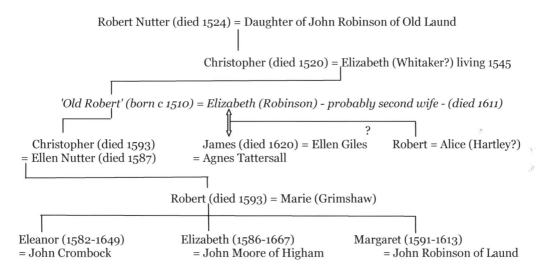

Robert Nutter (died 1524) = Daughter of John Robinson of Old Laund

Christopher (died 1520) = Elizabeth (Whitaker?) living 1545

'Old Robert' (born c 1510) = Elizabeth (Robinson) - probably second wife - (died 1611)

Christopher (died 1593)
= Ellen Nutter (died 1587)

James (died 1620) = Ellen Giles
= Agnes Tattersall

?

Robert = Alice (Hartley?)

Robert (died 1593) = Marie (Grimshaw)

Eleanor (1582-1649)
= John Crombock

Elizabeth (1586-1667)
= John Moore of Higham

Margaret (1591-1613)
= John Robinson of Laund

The above Nutter of Greenhead family tree is by no means comprehensive, nor is it claimed to be totally accurate; as is the way with records of this date it is not possible to furnish an absolute genealogy. However, the basis of our story begins to make sense when we look at Old Robert and his wife, Elizabeth. It is highly probable that Elizabeth was not the mother of old Robert's frst son, Christopher - she would have been Robert's second wife and already had sons James Robinson and Robert Robinson (alias Nutter). It is clear, therefore, that were 'young' Robert Nutter to die then there would have been no male heir to the Greenhead estate through Christopher; in accordance with Old Robert's will, therefore, the eldest son, James (Robinson) Nutter, would have inherited.

The Robinsons of Old Laund Hall were close neighbours to the Greenhead family and, as social equals, it is little wonder that the two families intermarried on a regular basis. For the main branches of these landed families (the direct heirs) there would be few reasons for jealousy between family members. However, the minor family members, such as younger sons and daughters, were often placed in a position of having to make their own way in the world while their inheriting sibling would take over the family estates. This often led to tensions within the extended families and this is almost certainly what we see in the Nutter/Robinson case. Again, certain members of Pendle Forest society were prepared to commit virtual murder in order to gain property or revenge.

Whether the 'witches' actually practised the black arts as suggested in the prosecution cases is irrelevant - the fact is that these people believed that they could bring about the deaths of those who stood in their way. In other words, the *intent* to kill was clear, the motive was transparent and this ran against all religious and civil law. Elizabeth Robinson Nutter, Lomashaye's Wife and Jane Boothman, then, were prepared to bring about the death of Robert Nutter in order to obtain land for their family. The intent here is plain to see and if these women had been alive at the time of the Pendle trials they would surely have hanged in consequence of the testimony of Old Chattox.

The Clitheroe court rolls show that Christopher Nutter was named as co-trustee of Henry Mitton's estate in 1562 - this was the Henry Mitton, of Roughlee, who was supposedly bewitched by Demdike and company.

Two years later Christopher and Ellen Nutter signed over land and houses in Fence to Richard and James Crook; this is the family into which Christopher and Ellen's daughter, Margaret would marry. Richard Crook's son, John (cousin to Margaret's husband, John), of Old Laund, left a grey coat in his will to Thomas Redfearn. Within the Chattox family her son-in-law, at least, appears not have been at loggerheads with the Nutter family.

The transfer of the Nutter land and property at Fence was limited to twenty-one years and was further subject to limitations created in indentures made between Christopher and Ellen Nutter and Roger Nowell. Here, then, we have evidence for a relationship between the Greenhead Nutters and Roger Nowell and this suggests that Nowell would have been fully aware of the rumours surrounding the deaths of both Robert and Christopher Nutter. This puts a new light on the first interviews involving the Demdike/Device clan; Potts suggests that Chattox only became involved as a suspect following the Device statements. It could well be, however, that Nowell had Chattox within his sights all along and coerced the Device family into embroiling Chattox and her daughter.

We also see a land-based connection between the Nutter family and Roger Nowell which could possibly have been a reason for the legend that Nowell indicted Alice Nutter, of Roughlee i.e. because of a land boundary dispute between them.

Following the death of Demdike in Lancaster Jail, Chattox was interviewed by the prison governor and began to embroil her deceased foe in all manner of bewitchments. It is significant that Chattox did not accuse Demdike until after her death and it is almost certain that her examiner promised leniency in return for her admission of guilt - Chattox, in blaming Demdike, would have hoped to escape the death penalty. Further to this, Chattox stated that she had become a witch through the persuasions of Demdike some fourteen year ago (1598). However, in her account of the Elizabeth (Robinson) Nutter affair she was consulted by Elizabeth because of her perceived ability to bring about someone's death. In other words, she was known at that time as a practicing witch and this would probably have been in the 1580s - certainly prior to 1593 when young Robert Nutter died. Chattox also said that Demdike had been involved in this incident but this can be ruled out with a degree of confidence. Almost all of the statement supposedly given by Chattox in Lancaster Jail is fiction - even the few facts that can be substantiated are garbled and cobbled together and so we see yet another example of discrepancy within the witness statements as reported by Thomas Potts.

CHATTOX AND THE MOOR FAMILY

And further, this Examinate (Alison Device) saith, That about two yeares agoe, she, this Examinate, hath heard, That the said Anne Whittle, alias Chattox, was suspected for bewitching the drinke of Iohn Moore of Higham Gentleman: and not long after, shee this Examinate heard the said Chattox say, that she would meet with the said Iohn Moore, or his. Whereupon a child of the said Iohn Moores, called Iohn, fell sick, and languished about halfe a yeare, and then died: during which languishing, this Examinate saw the said Chattox sitting in her owne garden, and a picture of Clay like vnto a child in her Apron; which this Examinate espying, the said Anne Chattox would haue hidde with her Apron: and this Examinate declaring the same to her mother, her mother thought it was the picture of the said Iohn Moores childe.

And she this Examinate further saith, That about six or seuen yeares agoe, the said Chattox did fall out with one Hugh Moore of Pendle, as aforesaid, about certaine cattell of the said Moores, which the said Moore did charge the said Chattox to haue bewitched: for which the said Chattox did curse and worry the said Moore, and said she would be Reuenged of the said Moore: whereupon the said Moore presently fell sicke, and languished about halfe a yeare, and then died. Which Moore vpon his death-bed said, that the said Chattox had bewitched him to death.

Here is yet another example of the apparent enmity between the Demdike and Chattox clans. Accusations between the two flew like feathers in a pillow fight and must have been music to the ears of the magistrates. In the above case, Alison Device stated that Chattox had unceremoniously bumped off young John Moor of Higham and his father's uncle, Hugh Moor of White Lees. Again, as we saw with the Nutters of Greenhead, Chattox was at odds with her yeoman neighbours who, whenever they had the temerity to accuse her of some misdeed, felt the sharp-edge of her tongue. This would have been an almost daily occurrence – as Chattox would have wandered her part of the forest, muttering and grumbling and generally being a nuisance, she would have found herself in many situations where she was not wanted and would have been told in no uncertain terms to 'clear off.'

In her usual inimitable fashion Chattox would respond in the only way that she knew how, by the employment of a vitriolic stream of expletives. In ninety nine out of one hundred cases this would have been the end of the matter but, as happened in the Nutter and Moor incidents, young and apparently fit people could be stricken down by disease in a very short time. The dank winter months within the Pendle Forest aided the health of neither man nor beast; pneumonia was a swift and deadly foe but the enemy that everyone feared, rich and poor alike, were the unholy trinity of tuberculosis, typhus and smallpox. It is significant that not a single person actually dropped dead on the spot following a tongue-lashing by any of the accused; John Lawe is the only reported case where the accursed suffered an instant and obvious affliction.

We have to conclude, therefore, that most of those who died of supposed witchcraft were already ill when they were said to have been cursed; the statements of the accused in relation to this reinforce this argument as the bewitched person would have *'languished half a year'* or *'died presently.'* So, the people who were seen to have died as a direct consequence of having crossed a witch would have almost invariably been suffering from some terminal ailment – should the victim be aware that they had been cursed then their condition would have been likely to have deteriorated rapidly.

The prosecution stated that feuding matriarchs were intent on chalking up more assassinations than their opponents - anyone unfortunate enough to have been within the periphery of their enemies would become victims by association. Thus we see that the entirely innocent child of John Moor had allegedly fallen prey to Chattox, this is an identical situation to the 'killing' of Richard Baldwin's child by Demdike. This was manipulated into an apparent willingness of the accused to bolster their reputations by accepting responsibility for individual deaths and the strength of feeling held by the otherwise down-to-earth forest people towards the existence of malevolent witchcraft.

Alison Device stated that Hugh Moor died at the hands of Chattox *'about six or seven yeares agoe'* (1605). Hugh was the son of Richard Moor of Fence and this is probably Hugh Moor of White Lees, a neighbour of the Chattox family at West Close. As such Moor's cattle on White Lees land would have grazed up to the garden fence of the Chattox home and when they began to show signs of disease (probably murrain) Moor immediately suspected Chattox of bewitching them. This Hugh Moor was married in 1590 to Mary Nutter, of the Waterside family of Ellis Nutter, and buried at Newhurch in 1599, supposedly following his un-neighbourly bewitchment by Chattox. From the White Lees family of Moors came the famous mathematician, Sir Jonas Moor (1517-1579).

Chattox appears to have been friendly with John Moor's wife, Elizabeth, who invited Chattox to her home in order for her to cure the household ale, which had gone sour - John Moor lived at one of his two neighbouring properties in north of Higham, Heights and Dean. Chattox muttered a garbled Catholic prayer over the drink and cured it; according to the Chattox statement Elizabeth Moor then chided her for having bewitched it in the first place. Chattox said that she then bewitched one of the Moor's cows in revenge. However, Alison Device upped the ante by stating that Chattox had also bewitched the Moor's young son, John Moor, who died a short while later. Elizabeth Moor (1586-1667) was young Robert Nutter's middle daughter and, therefore, Chattox had been accused by both her father and grandfather of bewitching them to death.

This raises an interesting question with regard to the prosecution case against Chattox. In 1612 the brother and sister of young Robert Nutter were adamant that Robert was convinced that Chattox and her daughter had bewitched him; their father also repeatedly blamed his fatal illness on bewitchment. Why, then, some years later did young Robert's daughter, Elizabeth Moor, invite the clearly dangerous Chattox into her home on the pretext of sweetening a few gallons of beer? This is not something that most people would do given the fact that Chattox was supposedly a dangerous witch responsible for the deaths of their father and grandfather!

Yet again the evidence does not stack up; in this instance the supposed statement of Alison Device quoted hearsay 'evidence' against Chattox. It must be said that either Elizabeth Nutter Moor was very naive in employing Chattox or she knew nothing about the accusations made by her father. Is it possible that the suspicion of witchcraft was kept from young Elizabeth? After all, she would have been barely seven years of age when her father died and it was probably not something that her family would want the child to know. However, it would be expected that if the diabolical accusations against Chattox were as widely accepted in the community as the prosecution evidence would have it, then Elizabeth would certainly have heard of them by the time she had become an adult.

Further to this, James Robinson (Nutter), in his evidence against Chattox, said that around 1606 his wife (either Ellen or Agnes) invited Chattox to their house (probably in Wheatley Lane) to help in the carding of wool. Chattox and James' wife happily worked together for a few days and, during the weekend break, James' wife brewed a batch of ale. On the following Monday the women resumed carding and Chattox helped herself to a few scoops of the new drink, which was on a stillage nearby. Unfortunately, the drink went quickly sour and so did the relationship between Chattox and Mrs. Robinson. Each subsequent brew for the following two months was also spoiled.

Of course, it was only natural to blame Chattox for having bewitched the drink - it didn't cross the Robinson's minds that they could possibly have been unhygienic when preparing the brew - they probably used barrels and equipment that had not been adequately sterilised. James Robinson justified his accusation by saying that Chattox and her daughter were *'commonly reputed and reported to be witches.'* In this case, as in the Moor case, it is difficult to accept that the family of Robert and Christopher Nutter would invite a murderous witch into their home and work with her for days on end.

In 1593 it is very possible that the story of young Robert Nutter (who died many miles from Pendle) was not known outside of the family and equally the deathbed ramblings of Christopher were not broadcast for fear of ridicule. This raises the possibility that none of the supposed deaths by witchcraft within Pendle were given much credence by the populace - until the authorities decided to act firmly upon the noted Godless activities of the Forest poor. Roger Nowell and company would be fully aware of the folk tales of bewitchment among his acquaintances, such as the Towneleys, Nutters, Moors and Baldwins, and it was then a simple matter to interpolate this knowledge into his examinations of the accused.

In other words, Demdike *et al* never actually owned up to having killed or bewitched anyone - they were, instead, coerced into saying that others had killed so-and-so or such-and-such a body had made clay pictures with which they supposed they had bewitched someone. When Nowell began his interrogations, initially with Alison Device, he probably had a list, supplied by his friends, of the people supposedly killed by witchcraft. It was then simply a case of manipulating the examinations and adding in a few people from the 'bewitched list' where he saw fit. On top of this, a mass of fanciful gobbledegook was also added to dramatise the statements.

The unfortunate demise of young John Moor at the hands of Chattox (in actual fact she was not charged with the killing of the Moors) did not deter the family from raising another child named John as later records show a John Moor,

Overseer of the Poor, of Higham Booth. The Moor family also appeared in other parts of the Forest in their role as minor local gentry; they appear in Foulridge where John Moor, and his wife Ann, built Ball House in 1627. This property is of interest as it boasts a number of features (such as the central entrance via a storied porch) that were of an unusually high-status for such a small house. The old Nutter property of Greenhead passed into the Moor family upon the marriage of Elizabeth Nutter (born 1585) and John Moor; it was almost certainly this family who built the present Greenhead Manor.

At her trial Chattox was actually found not guilty of the first charge of murder but Demdike had made a tit-for-tat confession stating that she had seen Chattox and Anne Redfearn makingclay 'pictures' of the Nutters to facilitate their deaths. This proved to be more than enough to convict Chattox and her daughter and both were duly hanged.

We have seen that there is a sound etymological basis within Elizabeth Southern's name of Demdike (Demon Woman). The case with Chattox, however, is far from clear. Many of the landscape and field descriptions of the Medieval and Early Modern periods still carried either the original Anglo Saxon or Middle French names and, if this was the case with the Chattox appellation then we could have the Old English word *cýte* meaning *hut/cottage/cabin*. The word *oxa* means *oxe/cow* while *oxn* relates to a hollow or arm-pit. This would provide a description for Anne Whittle's dwelling of *cottage in a hollow* or *cow shed* - this latter might have been used at West Close, given that it was the main Medieval grazing area of the Pendle vaccaries. Old Chattox, in this case, could have been known by the name of the ancient site upon which her dwelling stood (see Part Three).

Alternatively, it has been suggested that Chattox is a corruption of the surname Chadwick. This takes on a modicum of credence when the publication *'The Spending of Robert Nowell's Money'* is taken into consideration. The editor relates his research on the Nowell family and states that an Elizabeth Nowell was the sister of Roger Nowell's grandfather or great-grandfather, John Nowell. Elizabeth married a Henry Redfearn, but survived him, she then married a man by the name of Chadwick by whom she had a number of children; the family were in the Bacup area of east Rochdale in the 1560s and 1570s.

Meanwhile, Elizabeth's Redfearn's offspring (the eldest son was traditionally named Thomas) were farming at Spotland, this is the district around Whitworth, a few miles to the west of Burnley. By the 1590s we see members of a Redfearn family at Burnley where Ellis Redfeirne, son of Robert, was baptised and John

Redfeirne was buried. Thomas, John and Ellis were principal names of the Rochdale family of Redfearns and it has to be worth considering that the Thomas Redfearn of Pendle, husband of Anne and son-in-law of Chattox, was related to this family. If so, he was also related to Roger Nowell. As far as Chattox and Chadwick go it is perhaps somewhat coincidental that we have in Elizabeth (née Nowell) a woman with the names of both Chadwick and Redfearn. On the other hand it is possible that Chattox was a Chadwick and related to Elizabeth's second husband - if so Chattox was would have known the Redfearns and this might have been the reason for her daughter marrying Thomas Redfearn.

We saw earlier that a man by the name of Christopher Whittle rented land in Goldshaw in 1563 and then found himself in front of the magistrates in 1567 when he and James Moor, of Higham, were each fined for making an affray together. A Jenneta Whyttle was buried at Newchurch in 1576 and, given the rarity of the name in Pendle, it very possible that we see in Christopher and Jenneta the family of Anne Whittle - possibly parents or siblings. We also see that the Whittles and Moors had a long history of mutual enmity.

ANNE AND THOMAS REDFEARN

Anne Redfearn, and her husband Thomas, lived at West Close along with Anne's mother, Old Chattox; it is not clear if they all actually occupied the same property but this is probably the case. It is reasonably sure that Anne and Thomas had a daughter as the testimony of James Device stated that he saw the three Redfearns together i.e. Anne, Thomas and daughter Marie. Marie Redfearn married Richard Clayton in 1609 and this seems to have removed her from the danger of becoming embroiled within the family's dealings in witchcraft.

According to witness statements Chattox had at least one other daughter, Elizabeth (Bessie). For some unknown reason Bessie was imprisoned at Lancaster in 1613 and Richard Shuttleworth, of Gawthorpe Hall, was charged with sending her clothes to the jail. This shows that the West Close property where Chattox lived was still occupied by the family after Chattox and Anne Redfearn had been executed - it also suggests that Bessie might have up to her old tricks as a 'tea leaf', as was the case when she pinched the Device property from Malkin Tower. This bolsters the argument for John Device having been wary enough of the Chattox family to pay them a security of an annual aghendole of oatmeal.

In 1583 we find the marriage at Newchurch of Thomas Redfearn and Ann Brown and this is interesting; does this provide us with the marriage of Chattox's daughter? Given the fact that there were very few people with the name Redfearn within the whole district it is certainly tempting to take this as being the case. If Ann did indeed carry the maiden name of Brown then this would indicate that she was a widow or her mother could have had this name before marrying a Whittle.

Alternatively, as it was common practice for unmarried women to give the father's surname to a child then Whittle could have been Chattox's birth-name, thus she had her children by a man named Brown. The main family of Browns farmed at Barley, on the slopes of Pendle Hill; the head of the family during the latter part of the sixteenth century was Ellis Brown who was buried at Newchurch in 1576.

KATHERINE HEWITT ~ MOULDHEELS' WIFE

Katherine Hewitt, of Colne, was the wife of clothier John Hewitt. She appears to have been a friend of Alice Grey who, having been found not guilty (although arraigned on much the same evidence as Hewitt), figures little in the trial reports. Hewitt was accused of bewitching to death one Anne Foulds and on the 4th July 1608 the Colne church records show that *Anna Ffouldes, daughter of Nicholai,* was buried. Hewitt was also accused of *'having in hanck a child of Michael Hartley's of Colne.'* The meaning of this term is clear whereby *hanck* means *'in hand'* but the origin is rather dubious; it may come from the Scots word *'to hanck,'* i.e. *'to have,'* *'to holdfast'* or *'secure.'* Jamieson's Scotch Dictionary also shows hanck as possibly being from *'handkill'* meaning *'to murder,'* or the meaning may be metaphorically taken from the *'hanck'* signifying a skein of yarn or wool which is tied or trussed up.

Katherine Hewitt is said to have been known as Old Mouldheels but this incorrect. She was described by James Device as *'Mouldheels wife'* which means that her husband, clothier John Hewitt, was nick-named Mouldheels. Handloom warps had a size of animal-fat applied to them to stiffen and strengthen the thread and this was sometimes over-applied by unscrupulous merchants in order to bulk out the cloth. As a consequence of this the warp became shiny and susceptible to the growth of mould on the surface of the textile. The warp was then known as a *'mouldy warp.'* The word *'Heels'* was a suffix commonly applied to a nickname relating to the nature of an individual, for example *'Leaden Heels'* described someone who moved slowly or dawdled. John Hewitt, then, would have been known for his tendency to doctor his cloth in order to gain maximum profit - in other words he was slippery and untrustworthy.

Victorian novelists often used the term *'as shiny as a mouldy warp.'* In certain counties of England the farmer's enemy, the mole, is colloquially known as a *'mouldy'* but it was previously uncertain that the name applied within this part of Lancashire. However, reading the Shuttleworth of Gawthorpe accounts it is clear that this was the case; in the 1620s a worker was paid a small sum for *'skayling the moulde hilles'* or raking flat the mole hills. The term *moulde hilles,* of course, is very similar to *mould heels* and this raises the question as to whether mole catchers were also known as *mouldheels?*

It is likely that the Hewitts lived in the Waterside area of Colne as there is a record of a John Kenyon having illegally erected a number of cottages there in the later part of the sixteenth century and one of the tenants there was one John Hewytte, clothier, and his family. A land transfer of May 1561 shows that Thomas Robinson of Goldshaw and his brother, John Robinson, surrendered to Agnes Hewitt, formerly the wife of Nicholas Blakey and now the wife of John Hewitt, the tenancy of a farm, garden and fifteen acres of land in Colne.

It is probable that John and Agnes Hewitt were related to John and Katherine Hewitt. Further, Agnes was probably the sister of the Robinson brothers of Newchurch-in-Pendle. Demdike's son, Christopher Holgate, married a Robinson and this could mean that the Katherine Hewitt who was hanged for witchcraft in 1612 was related to Demdike - this would explain the mystery of how 'Mouldheels wife,' from the town of Colne, came to be embroiled within the Pendle witch trials.

GRACE HEY

One of the people said to have been in attendance at the Good Friday meeting at Malkin Tower was Grace Hey of Padiham; Grace was the daughter of Miles Hey and was baptised in 1568. The Heys were a well established family in the West Close area of Pendle and the modern farm of Heys Acre, on the ancient Ightenhill to Higham trackway, echoes this fact.

A Christopher Holgate (son of John) and Hugh Hey (with his wife Jennet) were co-tenants of a farm in Rossendale in 1570 and it is possible that the two families were related by marriage. This would raise the possibility that the Christopher Holgate above was related to Demdike's son, Christopher Holgate and therefore Grace Hey might have been related to Demdike. This would explain why she attended the Good Friday meeting at Malkin where many of the people were related to the Demdike/Device clan. Interestingly enough a Lawrence Hey was one of the people accused of being a witch at the 1612 Samlesbury Witch trial.

ANN CRONCKSHAW

Ann Cronckshaw, of Marsden, was another member of the group at the infamous Good Friday gathering. Ann was closely related to the Cronckshaw family of Hollins Farm, in West Close who were descended from Gilbert de Cronkshawe, a tenant there in 1332 - an area of West Close was called Cronckshaw and this illustrates the length of time in which the family had lived in the Forest. They were granted the farm of West Close at a very early stage in the forest development and had long been major landholders in the area. Ann's mother was Agnes Brown and had married her father, Miles Cronckshaw, in 1567 – was Agnes closely related to

Chattox whose possible Brown family lineage we explored earlier? A Jennet Cronkshaw was accused of being a witch in the Pendle witch trials of 1633.

In 1600 Leonard Cronckshaw, gent, was listed as one of the freeholders of West Close and his wife, Elizabeth, had been buried at Padiham in 1573. Elizabeth was the daughter of Elizabeth Nowell, sister to Dean Alexander Nowell who oversaw the payments of brother Robert Nowells' legacy. This latter Elizabeth married Thomas Whitaker of Holme-in-Cliviger, gent, and ancestor to the historian, Thomas Dunham Whitaker. This means that Leonard Cronckshaw's family were related to Alice Nutter, of Roughlee, and Roger Nowell.

JOHN AND JANE BULCOCK

In 1612 Christopher Bulcock was living with his wife, Jane, and son John at Moss End which is often taken to be Moss End Farm to the south of the village of Newchurch-in-Pendle. This farm, which had become derelict by the middle of the twentieth century, was sited where Spen Brook Mill now stands.

Both James and Jennet Device accused John Bulcock and his mother, Jane, of having attended the Malkin Tower Good Friday. At the 1612 trial the accused were lined up in an identity parade and young Jennet was asked if she recognised any of the people there. Having failed to name the Bulcocks in her 'evidence' Jennet proceeded to identify Jane Bulcock as having been at Malkin Tower - she also added that John Bulcock turned the roasting spit for the feast. This latter information was another contrivance on behalf of the magistrates in order to paint the Good Friday meeting as a witches' Sabbath - roasting spits being a favourite of those who wished to dramatise these diabolical gatherings.

Both mother and son were accused of '*practising their devilish and wicked art upon the body of Jennet Deane of Newfield Edge in Middop*' so that she was eventually driven mad. It is clear that poor Jennet Dean had psychological problems and the Bulcocks took the blame for this. Yet another illustration of the contrived nature of the statements taken from the accused is provided when the confession of James Device was read to the court:

> The said John Bulcock, and Jane his said Mother, did confesse vpon Goode-Friday last at the said Malking Tower, in the hearing of this Examinate, That they had bewitched, at the Newfield Edge in Yorkshire, a woman called Iennet, wife of Iohn Deyne, besides her reason; and the said Woman's name so bewitched he did not heare them speake of.

James (or at least his so-called statement) was saying that he did not hear the Bulcocks speak the name of Jennet Dean at the same time that he heard them speak her name! John and his mother vociferously protested their innocence; they denied ever having been at the Good Friday meeting and, as might be expected under those circumstances, they protested (according to Potts) *'even unto the gallows'*. Rather than pricking the conscience of the prosecution into considering that these unfortunates might just have been innocent after all, quite the opposite reaction is apparent; Potts used the fact that they protested as a sign of their belligerence and an illustration of their extreme wickedness!

It is fair to say that the majority of those attending the Good Friday meeting were friends and relatives of the Demdike clan. We have seen that Alice Nutter's sister-in-law, Jane Nutter was widowed and re-married to Christopher Bulcock of Roughlee. Jane and her step-son, John Bulcock (of Moss End Farm), attended the Malkin Tower meeting and for this alone they were hanged. Jane had a daughter, Maria Nutter, with her first husband and Maria married Henry Robinson of Roughlee who was, in turn, probably related to Demdike's daughter-in-law. Further, Jane Bulcock's step-son, John, was married to Margaret Hartley of Roughlee who was related to Alice Nutter while another of Jane's step-sons, Henry Bulcock, married Alice, the daughter of John Nutter (another relative of Alice Nutter's family) of Bullhole Farm in Newchurch. This John was stated by Old Chattox to 'favour Demdikes' services over her own' and this is probably because John was related to both Alice Nutter and Demdike

MARGARET PEARSON

The Iudgement of the Court against you, is, You shall stand vpon the Pillarie in open Market, at Clitheroe, Paddiham, Whalley, and Lancaster, foure Market dayes, with a Paper vpon your head, in great Letters, declaring your offence, and there you shall confesse your offence, and after to remaine in Prison for one yeare without Baile, and after to be bound with good Sureties, to be of the good behauiour.

Margaret Pearson lived in Padiham, just outside the Forest of Pendle but, as this bounds onto the Higham and West Close areas of the western Forest, she would be familiar to the Pendle accused. This was the third time that Pearson had been arraigned on a case of witchcraft, on this latest occasion she was accused by Chattox of *'riding a mare of Dodgeson's to death.'* Another witness, Jennet Booth, also from Padiham, said that she had visited Pearson's husband while Pearson was in prison and a toad had hopped out of a pile of firewood. On the strength of this puerile 'evidence' Margaret Pearson received a sentence of pillory in the stocks of the main county towns, followed by imprisonment for twelve months. This might sound to have been a lenient sentence but it has to be remembered that Pearson never actually harmed anyone and a year in a filthy dungeon could often prove fatal when malnutrition and disease set in.

In the end the Lancaster trials of August 1612 saw ten people (eight women and two men) being judged as deserving of being summarily removed from the face of the earth. Elizabeth Southern would have brought the total number of executions to eleven but her demise in the stinking Lancaster Well Tower dungeon had spared her the rope. We must not forget also that Jennet Preston, of Gisburn, had been hanged at York a few days earlier (on the 29th of July). The wording of the death sentence passed by Sir Edward Bromley was designed to reflect his professional position where a need to rid the country of such damnable creatures was balanced by contrition. That the poor souls should have had the temerity to be poor in the first place was a source of great sadness to him!

History does not inform us as to how many people of the Forest area attended the Lancaster Assizes but there is no doubt that the affair would have caused a massive stir both locally and in the wider northern region. The court rooms were packed to bursting point and Monday the 17th August, the opening day, the broadsheet sellers and street-ballad singers were proffering their wares in all of the major towns of the North West.

In the afternoon of the 18th August Judge Bromley had heard the opening of the witch trials where Chattox, Elizabeth Device and James Device were found guilty; Ann Redfearn was tried and acquitted. The following day Ann Redfearn was tried on a second charge of witchcraft and convicted. The Samlesbury Witches were tried and acquitted whilst Alice Nutter and Katherine Hewitt were tried and found guilty. In the afternoon John Bulcock and his mother, Jane, Alison Device, Margaret Pearson and Isabel Roby were all tried and found guilty. This was followed by all of the convicted prisoners being brought before the judge who then passed the death sentence. On Thursday the 20th August Sir Edward Bromley confirmed the sentence of death by hanging upon the condemned prisoners and sentenced Margaret Pearson to the pillory to be followed by a period of incarceration.

Large crowds of onlookers would have attended the mass execution in Lancaster on that later-summer day in 1612. Many lined the streets as the cart passed with its sad payload of condemned prisoners; pathetic, starved and shivering with fear this once-proud group of Pendle Forest people sat with their backs to the horses. Surrounded by their own makeshift wooden coffins the prisoners stared blankly at the baying crowds as the unsprung dungeon cart rattled, bumped and swayed along the bone-shaking road to Gallows Hill.

Having left the Castle gates behind the pitiful procession would have passed along Moor Lane and Moor Gate before making a stop at the newly built Golden Lion Inn; the prisoners would possibly have been allowed a final drink at the inn along with their friends and relatives. A more heart-rending sight than this can hardly be imagined - mothers and daughters, mothers and sons, all on their way to certain death were spending a last few precious minutes with their loved ones while surrounded by drunken, rowdy revellers out for the day's 'entertainment.'

The nine condemned forest-folk were hanged together upon Gallows Hill; this was an area of moorland close to Lancaster's Williamson Park. As the sad group breathed out their last it is possible that their family and friends would have grabbed their legs and pulled as they dangled from the heavy wooden gallows, this hastened the process of strangulation and was seen as an act of mercy. Finally, the prisoners having been pronounced dead by both the Lancaster coroner, Thomas Covell, and the prison surgeon; the nine rough coffins would have then been unceremoniously piled into an open pit on the present site of Nightingale Hall Farm (now a Quaker graveyard). In the present day, on the site of the execution area, stands St. Martin's College and, within a short distance, an ancient row of cottages carries the emotive name of Golgotha. This translates from the Hebrew as *Place of the Skulls* and this surely reflects the grisly history of the area.

And so the curtain falls on a story that bequeaths only a dull smoky image of the actual events. Four long centuries have taken their toll upon the fears and the joys of a time long passed but it is now possible for us to part the mists - to a small degree at least. Hopefully we can now hear more clearly the voices of the common people whose true story has, for too long, left us only with grey reflections.

DEMDIKE'S LAMENT

THE RATS AND THE MICE, THE FLEAS AND THE LICE
DANCE TO HELL'S DUNGEON TUNE,
WHILE MOCKING CHAINS AND RATTLING LUNGS
RASP OUT A RHYTHMIC DRONE

DREAMS SWEEP IN AT LIFE'S DUSK HOUR,
I AM YOUNG AND FREE AGAIN,
TO RUN ALONG WITH THE MORNING SONG
OF THE MEADOWLARK AND WREN

NOW GABRIEL'S DOOR STANDS WIDE UNDONE,
WASHED BRIGHT WITH MY CHILDREN'S BLOOD,
THE HAND OF MAN WILL HANG THEM SOON,
IN THE NAME OF JUSTICE AND GOD

THE HIDDEN ROAD TO OLD MALKIN'S TOWER,
NOW ONLY THE RED KITE KNOWS,
A WEIGHT OF AGE DECAYS FOREST FLOWER
BUT SWEET BELLADONNA STILL GROWS

J A Clayton

Part Two ~ Conclusion

In Part One we saw that the Pendle witch trials were the culmination of a number of factors; as is often the case with signal historic events a final spark ignites the tinderbox of pent-up discontent. As Britain moved steadily toward that ultimate display of Puritanical political conflict, the Civil War (1642-1651), an increasingly dangerous attitude of mistrust percolated downward through society, from the Crown to the very bottom of the social heap.

The Chelmsford witch trials of 1566 set the scene for the Pendle trials of 1612; here we see many of the ridiculous assertions of diabolic imagery used by the gentlemen prosecutors to ensure that the poor wretches accused of witchcraft were forever damned. Chief among these gentlemen was one Gilbert Gerard whose descendant, Sir Thomas Gerard, would come to play his own part in the Pendle trials. To a large extent, then, it is fair to say that the story had already been written when young Alison Device met with the 'chapman' (priest?), John Lawe, on Colne Field in the March of 1612.

It cannot be pure coincidence that the people who complained of having been bewitched, or had lost a family member to witch spells, were all known personally by Roger Nowell. Many of these unfortunates were of the yeomanry class and these families were all interrelated to some degree or other. It is, therefore, a mistake to take the events within our story as isolated incidents. Within the background of the accusations of diabolical murder levelled at this witch or that witch there existed a seething tumult of family tensions.

The wealth of landowning families was concentrated through the eldest sons while other siblings were left to make their own way; this resulted in large junior branches of landed families. Some of these junior family members were reduced to working in the fields and houses of their wealthy cousins and they resented the fact that this position was due entirely to an accident of birth. As we saw with the Nutter family of Greenhead there were always disgruntled family members but not all of them were willing to enlist the services of a local witch in order to bring about the death of another family member!

Within the Pendle trial 'evidence' a great deal of coercement, interpolation of fantastical rubbish and downright lies are quite apparent. Stripped of the 90% of fiction contained within the 'evidence', to what extent can we say that the accused were deserving of the death penalty?

Despite the fact that the prosecution twisted their statements there is not a single case where the accused can be proved to have admitted to premeditated murder; direct accusations of killing were attributed by the accused to other people in the form of hearsay evidence. As the highly complex relationship between Pendle Forest families is studied so it becomes clear that those who were hanged at Lancaster were the scapegoats of a guilty, dystopian society. The gentry had issues with their religion and position within Crown authority; the yeomen had issues with the authorities and God while the poor had issues with just about everything.

The middling sort were not above enlisting the aid of those they called 'witch' but equally they were only too willing to let these people take the blame when necessary. When this happened there could only ever be one outcome - the authorities made sure that those who stood before them, accused of the religious crime of witchcraft, were charged instead with the new crime of murder or treason. In 1612 Sir Cuthbert Halsall, Sheriff of Lancashire, was instructed to hand-pick the trial jury from selected gentlemen. The accused were defenceless against the onslaught of a predetermined prosecution; they were often condemned before they stood trial and for the vast majority there would be no way back.

Notes Relating
to Part Two

1 Roper, L. *Witchcraft and the Western Imagination* Transactions of the RHS 16 (2006), pp. 117–41 Royal Historical Society doi:10.1017/S0080440106000442

2 Sosis, R. and Alcorta, C. *Signalling, Solidarity, and the Sacred:The Evolution of Religious Behaviour*. Paper in Evolutionary Anthropology 12:264-274 (2003)

3 Winkleman M, 1992. *Shamans, Priests and Witches: a cross-cultural study of magico-religious practitioners*. Tempe Arizona State University. Anthropological Research Papers No.44

4 *On The History of Witchcraft*. Wesleyan-Methodist magazine, 6 (1850:Dec.) p.1275

5 Edwards, L. *Flights of Angels: Varieties of a Fictional Paradigm* Feminist Studies, Vol. 5, No. 3, Toward a New Feminism for the Eighties. (Autumn, 1979), pp. 547-570.

6 *The Registers of Newchurch-in-Pendle*, 1574-1754, (Lancashire Parish Register Society –2002)

7 *The House of Commons: 1509 - 1558* Appendices, constituencies ..., Volume 4 Stanley T. Bindoff, John S. Roskell, Lewis Namier, Romney Sedgwick, David Hayton, Eveline Cruickshanks, R. G. Thorne, P. W. Hasler

8 Gilbert Gerard was an executor of the will of Robert Nowell, brother of Dean Alexander Nowell, in which money was provided to pay for woollen cloth to distribute among the people of the Pendle district between 1558 and 1580

9 Sepult (burial); interpolated entry means the burial was entered into the parish register at a later date

10 Whitaker, G. *Roughlee Hall, Fact and Fiction*. Marsden Antiquarians. (1980)

11 Farrar, W. *Court Rolls of the Honor of Clitheroe*. (Vols-1/3 - 1912)

PART THREE

BACKDROP

ASHLAR HOUSE

Ashlar House is the property in Fence where Roger Nowell interrogated Demdike and Chattox on the 2nd April 1612. They were probably detained overnight in the vaulted cellars here before being taken to Lancaster Jail. Also present as witnesses were siblings John Nutter and Margaret Crooke along with their half-brother, James Robinson. Accusations of witchcraft flew thick and fast and more local people were brought into the fray. Potts said that the suspects were examined at the house of James Wilsey but this is wrong. In another example of misinterpretation Potts had written Wilsey instead of Walmsley.

A stone plaque above the porch says that the house was built in 1594 by Richard Grimshaw and John Box but the rest of the property appears to have been rebuilt later in the seventeenth century. Grimshaw was a landowner from West Close and his new property was variously known as Fence, New House and Hewn Ashlar. The house passed to James Walmsley of the Coldcoats (west of Pendle) branch of the family in 1608. Thomas Walmsley (died 1575) had been a Justice in the Court of Common Pleas and in this capacity had gathered a great deal of wealth. His son, Thomas, followed his father into the law and married Ann, heiress to Sir Richard Shuttleworth of Gawthorpe. The family occupied Dunkenhalgh Hall and Robert of Coldcoats, the brother of Thomas, had a son, James Walmsley, who we see owning Ashlar House at the time of the 1612 trials. James eventually lived at Gawthorpe from where he was buried in 1646.

And so it becomes clear why Ashlar House was used by Roger Nowell to examine the Pendle accused - his fellow magistrates were quick to offer their services in the task of clearing the Forest of witches.

Ashlar House

WEST CLOSE

There are numerous references in Potts to the fact that Anne Whittle and her family lived in the southern Forest district of West Close. There is actually a twelve acre field above Higham village that was known as West Close Field but this was attached to the Lowerhouses Estate (Sabden Fold) and was not, therefore, on the Shuttleworth estates of West Close proper.

West Close Booth is now attached to the parish of Higham but the name originated in the twelfth century when the de Lacy family, lords of the Honor of Clitheroe, set up their cattle vaccary system within Pendle. The southern slopes running south from Higham down to the Calder formed some of the best stock grazing land within the whole Pendle district and it was here that cattle from other vaccaries within the Forest were sent to fatten. West Close, then, was so-called because of its position to the west of the deer enclosures of Old and New Laund.

The Ightenhill manor was the de Lacy headquarters of the Forest area and this is where the halmote courts were held - also the vaccary stewards were based here. The manor house at Ightenhill was situated a short distance to the south of the Calder and from here the ancient track of Higham Lane ran through West Close and Higham and onward into the further reaches of the Pendle Forest.

This ancient route from Ightenhill can still be made out through field work and air photographs and it is clear that the present day trackway of Foxen Dole Lane is not the original route. Higham Lane ran from Sabden Fold, over Haddings Head and past Heights Farm, down Blind Lane (where the modern A6066 has obliterated it) and down to Heys (not the modern Heys Acre Farm). From Heys the old route continues down to the Calder and, having forded the river, up towards Ightenhill manor.

The ancient Higham Lane heads up to the A6066 above Heys

The track is blocked by an old stone wall and this is an indicator of how long the trackway has been disused

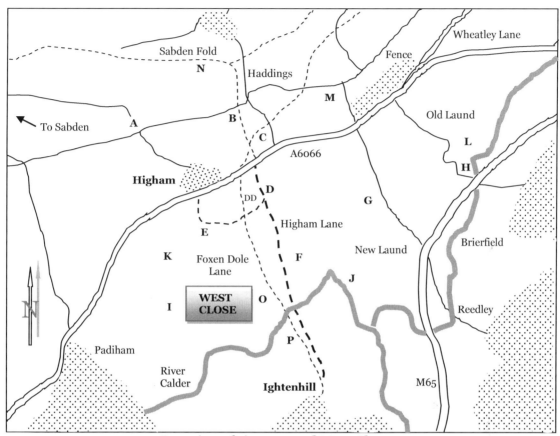

Location of sites around West Close

A	DEAN FARM
B	HEIGHTS FARM
C	HIGHER WHITE LEES
D	HEYS (DD HEYS ACRE)
E	WEST CLOSE FARM
F	MOOR ISLES
G	GREENHEAD
H	WATERSIDE
I	HIGH WHITAKER
J	INGHAMS HOUSE
K	HANCOCK HALL
L	OLD LAUND HALL
M	HOARSTONES
N	LOWERHOUSE
O	PENDLE HALL
P	HUNTERS OAK
R	ASHLAR HOUSE

Eventually West Close passed to the Gawthorpe estate and at the time of the witch trials Richard Shuttleworth was the landowner. Scattered across the general area of West Close were the high status farms of West Close Farm, Pendle Hall, Moor Isles, High Whittaker, Inghams, Hollins and Higham Hall.

On the periphery were the Nutter's Greenhead property, Ashlar House, White Lees, Northwood, Old Laund Hall, Hunters Oak, Fence Gate and others. It is clear from this that West Close was a prosperous area that attracted the yeomanry and the gentry alike.

Courtesy of R J Hayhurst

West Close Farm

Old Laund Hall

Courtesy of R J Hayhurst

Fence Gate House

Greenhead

Among the residents and neighbours of West Close around 1612 were: the Crook families - Christopher Kendal - Henry, James and Richard Hey of Northwood - Lawrence Booth - John Whittaker - James Baley (alias Moore) - Robert Smith - Parkers of White Lee - Hugh Moore of White Lee - John Moore of Higham - John Cross - William Riley of Pendle Hall - James Roe - John Ingham - James Robert - John Dickinson - Hugh Dickinson - Geoffrey Birch - John Cronkshaw of Hollins - James Pollard - Bernard Parker - Isabella Hancock (wife of Richard Assheton) owner of Pendle Hall - Richard Grimshaw of High Whitaker and Fence (Ashlar) - the Hartleys of Fence Gate.

The above residents can reasonably be multiplied by a factor of four which means that there would have been at least eighty people within the immediate neighbourhood of the Chattox homestead. The fields would have been bustling with the busy coming and going of plough teams, labourers hedging and ditching, stockmen tending to their cattle and sheep, haymaking, carts taking produce to market, masons working on the new stone buildings, muck spreading, quarrymen extracting and carting building stone, coal hewers digging the black stuff from shallow surface pits and pit shafts, 'penny men' digging marl fertiliser from sand pits and carpenters felling trees and carting large roofing timbers.

Pendle Hall: home of the Hancocks - described as 'Higham Tower' in 1564

Beside all this daily activity there would also have been considerable movement through the area as traders, cattlemen and others journeyed from Burnley to Clitheroe and the towns of Blackburn, Preston and Manchester to Colne and Yorkshire. The solitude of West Close today, where only the upward burst of a skylark disturbs the quiet, belies its importance at the time of the witch trials.

To the landscape archaeologist the West Close area is of interest as, not only do early field patterns survive, but air photographs and field work show a number of long forgotten trackways, land terracing and levelled platforms. West Close Farm appears to have been at the hub of a network of early trackways and on the old lane above the farm the practised eye can discern a rectilinear platform at the terminal of a denuded hollow way. The platform overlooks the deep clough of Fir Trees Brook and could well have been an early occupation site.

A long abandoned lane near to West Close Farm. This sunken road ran from the ancient Higham Lane through West Close Farm and up to Higham Old Hall. The depth and width indicate that the lane had been an important route for a long period

Our particular interest at West Close, however, is to locate the home of Old Chattox and her family and this is not a simple task. When it comes to the actual site we are left with little to go on other than fragments of information gleaned from the Potts account. The place where Chattox called home could have been anywhere within the extended area of West Close but Demdike's description of the place narrows the search somewhat. In one of her statements Demdike says that she was going home one day, with a full piggin of milk scrounged from a local farm, and her way happened to take her past Chattox's house. The garden was some ten feet from a ditch and when Demdike saw Chattox preparing clay images, reputedly of Robert Nutter, she fell into the ditch in her haste to get away. This raises the question as to why such a supposedly dangerous witch such as Demdike would be spooked by Chattox forming a doll from clay?

The Chattox house, then, stood by a ditch and near to a track or path - this at least enables a more focused search to be carried out. During the early part of the twentieth century a large swaith of land around the lower length of Foxen Dole Lane was stripped for drainage and removal of hedges and ditches and, were the Chattox residence to have been situated here, it would be lost forever. However, all is not lost - the large strip of land running east-west between West Close Farm and Higham has retained much of its Medieval nature.

It is here that we find a ruined building by the name of Heys - a surname that we have seen before in relation to the West Close area. At first sight the Heys building appears to be set in isolation, some two fields distant from the nearest road of Foxen Dole Lane and with no access track. However, the 1847 OS map shows that a trackway ran directly westward from the building to Foxen Dole Lane - this is now the location of the modern property of Heys Acre Farm.

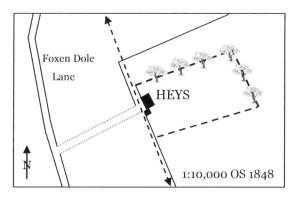

Heys in 1847 showing access track.

The building is situated within a ditched enclosure of 2.5 acres.

The arrowed dotted line indicates the line of the original trackway

Now that we know the route of the original Higham Lane it becomes clear that the Heys building stands directly upon it, the axis of the building respecting the original trackway (indicated above). The Heys building incorporates two separate dwellings, one being known as Heys Farm in the nineteenth century and the other as Heys Farm Cottage. However, the building was not erected as a traditional farm as there was no barn - there were outbuildings of sorts and this indicates that the property took the form of a smallholding with 2.5 acres attached.

Heys - southern aspect

Heys - northern aspect

It is possible that Heys was erected around 1800-1820 to house workers of the Huntroyd estates (who owned most of the land and property in the district at this time). In 1891 Robert Ree, a gamekeeper, lived in Heys Farm while the family of Luther Horsfield, a weaver, occupied Heys Farm Cottage. The age of the building, then, is not contemporary with the enclosure it occupies and would not be expected to respect the line of the ancient trackway in the way that it does. The enclosure is a true example of a parcel of land commonly referred to in farm records as a 'close.'

The Heys enclosure is formed on three sides by Medieval ditches with earthen banks topped with stone walls and thorn hedging - the fourth side was formed by the early trackway.

The ditch running along the northern side of the Heys enclosure

The stone from the banking was robbed out to erect the later walls of the area around the time that Heys Farm was built

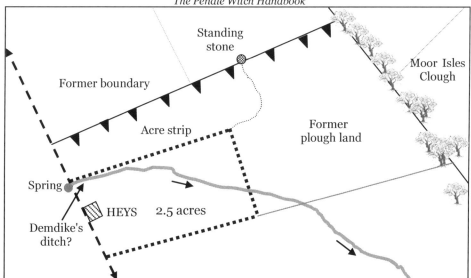

On close inspection the Heys area retains a number of remnants relating to its early agricultural days. The plan above shows that originally a spring rose in the north-west corner of the Heys enclosure and ran south-east into Moor Isles Clough. The presence of this stream was probably the reason why this particular close of land was enclosed as it would provide water for the stock - the stream has now been culverted but its former course can still be made out.

The 2.5 acre Heys enclosure is set within a larger enclosure and this is separated from the land to the north by a drainage ditch. The ground to the north of this feature is higher than that to the south and this suggests that the ditch has been cut into a former lynchet or terrace formed by ploughing across the slope. A large broken standing stone is present to the side of the ditch and its size indicates that it was originally of some importance, probably as a boundary marker.

The remaining standing stone base

Between this ditch and the Heys enclosure another enclosure is evident from the traces of another ditch. This ran to an acre in extent and would probably have formed one of a series of feudal land divisions used by the people of Higham during the Medieval and possibly in the Anglo Saxon period. Ploughing of the furlong strips within this acre enclosure would account for the difference in ground level between the north and south fields and this further suggests that the

159

standing stone marked the extent of the 'manor' land attached to Higham Hall. Beyond this stone was the poorer or 'outer' land reserved for the village cottars.

The suggestion is, then, that Heys stands on an enclosure which dates back to at least the sixteenth century, and possibly much earlier. At some stage the land at Heys was selected as a farm site because of the supply of fresh water; ditches and banks formed the enclosure, retained stock and drained the land. It is highly probable that a small complex of buildings were erected upon the enclosure to house a stockman. The present Heys building respects the ancient Ightenhill trackway, it stands within a well defined early enclosure, it is sited by a spring and was located on the Shuttleworth estate while being outside of the better quality Higham 'manor' lands. This strongly suggests that the Heys enclosure stands on the footprint of an earlier smallholding and it is very possible that this was the sight of the Chattox dwelling.

In 1612 we know that Chattox's house had a garden running up to a ditch and this fits the Heys site exactly - the ditch at that time would have been the open stream produced by the spring. Thomas Redfearn gave the schoolmaster a capon - the probability is that the house had enough ground on which to run hens. The Chattox home, then, would have been a humble wattle and daub cottage with a fern-thatched roof, a garden area and a couple of acres on which to keep a cow, hens and possibly a pig or two. It was situated next to what was still at the time the equivalent of a main highway.

A peculiar stone from the embankment at Heys.

The holes are possibly 'wuzzin hoiles' created by spinning soaked woollen pieces around a stick to dry them.

This would mean that the stone was incorporated into a building or perhaps the top of an upright post.

Further to this, we could possibly have the situation where the Demdike clan, in the form of daughter Bessie and son-in-law Thomas Redfearn, carried on living at the family home following the execution of Chattox and daughter Ann. Within a reasonably short period, however, Bessie and Thomas tired of the finger-pointing and whispering of their neighbours and left the smallholding. Perhaps by around 1620 one of the local Heys families acquired the tenancy of the now unoccupied Chattox house and, after demolishing the old cottage, erected a small building in which to house his family. Because of the dilapidated nature of the old roadway running by the house it could have been at this time that a new parallel trackway was being developed through Foxen Dole - certainly by the first quarter of the eighteenth century the trackway past Heys had been abandoned leaving the building there two fields distant from the new road.

The building erected by Heys might have been extant, albeit in a ruinous state, at the end of the eighteenth century when the present building replaced it. If the suggestion that Chattox lived here is correct then the Ightenhill track would have connected her home directly with the houses of John and Hugh Moor with whom she is indelibly linked. It was also the track along which Demdike was walking with her piggin of milk when she saw Chattox making a clay doll of Robert Nutter.

Is this the spot where Demdike fell into the ditch?

As a caveat it must be said that the building at Heys is in an extremely dangerous condition - it is also on private land. A footpath runs along the west gable but it is strongly advised that anyone passing the site should keep to the path and stay as far away from the building as possible!

Malkin Tower

'Malkin's Tower, a little cottage, where
Reporte makes caitive witches meete to swear
Their homage to ye devil'

The Reverend Richard James, Fellow of Oxford, visited Pendle at the time of the 1633 trials and wrote the above description of Malkin Tower in a first-hand account. He also said *'Whatever the truth may be, those poor wretches find pittie and apologie from manye.'* Within these words there is probably an accurate contemporary report of the type of dwelling occupied by Demdike and the emotions of the forest people following the 1612 and 1633 trials.

The site of the long-lost Malkin Tower has occupied historians and local people alike for centuries. Until now there have been two main contenders when it comes to claiming the site - the first is at Malkin Tower Farm in Blacko and the other is the Saddlers Farm area of Newchurch-in-Pendle. The basis of this latter site is found in the writings of Dr. Laycock of Sabden who stated that fields at Saddlers Farm were named Malkin Fields; however, in their *Trials of The Lancashire Witches* the authors, Edgar Peel and Pat Southern, say that they inspected the Saddlers Farm deeds and the attached field name plan does not bear this out. It is possible, then, that there is more folklore than fact here.

In *The Lancashire Witch Conspiracy* the case for the site of Malkin Tower having been at Blacko was covered in great detail and, at the time of writing, this was the favoured theory. The main reason for this is that the Clitheroe Court Rolls for 1508 show that *'a place to the north of Colne'* was known as *Malkenyerd* and in 1564 the same place was given as *Mawkynyarde*. This was the only firm example found of the description of Malkin being applied to a site within the Pendle district. Slightly to the north of Malkin Tower Farm (SD 866 424) is a large hollow feature shown as *Heynslack* on a map of 1581 and *Mawkin Hole* on the nineteenth century Malkin Tower Farm property deeds; this hollow is large enough to accommodate a small cathedral. The two terms of Heynslack and Mawkin Hole appear to emanate from different periods within our history although they both describe exactly the topography of the site.

The site falls within the north-eastern corner of the Forest of Pendle. The Heynslack name has two derivations - the first is from the Saxon where *haie* means *a hedged place* while the Norse word *slack* is commonly used in our area as a description of a *hollow on a hillside*. We have, then, a Skandiwegian term for the Blacko Hill feature of *hollow on the boundary* and this is apt given that the pre 1974 Yorkshire/Lancashire boundary ran through the hollow. The name of Mawkin Hole is a later description of the site and would have first been used in the Medieval period.

We have at Blacko, then, an early written source giving the name of Mawken to the north of Colne (Blacko). Further, through the generosity of the owners of Malkin Tower Farm, we know that the name of Mawkin Hole applies to an area of land to the north of the farm.

However . . . as is usually the way with these things, the dynamics of ongoing research has altered the focus of the search for Demdike's lair. *'I have vowed to change my mind and to keep on changing my mind with every instance of new evidence that presents itself.'* These are the wise words of a nineteenth century historian and, as we shall see, are as true today as they ever were.

The variations of the Malkin term are many and varied but recent research by Hubert Mankin into the origins of his family name (*www.mankin.org*) shows a very interesting and apposite meaning of the name:

> At first glance, one might think *Mankin* means either *akin to man* or that it is a diminutive form of man in the same way that *lambkin* means a little lamb. This would be the case if the origin of the word were Dutch as in *manikin,* or French *mannequin,* but it has been stated in excellent sources on the etymology of names that *mankin* comes from Celtic origin. The *kin* actually means *leader* or *head* and in the combined form *man-kin* means *head of a group* or *headman.*
>
> In the Oxford Old English Dictionary (OOED), where the first known uses of the word are recorded, a *mankin* was a *fierce wild man.*
>
> In heraldry a *mankin* is always shown as a forest being with a crown of leaves and a wild-eyed expression. As cited in the OOED in Sleq.Inf.Chr.(Ld)57 written in the year about 1300 AD, it talks about *Mankin Beasts* coming out of woods and fields: *Ne hadden huy nout ful longue I fare yat huy ne seien wondres yare; ye Bestes Mankene and eke wilde Comen out of wodes and of felde.*
>
> There is in Yorkshire (Todmorden) a placename, *Mankinholes,* which identifies an area of caverns not uncommon in the Pennine hills of that region, where *mankin holes* appear to have been made or inhabited by *mankins* now gone, and leaving deep pits or openings descending to connected caverns in the ground. *Mankin holes* are often quite deep, such as the well-known, Witches Cave which is many hundreds of feet in depth. In other sources, the Celtic meaning is that *mankinholes* are defined as air pockets in bread, giving one the impression or superstition that something or someone was living there. *Mankinholes* in Yorkshire is related to that superstition.

So here we have a simple and very plausible reason for the name applied to the massive hollow on Blacko Hillside; Mawkin Hole has the same root as Mankinholes near Todmorden. This would have been a generic description for natural holes and hollows in the landscape where the wild *mankin* lived. The name of Mawken at Blacko had been absorbed into local culture by the end of the fifteenth century but a 1581 map of the area shows the hollow was called Haynslack - Mawkin Hole, then, was a colloquial term. We are left with the fact, however, that Blacko is the only known site locally that can boast of a Mawkin/Malkin name in relation to a landscape feature and it stands to reason that any tower-like structure here would be known as Malkin Tower.

That said, there has always been one serious stumbling block when it comes to the location of Malkin Tower having been at Blacko and that is the fact that the Potts accounts do not relate to this part of the Forest. Within the statements of the accused it is possible to discern a spacial pattern where events were reported near to (say) the 'new kirk' or 'Bull Hole' etc. To further this all of the sites mentioned by the examinates have been collated and plotted onto a plan of Pendle Forest and the results are very interesting.

Reported incidences taken from Potts.
Squares represent focal points within each Forest parish

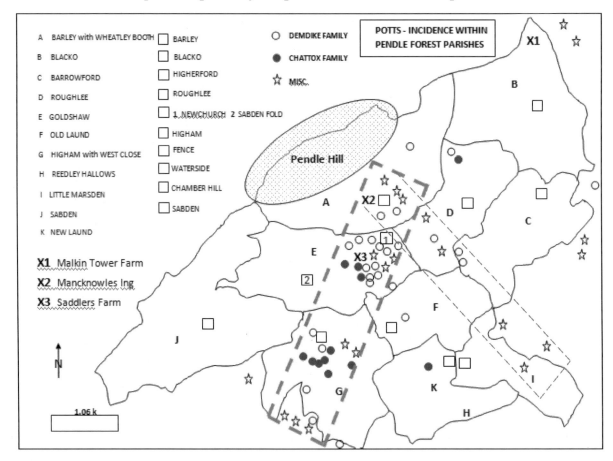

The plan can only provide an indication of the movements of the accused as we see the related in Potts' *Wonderfull Discoverie*. Nevertheless it serves to illustrate the point that they were mainly active within a clearly defined corridor roughly four kilometres in length and one kilometre wide and running from Ightenhill and Padiham, in the south, up to Barley. A secondary corridor runs from Great and Little Marsden, in the south-east, to Barley. The plotted locations of the accused who were not part of the Demdike or Chattox families are represented by star symbols - it is clear that these originate within the urban districts outside of the Forest and follow the corridors deep into the Forest.

Further to this, there are three apparent groupings in the areas of West Close, Goldshaw and Barley. The West Close group is to be expected as the Chattox family lived there while the Goldshaw group is the largest - this can be explained by the fact that there are a number of incidences relating to Bull Hole Farm. Furthermore, the village of Newchurch, with its parish church, was the focal point of the western Forest and those travelling south from Barley, or north from West Close would pass through the village.

Running counter to the concentrated pattern of incidence in the west we find that there is not a single reported incidence within the north-eastern Forest district of Blacko. In fact the two corridors converge on the parish of Barley which, with its back to Pendle Hill, forms the very heart of the Forest parishes.

In *The Lancashire Witch Conspiracy* it was suggested that the reason for this lack of reported movement around Blacko was that Demdike moved to that area after having lived in the western Forest for many years. However, it has to be said that we might expect at least a few reported incidences to have occurred in the Blacko district.

Malkin Tower from 'The Lancashire Witches'

This, then, leaves the thorny issue of Blacko having been the only written source of a name that could be reasonably applied to the Malkin Tower of Potts account. Well, perhaps this is not actually the case - the truth might have been staring us in the face all along. In the village of Barley stands a ruined farmstead by the name of Mancknowles Ing and it is to this site that attention will now be turned in the search for the elusive Malkin Tower.

When the new system of land tenure was introduced in 1507 the Forest lands were re-let to those who had held them previously. Thus we see that Barley Booth was rented out to the existing tenants at the annual sum of £10. These tenants were:

John Robinson the elder, John Robinson the younger, Richard Varley, William Varley, Roger Bollard, Margaret Bollard, Richard Bollard, James Healey and Margaret Bollard and James Manknowles. The two parcels of pasture called Haybooth and Wheatley Haybooth, both attached to Barley Booth, were demised by copy of Court Roll for £8 to James Hargreaves, Robert Bulcock, John Bulcock, William Holgate, John Robinson the elder, John Robinson the younger, Thomas Varley, Robert Varley and Roger Hartley.

By 1607 Christopher Bulcock was the largest copyholder in Barley and Wheatley while other tenants were the wife of William Robinson, James Hartley, Robert Swire, Richard Bollard, James Bollard, Miles Crabtree, Richard Woodroffe, gent., James Hartley, Christopher Robinson, John Robinson, Agnes and Lawrence Hargreaves, John Robinson senior and junior, William and Roger Hartley, Robert and Thomas Varley, John Bulcock and John Manknowles.

And so it can be seen that many of the names relating to the witch story were old tenants of Barley Booth. The particular name that interests us for now is that of Mancknowles. A John Mancknowles was listed as a freeholder of the Honor of Clitheroe in 1443 and by 1453 he was living at Townhouse in Great Marsden. In 1480 John owned land in Trawden and Great Marsden and in 1497 the Abbey of Pontefract demised to John's son, Henry, forty acres in Great Marsden and Southfield.

By 1567 John Mancknowles, a branch of the Townhouse family, had married Alice Bollard, sister to James of Whitehough, and owned land in Barley. This land was part of an area known as Ing, from the fact that it was meadow land lying to either side of the infant Pendle Water. During the 1500s the larger area of Ing was split between the three farms of Ing Ends and Ing Head while John Mancknowles retained the parcel that became known as Mancknowles Ing. It is probable that a dwelling of sorts was erected on this parcel of land; this was more likely to have been of lower status that a fully working farm.

Today we find a semi-ruined building on the site, part of which appears to originate in the latter part of the eighteenth century. This is Mancknowles Ing Farm and was occupied well into the twentieth century (a farm survey of 1969 shows it to have been abandoned by then). However, the building as we see it appears to be of different phases and there is a suggestion that the property began life as a cottage and integral barn taking the form of a smallholding upon a small close of land - in fact very much like the proposed situation at the Chattox home in West Close. Another cottage appears to have been added to the original, this is the central bay with downstairs 'weaving' windows.

Mancknowles Ing Farm as it stands today

It is apparent that this central bay was opened up into the barn at some stage as this latter structure contains newish roof timbers and an iron girder above the door. The original cottage front has stepped three-light widows, or Pennine windows, and this would suggest a date of around 1790.

A smaller structure stood to the rear of the extant Mancknowles building. The evidence of large scattered building stone here suggests that this lost building could possibly have had an industrial purpose

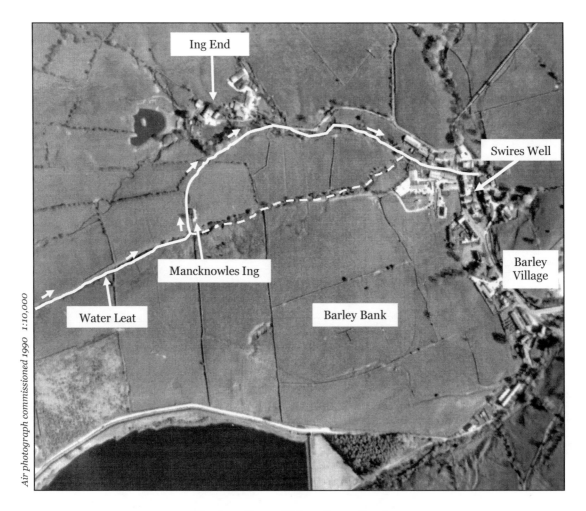

Air photograph commissioned 1990 1:10,000

The location of Mancknowles Ing

And so we find the sixteenth century site of Mancknowles Ing. Sandwiched as it is between the Pendleside village of Barley, and the foot of Pendle Hill, the site is now little more than sheep grazing with the ruins of an unremarkable farm building thereon. However, it is suggested that this unprepossessing site was actually the place where Elizabeth Southern and her Device family lived and from where they were dragged unceremoniously to meet their fate at Lancaster.

The argument for this having been the site of Malkin Tower, then, goes as follows:

Perhaps of most importance, we have a name of three syllables in *Manc-knowles-Ing*. This is rather a mouthful and it is almost certain that the name would have been colloquially shortened to *Mank-ing* or *Mank-ling*. Thus we have a second example of the name within Pendle - and at the very heart of Pendle at that!

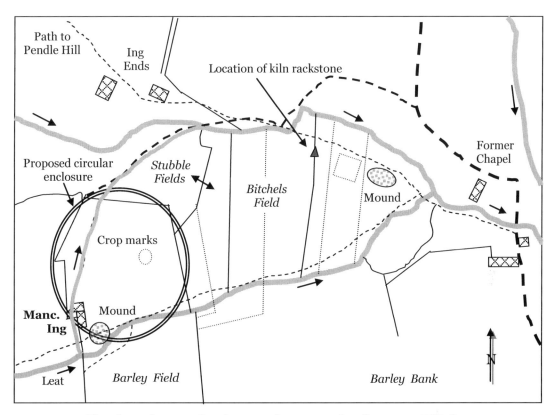

Path to Pendle Hill

Ing Ends

Location of kiln rackstone

Proposed circular enclosure

Stubble Fields

Bitchels Field

Former Chapel

Mound

Crop marks

Mound

Manc. Ing

Leat

Barley Field

Barley Bank

N

Plan based on early nineteenth century land survey. The fine dotted lines represent field boundaries that have now disappeared

The building at Mancknowles Ing stands within the south-western corner of a series of enclosure walls. It is apparent from air photographs that the walls were erected to enclose what would have originally been a circular enclosure as illustrated on the above plan. The land within this circle does not display the same division axis as its neighbours - in other words the other fields were formerly divided into north-south orientated strips while the Mancknowles enclosure was void of these strips. Further to this, air photographs again show that there is a distinct possibility of there having been a rectilinear enclosure within the larger circle and on the western edge of this feature can be seen the outline of a smaller circle.

There is also evidence of occupation, or building, to the west of the Mancknowles enclosure where a mound sits adjacent to the footpath from Barley to Pendle hill. This feature takes the form of an elongated ridge culminating in a defined mound and this is surrounded by a ditch. On the flanks of the mound is what looks very much like an early quern stone used for grinding grain into flour. The mound suggests a former site of occupation, as does the Mancknowles enclosure - the question is, if this is indeed the case, what date can be assigned to these sites?

169

*Probable quadrant of
a broken saddle quern*

The simple answer to the question of dating is that we do not know. Without the benefit of geophysical survey and archaeological assessment it is not possible to confirm the suggested features or to date the continuity of the site. However, what we can say is that it is very likely that a smallholding or industrial building stood within the immediate location of Mancknowles Ing during the sixteenth century.

A man-made watercourse runs from the slopes of Pendle Hill in an almost straight one-kilometre line down to meet Barley Water to the rear of Wilkinsons Farm. A straight watercourse of this nature was commonly created as a leat in order to supply power to a water mill. At Mancknowles Ing there is evidence for the leat having been diverted down the hill directly past the site of the present building and this raises the question as to whether a former building on the present site was water-powered. If this was the case then we would expect there to have been a water corn mill, a woollen fulling mill or perhaps a blacksmithing operation. On the other hand water could have been required for other purposes such as brewing ale or sheep dipping.

The subject of a possible mill at Mancknowles, or somewhere in the vicinity, is particularly interesting when we see that the field to the west of the site was known as *'Bitchels Field.'* The first thing that springs to mind here is that the name is a derogatory term for a certain type of woman - if this had indeed been the site of Malkin Tower than is easy to see that it would have been given a less than flattering appellation following the 1612 trials. However, as usual, there is a caveat; the Old English word *bæcestre* (*bakester* becoming *baxter)* means *baker* while *bæcel* is related to the *baker's place.* This becomes particularly interesting as I found a rackstone in one of the walls enclosing the Bitchels Field. Rackstones are stones of uniform thickness (typically around fifteen centimetres) and width (around 30 centimetres); along the flat surfaces are deep grooves chiselled into both faces of the rackstone and these are designed to allow the passage of hot air. A number of these stones were laid as flooring in grain drying kilns where the circulating air from a fire below would dry wheat or malt barley.

The broken length of rackstone found in the wall of Bitchels Field

Leaving the village of Barley and heading past the Mancknowles Ing area it is difficult to imagine that this was probably a hive of industry during the Medieval period. The large areas of extant ridge and furrow crop marks stand testimony to the fact that Barley Booth always provided more than its fair share of arable crops within the Pendle Forest vaccary system. It is reasonable, then, to expect that the conversion of a proportion of the corn crops grown here would have been carried out on site. In other words much of the local grain was stored, dried, ground and converted to bread, flour and meal within what now appears to be an isolated backwater. The streams running from Pendle down through Barley were ideal for the industrial processes required for grain conversion and it would be surprising, therefore, if there had been no industry here.

So . . . returning to possibility that we have the site of Malkin Tower it is reasonable to propose that the Mancknowles area had at least one kiln, possibly a bakehouse and water mill. The two storied structure of a grain kiln in particular would have stood out in relation to the single storey dwellings of the district and it would be reasonable to suggest that such a building would have been known as a 'tower.'

This is a northern type of grain kiln and the reason why they were known as grain 'towers' is clear.

Bessie Whittle was accused of breaking into the *fire-house* at Malkin Tower and stealing clothes and oatmeal. This begs the question as to whether the *fire-house* was the *'dryster's house'* as the single storey building was known.

Was Malkin Tower an abandoned grain kiln of this type?

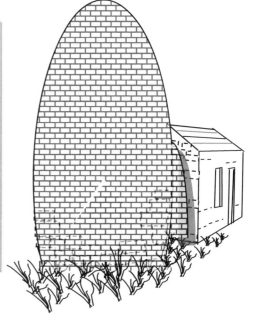

So far, then, the argument for Mancknowles includes the name having been shortened to *Mank -Ing*, which is almost identical to the *Mawking, Malking* and *Malkin* given in Potts. We have also seen a possibility for the 'tower' appellation in that the Barley site would have contained industrial buildings. Furthermore, there is a strong probability that the site has been occupied in one way or another for a very long time - the stone from a kiln structure, and the probably quern stone were found within metres of each other and indicate that the conversion of grain has been going on here for over two thousand years.

To press on with Malkin Tower mystery, the following is the abridged statement given by James Device in relation to the Good Friday meeting at Malkin Tower:

The said Iames Deuice saith, That on Good-Friday last, about twelue of the clocke in the day time, there dined in this Examinates said mothers house, at Malking-Tower, a number of persons, whereof three were men, with this Examinate, and the rest women . . . And he also sayth, That the names of the said Witches as were on Good-Friday at this Examinates said Grandmothers house, and now this Examinates owne mothers, for so many of them as hee did know, were these, viz.

The wife of Hugh Hargreiues of Burley; the wife of Christopher Bulcock, of the Mosse end, and Iohn her sonne; the mother of Myles Nutter; Elizabeth, the wife of Christopher Hargreiues, of Thurniholme; Christopher Howgate, and Elizabeth, his wife; Alice Graye of Coulne, and one Mould-heeles wife, of the same: and this Examinate, and his Mother. And this Examinate further sayth, That all the Witches went out of the said House in their owne shapes and likenesses. And they all, by that they were forth of the dores, gotten on Horsebacke, like vnto Foales, some of one colour, some of another; and Prestons wife was the last: and when shee got on Horsebacke, they all presently vanished out of this Examinates sight.

According to James those present were the wife of Hugh Hargreaves of Barley, Jane Bulcock and her son John Bulcock of Moss End, Alice Nutter of Roughlee, Elizabeth Hargreaves of Thorneyholme (Roughlee), Christopher Holgate and his wife (actually Isobell not Elizabeth), Alice Gray of Colne, Katherine Hewitt of Colne, Jennet Preston of Gisburn, James Device, his mother Elizabeth Device and young sister Jennet Device. When the 'innocent' Jennet Device is taken out of the equation we have, interestingly enough, twelve people - the optimum number for a diabolical meeting.

Young Jennet said that there were twenty people at the meeting but she only knew six of them (her own family apart) - she included Christopher 'Jackes' Hargreaves where James had omitted to say that he was actually at the meeting. James Device, then, knew more of the people at the meeting than did his youngest sister; this is not surprising as he was grown man and would have had a wider social contact. The people that Jennet did know were: the wife of Hugh Hargreaves of Barley, Christopher Holgate of Barley and his wife, Alice Nutter of Roughlee, Christopher and Elizabeth Hargreaves of Thorneyholme, her brother James Device and mother Elizabeth Device. Leaving out the family this number consists of three people from Roughlee and three people from Barley. It is suggested, therefore, that young Jennet's social breadth had not expanded beyond the immediate neighbourhood - she was aware only of her neighbours and this puts her home of Malkin Tower between Roughlee and Barley.

Taking another look at James' statement we see that he included John and Jane Bulcock where Jennet did not. It is usually taken that the Bulcock home of Moss End was situated below the village of Newchurch, at Goldshaw, but it has to be said that this is not proven. The farm could also have been one of the Black Moss properties on the outskirts of Barley; farms here were occupied by the Bulcock families for many generations. If this is correct then James described five people from Barley and two from Roughlee. The remainder of the assembly described by James were friends and relatives of the Southern/Device family.

It is also pertinent to the issue that James Device stole a whether from Christopher Swire (alias Robinson) of Barley in order to feed the guests at the Malkin meeting. Both the Robinsons and Swires farmed around the vicinity of the Barley hamlet, including the land on which the old Pendle Inn stood and the new inn now stands, and a Swires Well exists near to the garage to this day. James, then, had only to go a hundred metres or so to find the sheep on the night before Good Friday.

―――――――――

The Clitheroe Court Rolls contain a link between the gentry and Mancknowles Ing. A member of the landowning gentry by the name of Randle Holker was a close neighbour and relative of Roger Nowell in Read. Randle, and his wife Jennet, had a son John and we find that in 1610 John married Elizabeth, the daughter of James Hartley. There is nothing remarkable about this until it is realised that this James Hartley, of Barley, owned Mancknowles Ing.

John Holker took over the family lands in Read and Simonstone and these were rented out to John Robinson (son of Edmund) of Old Laund in Pendle and Robert Bulcock of Whitehough in Barley. The Moss End family of John and Jane Bulcock, of Good Friday fame, was related to the Bulcock family of Whitehough which lay to the east of Barley, in the Pendle Water valley. In 1610 Christopher Bulcock of Whitehough, the son of Christopher who was, in turn, the son of Robert of Whitehough, was granted lands belonging to Randal Holker, gent, of Read. Christopher senior built the earlier part of the extant Whitehough Grange the south porch of which carries an inscription; *This house was builded by Christofer Bulcocke and Jennet his wife 1593.*

We have, then, a very interesting scenario relating to the proposed site of Malking Tower. Elizabeth Device was said to have bewitched brothers John and James Robinson of Barley. James Device implicated John and Jane Bulcock in the Good Friday meeting when it appears that they were never there. Henry Bulcock, of Whitehough or Black Moss, came one day to Malkin Tower to ask Alison Device to remove a spell that she had supposedly placed on his daughter.

This gives the distinct impression that there was little love lost between the Malkin Tower crew, the Bulcocks and the Robinsons. We then see that the daughter of the owner of Mancknowles Ing, the proposed Malkin site, was married to a close friend and neighbour of Roger Nowell who rented land out to the enemies of the Demdikes. Is the date of 1610, when James Hartley's daughter married John Holker of Read, of significance? Well, it is probable that within a period of the following eighteen months the Malkin Tower property reverted back to its owner - perhaps what we see here is the reason why the witch roundup of 1612 was instigated. James Hartley, the Bulcocks and the Robinsons wanted the Demdikes removing from the neighbourhood and their chance came when Hartley's daughter began to move in influential circles.

Whitehough - built by the Bulcock family

Upper Houses - Barley

Roughlee Old Hall

Bridge End - Barley

Original Pendle Inn - Barley

Mancknowles Ing remained in the Hartley family until 1812 when William Hartley, of Fencegate House, convened the property to Thomas Grimshaw of Barrowford. In 1824 Grimshaw was to build Higherford Mill at Barrowford upon land he had gained through his marriage to Grace Gibson, niece of two Bulcock brothers. These latter were a branch of the Whitehough family of Bulcocks. The property of Mancknowles Ing was described as one messuage or dwelling house, one garden, one close of land called Higgin Ing, one barn with house adjoining and closes called Mancknowles Ing in Barley Booth.

175

Roof timbers over the Mancknowles Ing cottage

Hewn ridge plate   Hewn slate lathes   Hewn rafters   Sawn plaster lathes

The same caveat applies to the Mancknowles Ing building as it does to the Heys property in West Close. A raised trackway has now become a footpath and passes within metres of the building, however, the building itself is on private land. Furthermore, the roof is in an extremely dangerous condition and could easily collapse - the building should not be approached.

For the sake of safety the above photograph, showing the rafters in the roof of the cottage, was taken by means of a remote boom through the upstairs window. Here it can be seen that the rough-hewn rafters, slate lathes and ridge plate do not appear to be contemporary with the building. Other timber components, such as the purlins, joists, floor boards and plaster lathes are of sawn timber, as would be expected of a house of this period. The downstairs ceilings have hewn beams but these were added post-construction for decorative purposes only.

The exposed rafters in the above photograph are, as far as can be seen from the limitations of the survey, from an earlier building and have been reused in their present position. Without safe access to the internal roof it is not possible to inspect the hewn rafters; if this had been possible then the timbers could be used to extrapolate the size and type of the building from which they originated. The question will be asked, of course, are these early timbers actually remnants of Malkin Tower?

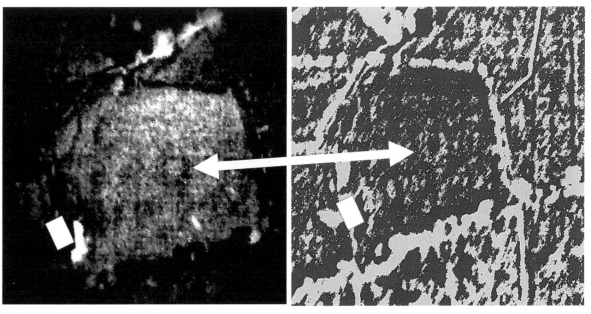

The Mancknowles enclosure

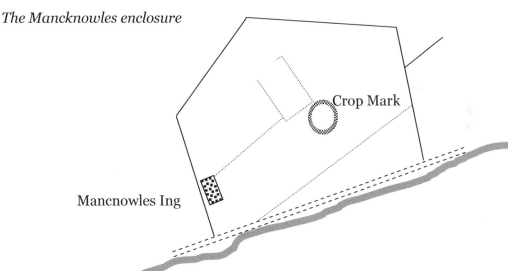

The two images above are reversed versions of the same image of the Mancknowles Ing enclosure, taken from a 1990 1:10,000 air photograph. A circular feature thirteen metres in diameter can be clearly seen toward the middle of the enclosure - the outline of this feature appears to take the form of a double ditch and this would suggest a very early date. However, the outline could also be a crop mark caused by the stone foundations of a circular building - a grain kiln? Only archaeological assessment can answer this question and this would make a fascinating project for the future.

PART THREE ~ CONCLUSION

We do not know the full background of the two main characers within our story. Within the foregoing text an attempt has been made to provide a best scenario based upon the available records and this is, perhaps, as close as we will get without an extensive archaeological survey.

Demdike and her family lived at Malkin Tower in 1612 but it is not clear how she came to be there. It is likely that her daughter, Elizabeth Device, lived with her husband John in a cottage attached to the farm on which he worked. This could well have been somewhere within the Barley and Goldshaw districts - Elizabeth had a child by a Sellers and there were two suspects here. A family of Sellers lived at Dean Farm, a short distance along the Sabden valley from Newchurch, while another Sellers family could be found on one of the Under Pendle farms, a few fields to the west of Mancknowles Ing.

Demdike's son, Christopher Holgate, would have worked the Holgate farm at Barley, or one of the Robinson farms of his wife's family at Barley. This would have given him the opportunity to arrange for his mother to live in the abandoned property of a grain kiln which stood somewhere within the Mancknowles Ing site. Following the death of John Device, his widow Elizabeth would have needed to find a new home for herself and her children and it appears that she moved into Malkin Tower (Mank Ing?) with her mother.

Recorded evidence for the site of the Chattox homestead, and Demdike's Malkin Tower, is scanty indeed but perhaps we are now as near to them as we have ever been. The Malkin Tower Farm at Blacko proudly carries the name we have been in search of and this is the obvious place to look. However, despite the fact that the area does have a fascinating history of its own this site is miles in distance from the focus of the story. The neighbours of the Demdike clan were clustered around Newchurch and Barley and this has to be taken as firm evidence.

The suggestion that Malkin was situated at Saddlers in Newchurch is tempered by the fact that there does not appear to be any *written evidence* for a Malkin site here, only hearsay. If pushed, then, on present available evidence I would rate each site at a probability of:

Blacko = 5%   Saddlers area = 30%   Mancknowles area= 65%

FINAL CONCLUSION

Where there is history there is an extremely tangled web of truth and half-truth, the gaps often being filled with supposition. Such is the case within the popular view of the Pendle Witches.

Our view of the witches has a basis within fiction and fantasy where the image of the black-clad, pointy-hatted, broomstick-bound hag with a huge warty hooter is as accurate as the description of Cinderella with hobnailed boots and smoking an opium pipe. For centuries Medieval dramatists and social commentators propounded our perceived version of the witch attending the diabolical Sabbath, consulting demonic familiars and selling their souls to the devil.

The Demdike brood were not popular with their farming neighbours and it appears that by 1612 certain members of the community had come to the end of their tether. For a long time magistrate Roger Nowell had been hearing of the exploits of Elizabeth Southern and her Device family. Complaints had been made to him by the gentry family of Towneley and these sat alongside reports made by the local yeomen farmers of Baldwin, Bulcock, Mitton, Hargreaves and Robinson *et al.* Nowell was also in receipt of a number of complaints by his fellow magistrate, Richard Shuttleworth, concerning the misdeeds on his land of Old Chattox and her family. The further reports of the gentry family of John and Hugh Moor, of Higham, meant that Nowell was under increasing pressure to act.

The Elizabethan period was one in which espionage had reached new heights of sophistication - spies acting for the church or the Crown were everywhere. This situation did not diminish during the reign of James I and it is clear that the local gentry had their spies also. The Gawthorpe accounts for 1620 show that half-a-fifteenth was paid to the constable of Padiham for *'watching the supposed witches.'* There had been a levy on the township of Padiham to the sum of 2½d for the purpose of keeping a close eye on certain members of the community who were suspected of practising witchcraft and the half-a-fifteenth was Richard Shuttleworth's quota towards this.

There is every likelihood, therefore, that a similar system was in operation in the run-up to the 1612 witch roundup.

By the end of 1611 Roger Nowell had a full list of people accused by their neighbours of being witches. Perhaps the final straw came when his friend and neighbour, Randal Holker, told him that his son's father-in-law wanted to rid his land of the witches at Malkin Tower.

In the meantime, another friend of Nowell's, Sir Thomas Gerard of Bryn, had been relating diabolical stories of the Chelmsford witch trials over which his uncle, Gilbert Gerard, had presided. This latter was a man who had married into the powerful Radcliffe family and as such he owned a great deal of land and property within Pendle Forest.This meant that the Gerards had their own axe to grind when it came to removing a public nuisance in the form of a local group of witches.

All the fantastical elements of the Pendle trials were present at the earlier trial; demonic familiars called Tibb and Sathan, Sabbatical meetings, innocent people bewitched to death. Nowell saw his chance of solving the problem of an apparent witchcraft outbreak on his own patch - he enlisted the help of Sir Thomas Gerard whose experience was to be put to good use.

Nowell now had a clear plan in as much as he would find an excuse to arrest a younger member of the so-called witch clans and in so doing would be able to manipulate the evidence. He would ensure that his examinate would incriminate others by placing before them the names on his list. Once he had gathered 'evidence' against all of those people who had been reported to him it would be time to take the next step - a show trial which would include all the titillating diabolism of the Chelmsford trial before it.

Nowell's plan went like clockwork. Thomas Gerard was brought into the affair and probably laised with the Lawe family to get the ball rolling. The initial arrest followed the Colne Field affair where Alison Device's dog chased John Lawe. Almost as a throwaway line in Potts we see that Lawe's son, Abraham Lawe, mentioned that Alison was accompanied by *'one other old woman who this examinate did not know'* and so Alison was probably accompanied by her grandmother, Demdike. This is never picked up on in the story but it could very well point to the fact that Alison was to be the scapegoat - why was Demdike herself not immediately blamed for laming Lawe?

The reason why Alison was blamed was probably because Nowell knew that a youngster would be far more likely to tell him what he wanted to hear than a taciturn and wily old woman. And so it proved - Alison sang like a canary and soon the main contenders on Nowell's list were safely locked away at Lancaster. However, this was not good enough; Elizabeth Device and her two children were still in residence at Mank Ing Tower and the neighbours were not happy.

However, this would be short-lived. When a few friends and relatives gathered at Mank Ing to discuss the situation of Demdike and Alison being incarcerated the matter was reported Nowell by his constable, Henry Hargreaves. In another master-stroke Nowell arrested Elizabeth and James Device and the others they so willingly reported as having been at the meeting - including Jennet Preston of Gisburn who Nowell's friend, Lister of Westby, wanted arresting (although it is possible that Jennet Preston never was at the Good Friday meeting).

The fact that there had been a gathering of people played right into Nowell's hands as he was able to show his trump card; the affair was played up into a full-blown Sabbath and this was sure to convince any jury of the guilt of all those present. The icing on the cake was the fact that eleven year old Jennet Device allowed herself to be manipulated into giving evidence against everyone she knew.

Having embelished the 'evidence' of the accused Nowell took the case to trial where the judge instructed the apparent inveterate gambler, 'Bad Sir Cuthbert Halsall' to hand-pick a jury of *gentlemen suitable for the task'* - in other words he was charged with the task of rigging the jury.

The popular notion of the Pendle Witch legend, then, is nothing other than Medieval broadsheet fantasy. Very little of the evidence that Potts related was actually based on fact and, rather than the diabolical witches of legend, we see in 1612 a long-simmering revenge exacted upon what amounted to a public nuisance.

The Demdike clan would probably have been under ASBO supervision in this day and age, they were certainly not averse to thieving when the opportunity arose. The Chattox family were probably no better; Bessie Whittle had burgled Malkin Tower and was imprisoned at Lancaster in 1613 for some offence or other. We can be certain of one thing, however, if they had been living today they would not have paid with their lives.

BIBLIOGRAPHY

Ainsworth, W. H The Lancashire Witches - a Romance of Pendle Forest 1854
Bannister, F The Annals of Trawden Forest 1922
Bennet, W The History of Burnley - Vols 1 and 2 1946
Bennet, W The History of Marsden and Nelson 1957
Bennet, W The Pendle Witches 1957
Blakey, J Annals of Barrowford 1929
Brigg, M The Early History of the Forest of Pendle
Brigg, M The Forest of Pendle in the Seventeenth Century; Part Two (paper) 1963
Byrne, C H Newchurch-in-Pendle – Folklore fact and Fiction 1982
Camden, W Britannia - 1695 reprint of 1586 original
Carr, J Annals and Stories of Colne 1878
Chetham Soc. Wonderfull Discoverie of Witches in the Countie of Lancaster -
      written by Thomas Potts 1613 and republished 1845
Clayton, J. A Valley of the Drawn Sword - History of Burnley, Pendle & Craven 2006
Conroy, M. P Backcloth to Gawthorpe 1971
Crowther, D Various unpublished genealogies
Dyffy, E The Voices of Morebath 2001 Yale University Press
Farrar, W Clitheroe Court Rolls - Vols 1, 2 and 3 1912
Fell, J Window on Whalley
Harland & Wilkinson Lancashire Legends 1873
Harrison, D The History of Colne (Pendle Heritage) 1998
Hopwood, E The Lancashire Weaver's Story - Amalgamated Weavers Assoc. 1969
Kenyon, D The Origins of Lancashire 1991
Lambert, Ven. C H Whalley Abbey – Yesterday and Today
Lancashire Parish Register Soc. Indexes and Registers of Newchurch-in-Pendle 2002
Lumby, J The Lancashire Witch Craze 1995
Macvicar, J. R Colne Parish Church 1944
Moncrief, A. R. H Classic Myth and Legend - Gresham
Moorhouse, C The Birth of a Lancashire Village (Sabden) 1975
Mullett & Warren Martyrs of the Diocese of Lancaster 1987
Pearson, S Rural Houses of the Lancashire Pennines 1985
Peel & Southern The Trials of the Lancashire Witches 1969
Poole, R ed. The Lancashire Witches - Histories and Stories 2002
Smith, R Blackburnshire - occasional paper of 1961
Snape, A. W English Martyrs Whalley 2000
Spencer, K. G An Outline History of Habergham Eaves 1989
Starkey, D The Monarchy of England - Vol 1 2004
Whitaker, T. D The History of Whalley - 1st edition 1881
Whitaker, T. D The History of Craven 1885
Walton, J Pendle Forest Folk 1950
Welch, M Anglo-Saxon England (English Heritage) 1992
Whittaker, G Roughlee Hall - Fact and Fiction 1980
Williams, E Walks and Talks with Fellman 1951

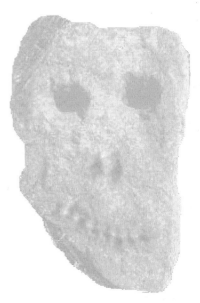

OTTOMAN EMBROIDERY

Roderick Taylor

with line drawings by Antony Maitland

STUDIO
VISTA

A STUDIO VISTA BOOK

First published in the UK
1993 by Studio Vista
(a Cassell imprint)
Villiers House
41/47 Strand
London
WC2N 5JE

Distributed in Australia
by Capricorn Link (Australia) Pty Ltd
P.O. Box 665, Lane Cove, NSW 2066

Designed and produced by
Alphabet & Image Ltd, Sherborne, Dorset DT9 3LU

British Library Cataloguing-in-Publication Data
A catalogue record for this book is available from
the British Library

ISBN 0-289-80084-6

Typeset by Kendalls, Milborne Port, Sherborne, Dorset DT9 5EB
Printed in Hong Kong by Regent Publishing Services.

Frontispiece A quilt facing made of four strips with a pattern based on an architectural ogival design which can be seen in drawings of Timurid carpets and in a Turkish carpet of
1600 attributed to Brusa. The four-lobed design is based on curving leaves filled with a
stylized flower head, the repeats on the left overflow the central ground. The border is
composed of a leaf tendril and formal flower heads. Silk single darning on linen. *c.* 1600.
230 x 137 cm. *cf.* Museum of Islamic Art, Berlin. Brusa carpet. Inv. 97, 58.

Contents

6

Foreword

The Ottoman Turks had a passion for decoration that allowed them to leave no surface undecorated; this passion is evident in every aspect of their lives. Their architecture is emphasized by painted and coloured stucco work inside and by coloured tiles both inside and out, and bright miniatures illuminate their books. They used woven textiles covered with elaborate designs for their costume and furnishings, and they spread patterned and multi-coloured knotted and flat-weave carpets in their mosques and palaces and even in the most modest of their houses.

The decoration in all these forms is bold and rich in both the patterns that were developed and in the colours used. The ability to use shapes and colours, to place them with surety and with an innate design sense, is the great strength of their decorative art, especially when it is combined, as it invariably is, with great technical skill. Their addiction to decoration in public is carried into their private life at home, which is more informal and less rigid than that in the Western world. Despite this informality there are clearly established conventions of behaviour and social status that are very carefully followed. Even the fragile and ephemeral articles used daily are decorated, prime among them being the many textiles which were in constant use in the house.

This book is mainly concerned with the various forms of the embroidered domestic textiles, although some reference is made to the larger, more public, textiles made for the palaces and the civil services. My intention is to show how the various textiles were used, the way they reflected the life of the people who used them and how they were altered to fit in with social changes during the centuries. The emphasis of the book will be on the embroideries made in the Turkish mainland in Asia and Europe during the six centuries that the Ottoman Empire endured, but it will also cover some of the embroideries made further afield in the Empire by the various peoples within it that were influenced by the Ottoman style.

The same articles were made over many centuries, retaining their original shapes and proportions. In many cases they are known today by the name they originally had even though the use to which they are put

One end of a woman's sash with a single motif of branches rising from a shallow tray with a narrow base panel of a small tendril design. Gold thread and gilded strip on a cotton ground. *c.* 1850. 30 x 30 cm.

may have changed. This book will show how a continuous tradition of embroidered textiles has persisted from before the capture of Istanbul in 1453 to the creation of the Turkish Republic in October 1923 and how some part of it has survived until today. It will not attempt to make a complete historical analysis of how the patterns used were developed, other than by placing them in an historical context. The book will identify the stitches used but will not attempt to show how they were all worked.

My interest in Ottoman embroidery started with my first visit to Turkey in 1957 and much of my information was collected, rather informally, at that time. The main sources of my information were the ladies in families that I met, other collectors and the dealers in the bazaars and street markets. At that time it was possible to find great piles of embroideries and textiles in most of the bazaars and markets. I found them not only in Istanbul and across the Bosphorus in Üsküdar, but also in Kayseri and the smaller towns in Cappadocia. All the dealers had wonderful stories about how they had found the pieces; usually they came from the last harem lady who had been expelled from Topkapi Palace and every piece that I was offered was invariably dated from the sixteenth century. New and old pieces were sold together, some of them looking as if they had been worn right up to the minute at which they were offered for sale.

Many of the houses I visited still used embroidered textiles for different purposes and in some of them they were still being made. Admittedly the work was more perfunctory than would have been acceptable in an earlier age. In reading accounts left by earlier collectors I see that this comment has been made many times before: it is certain that a collector in 1792 deplored the deterioration in design and workmanship from the great period of 1592.

I started to buy embroideries on my first visit there but, surprisingly, it was only on my return to England that I found it possible to indulge my new passion, the collecting of Ottoman and Greek Island embroideries. They were available in large quantities, appearing as the last, undesirable mixed lots in auctions or in street markets, presumably as a result of the clearing out of attics and the dissolution of large houses, a process which released many art treasures onto the general market. Many other objects may have been more valuable in terms of price but few rivalled the textiles in terms of charm, artistry and skill.

Sadly it is not as easy to find these textiles now, and they have become scarce even in Turkey. The asking price is beyond the means of most collectors; these and other textiles have now fallen into that group of objects that are bought as investments in the hope of substantial future profits. Many pieces have been butchered to make small pieces of trite tourist souvenirs, joining a large volume of commercially produced embroideries most of which are equally worthless.

The interest that does exist in these textiles is mainly channelled towards the oldest and grandest pieces, while the smaller, domestic pieces are neglected. Perhaps this book will help to redress the balance and show how wonderful the small domestic pieces are and how worthwhile they are to collect.

Language note

I have attempted to give the Turkish names of the various articles wherever possible, often with a literal translation, because I believe that knowing what the words mean allows one to understand them better. In order not to break the flow of the text this information has been added in notes at the bottom of the page, together with any etymological information that helps in understanding the usage or development of the piece.

I have used standard Turkish orthography even for words from Ottoman Turkish, Arabic and Persian which may not be in current use today. The transliteration is far more disputable: Turkish was never satisfactorily rendered in the Arabic script and romanised version also presents problems, particularly in words derived from Arabic. The name of the Head of the Islamic religion is written differently as Caliph, Calif, Khalif, Khaleef or even Kalif, and each of them can be justified under one system or another; it is a matter of choice which one uses. Equally the stitch called 'muşabak' can be written muşabek, mushabbek or musabbik.

Most consonants in Turkish are pronounced as in English, except:

c   is a hard j as in jar
ç   is a soft ch as in church
ğ   is hardly sounded at all, it is almost a breathed-in glottal stop
j   is a soft j as in the French je, and it is only used in introduced words
ş   is a soft sh as in ship
v   is pronounced softly, almost a w sound

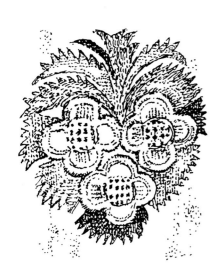

Turkish has more ways of writing the many vowel sounds that are covered in the Romance languages by the five vowels, but even these do not give the whole range of vowel sounds in the language. Turkish emphasizes the vowel harmony within words, changing the vowel in suffixes to harmonize with the dominant vowel sound in the main word. In addition to the five standard vowels Turkish also uses:

ı   is an unstressed e as in egg
ö   as the diphthong ea in earnest
ü   as the diphthong oo in shoot

In general all vowel sounds are short and words, if stressed, are stressed on the last syllable.

Marginal references are to relevant illustrations.

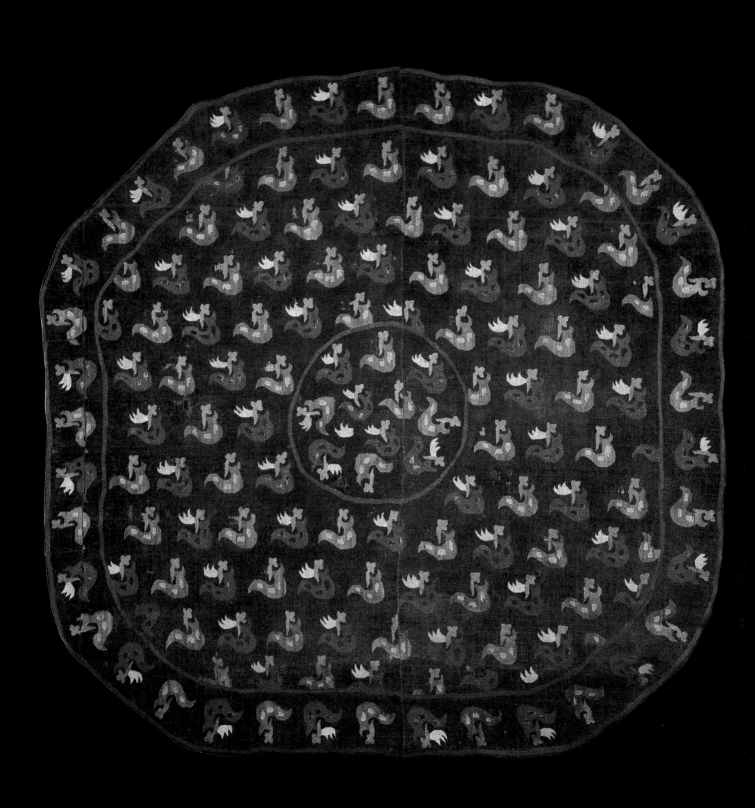

1 Background to an Empire

History

The Ottoman Empire lasted for over 600 years, from 1299 to 1923. The period from 1299 until the capture of Istanbul in 1453 can be seen as the time during which it established itself. It expanded until 1683, when it achieved its greatest power, and then slowly declined until the creation of the Republic of Turkey on 29 October 1923. At its height the Empire stretched from Morocco in the west to the Persian frontier in the east, from Vienna in the north to Aden in the south. At that time the Ottomans governed over 250,000 square miles with an estimated population of eight million people.

The peoples who became the Ottomans arrived in the Middle East as part of the great invasions of tribal nomadic peoples moving westwards out of Central Asia. These peoples arrived in waves as small groups of mercenaries who allied themselves to local rulers or as small armies who conquered territories on their own behalf.

The first of the great armies to create an empire in Asia Minor was that of the Seljuk Turks; they arrived in Turkey after having attacked a weak Persia and after having captured Baghdad from the Abbasid Caliph in 1055. They then attacked the eastern Roman Empire and under Alp Arslan defeated the Romans at Manzikert in 1071, capturing the Emperor Romanus Digenes. The Seljuk Empire eventually withdrew into Asia Minor and survived there as the Kingdom of Rum with twin capitals at Konya and Nicaea until the death of Ala-ud-din Kaikobad in 1307.

Within this kingdom a number of smaller principalities were established, one of which was that of the Oghuz Turks who had moved into Asia Minor about 1240. Under the tribal Chief, Toğrul, the Oghuz ruled an area around Ankara and started their conquests towards the west. At the dissolution of the Seljuk Empire the Oghuz were ruled by Toğrul's son, Osman, who had already captured Nicaea for the Seljuk Sultan. Osman and his son Orhan captured Bursa in 1326 and established the capital of their own empire there. Thus it was that the

A circular cover with a central circle and a broad outer border. The whole ground is covered with repeats of a very stylized form of a leaf and flower. Single darning in silk worked diagonally on a dark blue linen ground. Before 1700. 105 cm.

Ottoman Empire came to be regarded as named after Osman, the first independent ruler.

The Ottomans, even at this early date, had designs on the Byzantine Empire to the west. Orhan's second wife was Theodora, the daughter of John Cantacuzenos who was one of the claimants to the Byzantine throne, and through this marriage the Ottomans considered that they had a legal claim on Byzantium. In order to reinforce this claim they waged war on the Empire and in 1352 Orhan's son, Suleiman, captured Çimpe in Gallipoli, the first conquest made by the Ottomans in Europe. Orhan's second son, Murad, captured Edirne to the west of Constantinople (Istanbul) in 1361, starting the process of surrounding the City[1] and isolating it from its former Empire. After Murad became Sultan he extended the Empire into Bulgaria and Serbia before being killed at the Battle of Kossovo in 1389.

Between that date and 1453 seven successive Sultans continued their campaigns into Europe, conquering most of the Balkans and defeating a coalition of armies led by the Hungarians at Varna in 1444.

In 1453 Mehmed II the Conqueror captured Constantinople (Istanbul). This was the final defeat of the Byzantine Empire, which had been reduced to the City itself, having lost everything outside it. Mehmed moved his capital to the City, which became the centre of the Ottoman Empire. All power was centralized in the renamed Istanbul, and in the view of most foreigners at that time Istanbul *was* the Empire. It might even be said that for them it was the Sultan's palace at Topkapi, the Sublime Porte, that was the Empire.

The Empire grew in every direction from that date, achieving its greatest growth under Suleiman the Great between 1520 and 1560. The Franks had been removed from most of mainland Greece by 1461, the Knights Hospitallers were removed from their headquarters in Rhodes in 1523 and the Hungarians were defeated at Mohacz in 1526, leaving the Ottomans as rulers of the whole of the Balkans.

In the south the Ottomans conquered the Mamluk Empire in 1517, displacing the Turki Mamluks that had been established there since 1250. They acquired all its territories in Egypt, Syria and Palestine and gained control of Arabia from the Gulf Coast down to Muscat in the east and along the Red Sea down to south of the Holy Cities of Mecca and Medina. By this conquest they not only extended their Empire geographically and politically but gained religious control over the Islamic world. The Caliphate that had moved to Cairo from Baghdad was moved to Istanbul and the Ottoman Sultans became hereditary Caliphs. The fact that they also controlled the Holy Cities authorized and legitimized this action.

During this time the Ottoman fleet, under Barbarossa, sailed westwards across the Mediterranean, capturing Algiers in 1516 and Tunis in 1523. Control of these territories proved difficult, particularly as the Ottomans had failed to capture Malta after a long siege in 1566 and

were defeated by a European fleet at Lepanto in 1571. Algiers and Tunis were ruled by local Deys from that date and, although subject to the Sultan, in practice they ruled independently and established their own dynasties. The expansion of the Ottomans westwards was halted and they remained in the western Mediterranean only as pirates harassing the European trading traffic.

In the east the fortunes of the Ottomans changed continuously. They were expelled from Persia in 1585 by the Safavid Shahs after a decade of a debilitating war but they recaptured Baghdad in 1639. To the north they conquered a large part of the Caucasus, stretching from the Black Sea to the Caspian, including Daghestan and Georgia. They occupied parts of southern Russia, the principalities of Moldavia, Bessarabia and Wallachia. They controlled these areas by selling the Governorships to rich merchants from the Christian Phanar section of Istanbul who then installed themselves as Princes and rulers. Where the Ottomans did not conquer they established treaties, first with the Crimean Tartars and then with the Uzbek and Bokharan Sultans of Turkestan.

The expansion of the Empire in Europe was halted in 1683 when the army under the Grand Vizier, Ahmed Köprülü, failed to take Vienna after a long siege. This was seen as a great failure and the peace treaties of Karlovitz in 1699 and Passarowitz in 1717 started to exclude the Ottomans from Europe.

Not only was the Empire threatened from outside by losing battles but a number of internal changes were equally destructive. Selim III began to realise that the organisation of the Janissary Corps was partly responsible for the defeats and that the army was too powerful and

p. 144–7, 154, 155

A cushion cover, most probably part of a set of bed furnishings. A portion of regular trellis with stylized flowers at the intersections, each space filled with a decorated pomegranate. Single tight darning on cotton ground. Before 1650. 105 x 46 cm.

13

needed to be restrained. He was also affected by the new rationalism and liberalism in Europe and tried to institute a program of change that was resisted for twenty years. Eventually his successor, Mahmud II, was able to defeat and disband the Janissaries and replace them with the New Organisation, the Nizam Jedid, in 1826.

This was the start of the movement which culminated in the Tanzimat, the Reform Movement, which led to the first Ottoman Constitution in 1876 and to the first Parliament in 1877. This was abolished in the next year by Abdul Hamid II, who continued his oppressive regime until 1909 when he was deposed and the Constitution restored. In the Great War of 1914–18 Turkey was defeated by the Allied Armies and the Empire was dismembered.

In 1919 Greece invaded Turkey and a cruel war was fought between them, ending in 1922 with the establishment of new borders which further reduced the Turkish territory. The leader of the Turkish Army was Mustafa Kemal Pasha, who after the war seized power, abolishing the Sultanate in 1922 and later the Caliphate, in 1924. He secularized the clergy, abolishing many of the religious orders and seizing their property in 1924 for the new Republic of Turkey. He selected Ankara as the new capital and Istanbul was reduced to a commercial and artistic centre. After 600 years the great Ottoman Empire was reduced to about the size it had been in the middle of the fourteenth century. The Ottoman Empire can be seen to have followed the cycle that every great Empire has run: a rapid initial growth and expansion, a short period of stability and then a long gradual decline ending in some cataclysmic event. For the Ottomans this was the 1914–18 war.

The Ottomans left in their wake a disastrous system of public administration, a corrupt civil service and a legacy of national problems for the whole area of their Empire that is likely to take centuries to resolve. But they also left a lavish, exuberant and joyous artistic style.

A detail from a quilt facing with a pattern set out in rows. The main design is a pomegranate between two leaves alternating with a smaller row of çintamani and a pair of tulips. The pomegranates are worked in a heraldic pattern of red and white triangles. Double darning on a linen base. Before 1650. 219 x 155 cm, only one quarter shown.

NOTES

1. Constantinople (Istanbul) was always the 'City'. In the Greek of the period it was 'stin Poli', which by usage became the Istanbul of its conquerors.

16

Culture

Asia Minor is the point where Europe meets with Asia, not only geographically but also artistically, where the early Mesopotamian cultures link with that of the Greeks, where the art of China makes contact with the Roman Empire and where Christianity first meets Buddhism and later confronts Islam. Many of the earliest expressions of the art from the beginning of Western Civilization are to be found throughout the whole area.

Since earliest times Asia Minor has been populated with many different races, living side by side and freely inter-marrying. The Caucasian races mixed with the Semitic peoples from Egypt and Babylonia and later with the Asian invaders from China and Central Asia. Each wave of immigrants or conquerors brought with it a new culture and each was, in its turn, absorbed to some degree into the existing one, usually creating a different and greater culture. The fortunes of the various races changed from time to time, the rulers of one period becoming the subjugated of another.

The earliest recorded civilization in the area is that of the Hittites, followed by the Urartu peoples and various invaders from Persia and Babylon. The Greeks had colonized the west coast of Asia Minor from very early times; the war against Troy is thought to have taken place in 1200 BC. The Dorians and the Lydians had established empires east of the Aegean Sea many centuries before Alexander the Great passed through on his campaign of expansion to Persia and northern India in the third century BC. The Greeks were followed by the Romans who conquered both them and the native peoples. While the Armenians spread south from their homeland in the southern Caucasus to colonize southern Turkey, the Phoenicians extended their commercial empire by setting up colonies along the southern and western coasts of Turkey on their way to the west.

The advent of Christianity and its acceptance throughout the area was the first great unifying force; the earliest churches were established in Asia Minor and Syria, and nations in the Caucasus were among the first to adopt Christianity as their state religion. Constantinople (Istanbul), the New Rome,[1] became the centre of a Christian empire within which all its races and religions lived a fairly harmonious life, sharing a common culture.

The advent of Islam about seven centuries later was the second great

The central feature on this man's sash is a tent which rises from an urn like a flower. The field is covered with designs from nature; the flowers are drawn in one scale and willow trees, poplars and pines are scaled down. Silk stem stitch worked in horizontal rows, silver-wound silk and gilded silver strip on a linen ground. Edged with metal wire button-hole stitch. c. 1825. 39 x 32 cm.

event that led to the creation of an homogenous society, identified more by its adherence to a single religion than by any racial or nationalistic character. The Infidels, Christian and Jew, still found it possible to survive and to pursue their own religions within the Islamic state, having accepted the imposition of the head tax they had to pay.[2] The Christian Empire of Byzantium existed for nearly five hundred years alongside the Islamic states to its south; they exchanged diplomatic relations and traded with each other with an occasional small-scale military skirmish. This stable society was totally disrupted in the eleventh century by invaders from the east who attacked both religions, being eventually converted to Islam.

One of these tribes, the Seljuks, was the first to invade the Byzantine Empire and establish itself in Asia Minor. Seljuks had initially been persecutors of Islam and attacked and captured the Caliph in Baghdad, but they were soon converted from their tribal shamanist and animist religion and arrived in Turkey as fervent follows of Islam. They also captured Jerusalem from the Fatimids of Egypt who held it for a hundred years, and it was this event in 1071 that disturbed the relative harmony in which the three great religions had lived, and disrupted the established Pilgrim traffic to the Holy Lands. The Europeans, mainly the Italians of the City States, had had trading agreements with the Byzantine Empire since the end of the tenth century. They were established within it as merchants and had travelled through it as Pilgrims for

A napkin end decorated with four repeats of a sugar melon set in a bowl. The melon has had a slice cut from it and the knife is still stuck in the fruit. This design is used as a symbol of hospitality and generosity. Silk and metal thread on a cotton ground with supplementary wefts in slubbed cotton to form a diaper pattern. *c.* 1850. 48 x 15 cm.

This napkin end has three repeats of the sun pattern worked in gold thread with a little silk used to emphasize the shape. The sun usually represents good fortune and happiness. The cotton ground cloth is woven with extra thick cotton wefts in a regular stripe. *c.* 1850. 45 x 12 cm.

over four hundred years. Once the Seljuks had control over Jerusalem the Pilgrim traffic was changed from religious tourism into a more militant movement, the Crusades, which started in 1099 with the recapture of Jerusalem by Godfrey de Bouillon.

During the Crusades large armies of Europeans moved through the Byzantine Empire and their zeal to reconquer the Holy Lands was mixed with an awareness of how rich the Empire was and how easy it would be to profit from it. In 1204, during the disgraceful Fourth Crusade, the Crusaders, instigated by the Venetians, sacked and captured Constantinople (Istanbul) rather than pursue their original sacred aim of saving the Holy Places.

The militant Crusaders caused greater damage to the Byzantine Empire than they did to the Seljuk and Ottoman Empires. After sacking Constantinople (Istanbul) the Franks established themselves in Greece, the Aegean, Cyprus and Syria as occupying forces, but it was their continued activity as traders that caused more real change in the Ottoman Empire than had ever been occasioned by their armies. They set up companies and trading posts in Constantinople (Istanbul) and throughout the Aegean and they also moved into the Black Sea and traded directly with the nations around the Caspian Sea. They brought with them concepts that were alien to Ottoman thought, the most formidable of which was the independence and rights of the individual. For the first time the power of the Sultan and the State had to confront

19

the concepts of a City State which was run by its inhabitants rather than by a despot, and of commercial organisations which were separate from the state and not controlled by it.

The Turki invaders had arrived in hordes that were numerically far inferior to the populations already established in the lands they conquered. They arrived as warriors on horses and although they must have been supported by wagons and carts it has always been accepted that very few of their own women came with them. The process of absorption was therefore considerably accelerated by the inevitable inter-marriage of male Turks and local women. The accepted tribal usage that the Sultan could marry many times made the creation of links with the existing aristocracy very easy. Orhan, Osman's son, first married Nilufer, the daughter of a local Christian ruler, and then the daughter of John Cantacuzenos, a pretender to the Byzantine throne. Orhan's grandson Bayazit married, among others both Christian and Muslim, the daughter of the Serbian King Lazar. Most of the other Sultans up to Suleiman married into local Anatolian patrician families established before the Seljuk invasion. After Suleiman the Sultans did not technically marry: they had harems and the children born within the harem were acknowledged as 'family', and their mothers were given high rank. Selim II's mother was Russian, and both his son and grandson who succeeded him had Italian mothers.

A similar situation arose with the Crusaders who had also arrived as a male army and they, once settled, married, or as the genteel phrase of the time had it, they 'took as consorts' the local women. These unions created a crossbreed known as the 'gasmouli', a form of racial distinction which was never made with the children of Turki-local marriages. Once the gasmouli were absorbed into the Ottoman Empire after the fall of Rhodes even that distinction was lost.

Over the next six centuries small groups of Turki tribesmen continued to arrive from the east, either as immigrants or mercenaries, attracted by tales of wealth and an easy life. These later arrivals had often been converted to Islam even before arriving in Asia Minor.

The Ottoman Empire was the flowering of all these mixed cultures, an amalgam of all that had gone on before. The influx of the Seljuks and the Ottomans and the introduction of Islam created one of the greatest empires, vying with the Roman and later Spanish empires, both in its extent and in the way that it influenced those living within it. At the conquest of Constantinople (Istanbul) in 1453 this amalgam of peoples and cultures gained a centre and became an identified whole. It is about this time that the area starts to be known as Turkey, and Turk no longer means the Turki-speaking peoples of Central Asia but inhabitants of this country. The Empire continued to grow for a further 230 years and during all that time it influenced the many and diverse peoples within it, modifying their own cultures but everywhere remaining clearly identifiable as Ottoman. Although the Europeans remained in

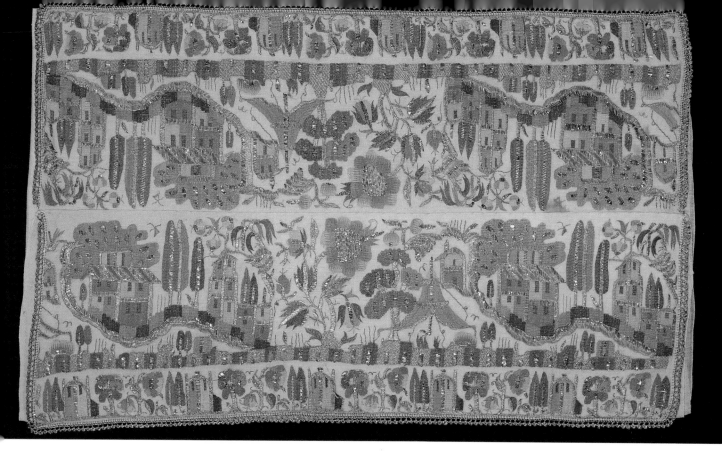

Summer houses alongside the Bosphorus with tents set up in the garden decorate both ends of this rich napkin. The border is composed of kiosks, trees and out of scale flowers. Silk in brick stitch and four varieties of metal strip on a cotton ground edged with a metal crochet lace. *c.* 1830. 45 x 30 cm.

the Empire as traders, initially very few of them established formal residence because they were then deemed subject to the local laws. It was only after Suleiman signed treaties with the Europeans, allowing them to remain subject to their own laws rather than to his, that a European population settled and grew.

The two great pillars of this culture were the central figure of the Sultan, and Sunni Islam. The Sultan was the sole authority and technically owned everything: all his public administrators, even those at the highest level, were his personal slaves, a survival of the Mamluk slave system that the Seljuks had brought with them. These administrators were originally boys who had been taken from the provinces as part of the annual compulsory gathering of the children, the 'devsirme'. This gathering mainly supplied soldiers for the Janissary Corps, but it also provided recruits for the civil service and the palace administration. They were all converted to Islam and received the best formal education that was available. All these recruits would have considered themselves to be Ottoman Turks and fervent adherents to the faith of Islam, but in origin they may have been Greeks, Armenians, Caucasians, Albanians, Slavs or any of the Balkan peoples, and were most probably born into Christian families.

This system ensured that no matter how wealthy any individual became in the service of the Sultan, on his death all his property reverted to the Sultan and not to his own children. They were all tied to the person of the Sultan as slaves, and the most powerful were drawn even closer to him by being married to one or other of the Sultan's sisters or relatives.

Not only was the Sultan the centre of the Empire but the Palace at Topkapi was the only place where decisions could be made. It was consequently full of provincial administrators, keeping 'in the eye' of the Sultan, and crowded by the groups of lobbyists pleading their various causes.

The Empire was always centrally controlled and administered by a handful of governors appointed by Istanbul and a larger number of locally appointed officials who were not necessarily Muslims. They were the local judges and senior civil servants and their main concerns were to collect the taxes and to maintain a trouble-free society. The Ottoman rule was in most respects fairly liberal; the local religions were permitted and native languages and customs continued as before.

For the adherents to Islam personal identity was a matter of belonging to a family or to a tribal group. The only larger sense of community came from being a member of Sunni Islam and not from being a member of the Ottoman Empire. The concept of national identity was much more central to the lives of the non-Muslim populations. It was only after the disintegration of the Empire in 1919 and the creation of the new states and nations in the Middle East that a sense of a national identity was developed for the Muslims that superseded family or tribal identity.

Both of the central pillars of the society were displaced with the establishment of the Republic of Turkey in October 1923, when the new state was declared to have no official religion and the Sultanate was abolished, with Mehmed VI as the last Sultan. His nephew, Abdul Mecid II, remained only as titular Caliph from 1922 to 1924.

An idyllic rural scene of a house set in a garden with a pond surrounded by poplars and a weeping willow. A stream with small rowing boats and a three-arched bridge fill the border frieze. Silk and metal thread on a fine cotton ground. *c.* 1850. 45 x 13 cm.

The culture of the Empire was a homogenous one; the arts and sciences, even decoration, drew their inspiration from the same repertory of artistic ideas and pattern. The practice of the religion, its architecture, symbols, language and script were all the most powerful influences.

It would be naive to suggest that this was an ideal society; in theory the Sultan ruled and possessed everything. The society was constructed for males and Islam reinforced this concept, although women could become extremely powerful, but only as part of the royal family. The Seljuks brought with them the powerful concept of tribe and family from their Central Asian homeland together with the art and technology of China.

Their passage through Persia and Baghdad had introduced them to Islam and to its literature in Persian and Arabic, preparing them for their change to a settled non-nomadic life. They retained Turkish as their tribal and administrative language: Arabic was the language of religion and Persian that of literature and cultivated thought. Greek remained the language of commerce and the *lingua franca* of most of the population.

The Ottoman style was introduced throughout the Empire, percolating down from the Court and the provincial seats of government. Local traditions persisted and were often absorbed into the standard repertory, together with outside influences from Venice and Italy and later from France.

The cultural end of the Empire was clearly to be seen when Sultan Selim III was defeated, not by superior military forces but by the attraction of the new, European, ideas which he attempted to introduce. The ideas were not only political and social but also artistic and cultural and had first been encountered by the Ottomans when the Italian traders of the eleventh century had introduced them, but they became invincible only when combined with the development of industrialization.

p.174

It was only after 1850 that styles changed dramatically in response to the new influences from Europe. The distinctive Ottoman art slowly disappeared, to be replaced by a universal European style that stretched from Spain to Moscow and from Cairo to Helsinki. It was not a change brought about by an intellectual or emotional decision: the main factor was industrialization, the availability of cheap and perfectly adequate products. Sadly this also had the effect of destroying most of the crafts that had existed throughout the Ottoman world for seven centuries.

NOTES

1. The City was known as Rum by the local peoples and the word in the form Rumi means Western. The Province of Rumeli was the Western Province of the Empire, Anatolia was the Eastern Province.

2. The jeziya was an annual tax paid by all non-Muslims. A further tax, the haraç, was paid by adult non-Muslims as an exemption from military service.

2 The Embroidered Textiles

The trade in textiles was the most important international trade throughout the centuries before industrialization and it represented an even greater trade value than the movement of agricultural products. If one includes the growing and processing of the raw materials for making cloth then the textile industry throughout the world employed the largest number of people and represented the greatest wealth for the producing countries. Textile production was carried out at every level of quality, from the most modest weaving in a village house to the production of elaborate tapestries, sumptuous carpets and precious embroideries.

Although embroideries were also produced by machine during the twentieth century it was embroidery that persisted as a hand craft long after all cloth was made by machine. Throughout both the Ottoman Empire and the contemporary Chinese Empire embroidery was the most common method of decorating textiles, mainly because this method involved no capital expenditure and only took time which, unlike the raw materials used, was not calculated as having any value.

In the Ottoman Empire embroidery was carried out at a number of levels both of skill and volume of production. The lowest level of skill and the greatest volume of production are found in the domestic work and because this work was used daily most of it has vanished. Professional embroidery was made in all the main centres of population, usually in ateliers run as family units or as small workshops. This production was very skilled and was invariably done by men who also made all the large pieces and those that included precious metals. All the domestic work was carried out by the women of the household, the training starting for girls at the age of four or five.

Earlier foreign writers on embroidery in Turkey always refer to Harem or Court work and praise its high quality and desirability. The Court was the arbiter of fashion and style and a great deal of high quality embroidery was made for consumption at Court. Although some of it was made by the professionals who worked in the workshops at Topkapi a great deal was made outside in the City's embroidery ateliers,

A detail from a large bath sheet with a border covered in sprays of hyacinths, roses, daisies, carnations, lilies and long-petalled tulips in gold. Silk and gold thread on cotton. Highest quality professional work, most probably Tepebaşi. *c.* 1850. 54 x 45 cm, portion shown.

25

in Tepebaşi, Galata and Kasimpaşa. The term 'Court work' therefore implies a standard of work rather than a statement that the work was made at Court. The ladies of the harem certainly worked at embroidery, as they did occasionally at making clothes, sweetmeats and jams, and they may have produced high quality work, but 'Harem work' must imply work used in the harem and not necessarily work produced by the wives of the Sultan.

The various levels of work can be found in every one of the categories of embroideries throughout the whole book. The fact that no inferior examples have survived from the early period does not mean that none was made, they have merely been consumed. A few examples do remain as scraps in composite pieces but they are difficult to date with assurance.

26

p.104

A decorated china urn supports a large bouquet of flowers with apples and pears clustered around the stem. This is repeated three times above a narrow panel of a tendril with fruit and flowers. Highest quality professional work, silk, gold and silver thread in muşabak and stem stitch on a fine cotton woven in a diamond pattern. *c.* 1850. 45 x 20 cm.

Costume

The standard costume of the Byzantine Empire was based on that of the classical Greeks, adapted for the local climate and influenced by the existing costumes of the native inhabitants. It was based on a long chemise for women and a shorter one for men with the legs covered by leggings or stockings. More than one chemise could be worn at a time and both sexes wore scarves and shawls around the head and body. Women did not cover their heads or hide their faces on religious grounds. Many of the regional costumes survived and the most different of them were those which included trousers, which were considered as barbaric and foreign, worn by northerners and peasants.

After the invasion of the Turki peoples the costume was gradually standardized to be very similar to that worn by most of the peoples who lived from western China to the Mediterranean and in northern India. This introduced style established the shirt and trousers as the universal dress. Ethnic differences did survive but mainly as variations in the decorations applied to the costume. The exceptions to this were the clothes worn by the religious leaders of all sects, who invariably preserved a more ancient, traditional style of dress.

p.42

p.56, 57

The standard costume worn by both men and women was basically a pair of loosely fitting trousers reaching to just below the knee, a loose shirt that fell to mid-thigh with full sleeves and a coat that covered both of them. Each article of clothing was secured by cloth ties or strings and each layer was bound around the waist by sashes or belts. It was common for more than one shirt or coat to be worn at the same time, either for warmth or as decoration, and for each layer to be secured by a wrap-around sash. These layers of clothing give a very bulky silhouette to both sexes. This style remained the standard costume of the Turks from their arrival in the West until the introduction of European dress for men at the Court of Sultan Mahmud II in 1829 and its universal diffusion after the 1922 reforms under Ataturk.

The passing of a distinctive national style was apparently more regretted by the European visitor than by the Turks themselves. Miss Pardoe

27

in *The City of the Sultan*, which was published in 1854, when the first changes had had 25 years in which to become established, wrote:

> The flowing robe of silk or of woollen material has been flung aside for the ill-made and awkward surtout of blue cloth, and the waist, which was once girdled with a shawl of cachemire, is now encompassed by two brass buttons.

This change in national costume introduced into the bazaars a new trader: the 'kapamaci' who sold suits for men, rather than the number of smaller tailors that each produced one or two of the many different articles that had been worn before.

There were, of course, frequent changes in fashion over the centuries, usually introduced by the Court, but the basic costume remained the same for most of the population and can still be seen in Turkey today in country districts. These changes were mainly in detail and in the basic materials used; there were no dramatic changes in either the single garments or in the outline they created. The costume worn indoors differed from that worn outside the house mainly in the weight of the materials used and in the number of layers of clothing.

Muslim women were required by religious obligation to cover themselves from strangers,[1] which meant that when they went outside the house they were completely enveloped in a large disguising coat or cloak, usually with a separate cloth to cover their head and eyes. Even non-Muslim women wore the cloak so as not to draw attention to themselves on the street. Contrary to popular belief the yaşmak was not imposed on women as part of the purdah system, it was most probably a much older veil worn by aristocratic women to avoid having their skin darkened from exposure to the sun. Aristocratic women in Greece and Rome, and later in Byzantium, wore a veil that was very similar to the yaşmak. Early literature in Turkish always refers to this veil as an aid to coquetry and fascination, which was in direct contradiction to the strict purdah system.

The Ottoman court was very fond of uniforms and they were obligatory to the military, the civil servants and the bureaucracy, the religious orders and palace servants. Uniforms identified their wearers by profession, rank and social standing and even by race. Suleiman regulated costume for the Court and for all official positions by law in the Kanuni Teshrifat.[2] In that codex details were given of the shape and cut of every garment, its colour and the material of which it could be made. Even the length and width of the cloth from which the turban could be made were set out. Not only were costume details given in the Kanun but also the various orders of precedence and the complicated rules that were to be observed regarding costume. Within the Empire foreigners and strangers were immediately identifiable by their dress because it followed none of the regulations.

Most clothing would have been made at home, much of it on fabric

A detail from the kaftan on p. 57.

that had been woven in the house or in the village. The women of the household would have all the necessary needlework skills to make clothes, particularly as garments were mainly made of straight lengths of material sewn together with very little tailoring being involved. The decoration on most garments was provided by the colour and texture of the fabrics from which they were made. Where it was considered necessary to have further decoration this was usually achieved by embroidery, which was a cheap and efficient method of adding colour and pattern. Practically every piece of clothing could be embroidered, but a pragmatic society only embroidered that portion of them which would be seen: trouser legs were only embroidered below where the shirt would fall, scarfs and handkerchiefs were embroidered only around the edges and in the corners, sashes were decorated at the ends, whereas cushion covers were embroidered all over. This pragmatism extended also to the form that the embroidery took: pieces that were to hang casually and which may be seen from both sides, such as sashes, scarves, towels and handkerchiefs, were worked on both sides to make a two-faced decoration, whereas trousers, shirts and cushion covers were single-faced. As the intention of the outdoor cloak that women wore was to distract attention from them they were never embroidered, whereas the men's cloaks and uniform jackets were heavily decorated.

The various embroidered cloths that were worn as part of the costume or which were worn casually about the body all have different names, usually related to their shape and size, but this does not mean that their use was exclusive to what the name would suggest. Scarves were used as sashes, towels as scarfs, sashes as headbands and any of them used to decorate the house or to be wrapped around a gift. Each household would have a collection of decorated cloths that would be brought out and used when needed.

There was a wide range of shoes made, from the delicate velvet slippers of the harem ladies, which were heavily embroidered, to the coarse leather over-shoes for out-door wear. Relatively few pairs of footwear have survived: shoes are considered to be base articles; their contact with the dirty world outside defiles them and they are always the first personal possession to be thrown away after a funeral.

The different names used for the same article caused great confusion to the Europeans when trying to describe the various costumes and household decorations that they saw. An Italian visitor in 1540 writes:

They [the women] wear a towel (sciugatoio) round the neck and head, so that one can see their eyes and mouth, and these they cover with a thin silk scarf a palm's width each way, through which they can see but not be seen by others. The scarf is fastened by three pins (aciucchie) to a suitable part of the head above the forehead.... The scarfs are of silk, as wide as towels, like those the men wear and are called Chussech.[3]

30

The costumes of the metropolis were copied throughout the Empire; officials in the Balkans and Algiers wore uniforms very similar to those at the centre and their women wore the current styles of the Court. These styles percolated down through society so that one finds Polish and Hungarian traders wearing costumes very similar to peasants in the Peloponnese or to officials in Syria and Aden. Official uniforms were made in the semi-industrial centres of Yanina and Bursa and were exported throughout the Empire, so not only were the costumes similar but so also was the majority of decoration, the repertory of patterns remaining the same in Algiers as it was in Bosnia. It is only as the Empire disintegrated that the native styles changed and started to dominate the received style.

In general the majority of the prints and paintings that European visitors made to illustrate the Ottoman world were of the Court and of rich society. The costumes portrayed are therefore those of a very small section of the population. Most of the people were poorly dressed in monochrome homespun and very seldom carried any decoration.

The regional variations in costume virtually died out when ready-made cloth and clothing became universally available. The traditional daily wear became the costume for celebrations and festivity and was worn by the descendants of those who had made them. The old costumes were not made any more and have either been preserved in museums or have disappeared.

There was great concern to record the regional costumes that had existed before the change. During the reign of Abdul Mecid a collection of 143 full-size male figures was made and dressed in the various regional costumes and taken around Turkey as a travelling exhibition.[4] The figures gradually deteriorated and were finally put on display in 1935 in the Church of St Irene, next to the Ayia Sophia Mosque. I do not know where they are now, but they would have been an invaluable record of the costumes that have now gone forever, even if no women's clothing was included.

The costumes of the Ottomans were of great interest and curiosity to the European travellers, and there are many books and collections of paintings illustrating the costume. Not all of the illustrations are necessarily true to life, and many of them are repeated copies of a small number of original costumes. They become more and more fictional as the later illustrators, who had never seen the costumes, drew what they believed could be possible; so the illustrations look more and more like what Europe was wearing. Even painters introduced Ottoman costumes into their work, the best known and earliest being 'The Reception of a Venetian Embassy', attributed to Gentile Bellini, which appears to have been drawn from direct observation. The tradition continued through every century as painters were attracted to the Court, and a list of the major painters and publications is given in the bibliography, in the section Costume Illustrations.

The Turkish drawings of their own costumes are very repetitive. There are a number of fixed poses which are repeated endlessly, with costumes drawn onto them which differ only slightly in detail. They are mainly used to show the official costumes of Court officials and the military as described in the Kanun.

NOTES

1. The clothing regulations for women are mainly contained in the Koran, in Sura 24, The Light.

2. The Canon of Protocol or Ceremonies which was promulgated about 1540. Although established for the Court in Istanbul it was used in newly conquered Egypt where the Kanun replaced and augmented the established laws on costume, which were called 'The Regulations of the Caliph Umar', dating from some time before 1300 AD.

3. From Luigi Bassano's *Costumi Turchi*, Rome 1545, ed. Franz Babinger Munch 1963. Chussech must be an attempt at kuşak, the modern word for a long sash.

4. The collection was called the 'Elbise-i Atika' and was originally in the Armoury of Topkapi Palace. Jean Brindesi published a collection of 22 of these costumes in 1855, called *Musée des Anciens Costumes Turcs de Constantinople*.

A flower and a leaf are repeated and combined to make a pair of tall candelabra with a small column of leaves set between them. Good quality domestic work signed with a single 'L'. Silk stem stitch with fillings and outlines in gold wire and thread. *c.* 1850. 24 x 24 cm.

Sashes and belts

The most common fixing for the layers of clothing were sashes. They were made of either a length of narrow patterned weave or of a plain weave embroidered at both ends. They were worn by both men and women, and early miniatures show both the Sultan and the ladies of his Court wearing them. The belt was more substantial, usually a narrow band of a plain or coloured woven fabric, or even a length of tablet weaving, and was fixed by being tied into a knot or, more usually, by the loose end being tucked into its tightly wrapped folds. When the belt was to be seen it was fitted with an elaborate metal clasp composed of two halves, one hooking into another. These buckles were often very elaborate, made of silver and decorated with gold and precious stones. They were also worn by both women and men. The belts worn by men as part of their civil uniforms were of leather and were fitted with harnesses to carry swords, powder horns and ammunition.

As each layer of clothing was held by sashes or belts the typical silhouette of the Ottoman, male and female, was very wide around the waist. This silhouette was seen as imposing in men, when being well fleshed was an outward sign of importance, affluence and power; the female silhouette of a substantial middle and thighs tapering down to small ankles and feet in flimsy slippers was seen as an ideal of beauty and vulnerability. Turkish women managed this bulky arrangement of clothes decorously and seductively.

The unembroidered sashes, the 'kemer',[1] were most commonly a striped shawl fabric which was twisted into a fat coil and wound around the body. The 'peştemal'[2] was a wide, long length of plain white cotton

Two men's sashes worked in silk filling stitch with every part of the design outlined in gözeme, the end borders worked with needle weaving on a coarse linen.

Top A pair of identical tiered bouquets set on flat dishes. Metal wire and silvered copper strip. Before 1870. 40 x 22 cm.

Bottom Two versions of a similar design set side by side. Worked with metal wire and brown copper strip and metal 'Z' forms scattered all over. Before 1870. 50 x 42 cm.

weave worn by men only. This was also twisted into a rope of fabric and then wrapped around and around the waist on top of the last layer of clothes with the end tucked into the folds.

More refined sashes were made of much narrower widths of fine cotton and linen and were usually only long enough to allow one turn around the waist with two long lengths falling from the waist. They were not twisted into coils. These lighter sashes were very often worn together with the metal buckles, through which they were threaded, then to fall gracefully down the legs. These sashes were most decoratively embroidered at both ends and because they were to be seen from either direction they are always worked as two-faced embroideries. They are called either 'uçkur' or 'kuşak'.[3] Uçkur is the more common name for the shorter sash worn by women, kuşak is the girdle worn by men, usually longer and made of a more robust fabric. In Mamluk Egypt and in the Ottoman Empire in the sixteenth century non-Muslim residents had to wear these sashes dyed in different colours to identify their various creeds.[4]

The embroidered sashes were made of a single width of fabric no more than 20 cm wide, although during the nineteenth century they were made as wide as 42 cm, possibly because no hand-woven fabric was being made in the narrower width. The sashes may be as long as 300 cm but the usual length is about 150 cm. The decoration on both ends is always identical and the embroidery occurs in many degrees of

A pair of large angular motifs of stylized leaf shapes. The design is worked in silk by interweaving an extra silk thread into the loose cotton ground. The impression is that it has been worked on the loom but it is worked in the hand. Before 1850. 50 x 30 cm.

p.36

p.33

Four women's sashes, all domestic work on homespun cotton. Conventional motifs are worked rather naively in stem stitch and muşabak with metal wire used sparingly. They are all *c.* 1870 and measure 23 x 23 cm.

34

35

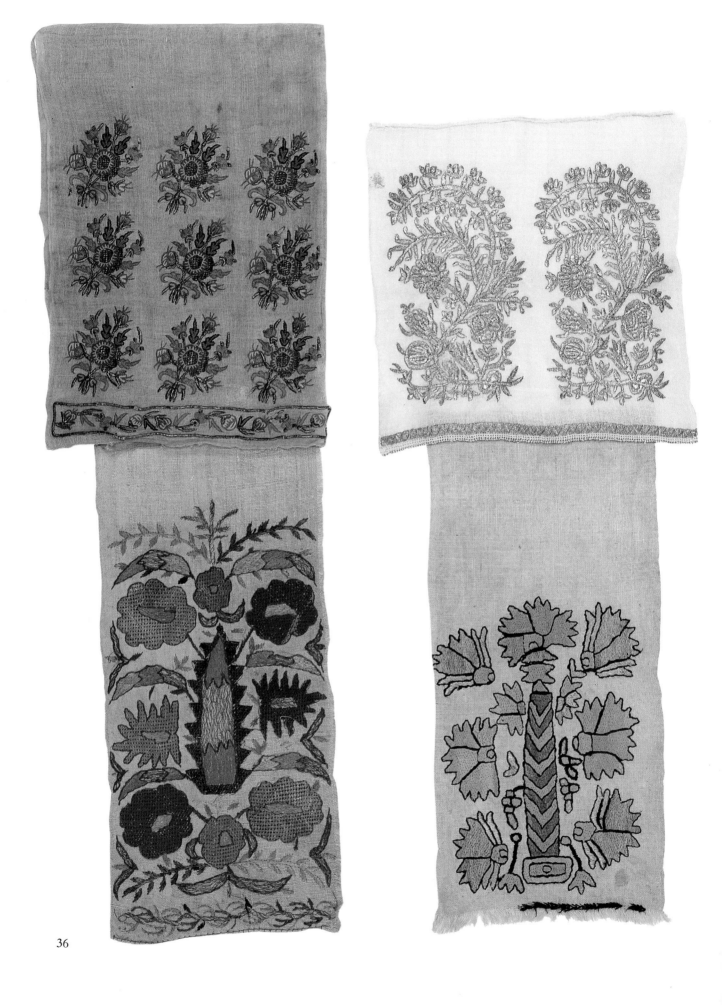

36

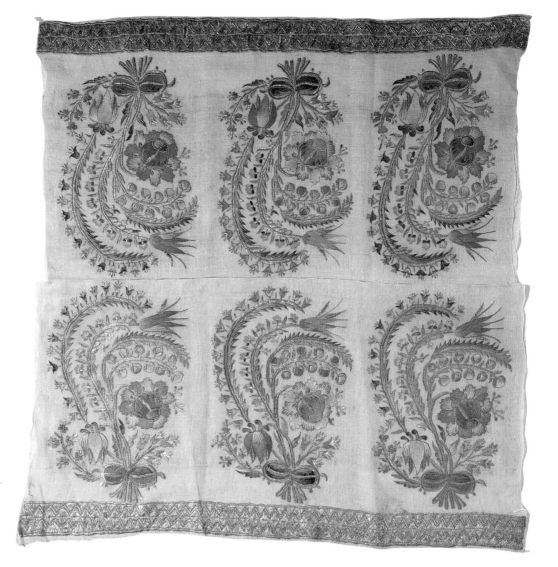

Two joined sash ends, each worked with three sprays of flowers and leaves tied with a bow. Professional work in gold, silver and silk thread on a fine silk ground. *c.* 1850. 45 x 44 cm.

Left: Four sashes: the top two are professional work and the lower two domestic.

Top left A single small spray is repeated nine times. Silk and metal strip on cotton. *c.* 1800. 26 x 24 cm.

Top right Two separated motifs of a bent branch with flowers and leaves, worked entirely in gold and silver thread. *c.* 1850. 26 x 22 cm.

Bottom left A single motif based on a Roman column with large flower heads and leaves. Silk and metal muşabak work. *c.* 1900. 35 x 18 cm.

Bottom right The same motif but worked in three-ply thick floss silk. *c.* 1900. 25 x 20 cm.

quality, as they were produced both by professionals and by home embroiderers. The decoration is composed of a single large motif, a pair of identical small motifs or of a smaller motif repeated in vertical rows. All the various versions are directional and are set upright above a narrow border and very seldom have a restraining border above them.

The large single motif is the rarer form, and from the style in which it was usually worked it would appear to be an early version, dating from the end of the sixteenth century. The motif varies between being a scene with a tent or a house and pond, or even a Roman column, to one of the most common of Turkish motifs — a complicated spray of flowers and leaves rising out of a realistic or stylized container, occasionally with a pair of opposed birds set among the foliage. Both the scene and spray are always worked so that one half is the mirror image of the other. The version worn by women is invariably floral whereas the longer sash for men can have a much wider range of architectural and landscape patterns. The design composed of a single motif repeated twice at each end usually indicates that the sash has been made professionally and the quality of the work is very high. The pattern is usually of a single branch curving around a flower with smaller flowers and leaves springing from the outside of the curve, the whole appearance

37

being slightly hunched and incurving. The pattern is usually narrow and tall with the repeats contrasted only in the colours used. The motifs can be isolated and worked alongside each other or they can be squashed together to form a solid block of decoration.

Another version is the sash with a design of small motifs set out in three or four rows, sometimes staggered, each of four or five repeats of the same motif which differ only in the range of colours used. This is the most popular version for working at home and it was most used when the fashion of printing rather than embroidering textiles was introduced. Sashes in this style are reminiscent of the panels found on the embroidered legs of the baggy trousers which were held up by these sashes.

The ends of the sashes are usually sewn as a rolled edge, although in some of the more domestic sashes a short weft fringe is left which is sometimes knotted to stop the fabric unravelling.

NOTES

1. Kemer is derived from the Persian word kamar, the waist, which produces the usage 'Kamarband' a waist band, a word which survives through the Raj into modern English as cummerbund.

2. In Ottoman Turkish the word was originally destemal, derived from the Persian. Apart from being a type of sash it is also the word for a wrap-around plain towel, described in the section on towels for the bath.

3. Uçkur is the more common name. The band on the trousers through which the cord is passed is called the uçkurluk. The usage 'uçkur çözmek' — to untie one's sash — has an immoral connotation.

4. The Mamluk code of clothing ordained yellow for the Jew, blue for Christian and red for the Samaritan. It also contained regulations as to how long the kuşak could be and the materials of which it could be made.

p.75, 188

A woman's sash end with four vertical rows of roses or strawberries between green fronds. Silk and metal thread on cotton. Rumeli, c. 1870. 35 x 29 cm.

40

Trousers

Trousers were the universal article of clothing worn by both men and women. They were shaped more like breeches in that they usually terminated just below the knee, fitting snugly to the top of the calf. They were worn at all levels of society; even members of the professional classes such as religious leaders and Court officials, who are conventionally portrayed as wearing long flowing coats, always wore trousers underneath their kaftans or the loose, all-covering large cloak, the 'ferace'.[1] Because of the hard wear that trousers would have received it is not surprising that very few complete pairs have survived. Those that have are usually the formal, broadcloth uniform trousers worn by men.

The trousers or breeches, 'şalvar',[2] were made on a standard pattern based on full-width lengths of a basic fabric sewn together at the selvedge. The trousers were neither shaped nor tailored, and only the section forming the baggy crutch was not a straight uncut length of material. The convention was that clothing should hide and not reveal the shape of the body within, and these loose trousers sometimes had a waist circumference twice the size of the wearer's waist, allowing them to be worn in loose body-hiding folds. One spectacular pair of embroidered wedding trousers, which is also reversible, has the waist four times the standard size. These trousers were held up by a cord that passed through the broad hem at the waist and knotted at the front. This

Ceremonial woman's trousers covered over all with a design of lilies and double straps derived from a brocade of the seventeenth century. The trousers are worked identically on two sides, the blue side to be worn at the wedding and the white at the presentation of new-born male children and at the Sünnet ceremony. c. 1900. Total waist circumference 3.2 m, leg 1.08 m.

Left Very elaborate decoration on a pair of Anatolian women's trousers. Flowers, leaves, buds and small wreaths, each filled with another pattern, are stacked to fill the whole panel, copying a sixteenth-century model. Single couching and stem stitch in silk with gold and silver thread on a sturdy linen ground. c. 1850. 86 x 48 cm.

cord was usually a narrow, loosely woven white band which, when stretched, became very strong.

Men's trousers were usually made of a robust fabric varying from a coarse woven cotton to a very fine baize or barathea fabric for the uniform or court dress. They were all cut to the same pattern. The baggy crutch of the men's trousers was very large, and in examples worn by the Muslim populations of the Balkans, Crete and some parts of Anatolia the crutch is even larger and lies in concertina folds between the knees and thighs.

The women's version was usually made of a medium-weight cotton or a cotton and linen mixture. They are 90-100 cm in length and of four widths of the standard 45-50 cm wide fabric, giving a waist measurement of about 2 metres. Trousers that were to be worn indoors, or by the non-working women of the grander houses, were made of a lighter fabric and were decorated either in the weave by the addition of warp threads in silk or, more rarely, by embroidery.

When the women's trousers are embroidered it is only the two outer leg panels which are decorated, and even then it is only carried up the leg to a level with the natural crotch, as the rest of the trousers would be covered by the loose shirt. These decorated panels sustained very little wear so when the rest of the trousers had deteriorated the panels were recovered and another pair of trousers were made incorporating them. Many of these embroidered panels have survived and are usually mistakenly identified as napkins or towel ends. Rather like the Persian 'nakshe', they were extensively collected as decorative pieces with no realization of their original use.

Far left: A pair of Anatolian women's trousers, decorated with a sprig of carnations and leaves set in five rows on each leg. Silk stem stitch with gold and silver thread on a cotton ground. *c.* 1860. 166 cm total waist circumference x 90 cm leg.

Above: A pair of Rumeli women's trousers, each leg decorated with five columns of a single motif set within a narrow meander. Mercerized cotton and gold thread on a crimped cotton ground. *c.* 1870. 166 cm total waist circumference x 92 cm leg.

p.40

A single motif of three flower heads and leaves rising from a rooted branch covers the whole leg in four rows. Diagonal stem stitch and outline stitch in silk on a cotton ground. *c.* 1850. 60 x 45 cm.

43

The patterns on these trousers were worked in two styles, the eastern, Anadollu, and the western, Rumeli. The eastern style is, rather like the sash ends, either one large motif ascending the trouser leg or a smaller repeat pattern set out in staggered rows. The size and shape of these panels allows them to be embroidered with large elaborate motifs that are seldom found on any other domestic textiles. They are invariably embroideries made at home for personal use, and thus escape the rigidity of the more formal embroideries. The version with repeated patterns is always composed of small motifs of sprays of leaves and single flowers which are set out in rows all facing in the same direction. The number of repeats and rows depends on the scale and size of the basic motif.

The western style, that worn in Turkey in Europe and in those Balkan States that were part of the Ottoman Empire, differs primarily in that the pattern is composed of vertical embroidered strips, usually four to each leg. These strips are either worked in a drawn-thread technique filled with needle weaving or made up of lines of chain and brick stitch worked in contrasting alternate colours. In both cases the spaces

p.42

A leg panel from a pair of Anatolian women's trousers. A single carnation placed between two hyacinth stems rising from a metallic stylized tulip acting as an urn is set out in four staggered rows. Silk and silver on a silk core on a cotton tabby weave. *c.* 1870. 58 x 46 cm.

44

between the vertical strips are filled with vertical lines of isolated small floral or simple geometric motifs. These panels have been extensively recycled for making into large covers and table cloths, as the geometric format is most suitable for making square designs.

p.40

In both versions of these panels the leg cuff is defined by a thin embroidered line which usually does not run the whole width of the panel, allowing for the slight tapering that is used to adjust the fit to the calf. This short line of embroidery is almost the only remaining evidence that these panels were originally part of a pair of breeches. As the trouser panels are only ever seen from one side the embroidery is single-faced and so a larger range of stitches can be used than for the two-sided pieces.

The men's trousers worn in the house were always plain. They are embroidered only when they form part of a formal uniform or costume, and in these circumstances the breeches are made of a thick worsted dyed in one of the solid colours that identifies the wearer's arm of the civil or government service. The decorative embroidery, both in its quantity and form, identifies the rank of the wearer. These costumes are always embroidered in a couched technique using either a metal wound thread, a silk corded thread or a very glossy floss silk. These garments were invariably made by professional embroiderers in the specialist workshops of Istanbul and Bursa.

Many of the uniforms for use by the Ottoman officials in the Balkans were made in the semi-industrialized ateliers of Yanina in Epirus. The maker of the uniform was the terzi, the workers in metal thread were the sırmakesci, and the workers in silk the kazzazci. These were among the most prestigious and most highly paid of all the craftsmen employed in the clothing trade.

NOTES

1. Ferace is the large all-enveloping overgown worn outdoors. It was worn by all classes, invariably in a solid dark colour without embroidery. It is the same as the chodor of Iran and the faldetta of Malta.

2. The word şalvar is used for trousers throughout the Islamic world, from Pakistan to Morocco.

46

Scarves and veils

A scarf in a French Empire style, a geometric panel edged with a ribbon meander. Feather stitch in silver thread, the central flowers in silvered strip, on blue dyed cotton. Edged in a metal-thread-fringed braid. *c.* 1860. 60 x 12 cm.

Left: **a** A scarf in a foreign style, copying a Lyons brocade with ribbons, bows and stylized floral shapes. Silk with gold wire, thread and strip. Edged in metal button-hole stitch. After 1850. 80 x 65 cm. **b** A scarf in a debased French style retaining bows and ribbons. A separate bouquet motif with a bow is set in each corner. Silk and metal strip. *c.* 1870. 96 cm square. **c** A scarf with each border decorated with a stylized tray of fruit outlined in gold strip. The scalloped edge has a wavy metal strip. The work is extremely coarse and perfunctory. After 1900. 80 cm square. **d** A wedding scarf with a meander of a leaf and flower. A large motif is set in each corner. Silk and metal strip on cotton with small scattered motifs. Each corner edged in crochet lace and sequins. *c.* 1870. 94 cm square.

Scarves and veils were part of the standard dress both in the homelands of the Ottomans and in the Byzantine lands they conquered; in both areas they were also used in social ceremonies and appear in religious ceremonies in all the major local faiths. They can also be seen in various manifestations of folk religion, when they are hung as tokens and votive flags at holy places.

Normally scarves, 'çevre',[1] were worn by women to cover their head and face in public. They were folded in half to form a triangle with the longest edge pulled tight at the forehead. The folded corners are then tied in a knot either under the chin or behind the neck and the other corners displayed on the shoulders. Although scarves were mainly worn by women, larger versions were also worn by men; these are usually made of a plain weave or a printed cloth with a fancy edge. Men would wear them wound round and round the head to form an informal turban, which acted as a cap.

The most common decoration found on scarves is embroidered, consisting of narrow borders on all four sides with repeated ornaments set either in one or in all four corners. The designs used on most of the scarves were those in the usual Turkish repertory of patterns, the borders being running meanders or stylized twisted ribbons sprouting small flowers all along the length. The corner ornaments are either single flowers or a large floral spray. The whole field of the scarf is sometimes covered with a small repeat of a single flower but this is less common. When the European French style was taken up a different range of decoration was introduced, mainly copies or adaptations of the motifs that were seen on the imported French damasks — large tendrils with flowers and elongated designs to replace the squatter Ottoman ones.

SCARVES AND VEILS

Scarves were always square, made of a fine cotton or a cotton-silk mixture in sizes from 50 cm to nearly a metre square, with a plain rolled hem. It later became the fashion to edge them with fancy needle lace or a fringe and many even had the edge scalloped around the embroidered motifs. After about 1850 a rectangular scarf was introduced, copying the dominant French fashion. As the court ladies and those in society took to wearing hats in the European style these new scarves were also worn differently: they were not required to cover the head and so became worn around the neck. They were even used to tie the European-style hats onto the head in the fashion sanctified by Paris.

During the nineteenth century embroidered scarves were replaced by the more easily manufactured and cheaper printed ones, which were initially imported and later manufactured in vast quantities in Turkey. However, they still retained the same decorative style of the embroidered versions.

In strict Muslim circles the scarf was also used as a veil to hide the faces of women in public. It was used to cover the face, particularly the eyes, operating as a form of yaşmak. This normally hung over the whole head, or was wrapped around the mouth. The western idea of the yaşmak tucked around the ears like a curtain is not shown in any early local illustrations. The veil, 'peçe',[2] was usually made of a very fine muslin and decorated like a scarf. A richer, more elaborately embroidered veil, the 'duvak', was worn by a bride during the marriage ceremony. Many of the veils worn in the Malatya region of eastern Turkey have a more densely embroidered area in one quarter that is meant to hang over the upper face, allowing the woman to see but not to be seen. These veils are often embroidered in metal thread or metal strip instead of silk. The heaviness and sharpness of the metal used has so often torn the fabric that few of these veils have survived. A particular form of the veil was made on a black coarser fabric which was intended to be worn by widows.

A larger version of the çevre was the 'mücessem', which was more like a body shawl. It was usually a rectangle over a metre long by 50 cm wide and was worn wrapped around the head or upper body. The embroidered decoration was contained in a broad band at each end, sometimes filling one corner, with only a thin single line of stitching along the sides. The mücessem is often made on a pre-printed cloth and the name is also used for these pieces without embroidery.

NOTES

1. The standard word for a square scarf is çevre. The larger rectangular scarf is called mücessem, implying a firmer, more solid fabric. The çevre was adapted everywhere throughout the Ottoman world and appears as a common article in the Balkans, the Greek Islands and in Palestine. In the islands of the Aegean, when they were under Ottoman control, the mücessem was worn in Astypalaia and Castellorizo as a wedding veil and was called the golden handkerchief, the 'chrysomandilo'.

2. The veil is called 'peçe' generally, but when worn by women in public it is also called 'yüz örtüsü', the cover for the face.

A large body shawl in printed cotton with a red flower on a black ground embroidered at both ends. A large branch motif is worked three times in two directions in a gold-covered silk, with a wide border on two sides also in a heavy gold thread. Before 1900. 280 x 70 cm.

Right, top A motif of fritillaries, hyacinths and a rose is repeated on this napkin. Silk and metal thread in two colours worked on a patterned slubbed cotton ground. *c.* 1850. 50 x 16 cm.

Middle A kiosk flanked by poplars set in a walled garden repeated three times. The work is very simple and economical, a simplification of an earlier, more accomplished technique but still most attractive. Silk and mercerized cotton worked with low grade tinsel. *c.* 1920. 42 x 18 cm.

Bottom A rectangular vase motif delicately drawn and executed in silk, using soft colours and fine silk wire in stem stitch. Aegean Coast *c.* 1900. 42 x 16 cm.

49

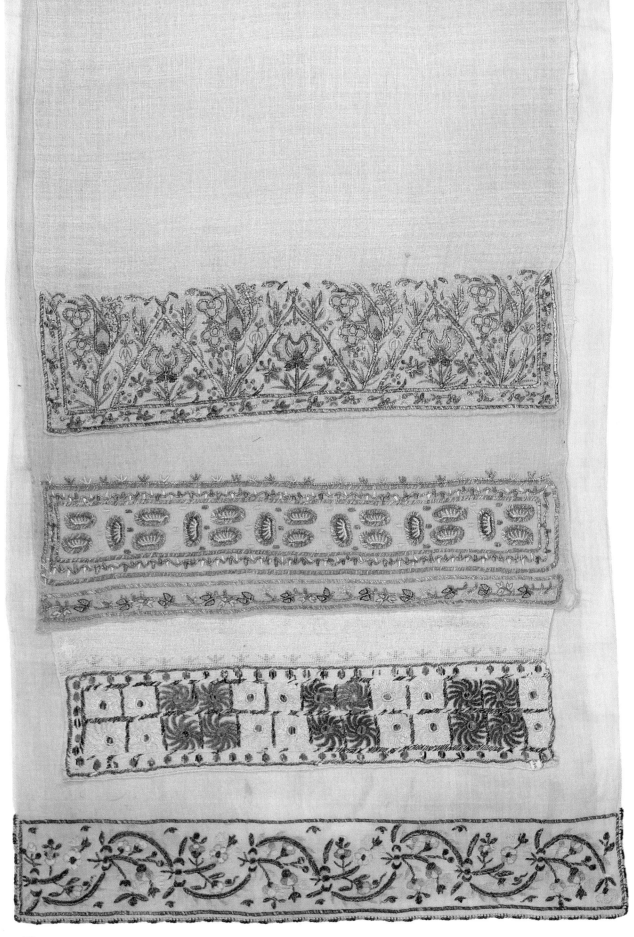

50

Handkerchiefs

A small handkerchief decorated with coffee pots and flower sprigs. Naïve work very similar to Turkish work from Skyros. Eyelet, stem and filling stitch in silk on silk. *c.* 1850. 56 x 46 cm.

Left Four small napkins to be used as handkerchiefs.

a A panel of flowers and leaves worked around three pyramid shapes set inside a border on three sides. Silk and metal thread on cotton. *c.* 1800. 44 x 11 cm.

b Isolated flower heads set in a large bordered cartouche. Silk and metal thread on a cotton ground. *c.* 1870. 45 x 11 cm.

c Groups of four squared flower heads in two colours set within a bordered panel. Silk and metal strip on cotton homespun. *c.* 1900. 40 x 10 cm.

d A simplified French brocade pattern with bows set in a panel. Silk and metal wire on a cotton ground. *c.* 1900. 54 x 8 cm.

The handkerchief, 'mendil', was introduced into Ottoman society and usage from Byzantium, where it was primarily a ritual cloth associated with religious services.[1] The main secular purpose was exactly that of today, a cloth to be carried for incidental use; it also offered an opportunity for decoration and display and it is in this sense that it will be discussed here. There were many other forms of this cloth, with different names, which could be used in virtually the same way and these are the napkins and hand towels which will be discussed later.

The best known early European reference to a handkerchief is in one of the letters that Ogier Busbecq wrote while he was Ambassador of the Emperor Ferdinand I at the Porte in 1560. He refers to the archery competitions held at the Spring Easter Festival either on Okmeidan or in the grounds of Topkapi Palace. He makes the comment that the victor is awarded an embroidered cloth by the Sultan: 'such as we use to wipe our faces.'[2] These awards could have been handkerchiefs, or perhaps small napkins or even the scarves that are to be seen in miniatures.

The handkerchief is basically a small piece of woven cotton or linen ranging in quality from the finest lawn to a coarse cotton. The earliest Ottoman illustrations of a handkerchief are in miniatures of the fifteenth century where they are shown, always held in the hand, as white, rectangular cloths with a little coloured decoration at both ends.

The most famous of all the Ottoman handkerchiefs are the four that were recovered from the tomb of Şehzade Mehmed, who was buried in 1543, and the one from the tomb of Hürrem Sultan, also known as Roxellane, who was buried in 1561. She was the wife of Suleiman the

Magnificent and the mother of Şehzade Mehmed, who died before her. These five handkerchiefs are all from the same tradition of embroidery: they are of fine, rather loosely woven linen all about 50 cm square, with blank centres and a band of embroidery about 5 cm wide on all four sides. The quality of the embroidery is very fine, although in a different technique and style to the embroideries found on other pieces which are called Ottoman from the same period. The handkerchiefs are square and very lightly worked in diagonal and stem stitch, leaving large areas of the ground cloth unworked, with eyelet and buttonhole stitches used to make small holes in the pattern. In Roxellane's handkerchief a narrow gilded metal strip is used to accentuate the diagonal pattern, using the technique called 'tel kırma'.

An unusual feature of these handkerchiefs is that the ground material has been partially dyed, presumably by printing, so that in two of them the blank centre is a dark blue and the borders off-white, almost brown but with areas also printed blue. In the other two the borders have been partially printed in blue, leaving a pattern of cartouches in one and a meander in the other. No other pieces of this complicated technique at such an early date have been found. It is very likely that these handkerchiefs copy a conventional Italian handkerchief of the period and introduce the square shape which is not evident until then.

After the sixteenth century the mendil becomes interchangeable with the small hand cloth, the 'peşkir', and by the nineteenth century they become the common article they are today. After 1830 they are always square; the women's version is usually very small and the man's version becomes as large as 45 cm square.

Apart from the square fifteenth-century handkerchiefs found in the royal tombs, the standard rectangular handkerchiefs are white and embroidered at both ends in a narrow band. Once the shape changes to being square they are embroidered with a border on all four edges, and occasionally over all with a small motif. Sometimes the handkerchief is embroidered with motifs that are appropriate to its use, such as small coffee pots or fruit.

The story that the Sultan gave a handkerchief to the harem lady who was to spend the night with him has been repeated in European literature since its first mention by Rycaut in 1540; in 1766 Flachat repeats it, mentioning that the information was given him by the Chief Black Eunuch in charge of the harem: 'The handkerchief that he [the Sultan] throws to her signifies his desire to be left alone with her.'[3]

Once they become very common objects they are seldom embroidered but are decorated by printing, 'yazma',[4] usually with a decoration of isolated motifs of flowers set along the four sides and printed with a plain colour over all.

As in all domestic textiles it is very dangerous to be dogmatic about either usage or names: the various social or racial groups in the Ottoman world used the names differently. Mendil was used in Greece

p.51, 189

Two snuff handkerchiefs on dark printed grounds. The upper one is printed with small multi-coloured bouquets on a green-brown ground and the lower one has a small two-coloured bud on a black ground. Both have been over-embroidered with metal thread and a little silk. Both c. 1850 on contemporary prints. The embroidered ends are 46 x 7 cm and 48 x 9 cm.

and the Balkans as the word for a large cloth spread on a table or for the cloth spread over furniture in the summer.

There is one group of handkerchiefs that does have a very special use and which were made for that specific purpose. These are the snuff handkerchiefs,[5] small rectangular handkerchiefs originally printed in a dark colour, black or brown, so that when they were used they did not show the snuff stains. The printing sometimes contains a multi-coloured small floral motif,[6] and a border pattern printed on the two short ends. Grander versions of the standard snuff handkerchief have these borders over-embroidered in metal strip and wire with a pattern that is quite different to the basic printed pattern.

p.53

NOTES

1. The word 'mandil' entered the languages of the eastern Mediterranean from the Latin 'mantele', or 'mantelium', which was the name for the end of the sleeve or of a cloth added to the end of the sleeve and used as a handkerchief. As 'mandylion' the word was absorbed into the Byzantine Empire, and was used in the eastern Mediterranean and pre-dated the establishment of Islam. Variations of this word are still used throughout the area for a handkerchief. In Turkish it is 'mendil'.

When the Latin word was used in Greek it became mandylion and was the name for the cloth used during the Communion Service. By extension it came to be the name given to many other cloths used in the Church, including the veils which carried, by divine means, the face of Christ. The word was extended in use to name the over-cloth worn by the Church soldiers and even the Crusaders.

Once the word entered Arabic as a common noun the form used was mandil. This was perfectly acceptable in Arabic as a substantive of the verb 'ndl', although such a triliteral root did not exist.

2. *The Turkish Letters of Ogier Ghiselin de Busbecq.* Translation of the Elzevir Edition of 1633, Edward Seymour Forster. Oxford 1927.

The word used is mappe, which is always translated as towel although it is more likely to have been a scarf, which the victor would have worn around his neck or at his waist. The usage is very similar to that in jousting and in the wearing of a colour.

3. This gesture has given a phrase to the Turkish language; 'mendil atmak', to throw the handkerchief, means to select for a special purpose.

4. Yazma is the standard word for handprinting derived from the verb 'yazmak', to write, and is the name given to all cloths printed with a pattern or with plain colours. The same type of work that follows a Persian style is called 'kalemkar' — pen work.

5. Snuff handkerchiefs are called 'mendil burunotu' from the Turkish word for nose, 'burun', or 'mendil enfiye' from the word for snuff, which in itself is derived from the classical Arabic word for nose, 'enfi'.

6. Multi-coloured prints are called 'elvan', the Turkish plural of the Arabic word 'laun', colour.

Formal costume

The clothes worn in the early years of the Ottoman Empire are best known from the pictures of costumes that European visitors used to illustrate their accounts of travels in the area.[1] A large number of water-colours and paintings were also made by travellers, most of which have never been reproduced commercially and are only known from the occasional exhibition and catalogues of various collections. Both men's and women's costumes are shown, but in view of the limited opportunities that these travellers would have had to see any of the women it is not surprising that most of the illustrations of their dress are repetitive and inaccurate in detail. The illustrations are mainly of the wives of the Sultans or of the ladies of the harem and of some of the palace staff. Those that are not of the palace women are of women of the minority groups; Greeks, Armenians, Jews and Slavs from the Balkans and the Caucasus.

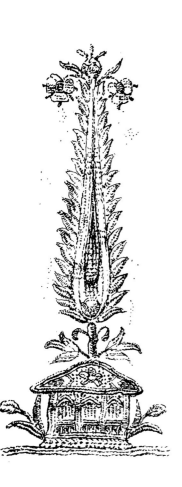

The costumes shown are invariably some version of the trouser and shirt combination which has usually been adapted to a European ideal. Other engravings rather indicate that the Court ladies wore European dress, and although there might have been considerable influence on costume in the harem from the wives and consorts who were European it is very unlikely that these engraved illustrations show the actual costumes worn. Women had no role in formal State occasions and if they did accompany the Sultan on the processions to the Mosque or to the various festivals, they were certainly not seen and it is unlikely that their costume could have been observed in detail. Unlike the clothing of the Sultans and his male relatives, there are virtually no garments left from his female relatives other than a rare embroidered handkerchief or head-band.

Costume started to change after about 1700, when the influence from Europe intensified and fashionable society dress became more and more like that worn in Western Europe. This change was clearly to be seen in the illustrations of contemporary travellers and of the new generation of watercolourists.[2] The dress of other women did not

change at all and remained rather monochrome and nondescript. Foreigners would only have seen non-Muslim women in the street and even they, like the Muslim women, would be covered from the crown of their heads to their feet with the all-covering cloak, the ferace.

Although women were more frequently seen in public after the move to Dolmabahçe they would have been women of a certain level in society who by then were always seen in European dress, slightly adapted to include some Oriental touches. Even before that time two garments had become more common, although some versions of them had existed earlier. They were a long open coat-like dress and a long

An open-fronted silk gown to be worn indoors under another thicker one. The parts that would be seen, the neck and chest panels, are heavily decorated with silk, gold thread and gilded strip. The sleeves are joined to the body with panels of drawn thread weaving, the neck is edged with crochet lace and the front with a light fringe. *c.* 1850. 122 cm in length.

56

A woman's kaftan worn at Court. The dark red silk velvet is embroidered with gold wire, gilded strip and sequins in dival work and in stem stitch. The pattern is 'Shah's Pleasure'. *c.* 1850. 135 cm in length, 232 cm total bottom circumference.

closed chemise, both with long sleeves. The open version, the 'entari', was an inner dress and it was continuously developed from the open coat, the 'maşlah', until in its last version it was composed of a coat with three tails which could trail a metre on the ground, with excessively long sleeves cut open from just below the elbow. It was always made of a fine brocaded silk and finished around the edge with elaborate gold and silver needle lace. The elaborateness of the patterned cloth from which these were made meant that there was no need for additional embroidered decorations.

The other garment, the closed kaftan, was a development of the robes of honour, the 'khilat',[3] usually made of a heavily embroidered monochrome silk velvet. The designs were always elaborate floral patterns with many branches and flowers. This pattern is called 'bindallı', meaning a thousand branches, and the garments embroidered in this style are now generally called bindallı.

The designs are all made in dival work of varying quality, based on patterns pre-constructed on thin card which was sold in sheets fixed to thin blue crêpe paper. An infinite variety of these patterns was available and usually had some fanciful name such as 'a handful of gold' (which was based on small gold coins), 'birds in a tree' and 'Shah's Pleasure'. The pattern can cover the whole of the dress, front and back and over the sleeves, although it is more usual for it to cover only the front, the shoulders and the bottom of the sleeves. This style of work was copied throughout the Empire and became the standard decoration worn by women for all public or formal occasions. The style was adopted in Morocco and Algeria, where it survives to the present day. Court costume in the principalities of the Balkans and Southern Russia was developed from this style and can even be found in the work of the Islamic embroiderers of Mauretania and northern Nigeria.

The standard wedding dress was also worked in the bindallı style, and when Ottoman officials were presented abroad with their wives they invariably wore this embroidered dress. The fashion still persists today and can be seen in many of the formal wedding photographs shown in the windows of fashionable photographic studios.

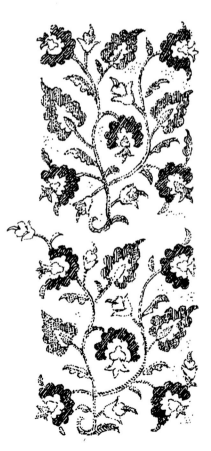

NOTES

1. The earliest editions are by the Fleming, Peter van Aelst, the Dane, Melchior Lorch, 1559 and the Frenchman, Nicholas de Nicolay, Seigneur d'Afreville, 1567.

2. The main illustrators of this period were the Frenchmen, George de la Chapelle, 1684, and Charles Silvestre, 1710; the Dutchman, Jean Baptiste van Mour, 1714, the Swiss, Jean Liotard, about 1750, the Englishman, Thomas Allom, 1841 and the Italian, Amadeo Preziosi, 1865. See Bibliography.

3. The custom of presenting robes of honour, the khilat, survived from the customs that the Turki invaders brought with them from Central Asia. These robes, which would have been made of the finest materials and lavishly decorated, were presented to foreign visitors, to neighbours and to loyal subjects as marks of esteem. There are accounts of as many as twenty of these robes being presented to European visitors at the courts of the Khans of Turkestan. The tradition in many countries was that the same robes were returned to the giver the next day.

Textiles in the home

Throughout the Ottoman Empire until the beginning of the nineteenth century most of the population lived in the country in modest, single-roomed houses within walking distance of a village or town. Town dwellers had slightly larger houses, but whereas the countryman gained his living from his animals and his fields, the townsman lived by his employment, usually a hand craft of some type. The city dweller lived alongside his neighbour and shared many facilities with him, usually travelling some distance away from his home to work: a pattern that was common in Europe and Asia before the industrial revolution. At every level most families owned very few household goods and made many of those that they needed themselves; it was only the richest merchants and landowners who had possessions and wealth in terms of physical objects.

The Turkish house was technically divided into two separate areas: an inner house which was the women's part and an outer house, the men's quarters, which was also used for entertaining guests.[1] These clearly divided areas were more likely to be found in the larger houses and this arrangement was developed most extravagantly in the palaces or houses of provincial governors, where the two quarters were very often made into separate houses, each with its own entrance. However, in the vast majority of houses this division into two areas was not practical; it was far more usual for the house to be considered as the private women's area; the men were expected to use the yard or to entertain their guests and meet friends in the coffee house. The equivalent meeting place for the women was the public bath house.

A towel end portraying the Ottoman ideal of civilization, a walled garden planted in compartments with small kiosks, fountains and water canals. Gold and silver thread and strip worked in muşabak and in interweaving, silk thread stem stitch all on a cotton ground showing some terry weave. *c.* 1840. 100 x 28 cm.

TEXTILES IN THE HOME

It is always assumed that this division of the house by sex is the result of the laws of Islam but, in fact, the tradition of separate quarters for the women was brought by the Turki peoples from their homelands and existed long before they were exposed to Islam. The same arrangement survives in Mongolia and China. A similar segregation had existed even in classical Greece and later in Byzantium, and the system was easily adopted by the Christians and Jews who lived in the Empire. The dividing of one's house into two became a sign of status and was therefore sought after.

A feature of the house was that the spaces within it were used as was necessary, with very little insistence on defined sleeping or working areas. As most houses had only one room it was used for every activity and operated dynamically. Even in the houses of the affluent, where there may have been many more than one room, none of them was reserved for one use only. It was not until the middle of the nineteenth century that the European idea of dedicated rooms was introduced and although this idea was received into high society at that time, it did not affect most of the population; it is still not universally accepted today in country districts.

This versatility in usage was made possible by the absence of fixed furniture in the house. Shelves and cupboards, such as they were, were built into the walls. Shelves were principally used to display even the commonest of domestic utensils, and cupboards were used to store the clothing and domestic furnishings, such as bedding, that was not in immediate use. There was no need for much storage space as families owned little that was not actually being used.

The vast majority of objects and domestic articles that have survived

A date palm with large fronds, silver fruit and flowers is repeated five times at each end of this napkin. This pattern is used in gifts and signifies abundance and prosperity. This style was developed in Istanbul after 1830. 100 x 55 cm.

60

from before 1830 had belonged to the rich, who formed a very small proportion of society. Most of the domestic textiles that have survived were made after 1830, when society was already changing. As in Europe, the movement from the country to the towns had started in response to the need for labour for the new centralized manufacturing processes. It was this new society that needed articles that the people were no longer able to make for themselves.

The most common image of Turkish life in the house is that of men and women, invariably in separate groups, sitting on long bench sofas composed of a number of separate cushions with carpets and rugs strewn on the floor. This image was supported by the many accounts sent back to Europe by the large number of diplomats and merchants who had established themselves throughout the Ottoman Empire. The accounts were mainly of life in the Court and gave an image of wealth and luxury that clearly satisfied the desire of the West for tales of the luxuriant East. In a letter to Sir Robert Cecil in 1599 Sir Henry Lello, the third English Ambassador, gives an account of an audience with the Grand Signior, Mehmed III, and says:

> I entered into the presence chamber, where the Grand Sigior satt uppon a cushion of red sattin most richly ymbroidered with pearls, and all his chamber floored with Redd sattin Ritchly ymbroidered with gould.

Chairs and tables were not part of the standard furniture until the early nineteenth century. Free-standing sofas did not replace the seating arranged around the wall until even later. Heating in the house was provided either by the fire used for cooking or by a portable small stove, the 'mangal'. This was a metalware dish on a stand that would be filled

Six pots standing on trays each with a basil plant are worked on each end of this napkin. A pot of basil was used to indicate a marriageable daughter in the house. Silk with silver thread and a strip on a fine cotton ground. *c.* 1800. 50 x 26 cm.

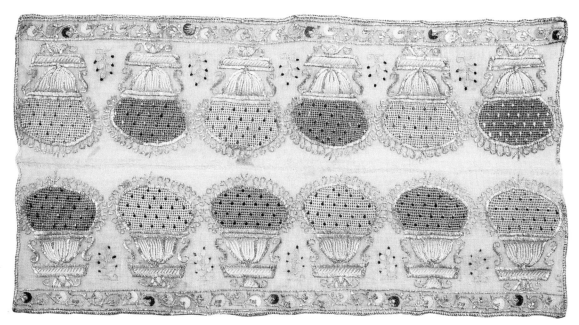

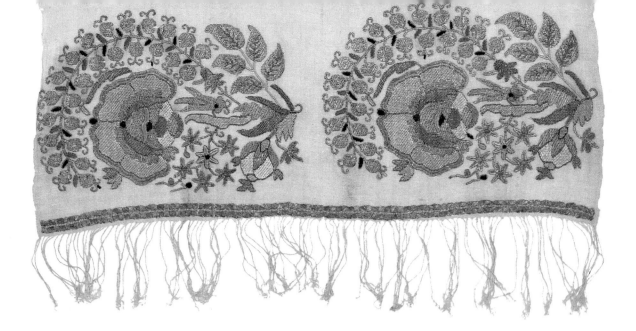

with burning charcoal and brought into the room. It would either be set on a stand with a metal cover or would be placed on the ground and covered by a quilted cloth around which one would sit with one's feet tucked in under the cover to keep warm.

In the absence of permanent furniture the floor was used to sit on and for meals and work. Food would be brought in on trays which would be set on the floor; there are descriptions of large leather mats that would be spread under the food trays to avoid soiling the carpets and floor coverings. At night the family bedding would be brought out and spread on the floor for sleeping. Even in the Palace at Topkapi and the grandest houses the family slept on the floor. Servants were relegated to sleeping in corridors or in doorways, acting as guards.

Windows were seldom glazed but were fitted with wooden leaf shutters that would be kept shut all day to keep out the heat. Curtains were not common as hangings in front of windows; they were occasionally used inside a room to create a small private area. They were only introduced in the nineteenth century as part of the change to living in an European style.

Textiles played a very important role in daily life, so much so that in the accounts of grand houses there was a position, the 'makramaci', who was responsible for having the various cloths made and then looking after them. They were universally used, cheap to make or buy and easy to store and could be adapted easily to every level of society. Most of the textiles were plain cotton or woollen weaves and many of them were decorated with embroidery. There existed very clear rules as to how these textiles were to be used in society, and specific cloths were made to be used for one purpose. Many of these are described in the following pages.

NOTES

1. The women's quarters were called the 'enderun', the inside, and the men's the 'selamlık'. The harem was a specific part of the enderun and the word was only used when it referred to the women's quarter in grand houses.

62

A fine example of the hunchback pattern based on a stylized rose and a budded branch. A good quality professional napkin worked in gold and silver thread and wire and silk in filling stem stitch laid diagonally on a ribbed cotton. *c.* 1830. 47 x 17 cm.

Right Three napkins from the Turkish Aegean Islands.

Top The hunchback pattern simply executed in silk and gold thread on a cotton ground. Finished with a tasselled fringe, a style that is usually associated with Mytilene. *c.* 1850. 45 x 11 cm.

Middle Five plants each bearing five flowers set in trays, all placed within a three-sided border of the same flower in a meander. Silk, silver thread and wire on a fine cotton ground. Usually called the 'Island' style. *c.* 1850. 43 x 13 cm.

Bottom Two bowls containing a bunch of grapes, a quince and a pear are worked on the end of this napkin within a broad continuous border. This has been worked onto the end of a Cretan panel in feather stitch. Silk and gold tinsel on linen. *c.* 1840. 40 x 20 cm.

63

64

Napkins

A napkin of exceptional quality. Six isolated bunches of flowers set horizontally above a narrow border of flowers strung on a silver rope. Silk and silver thread stem stitch and running darning on a fine cotton ground. Formerly part of F.H. Cook collection. Before 1750. 75 x 12 cm.

Left Two napkins worked after 1920 using imported silks. *Top* A motif of grapes and pomegranates repeated on both ends and worked over an inked sketch. Coarse dyed silk worked with considerable skill on rough slubbed cotton. *c.* 1920. 44 x 20 cm. *Bottom* A conventional motif worked in a new style. Each flower or grape is worked separately in a circular stem stitch and the leaves are filled with diagonal stitch. The gilded copper strip is laid flat or couched on a thick cotton. *c.* 1920. 47 x 37 cm.

Overleaf Both ends of this napkin are covered with a motif of two crossed cornucopias set in close reversed pairs. A common motif worked in Tepebaşi about 1860. Silk, gold and silver thread and strip on cotton edged in metal crochet lace. 56 x 36 cm.

The most common of all the domestic embroidered cloths are those called napkins, which is a convenient translation of the three Turkish words by which they are known; peşkir, makrama and yağlik. Napkins were the universal cloths in constant use in the home, in formal and domestic situations.

Charles White, in writing about his travels in *Three Years in Constantinople, or Domestic Manners of the Turks in 1844,* in three volumes, often mentions the great use that is made of textiles in the house. Although in historic terms the Turkey he is writing about is very late in the life of the Ottoman Empire and over-influenced by the new pursuit of European fashions, his observations refer to a style of living established centuries before which still persisted. He specifically talks about the napkins:

> Muslin and cotton handkerchiefs...are employed less, perhaps, for the purposes to which such articles are applied in Europe, than for that of folding up money, linen, and other things. In the houses of the great men, there is always a 'makramaci başi', whose principal duty is to take care of these and other similar articles. No object, great or small, is conveyed from one person to another, no present is made — even fees to a medical man — unless folded in an handkerchief, embroidered cloth or piece of gauze. The more rich the envelope, the higher the compliment to the receiver.

The napkins are all of the same basic pattern, a single width of a hand-woven fabric, cotton or linen, usually 40-50 cm wide and from 80 to 100 cm long, with a decorated panel at each end. The fabric was usually plain white although there are many examples of both coloured and patterned ground cloth being used. The napkin would usually be

65

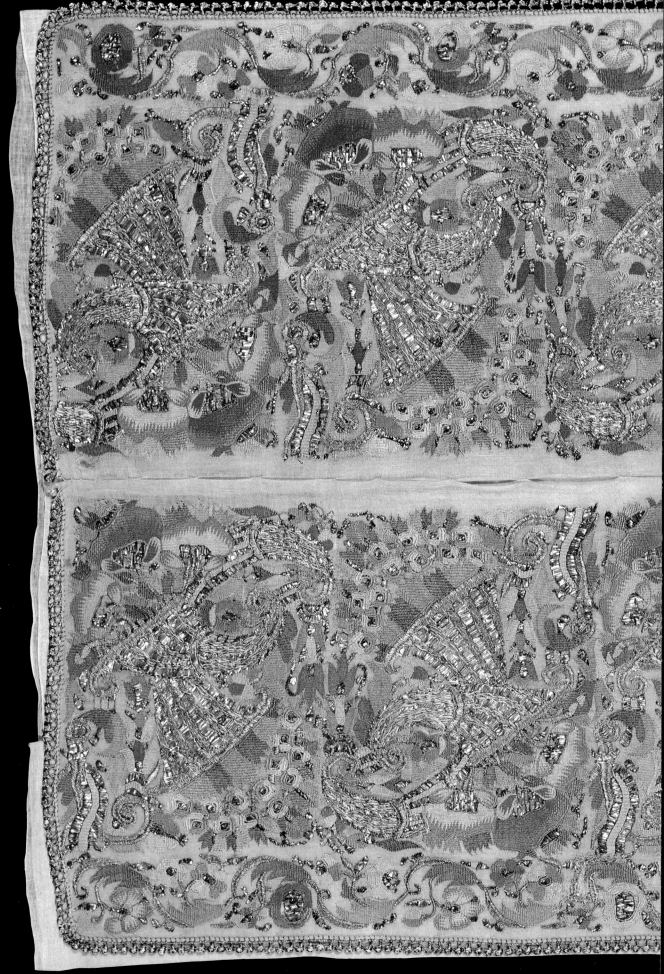

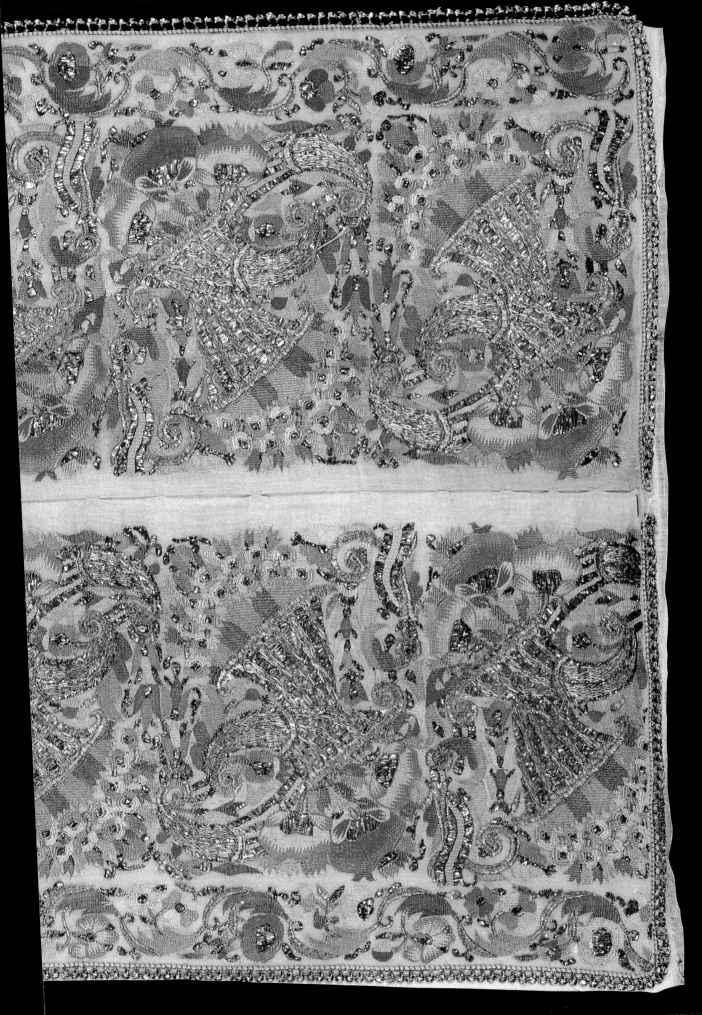

68

finished at both ends with the warp threads twisted into a fringe, sometimes with an added tassel. They were most commonly decorated in embroidery, which was found in every quality ranging from the most sumptuous gold and silver work to the very crudest, elementary work.

The grandest pieces would be used ceremonially to hold anything presented to a guest; no dish would be offered at table without it being held on a decorated cloth. Both before and after a meal a guest would be offered water to wet the fingers and a cloth on which to wipe them. It was vulgar to do more than just brush the fingers onto the cloth (presumably the washing had been done earlier and a proper towel used). At table the napkins were laid in the lap, folded under plates and dishes and hung alongside the ewers of water.

Another version of this table napkin is described by E.D. White in his book of travels published in London in 1816. In talking about the table and food in Turkey he says:

> The dinners, and indeed all other meals are wretched ... a long and coarse towel, very ill washed, about twelve inches wide, is spread around the table, in one entire piece, over the knees of the party seated.

This so-called towel is the napkin on which one actually cleaned one's fingers during the meal and where it still survives in use it is called yağlik.

Napkins were indispensable in the daily running of the house, and apart from the standard use at table they were used to cover books and documents and were often spread around as part of the furnishings. They were even used as decorations, hanging over cords that were stretched across the room behind where the bride was seated to receive her guests.

The version of napkins called makrama was originally a woven one from central Turkey, but the word was used to include the embroidered versions as well. In some parts of the Empire, particularly in the Aegean Islands, it came to mean a lavishly embroidered marriage head scarf.

All three names — peşkir, makrama and yağlik — are used and it is now futile to attempt to draw any distinctions between them, although it is certain that at one time they did have quite specific meanings. Today the napkins used in various circumstances all over Turkey can have quite different names. It may have once been possible to identify where each version of the napkin was made from its pattern of decoration, but it is not possible now as the same patterns can be found throughout Turkey; even the various embroidery techniques no longer specifically identify one place of production from another.

The embroidered motifs used in these napkins can be drawn from any of the various traditions used in all the other embroidered work, floral or geometric, landscape or pictorial. The embroidery is always

Top A large flowing motif from Renaissance Europe adapted to a napkin end. Stem stitch in silk in muted colours is contrasted with silver strip which would have filled most of the cotton ground to reinforce the appearance of an imported brocade with a silver ground. Before 1850. 52 x 19 cm.

Bottom A row of short columns joined at their tops by flower wreaths decorates each end of this large napkin. Bouquets of flowers are set in each arcade. *c.* 1860. 82 x 34 cm.

two-faced and worked on both ends of the napkin. It can be set either in a clearly delineated block or it can be a number of repeats of a single design set freely on a base line. The variety of designs is extremely large, usually following the current fashion. Even more of these napkins are woven than embroidered and often the weaving patterns are repeated in the embroidered ones.

Three napkins of apprentice or children's work.

Top A very simplified hunchback design is set in pairs on this napkin with an almost machine-worked border. This quality is usually called 'children's work'. Cheap metal tinsel and mercerized cotton have been used on a cotton ground. Weft threads have been withdrawn to make a voided panel of warp threads as a decorative end. *c.* 1920. 42 x 26 cm.

Middle Two debased hunchback patterns are set on each side of a striped Roman column. Apprentice work in silk and cotton with outlines and decorations in two-colour metal strip on a coarse cotton edged with a warp fringe. *c.* 1920. 47 x 11 cm.

Bottom This is another debased version of the pattern worked in mercerized cotton and metal thread on a coarse cotton. A very perfunctory border and a voided end panel. *c.* 1920. 45 x 12 cm.

Bath towels

The bath, the 'hamam', was a very important feature of Turkish life, attaining almost the position of a ritual. Very few houses had the amount of water, either hot or cold, that was necessary for a bath so the communal bath house provided them at a minimal cost. There were innumerable baths in every city and formed part of the services provided by the municipality or, more rarely, run by individuals. Many were designed by the most famous architects of the period, including Sinan. They were very sturdily built of stone and a large number of them have survived from the sixteenth century throughout Turkey and the Empire. Many were built on the sites of the bath houses of the Byzantines and, in a sense, continued the tradition that they had brought with them from Rome.

Men and women used separate bath houses or separated sections of the same building. These became centres of social life, particularly for the women who had no other meeting place. It was at the hamam that women gathered to talk and where, traditionally, marriages were arranged. The hamam in Western literature has acquired a reputation that is quite different to the reality, which was extremely conventional and modest and, in those used by the general public, the bathers remained partially covered at all times.

It was this need for the body to remain covered that has produced the large range of cloths necessary for the bath. The abundance of these cloths also allowed an opportunity of display and even ostentation that was usually not permitted for women outside the house. The weekly visit to the hamam by the women and young children of the household would be accompanied by the female servants, who were there to assist the family in their bath and also to bathe themselves. The progress to the bath would be accompanied by servants carrying piles of folded towels and cloths carefully arranged so that the richness of the embroidery could be seen, together with the copper, brass and even silver containers for sponges, soaps, oils and perfumes.

At the bath the bathers would move from one room to another, each of which had been heated to a different temperature. In some there was

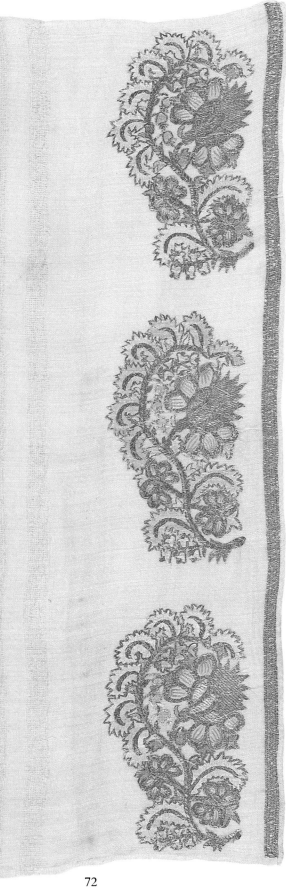

72

water available in basins or taps for washing and rinsing; other rooms were heated by steam for sweating, and finally there were the rooms for getting dry and relaxing after the rigours of the bath. In each of these rooms a different covering was required — these were the towels and bath sheets that covered one from head to toe.

During a stay in Constantinople (Istanbul) in 1836 Julia Pardoe wrote about a visit to a hamam:

> The busy slaves, passing and repassing, naked from the waist upwards and with their arms folded upon their bosoms, balancing on their heads piles of fringed or embroidered napkins...attentive slaves pour essence upon their [the bathers'] hair which they twist loosely without attempting to dislodge the wet, and then cover with handsome headkerchiefs of embroidered muslin.[1]

The towels also had a ritual and symbolic role in daily life. Rycaut observes in 1668 that when a commoner, invariably one who has attained a high position at Court, is made to marry a sister of the Sultan (usually as a means of binding him to the Sultan's service) he, the groom, is expected to make many very expensive gifts to her and she in return is only required to give him the linen to be used at his bath.

The towels were of two main types: those with a nap or pile and those without.[2] The napped towels, the smaller one called 'havlı' and a larger version called 'silecek', are woven in a single width in a combination of terry and plain weaving. The major central portion is terry weaving and there can be three or more bands of alternate terry and plain weaving at each end. All towels are woven in cotton; the smaller havlı are about 65 cm in width and a metre long, the silecek being usually a metre in width and anything up to 2.1 metres in length. The plain-weave towels without any nap, the 'peştemal', are usually made up of three separate woven lengths of about 40 cm width, again in cotton, which are joined together at the selvedge to make a bath sheet even larger than the silecek.

It is very usual for the plain ends of both types of towels to be embroidered: the ends of the napped towels are encrusted with silk and metal work and are clearly not meant to be used to dry oneself, they are to be draped around the body to absorb any water or sweat. The weight of the embroidery ensures that they fall gracefully about the body.

The embroidery is always two-faced, because both sides will be seen and the quality of the embroidery is usually very fine, almost certainly atelier professional work and not a domestic product. The design of the embroidery is either a single large isolated motif repeated as often as is necessary along the width of the towel or a broad, solid band of embroidery containing a repeated motif. In both cases the decoration stands just above a narrow, solid band of embroidery, usually including a vertical line of trees. There is never a second line of embroidery above the broad band.

Far left Three large flower and branch patterns fill the end of this large towel. The work is professional and constant washing has dimmed the colours. Silk and metal thread on a cotton weave with broad terry weave portions. The border is made of five rows of metallic flat stitch. *c.* 1870. 98 x 21 cm.

Left Three large encircling branches containing a sunflower with separated petals are set within a three-sided broad border on this large towel. The embroidery is mainly in wide gilded metal strip with a little silk diagonal stem stitch on a cotton weave with terry weave patches. A panel of voided weft threads has been left before the wide end. *c.* 1870. 86 x 25 cm.

BATH TOWELS

The motifs used in the decoration are either bunches of flowers standing in a container or, more grandly, an architectural feature. The favourite one is a kiosk standing at the water's edge with cypress trees on one side. Some of the professional pieces are very elaborate, showing large views of ruins with aqueducts, temples and colonades.

The plain towels, the peştemal, are also embroidered at both ends, identically on each of the three widths of which they are composed, but usually less elaborately and these are more likely to be worked at home. Both ends of each of the three lengths carry the same double-faced embroidery, usually a flower motif. Because the plain weave has no terry centre it is quite common for the main surface of the peştemal to be woven with a supplementary slubbed weft in an irregular pattern, sometimes even with weft threads of different gauges and textures being used. As this was the towel used for drying the body some irregularity in the surface would both accelerate the absorption of the water and act as a rough massage.

p.24, 88, 186

The embroidery is always carried out in silk in stem or satin stitch, identical on both sides. On the napped towels there is usually a great deal of ostentatious metal wire or strip. The colours of the silk have invariably faded because of the frequent washing that the towels must have received, but it is evident that they were always worked in rather subdued colours.

Another version of the peştemal is in a coarser plain weave and is always unembroidered.[3] This would be worn by both sexes in the wet rooms and would be frequently changed as it absorbed more water. The version used by men is about the size of the silecek, it is always in one piece and is often woven in an ikat technique. Some were originally woven in silk and later in synthetic yarn.

Large embroidered towels were seldom used at home; some versions of a napped towel the size of a napkin were used when indoor washing facilities became more common and these are quite late, most probably introduced after 1920. By that time commercial towelling was both made in Turkey and imported, and the embroidered version was replaced by a plain towel. Eventually towels were no longer embroidered at all, other than small hand cloths made for the tourist trade.

NOTES

1. Julia Pardoe, *The City of the Sultans and the Domestic Manners of the Turks in 1836*. London 1838. Vol 1, p.133.

2. The napped towels, 'havlı', from the Persian 'hav', nap. The Turkish word for nap is 'ölker'.

3. This plain towel is called 'futa', the generic word in Arabic for a cloth. In the Yemen it is the word for the universal sheath of material worn by men around the waist to cover their legs, and the same usage is common in the Maghreb.

74

A detail from a peştemal showing the central panel of three. Two stylized flowers, a rose and a tulip form, are set in four staggered rows to fill the end of this bath sheet. This is highest quality professional work involving very fine stitches with the best quality silk and metal thread on a fine cotton weave. The border is particularly fine. Before 1800. Central panel 45 cm square.

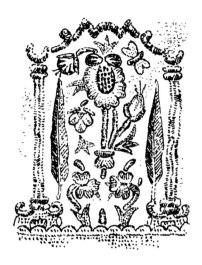

Cushion covers

The only formal part of the Turkish house was the area where visitors were entertained and where the family, or at least the male members of the family, gathered. In larger and richer households there was also a separate room where the women gathered and entertained their visitors, who were always other women and most usually close relatives. The visitors' area would be furnished with a raised bench-like couch[1] which ran along three sides of the room, usually quite low, with the windows set just above it. The seat and back of this continuous bench would be covered with hard stuffed cushions like mattress biscuits. The couch would often have decorative fabrics spread over it; paintings of these rooms are quite common and they often show knotted carpets and kilims spread over the seat. The back of the bench would be covered with softer cushions, virtually the only concession to comfort that was made in the house.

The two main versions of these cushions were the 'minder' and the 'uzun yastık'.[2]

The minder was the square or rectangular hard cushion used on the seat of the sofa as a fixed feature, but sometimes also set along the wall, on top of the base cushions, to make a firm back rest. They were very solid, being stuffed with scrap wool or cotton wadding or even with chopped straw and covered with a hard-wearing plain fabric, as it was usual for one to sit on them with one's unshod feet drawn up onto the sofa.

In the richer households minders would be covered with velvet or brocade covers made in Bursa and Istanbul. They were woven in long lengths on a fine cotton warp with a coarser cotton or even hemp weft, with each repeat separated from the next by a narrow band of warp threads alone, allowing them to be cut into single facings. The velvet facing was woven in silk usually in one colour, most commonly red. Later versions were made in two or three colours and many had silver or gold-covered wefts woven into the flat areas surrounding the tufted velvet patterns. The standard pattern for these cushions was a central

This cushion cover on a satin ground is a later version of those made in the sixteenth century on velvet. A single spray is arranged in four rows with one of the flowers set in the 'houses' at each end. Silk single couching and two-directional stem stitch on silk satin. *c.* 1800. 120 x 118 cm.

77

area of pattern filling the whole width, selvedge to selvedge, and a band of a repeat motif of vertical lappets at both ends. This pattern survived until the middle of the eighteenth century when the European influence developed different patterns.[3]

The demand for these new patterns was so great, both in Turkey and in Europe where the Turkish fashion had a short vogue in the nineteenth century, that new factories were set up to produce them. The best known of them was in Scutari on the Asian shore of the Bosphorus, but there were also manufacturing units in Chios, Aleppo and Damascus. The last two factories were run by Genoese Italians who produced cheaper versions with very thick wefts of coarse hemp and often with cotton rather than silk velvet pile.

Although the usual covering was the woven velvet one, embroidered versions of the covers are also found. Minders in Palaces were covered with plain red or blue silk velvet or satin covered with decorative patterns in gold or silver dival work. These are even referred to as being worked with pearls and precious stones, rather like the velvet carpets which covered the floor of the throne room. A more modest version of the embroidered velvet covers was made following the standard pattern of the covers, but embroidered on a stout cotton ground in a fairly thick 4-stranded cotton thread. They were made at home and were much cheaper than the commercially produced version worked with silk. Many cushion covers have perished because they received such hard wear.

p.76

p.186

p.191

These cushions and their covers have been described and used from the end of the fifteenth century and are clearly illustrated in many miniatures and paintings of the period.

The second version of the cushion, the long bolster, the uzun yastık, was made to be used in conjunction with the other cushion, not fixed but set out in an uneven number along the back of the sofa. They could be moved and were often used as arm rests. The bolster covers were made in cotton or linen and both outer faces were worked with identical designs. The decoration was usually confined to a narrow border on all four sides with a little ornament set into each corner. Versions are found with a pattern covering the whole surface. The bolsters were long and narrow and were much softer than minders, being filled with light fluffy wool or cotton, or later with feathers. They were to be found in use throughout the Ottoman Empire and the forms that they took were very influenced by the local tradition. The bolsters found in Morocco, Algiers and Tunis are very different to those of Epirus and the Balkans in shape, size and decoration.

p.161

p.169

The introduction in about 1850 of chairs and free-standing sofas so changed living style that the type of room with sofas running along the walls went out of fashion, and so reduced the demand for both the minder and its covers that they were no longer made. The factories which had been set up to make them were converted to producing

A small bolster cover which is entirely covered in an extended decoration, including kiosks, trees and flowers, with arches at both ends in the style of a hearth carpet. An unusual pattern entirely in small chain stitch on cotton. *c.* 1880. 86 x 41 cm.

79

A bolster cover decorated with five repeats, set vertically, of a flower flanked by two leaves within a mountain border. Silk couched stitch with outlining on an unbleached linen ground. Before 1720. 137 x 39 cm.

small velvet table carpets. The conventional European square cushion was introduced and the cover was changed to fit the new shape. Covers were made in every type of fabric, the most popular being the printed square, although embroidered versions are to be found, but they bear no particular feature that identifies them as part of the mainstream of Turkish embroidery. Some patterns are taken from traditional embroidery but it is much more common for them to copy imported patterns.

A detail of a large couch cover from Morocco. Large medallions are placed over a broad border. Floss silk worked in long stem stitch on a red cotton ground. Rabat, *c.* 1850. The whole cloth 180 x 90 cm.

NOTES

1. This long bench is called a 'sedir', and the room itself is often called a 'majlis', a place for sitting.

2. The word minder is often used in Turkish to denote official position and creates an image of the official lounging back on his cushions. 'Minder çikmek' is the phrase used for becoming an official and 'minder geçmek' means to rise to a more important heirarchial position.

3. *Turkish Velvet Cushion Covers* by Jennifer M. Wearden. Victoria and Albert Museum, Leaflet No.5.

Quilt facings and bedding

Before the middle of the nineteenth century no separate room was dedicated for sleeping in the standard Ottoman house. The common living area was adapted as was needed for any particular purpose. It was only at court and in the grandest of private houses that there were rooms in which beds were permanently set up and this was only so after the introduction of the European style after 1840; in Topkapi no particular room can be identified as the Sultan's bedchamber (as there would have been in a contemporary royal palace in Europe). Even in Dolmabahçe Palace the Sultan's bedroom is very modest, almost a cubicle off a passage on the ground floor, although there are about five bedrooms for the Sultan's wives on the first floor of the harem, doubling as their private quarters.

In all houses before then and in most until the 1930s it was usual for beds to be laid out at night in any space that was available. The family would have the beds made up in the living quarters, usually in the sofa; less important family members and the servants would sleep in corridors, across doors, on the roof or in the outside verandahs. During the day all the bedding would be stored in cupboards,[1] or kept in piles against the wall, covered with a cloth and used as seating.

The bedding was composed of a number of thick biscuit mattresses, pillows, a quilt and a top sheet.[2] The bed was made by spreading the mattress, covered with a thin blanket, a 'battaniye', on the floor, with the pillows at the head covered with a loose cloth. The quilt would have a cotton or linen, or even silk, sheet spread under it with all four sides folded up over the top and lightly tacked to it. Finally the quilt facing, the 'yorgan yüzü', would be spread over the quilt and tacked to the top surface to cover the turned-up edge of the sheet that had been folded over it. It is most likely that at the head of the quilt the facing was sewn under the turned oversheet so that it would not be directly handled. There is a description of this bed in M. Guer's *Moeurs et Usages des Turcs*, published in Paris in 1747:

Leur lit consiste dans un ou deux matelas, qu'ils étendent le soir sur les tapis:

A quilt facing patterned on a trellis made of a twisted wreath. The trellis has decomposed into a directionless framework filled with spotted red rhomboids which are deformed flower heads containing a bouquet rising from a vestigial urn. The wreath in its original form survives in the border. Single darning in silk on linen. The work is from the Ottoman Province of Epirus. Before 1700. 165 x 270 cm.

Leurs draps sont cousus l'un au matelat même, l'autre a la couverture qui est de toile peinte, d'étoffe de soie, ou de brocard....³

It is clear that Guer took his information from Rycaut's *State of the Ottoman Empire*, London, 1668, and like many writers about the Ottomans he had little direct experience of them and having seen only illustrations or prints had assumed from them that the decorated surface was a painted cloth and not embroidery.

John Morley, in his *Life of Gladstone*, quotes the passage in his secretary's diary of Gladstone's visit to 'the Old Lady of Filiates' in Albania during his Mission to the Ionian Islands in 1856:

> We all slept in the same room and that was not a large one, and we were packed tight on the floor under quilts of Bursa silk and gold, tucked up round us by gorgeous Albanians.

The quilt facing is one of the oldest surviving of all Ottoman domestic embroideries. The facings would have only been used in wealthy households and would have been made by professional embroiderers; they were very expensive to make and would therefore have been extremely prized. The way in which they were used meant that they sustained no hard wear and a large number of them have consequently survived. The fashion for using them lasted until about 1800 when they were replaced by the more conventional two-faced quilt cover like a bag, which persists today. The bag version was usually made in a printed or woven fabric, so the embroidered facings were kept and were not usually recycled for another use. The only changes they sustained were the occasional over-embroidery with metal thread when that fashion was thought to enhance their appearance and to make them suitable for use as table cloths or hangings.

Quilt facings have been usually described in the West as curtains, mainly because they are of an appropriate shape and size. In fact there was little use for curtains of this type in most Turkish houses. Such curtains as there were are always made of much stouter materials such as damasks and brocades and were used to keep the sun out of rooms. They were usually woven with a pattern or printed with a simple decoration.

Quilt facings were produced from the sixteenth century to the beginning of the nineteenth century. At the start of this period they were worked on a fine linen ground which was a hand-woven bleached gauze with a count of 24 x 22 per cm, and by the end of it they were made on a fairly coarse standard machine-woven cotton fabric with a count of 18 x 15 per cm. The facing is made by sewing three strips of this fabric, which is usually 42-48 cm wide, together to make a panel measuring 220-266 cm by 124-144 cm. There are occasionally pieces that are smaller, 185 x 126 cm, but these are more unusual.

These pieces are always worked on one face only, as the underside

A corner of a quilt facing in the most sophisticated sixteenth-century style, in the tradition of the great tile designs, which were copied in weavings and carpets for the next three centuries. The elegant cartouches are linked together by flower tendrils and the Chinese cloud band, both of which also appear in the broad border. Fine single darning on linen. Before 1700. 92 x 56 cm.

was never intended to be seen, unlike a curtain. The embroidered decoration is always in silk; in the early pieces it is an untwisted floss silk dyed in bright luminous colours, predominantly red and blue but also in a green, a soft yellow, white and black. In later pieces the silk used is a machine-twisted yarn which has been commercially dyed, and a number of new colours have been introduced: a shocking pink, a violet and a startling gold. In the older pieces the black silk, which was used both to outline some motifs in the design and to emphasize others, has deteriorated and fallen out. This is because the process of dyeing the black silk involved a number of stages, one of which involving boiling at a high temperature, which has weakened the threads of the yarn. Where this black has been replaced a heavily twisted modern yarn has been used which is too black and shiny, and the new embroidery has been worked too tightly in stem stitch. This throws the pattern out of balance and is, fortunately, quite easily detected.

p.64

p.185

The early pieces from the middle of the sixteenth century to about the beginning of the eighteenth century are worked in a counted darning stitch 'pesent', which is worked over three ground threads. There are some pieces where the embroidery is so exact that it has been suggested that they were in fact embroidered on the loom using a floating weft technique with separate bobbins for each colour. I do not think that this theory can now be supported; the way in which the pattern is worked on the selvedge edge and the way in which the panels match would indicate embroidery rather than weaving. During the eighteenth century the couched Bokhara stitch, 'atma', was introduced and the quilt facings became more substantial, carrying a heavier weight of embroidery, and suggesting the greater availability of cheaper silk. By the end of that century these cloths, which may no longer even have been used as quilt facings but as general covers, were worked in a range of satin and chain stitch which had been worked either in the hand or on a tambour frame with a hook.

p.204

The decoration of quilt facings is worked after the panel has been joined together. The embroidery is placed over a pattern that had been drawn in outline by hand. The basic form of the decoration is an overall pattern contained within a border. Because the quilt facing would be made so that the top edge would be under the top sheet it is not unusual for the border to run around only three sides, although this is not always so.

The border is usually contained within two thin embroidered lines, and the pattern can either be a continuous wreath or a band interspersed with single flowers. The border pattern often copies the pattern and colours of the main design in the field. A variant of this broad border is a row of a three-pointed or lobed motif set on a thick line facing out, with no line on the extreme edge of the panel. This must be a simplified version of a very sophisticated pattern derived from the mountain border found in Chinese textiles of the same period. It can be worked

One joined panel of a quilt facing in the fluid Saz style, so called after the calligrapher's reed pen. The ground is filled with thick upright stems supporting an acanthus and a peach leaf set in opposed pairs. Fine single darning on linen gauze. Before 1650. 186 x 56 cm.

86

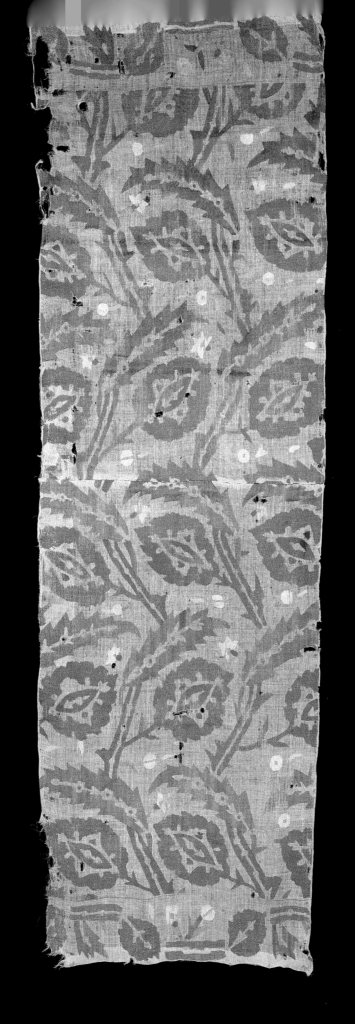

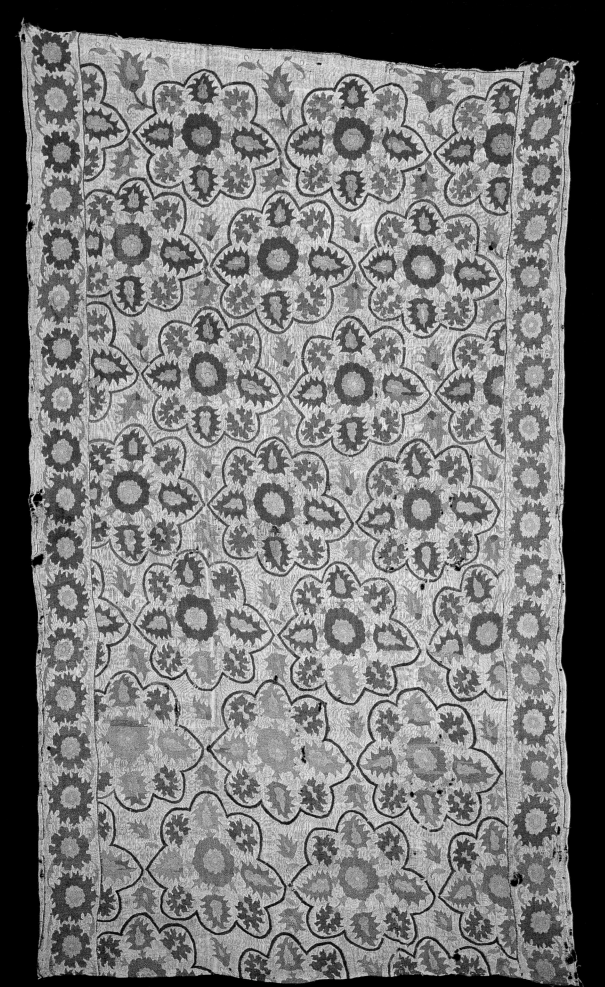

as either a thick or a thin line with the mountain peaks being either long or short. It is more often than not worked in a dark blue or black or very rarely in a dark red.

The patterns used on these quilt facings are those which were current from the fifteenth to the end of the eighteenth century on most household and ceremonial textiles, and as this is the first opportunity to describe them I shall do so here in detail and refer back to this section later, in the chapter on design and patterns.

The patterns used vary considerably and can be broken down into eight main groups.

p.87

LEAVES This pattern is found on some of the oldest pieces and is very similar to the woven textiles of the period. It is composed of rows of an acanthus or artichoke leaf loosely fixed to a continuous band.

OGIVAL This is a rare pattern, and unlike the other patterns is related to those found on carpets. The example shown on the title page has motifs similar to those found on Timurid carpets.

p.13, 15, 82, 116, 120

TRELLIS There are many variants on this basic pattern. The main form is a trellis — most commonly a broad, straight or sinuous strap — set diagonally in both directions to cover the whole surface of the cloth. It can either be set out in full with the straps crossing each other regularly, or the straps can be broken and interrupted by small motifs, such as crowns or flowers set at the intersections.

p.181

The diamond-shaped spaces created by the trellis are usually filled with either a single motif or by a more complicated arrangement of flowers and cartouches.

p.108, 119

WAVY BANDS In this version the regular trellis has disintegrated, losing its rigid structure. This results in the pattern becoming a series of vertical upright wavy bands running parallel, without touching. In rare cases the bands run horizontally, and sometimes the bands in both directions deteriorate and become disjointed into a series of half loops.

p.109

p.117

HORIZONTAL LEAVES Another development of the trellis pattern is where the vertical bands have been lost and the remaining horizontal bars have become elongated leaves set in opposing pairs, to make a pattern of a single motif in rows separated by rows of these leaves.

SINGLE MOTIFS In this group the simplest pattern of all has been used, of one motif repeated in rows horizontally, vertically or diagonally. The motifs are repeated exactly, the only variation is a change in colour.

ALTERNATE MOTIFS The pattern of the previous group is here varied by using two different motifs. They are set out in exactly the same way and the same colour contrasting is used. The two main variations are to have both motifs of the same weight and solidity (the most common example of this is the carnation and artichoke leaf pattern), or to have

A quilt facing with the ground covered in a staggered repeat of a pattern called 'çinili', based on an octagonal Kashan wall tile of nine flowers. The border is a simple repeat of two flowers joined with small green leaves. Split thread Bokhara couching and stem stitch in silk on a firm linen ground. Before 1750. 210 x 122 cm.

89

one motif a solid, such as a filled cartouche or medallion, and the other a floral spray or a thin branch.

OVER-ALL PATTERN This last version is one where the formal structure has been abandoned and the pattern is a repeat of a slight floral, vegetal motif used as it would be in a woven or printed fabric. When the embroidered quilt facing was replaced by the more familiar two-faced quilt cover it was this over-all pattern that was copied, as being easier to adapt to any size of quilt.

p.85, 100, 101

The patterns used in all eight groups were also used in the square covers, 'bohça', the turban covers, 'kavuk örtüsü', and the bolster covers which were sometimes made as a set with the quilt facing.

NOTES

1. These cupboards were called 'musandıra'.

2. The mattresses of which the bed was composed were called 'yatak' if they were in one piece and by the same name as the hard cushions, 'minder', when they were separated into two or three pieces. The pillows, of which there would be two or four, are called 'yastık'. They would be quite soft, filled with scraps of textile or wool; it was only much later that they were filled with feathers. The quilt is the 'yorgan' and was used throughout the Balkans. Quilts were known in Greece as 'paploma' and in central Europe as 'paplan'. The sheet, 'çarşaf' was not common, and was used on ceremonial occasions such as weddings or circumcisions. It was very often made of silk and can be found with a broad band of decorative embroidery at one end.

3. 'Their bed consists of one or two mattresses, that they stretch out at night on the carpet. Their sheets are sewn, one onto the mattress itself, the other to the cover which is made of painted cloth, the material of silk or brocade.' (Vol. 1, p.389)

A quilt facing filled with a very formal pattern composed of repeats of a two-branched spray reversed in alternate rows. A simple motif is used for the border. Silk couching on linen. c. 1800. 196 x 126 cm.

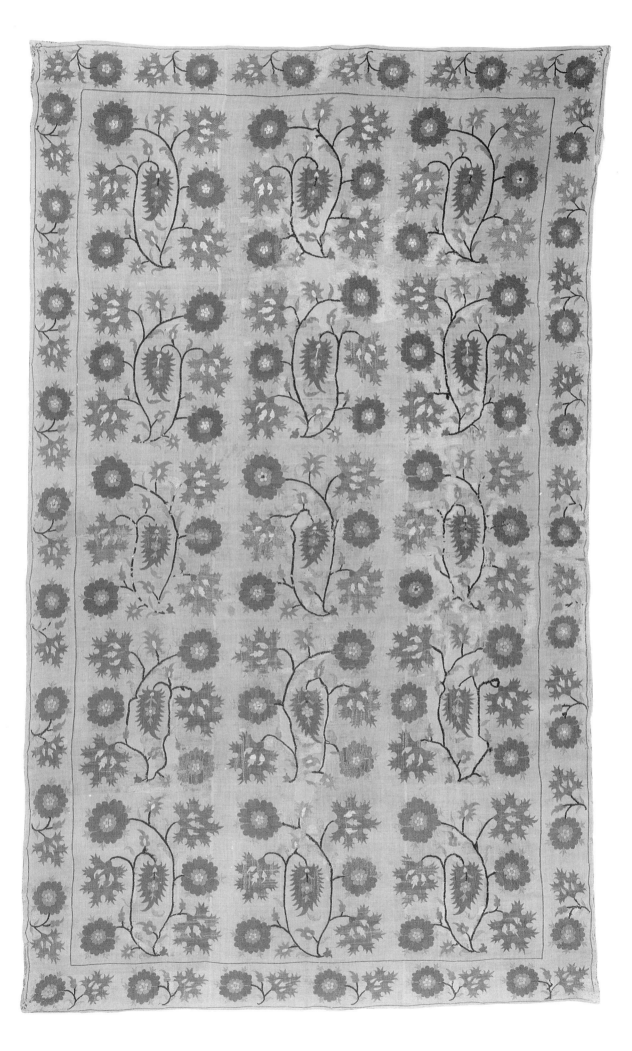

Turban covers

The turban was worn in Ottoman society as a sign of status, its form and shape indicating the rank and degree of the wearer. There were two main forms of the turban: that worn daily, the 'sarık', was formed of a length of finely woven cotton about 50 cm wide which was wound round and round the head, or around a small felt pill-box cap, to make a large solid hat. It was usually unwound at night and the cloth of which it was composed was washed whenever necessary. The other, larger formal version, the 'kavuk', was a much more prepossessing article, made of the same cloth as the sarık but differing in that the length of material was filled with cotton wadding to make thick soft cords which were then built up into a turban on a model.[1]

The first eyewitness account in English of a scene in Ottoman Turkey has been left by Anthony Jenkinson, who was a factor for the Turkey Merchants in Aleppo. He saw Sultan Suleiman passing through Aleppo on his way to 'give battel to the Great Sophi' Shah Tahmasp I in 1534, and recounts:

> Came the great Turke himself with great pompe and magnificence...having on each side of his person one page clothed with cloth of gold; he himselfe was mounted upon a goodly white horse, adorned with a robe of cloth of gold, embroidered most richly with the most precious stones, and upon his head a goodly white tucke, containing in length by estimation fifteene yards, which was of silke and linen woven together, resembling something Callicut cloth, but is more fine and rich, and in the top of his crowne a little pinnach of white Ostriche fethers and his horse most richly apparelled in all points correpondent to the same.

The many versions of the kavuk identified the rank, profession and even the race of the wearer. Some kavuk were extremely large and the tendency was for them to be made larger and larger to reflect the importance of the wearer. Eventually, in an attempt to limit their size, legislation was introduced that stipulated how much material could be

A round cover used on a tray or for covering food set on a tray. The most elegant version of the long tulip is placed between two artichoke leaves alternating with a plane tree leaf, all set around a central circle. A sparse style of decoration favoured in the seventeenth century. Fine diagonal single darning in silk on linen gauze. Before 1700. 98 x 89 cm.

used in each turban. This legislation had originated in Mamluk Egypt and was incorporated into the Kanuni Teshrifat by Suleiman. The maximum length of cotton permitted in each turban according to the Kanun was ten ells (over 12 metres) for the Faithful, while the maximum for Christians and Jews was only half that. These restrictions were not successful because the turbans still grew larger and larger by increasing the amount of padding. European paintings of the sixteenth century show how exaggerated the fashion had become.

So significant was the turban that the headstone placed on the grave of the Ottoman official was carved with the form of the turban he was entitled to in life so as to show his position in the society he had left. After the dress reforms of 1829 the turban was replaced by the conical, brimless cap, the 'tarbuş', for all except the religious leaders. Certain professions, such as teachers, who were considered as clerical staff, wore the tarbuş but wound a few feet of white cloth around its base to make it look like a clerical turban.

Once the kavuk was made, the various layered cords of the stuffed cloth were sewn in place and the kavuk was never dismantled. It was therefore not possible to wash it as it was to wash the material from which the sarık was made, so some form of protection had to be found to keep dust off the kavuk. When not being worn it was kept on a stand, the 'kavukluk', rather like the elaborate wigs of contemporary Europe, and both were stored in a cupboard. It was essential that the kavuk be covered and a special cover was introduced for this purpose, the 'kavuk örtüsü'. A painting by van Mour of 1708 shows the Sultan Ahmed III in his throne room wearing a complicated kavuk, but also having two other kavuks on their stands arranged behind him.

These turban covers were always square and their particular purpose was indicated by a circle set in the middle; this was usually 60 cm in diameter, but it was always arranged to fit in with the general pattern decided on for the whole cloth. In some pieces the single obligatory circle is developed into a number of concentric ones. The patterns used to decorate the whole surface of the cloth, including the area within the circle, are those contemporary ones found on quilt facings and wrappers — usually single flowers or sprays of flowers set on a hooked, curved branch. For the grander covers, usually those with multiple circles, a special design was developed that fitted into the design constraints.

The kavuk was a prestigious article; it represented authority and power and was imbued with an almost religious significance, so its cover became prestigious and was originally worked in the highest quality of professional embroidery. These covers are always known as 'harem' pieces, implying that they were used in the Palace, not that they were made by the ladies of the harem. It is more likely that they were made in the Palace by the professional embroiderers working there.

Women did not wear turbans. They had various other headgear,

p.96, 97

A turban cover composed of two concentric circles set in a rectangle. The inner circle is filled with a tight composite design of roses, sunflowers, daisies and lilies. A single spray of a carnation and a few hyacinth flowers fills the rest of the cloth. This is highest quality professional embroidery usually called 'harem' work. Silk and metal-covered yellow silk stem stitch, with the centre of the sunflowers filled with metal thread pulled stitch. Before 1830. 115 x 100 cm.

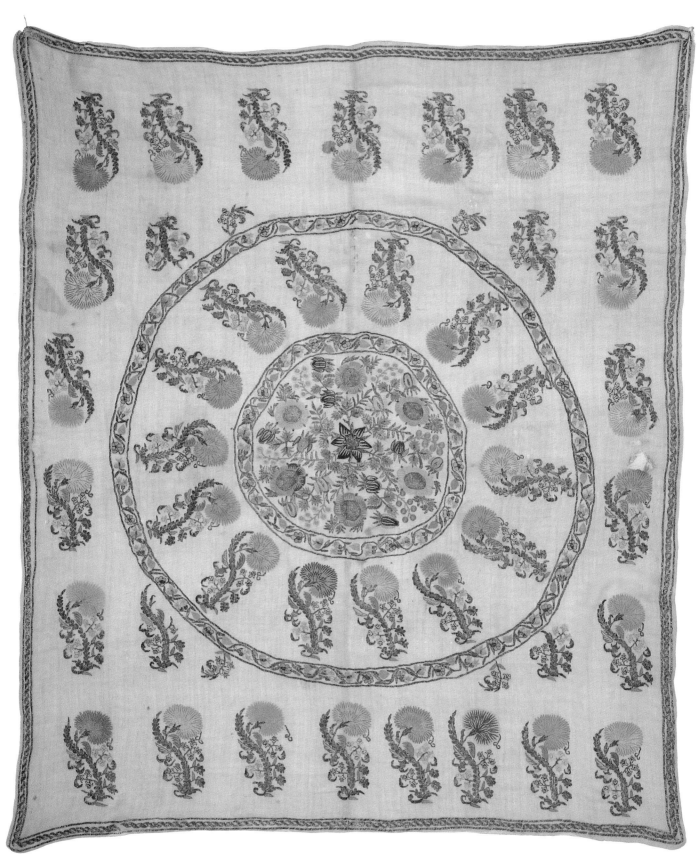

usually an embroidered cloth held in place by a ribbon.[2] The most impressive of the women's headgear was the 'hotoz' which was a construction some 60-80 cm tall worn on the head rather like a top hat. It had originally been made of horse or yak's hair and signified that the woman was a member of the Imperial family. Tall head-dresses became a sign of nobility and appeared in many different forms.[3] When these hotoz were stored they had covers made of fine gauze, usually white or green with very fine metal-thread embroidery on them. These covers are very rare, most having deteriorated as the embroidery has destroyed the gauze base but also because they were of such fine work that they were reused in other pieces.

This turban cover is in the same style as the previous one but was made by a domestic embroiderer. The complicated spray has been simplified to a small flower spray and a very simple design is placed in the inner circle. Mercerized cotton and cheap metal thread on a loose cotton ground. c. 1870. 94 x 88 cm.

The central circle of blue leaves contains a motif of three different flowers and green leaves. This motif is repeated eight times to fill the whole ground. Silk feather stitch worked in straight lines on a linen ground. *c.* 1720. 103 cm. square.

NOTES

1. The usual turban worn by most men was the 'sarık'. The more formal version worn by the Officials of the state and by religious leaders was the 'kavuk'.

2. These ribbons are called 'kaşbastı', and are worn above the eyebrow, 'kaş'. There are a number of classic headbands found in Imperial tombs of the second half of the sixteenth century, but they were not part of the standard costume and do not appear in descriptions or prints of later fashions.

3. Cornelius de Bruyn in his *Voyage au Levant*, published in Paris in 1714, reproduces a number of costume plates which are mainly of the different types of Turkish and Ottoman Greek head-dresses.

Mirror covers

Left A detail of the middle mirror cover on page 101.

Overleaf left Mirror covers.

Top A large hunchbacked branch with six blue carnations, six open roses and six in bud is repeated three times to fill the whole cover. Multi-directional stem stitch in silk on fine linen. Before 1720. 129 x 48 cm.

Middle A stem bearing five roses, five blue daisies and three yellow dianthus is repeated one and a half times in each of five rows. Stem stitch in silk on a loose linen ground. Before 1720. 128 x 48 cm.

Bottom Two curved branches bearing six roses and six blue chrysanthemums are repeated four times, reversing alternately, for the whole length of this cover. Stem stitch and pulled stitch in silk on a firm linen. Before 1720. 141 x 48 cm.

In the pre-Islamic world of the nomadic forefathers of the Seljuks and the Oghuz Turks, and before they spread to the West and conquered Turkey, the mirror was a powerful ritualistic object used in Shamanist ceremonies. It was usually made of polished metal or stone and was always kept covered when not being used. The mirror is a potent object in folk tales throughout Asia and appears in Central Asian as well as in Japanese and Chinese myths as a sacred article with great power. Even in the classical Greek and Roman world mirrors were valued and revered. They were made with heavily decorated backs in relief, so that when not being held in the hand they could not be put down with the reflecting surface uppermost.

The belief was, and persists in rural Turkey, that a mirror is the portal by which the Devil enters the house and therefore must not be left uncovered. As a lesser evil mirrors were thought to encourage vanity and deceit in women and were to be used sparingly. Before the availability of industrially manufactured glass, mirrors were made of small pieces of hand-made glass and then silvered by a manual process; they were consequently very expensive objects and were used with care. They were often protected by being incorporated into the folding lids of boxes or set into small frames. They would be used standing upright on the floor or on shelves and the surface would always be covered with a cloth when not in use.

In the Ottoman world, where every opportunity was taken to formalize and standardize objects, these covering cloths were developed into a very specific article of a special shape and with one unique function. They were made of a single length of a fine material that would hang over the mirror surface but which would be light enough to be easily lifted and folded back while the mirror was in use.

The earliest of these covers, 'ayna örtüsü', are those of the seventeenth century, and their original form persisted until about 1850. They were made of a single width of a fine linen hand-weave, 40 cm wide and about 1.5 m long. The selvedges were left in their original state and

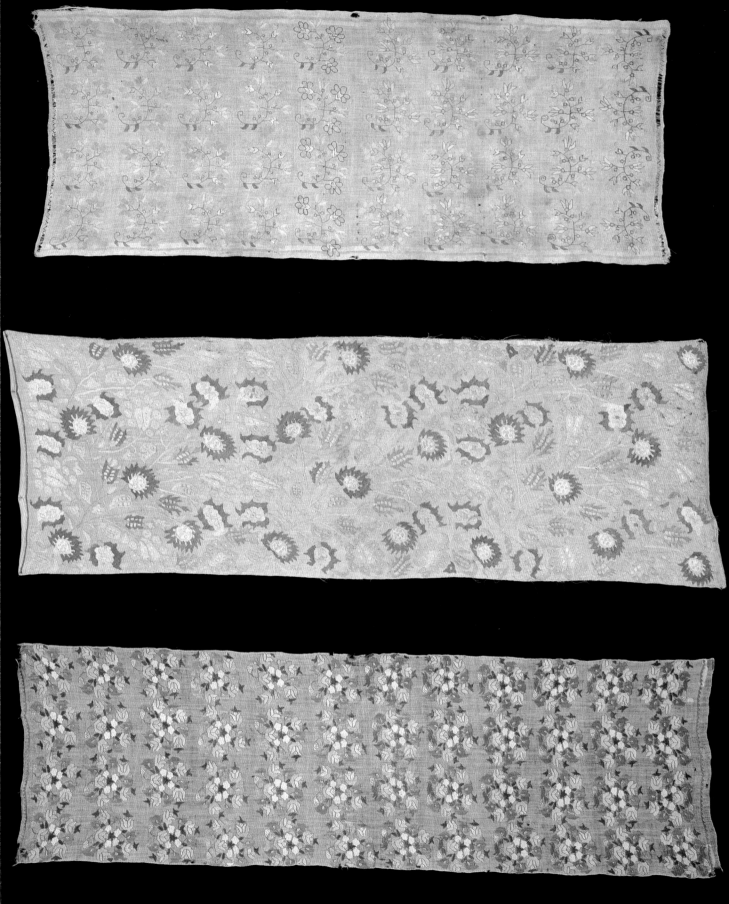

the two ends were finished in a rolled hem with one row of stem stitch in blue to define the end of the decorated area. To make the fine fabric more opaque the whole surface of the cover was covered with embroidery incorporating motifs that were used elsewhere in the other domestic textiles. The basic motif was usually the curved branch with flowers and leaves springing from it. Repeats of this motif were placed all over the cloth to make an over-all pattern, giving the appearance of a woven fabric with an irregular repeat. These covers were always worked on both sides in darning or stem stitch so that when turned over on the mirror they looked the same.

Towards the end of the eighteenth century the introduction of mechanically printed textiles from Europe changed the fashion of the decoration from the curling branch to motifs copying the new prints. These motifs were usually composed of a central flower surrounded by a number of other similar flowers, the motifs tending to be rather square, almost as if they had been made by a block. They were placed in rows, either regularly or staggered all over the cloth.

At the beginning of the nineteenth century the technology of glass-making changed so that larger sheets of glass could be produced from which much cheaper mirrors could be made. Larger mirrors came into fashion and they were either set into large frames to be hung on walls throughout the house, or into cheval fittings for use in dressing rooms. At that time the need for the original mirror coverings also changed and a different form of the cover was introduced. This new cover was much

One end of a mirror cover with a motif of quinces and leaves on a large branch alternating with small upright branches in pots, within a shaped border. Gold thread and strip with details in silk on cotton. *c.* 1870. 56 x 36 cm.

Previous page Mirror covers.

Top A single small hunchbacked motif like a block print repeated in ten rows. One half has red flowers and the other half pink with the last row reversed. Running stem stitch on linen. Before 1770. 125 x 48 cm.

Middle A many branched motif bearing four different flowers, the end version enlarged so that it bears nearly forty flowers. Multi-directional stem stitch on fine linen. Before 1720. 136 x 48 cm.

Bottom A tight multi-coloured bouquet copying a wood block print repeated four to a row for ten rows. A stronger red is used for half the repeats with the last row reversed. Stem stitch laid in rows on a very fine linen ground. Before 1750. 138 x 42 cm.

larger, and it also became less important that the covers be opaque: the original purpose of the covers became confused and they were now made of either machine lace or a fine transparent gauze. There was less need for embroidery, and if the new covers were embroidered it was restricted to one end only and was fairly perfunctory. The older covers were used either as table runners or were recycled into composite covers.

However, the idea that mirrors needed to be covered persisted and elaborate wall mirrors were provided with shutters or closeable screens. One can still see mirrors in Turkey with a cloth placed over them or draped in swags over the top. It is no longer possible to define the cloths as specifically mirror covers as they have no particular distinguishing features.

In the earlier mirror covers a soft palette of colours was used, predominantly blue, pale red and gold. It was standard practice for each repeat of the basic pattern to be worked in exactly the same colours. Although the curved-branch pattern used would have had a stalk worked in black on any other embroidered article of the period, in this case the stalk is very often worked in gold, giving a more harmonious appearance. When the isolated motif pattern was introduced it was worked in a much wider range of colours; strong reds and greens were used with highlights of many other colours. It was then quite common for the repeats to change colours in alternate rows, or even to alternate in colour within each row.

Relatively few of the embroidered versions of these cloths were made, and fewer have survived. Those that did are usually identified as separated panels from some larger object, such as a dismembered quilt facing, or more frequently and erroneously as a curtain.

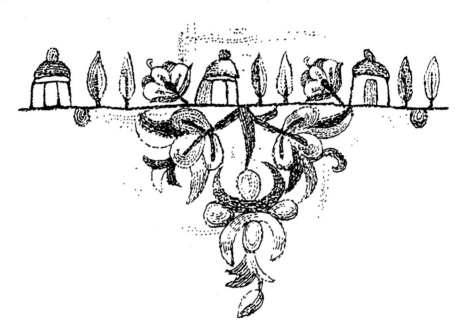

Ceremony

Ceremony and ritual were extremely important in Ottoman life. The year was regulated by two cycles of ceremonies, the obligatory one of religious observances that followed the religious year based on the lunar cycle, and the folk festivals of the land that followed the solar year. The religious festivals changed dates on the solar calendar from year to year and were therefore celebrated in different circumstances each year. The most important of these was the month of Ramazan and the Feast of Bayram which ended it.[1] The Bayram Greetings made by the State to the Sultan Caliph and by him to his subjects were the most spectacular of the annual Court ceremonies. They were originally held at the main inner gate of Topkapi Palace, the Babüsaade; after Abdul Mecid moved the Court to Dolmabahçe in 1853 they were held in the main Hall of the new Palace, the Muayede Hall.[2]

The Ottomans had very early started to celebrate the Persian New Year festival, which fell every year on 22 March. This Nevruz was the start of the secular year and the pivot around which all the festivals associated with the land and agriculture revolved. The Ottoman year was therefore filled with two different cycles of observances and festivities, the movable religious one and the annual cycle tied to the seasons and the land.

During the reign of Ahmed III, the high years of the Tulip Age, the Nevruz Festival was celebrated together with the Tulip Fêtes and the Imperial Viewing of the Tulips. Jean Claude Flachat, a French textile industrialist, visited Turkey between 1745 and 1755 and published an account of his travels in *Observations sur le Commerce* in 1766. He witnessed one of the combined Nevruz and Tulip festivals during the reign of Mahmud I and comments:

Wooden galleries are set up in the Courtyard of the New Serail with rows of shelves on both sides on which are placed vases of tulips. These are alternated with bowls full of coloured water, and cages of canaries and torches are set on the top shelves.... The Sultan's kiosk is placed in the centre and the presents made by Court Officials are

A very sumptuous and dramatic cover influenced by the Baroque style. Large curled feathers surround the elaborate stylized flowers and the jewellery-like motifs. Small running chain stitch in silk and stem stitch in silver-wrapped yellow silk on a woollen ground. *c.* 1800. 122 x 117 cm.

106

set out to be seen. When all is ready the Sultan calls for halvet. All the gates of the Palace leading to the gardens are closed. The Bostancis stand on guard outside and the harem Agas inside.... The women rush out of the Harem on all sides, like a swarm of bees from the hive, settling on the flowers and looking for honey.[3]

This Festival, like all the festivals of both cycles, was always associated with the wearing of new clothes, the giving of gifts and the display of decorations, all of which entailed new embroideries and the setting up of the great embroidered ceremonial tents. In later years and even today these are the few occasions when it is possible to see the old embroidered costumes and textile decorations.

The ceremonial aspect of daily life was also very strong. Inside the family there were strict observances of rituals and customs which were based on precedence and respect. They ensured the smooth running of large families in small houses where space was critical and in which many different activities had to fit. The outward signs of ceremony were therefore very important, as were the observances of tradition. Physical objects that contributed to ritual were essential: the embroidered cloths used for wrapping anything handed to a guest or to a senior member of the household, richly embroidered garments for special occasions, the display of finery to celebrate family festivals such as weddings and circumcision feasts, and even the embroidered tents for the garden festivals.

p.108, 109

A particularly pleasant group of textiles are those which were used for the shaving ritual of the Sultan and of those that aped the Palace ritual. This set of textiles, the 'traş takım' was composed of a large apron, a cloth to drape over the back and a number of hand towels. The most obvious piece of the whole set is the apron, the 'berber futası', which is over two metres long with an opening cut at the top to fit the neck. The whole set would have been embroidered over all with the same patterns.

A barber's apron decorated over all with a motif of a large flower set on a mound. The whole design is contained in a border of a vine bearing blossom-filled palmettes. *c.* 1820. 189 x 112 cm.

Overleaf, left On this barber's apron the design of a flower spray, with the flower shown hanging forward, is set between vertical wavy bands made of multi-coloured fat segments, which are also used for the border. The neck opening is filled with a flower spray on a solid silver ground edged with a flower set in a wreath. Silk and metal thread in running chain stitch on a silk satin ground. Before 1800. 165 x 93 cm. *Right* The formal trellis of this pattern has deteriorated into a series of compartments bordered by a segmented band in each of which there is a large flower spray. The neck band is filled with the same pattern on a solid gold ground. The apron has been altered by having the neck opening reversed to make a more acceptable piece for hanging. Before 1820. 180 x 72 cm.

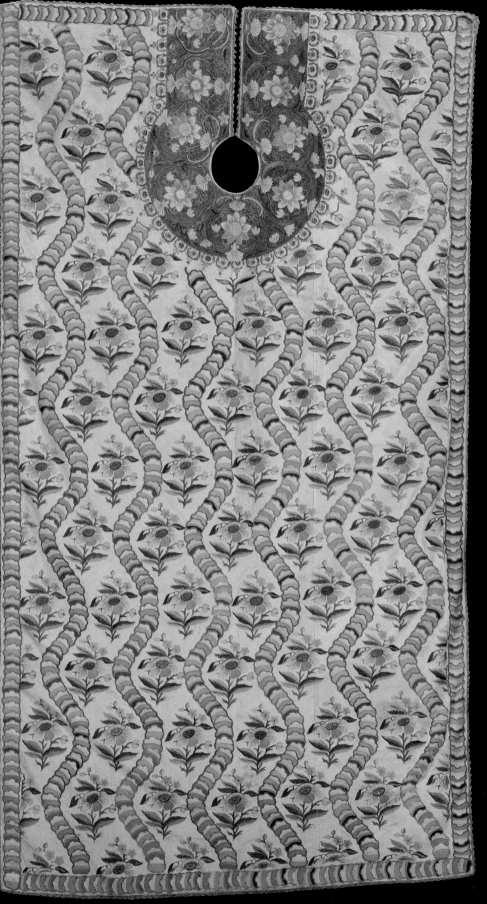

The most important of all the ceremonies for the male children was the circumcision ceremony, the 'Sünnet'.[4] This was always celebrated at home, usually in the women's quarters. The whole family would gather together and the women would be responsible for organising the ceremony. The centre of the ceremony was often a bed decorated with all the family embroideries. This was decorated by a professional who arrived the day before, who selected all the pieces and then used them to make a bed, with its posts and curtains covered with the family embroideries and often even the small knitted money purses.

A bed decorated for the 'Sünnet' ceremony and covered with a counterpane and valance from a dowry gift.

110

A series of highly stylized flower heads with quinces and muscari stems fill the ground of this formal cover. The broad border is filled with a flower and plane leaf. Gold thread and wire in a variety of techniques on a silk satin ground. Professional work from Bursa *c.* 1850. 75 cm square.

NOTES

1. Ramazan was the ninth month of the Muslim lunar year, during which Muslims were obliged to fast and abstain from many social activities during the daylight hours. It was terminated by the Feast of Bayram.

2. Muayede is the ceremony of making formal reciprocal greetings.

3. The Bostancis were the corps of personal bodyguards of the Sultan. Their name means 'gardener', presumably because the first guards were those who worked within the Palace grounds.

4. This ceremony, the Sünnet, was held when the male child was about eight years old. It was his formal acceptance into society as a man and as a full member of the Muslim congregation. In larger households he would then move out of the women's quarters to take up a place in the men's part of the house with the other unmarried males.

Wrappers

The recently urbanized Turks retained a nostalgia for their past nomadic origins, believing that the sense of impermanence and the acceptance of change which was part of that life gave them their greatest strength. They also wished to remind themselves of the rigours of the life that their ancestors had lived in their tents which they dismantled and moved about regularly. Ottoman poetry and literature often refer to that past nomadic life and to the annual change from season to season; images of travel are very common, life is compared to a journey or to the road on which the journey is made. The journey is often described as one without luggage and during which one must not accumulate material things.

While grand houses and palaces did have a certain amount of furniture, the houses of most of the population were simple and contained very little. What there was was only taken out when it was to be used; at all other times bedding, surplus clothing, tools and equipment were made into bundles and stored away. Each bundle was wrapped in a cloth both as protection and as identification; even when the bundles were kept in the rare cupboards they still had to be wrapped.

This wrapper, the 'bohça', was used continuously in the daily ritual of the house and, not surprisingly, is one of the most common of all decorated domestic textiles, and large numbers have survived in every style of both ground fabric and embroidery technique. Not only was it used for innumerable purposes in the house but custom demanded it was also used extensively in practically every transaction undertaken in public even if only as added decoration.[1]

In most cases the wrapper was merely a large square cloth, but the inability of the Turks to resist decoration meant that they were invariably decorated in a manner that became more and more elaborate. Bohças were made of either woven or embroidered cloths and were later made of machine-printed cloths. They were even made of contrasting scraps of cloth recycled from other articles which were then sewn together. Bohças can also be found in kilim work, in plain

A wrapper with a rich pattern derived from a silk brocade of the sixteenth century. Four conical flower heads set between two leaves with smaller round flowers placed in the corner fill the field, with a pattern of isolated leaves in the border. Split Bokhara couching in silk on linen. *c.* 1675. 115 x 97 cm.

tapestry technique and in the elaborate cicim and zile techniques. They are also seen in the knotted carpet technique where the pattern indicates how the carpet is to be folded to form the square envelope. However, the majority of them were worked on the same linen or cotton weave which was used for most of the other domestic textiles, although a large number were made of satin, silk or woollen weaves. By the middle of the nineteenth century satin became a favourite material for the more ostentatious bohças, even though it was a most unsuitable fabric: the silk surface wefts deteriorated and could not support the heavy metal work embroidered on it.

Sometimes these wrapped packages were themselves kept inside the sacks called 'yastık' which were made of a woven fabric itself over-embroidered. The stuffed sacks were used as cushions and those Turks that continued to live in tents used them as seating and also piled them up to form low walls separating the sleeping areas from the daily living quarters.

When Topkapi Palace was converted into a museum in 1924 many of the rooms that had not been touched since the Court moved to the new Palace at Dolmabahçe in 1853 were opened and their contents disclosed. A large number of wrapped bundles were discovered in these rooms, and found to contain clothing, ceremonial textiles and various objects from the reigns of previous Sultans, dating back to the death of Mehmed the Conqueror in 1481. Some of these bundles were wrapped in more than one cover: the often repeated, but inaccurate, story is that up to forty of these bohça were used in some of the bundles, having been wrapped one over the other.[2] The wrapped bundles had unfortunately been repacked on several occasions so, although many of them were labelled, the labels no longer related to the actual contents, nor could they be reconciled to the various registers of the bundles that had been made in 1505, 1570 and 1680. An invaluable aid to dating these textiles has therefore been lost.

Conventionally the bohça is decorated over all and the form of the decoration was always very stylized. The most common form of decoration is a pattern in the central field contained within a border on all four sides. Most frequently the central decoration is a repeat of an isolated floral motif which can be large or small and comes in an infinite variety of shapes and forms. These repeats are set out in staggered rows, usually changing direction in alternate rows. Sometimes the floral

Left A wrapper with a large curled branch and flowers set in each quarter. A thin line of chain stitch surrounds the decoration instead of the usual border. The style is very mannered and the motifs are reminiscent of Central Asian suzenis. *c.* 1830. 102 x 92 cm.

Overleaf, left A wrapper of almond-shaped cartouches of a blossom-filled pomegranate bordered by plum leaves placed on a background of blue and white triangles creating a trellis. *c.* 1700. 100 x 96 cm. *Right* A simple dianthus spray is set so that its two blue leaves make a formal trellis. Floral versions of the three çintamani pearls are placed at the intersections of the trellis. The border is filled with a tendril of tulips, roses, leaves and the floral çintamani. Single darning on linen. Before 1700. 107 x 95 cm.

motifs are connected with tendrils and trellises making a continuous pattern over all. This is more common in the earlier pieces. The pattern can also be a larger curvilinear pattern of flowers on a stalk repeated four or five times, or even one large motif filling the whole area, which is very rare. These last versions usually do not have a border but only a thin single line of stem stitch outlining the square. The border in all the other versions is usually a narrow band of a continuous linear pattern lying between two straight lines.

The earliest surviving bohça are from the sixteenth century and are decorated in the style of the period, sharing with all the other textiles made at that time a similar repertory of motifs. They are made of a fine tabby linen which is often of a loose weave in gauges from 12 to 20 threads per centimetre. They are embroidered in a two-strand floss silk worked in darning stitch over three ground threads using a very limited colour range: red and blue predominate, with small portions of the pattern picked out in white, a soft green and gold. In the seventeenth century designs changed gradually, the new ones being worked alongside the old. The great patterns which are like panels of tiles become stylized and start to look more like the woven textiles of each period, with the motifs set out in more regular repeats and consequently losing a great deal of their original clarity.

p.88

As society evolved with the creation of a property-owning middle class, the function of many of the traditional covers changed. The bohça remained as a symbolic formal wrapping for gifts, but there was no longer the same need for them in the house as cupboards and chests became more common, doing away with the need for wrappers. The cover changed from being a wrapper to being a decorative cloth. The ground fabric also changed from the simple linen and cotton to woollen worsted, fine silk, silk taffeta and unions of linen and cotton and cotton and silk. More often than not new covers were lined with a chintz or printed cloth and many of them were interlined with a woollen cloth. The lining became more and more necessary as less durable fabrics were being used, and the weight of the embroidery became heavier and heavier. How these other various covers were used will be described in the next section.

Although the darning stitch was still used right up to the end of the period of the production of bohças the change in patterns required that other stitches be used as well, and both stem stitch and 'atma' (the laid and couched surface stitch) became more common. This last stitch gives a richer raised surface for the large blocks of colour and contrasts with the fine stem stitch used for the lines connecting or defining shapes. Many of the individual motifs in the design are now outlined in a small tight stem stitch which gives a quite different effect to earlier work. These textiles are worked so that the pattern is only to be seen on one side.

From the eighteenth century onwards the variety of bohças becomes

Vertical bands filled with four-petalled flowers set with alternate large and small leaves fill the ground of this wrapper. The band also appears in the border and is adapted to turn at the corners. Tight single darning in silk on linen. Before 1700. 106 x 98 cm.

118

p.88

limitless. Patterns from many sources are used, copies are made of brocades and velvets, tile patterns are used as great panels and as individual octagonal tiles, copying work from Kashan. The classic motifs of earlier centuries are stylized and simplified; sometimes portions of one motif are worked with portions of another and are set sideways or even upside down. It becomes more and more difficult to date these bohça and impossible to assign them to any particular centre of production.

In the nineteenth century the use of the bohça becomes even more extended than before. They are not only used as wrappers but as covers for tables that are just being introduced into houses and as cloths thrown or draped over furniture. Metal-thread work becomes very common, either as embroidery carried out in metal-wrapped silk or as dival or zerduz work. The bohça is now related more closely to costume and upholstery carried out in the same technique rather than to the architecture of earlier centuries. The designs used now incorpo-p.60, 143rate images that are completely new, such as date palms, sailing ships and even stylized animals.

One version of the bohça had a ceremonial and commemorative function; this was the 'nişan bohça', where the central design becomes a badge or a large formal emblem. It was very heavily embroidered in metal, so much so that it must have been very difficult to fold it over in the way one would expect to use a wrapper.[3] These bohças were kept and used as part of the display of family treasures during festivals or visits.

Once the bohça becomes a cover rather than a wrapper many new uses are found for them, and they are made in new shapes for specific purposes: coffee tray covers, table cloths, desk covers and even covers p.125, 203for books.

A trellis formed of a flower-filled band merging at each joint is filled with an almond cartouche containing a smaller central one surrounded by a leafy wreath. Tight single darning on linen. *c.* 1700. 109 x 100 cm.

NOTES

1. One of the earliest uses of the word (1330) is Arabic and is found in Umari's description of a gift from a Moroccan Sultan, where 'bukhja' means a package. Ottoman Turkish distinguishes between a present being given upwards in the social scale, 'bohça baha' (wrapped at a price), and one exchanged between equals.

2. The figure forty was accepted by the Europeans as a factual figure, whereas it is used throughout the Islamic world merely to imply a large number. Ali Baba had a lot of companions, not specifically forty. Taksin Öz in *Turkish Textiles and Velvets* gives the exact details of the bundles and the number of wrappers used in the 1760 Palace inventory (pages 16 and 17).

3. The word 'nişan' means an order or a decoration and in this usage is a token given at a betrothal.

122

Covers

The natural grace and restraint of Ottoman art was affected by the change in the living style brought about by the closer contact with Europe in the middle of the nineteenth century. Earlier generations of Turks had been influenced by the initial flowering of European Renaissance art or by the elegance and splendour of the Napoleonic era, but the Turks of the Sultanates of Abdul Mecid, Abdul Aziz and Murad V, the period from 1839 to 1876, were influenced by the overblown oppressive styles of Victorian England and the Third Empire.

The developing industries of Europe, in an attempt to expand their total markets, not only imposed new products on their own populations but also promoted the idea of specialized products for specific purposes to a larger world market. The idea of different gowns for every hour of the day, or differently shaped or designed shawls for morning, midday and evening, or special sets of cutlery and china for different courses at different meals, were all the result of industries creating new demands and new needs for their enlarged mechanised production units.

Turkey fell subject to these pressures and, along with the disappearance of all the other products that were suited to a simpler life, the universal bohça lost its original purpose as a wrapper and was replaced by many covers, each with a specialized use. For example, there was a special round cover for the table or tray on which coffee was served, another to cover the small heater which burnt coal or lignite and was set in the middle of the room to provide heat, another for the oven and yet another for the cradle.[1] It is now quite difficult to decide which cover was intended for which purpose as they are mostly square or rectangular and the subtleties that distinguish them are no longer recognizable. It is almost easier to identify them by the ground cloth on which they are worked.

Before 1800 all the bohças were worked on a fine linen; the covers that replaced them were worked on cotton and weft-faced satins and later by a heavy woollen broadcloth. After 1930 a number of synthetic

A wrapper made from strips taken from five different garments, most probably Rumeli trouser legs, napkins and one sash. Assembled about 1900 by a dealer for sale. Small fillets of crochet lace are used to join the strips. Salonika or Kavala. 96 cm square.

fabrics were used for a short while. The covers in satin and broadcloth are very often lined with a printed cloth or with one of the striped materials woven in eastern Turkey, to act as protection for the surface of the table when hot pots and plates are placed on them. The form of the decoration also changed: the loose, open flowing patterns changed to the denser, solid, isolated motifs worked over the surface like wood blocks prints.

All of these covers are invariably late work made in embroidery workshops. They are mostly very fine work and clearly different from earlier pieces. The stitches used became heavier and more complicated; various forms of couching and feather stitching are used in addition to a coarse chain stitch worked with either a hook or a small awl, 'tığ'. Instead of the simple floss silks a large range of thicker spun and twisted silks was used and various metal wires and strips were introduced. In order to give the cloth a more important look, the new isolated patterns, particularly when they were mainly of metal, were stuffed with cotton wool or cardboard to make them stand out from the material.

The commonest of the new covers are the circular ones for the table.[2] A round cloth is certainly an introduction from Europe and follows on the introduction of the round table, although round leather mats for eating off on the floor had been made in the sixteenth century. The modern cover is usually divided into a number of concentric rings each filled with the same pattern. The heater 'mangal' cover is square and rather large, made up of an embroidered satin cover sewn onto a thick under-cloth of wool or even onto a padded quilt. Cradle covers are more likely to be rectangular but would have no other features on them that would specifically relate to this particular use.

p.10, 92

All these cloths formed part of the ceremonial and formal life of the family and, as in European households, the larger the range of these cloths that you could be seen using the more in fashion you were considered to be.

Throughout the Islamic world the custom that the social life of most families takes place outside the house meant that entertainment in the house was usually restricted to relations: women visiting women in the inner house, and men entertaining other men in the outer house. It was only into this outer house that strangers were ever admitted. The descriptions of home life given by European women who had penetrated the inner house clearly show that they saw very little of the real life and their introduction into the women's quarters was as much to entertain the Turkish ladies as the foreigner.

During such social meetings it was essential that refreshments be offered. In the women's area there would be spoonfuls of jam served with a glass of water, fruit, halvas, locums and nuts. In the men's quarters it would be coffee, sweetmeats and, in the more enlightened and less strict households, wine and even stronger drinks would be served. Covers exist which are decorated with emblems suitable for each of

A large round table cloth with a central medallion of four flower sprays on a solid silver ground. The three concentric bands are filled with repeats of a large and small flower spray. The rings are made of a continuous flowering vine. The cloth is worked in silk and silver on a yellow silk core in running chain stitch, most probably worked with a hook on a tambour. Professional work c. 1860. 284 cm diameter.

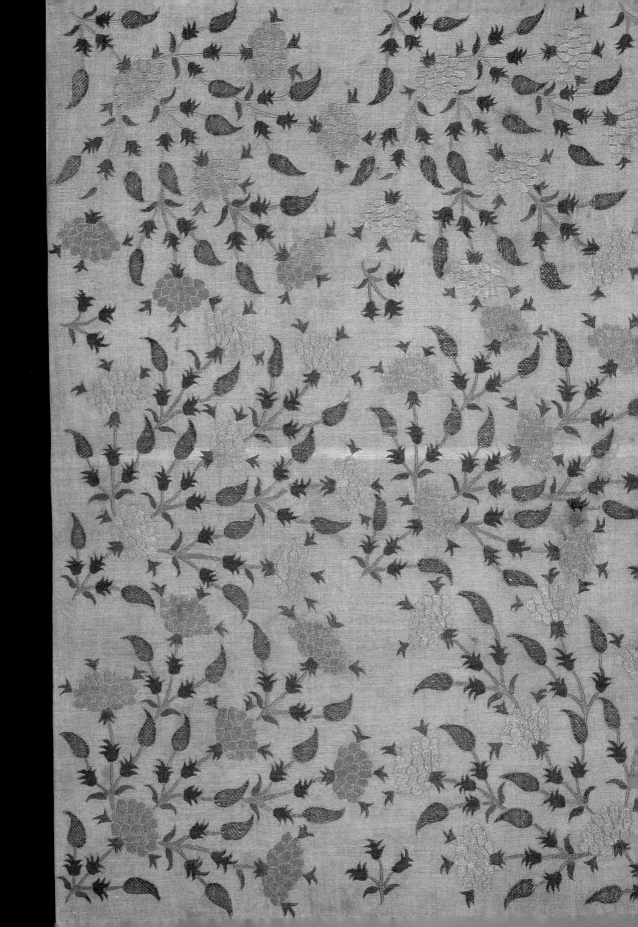

A wrapper of high quality professional work. A large branching spray of seven chrysanthemums and silver almond leaves is repeated nine times to fill the ground, with neither border nor edging. Silk and silver thread in tight stem stitch on a fine cotton. Before 1750. 105 x 99 cm.

127

these offerings – bowls of fruit and date palms, coffee pots and even bunches of grapes. Not only were the covers embroidered with these appropriate motifs but even the accompanying hand towels for touching the fingers to would also carry the same emblems.

Among the other specialist covers that were made were those for children's use. These are mainly the small satchels carried to school by both girls and boys. They were made of stout fabric, sometimes even leather, and would have an embroidery in zerduz or dival work in gold on them and may even carry a charm against the evil eye worked into the motif.[3] Special covers were made for the Koran, which was either kept on its stand or placed on a high shelf, and these covers often have a quotation from the Koran worked on them.

128

p.18, 26, 51

A small vine bearing a single monstrous bunch of grapes is the only pattern on this tray cloth. Seven of them radiate from the centre and repeats cover the green woollen ground. Silk and wool embroidery in small chain stitch and strap couching with metal strip. Edged in metal thread tatting. *c.* 1860. 106 x 102 cm.

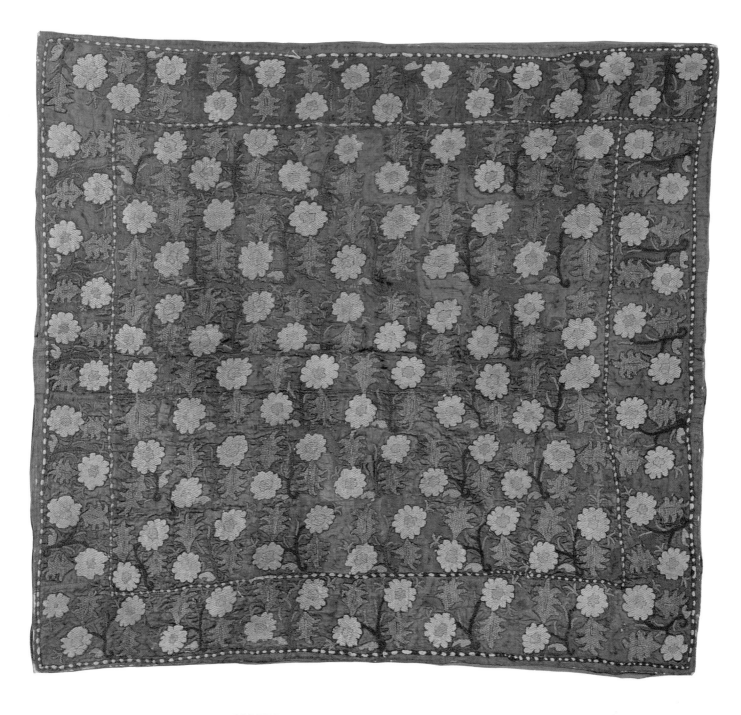

NOTES

1. The general word for the cover was örtü. A tray cover is 'tepsi örtüsü', the cover for the coffee tray or table is 'kahve örtüsü'. The portable heater is the 'mangal', the oven is 'tandır' and the cradle 'beşik'.

2. Table covers are called 'sofra bezi'. The usage of the word sofra implies that the cover is being used during a meal. The earlier meaning of the word sofra was the leather pad on which meals were served on the floor. Even these leather sofra were embroidered. Bez is the standard word for cloth, usually linen or cotton.

3. The most common charm is the word 'Maşallah', literally, 'what God had ordained', the implication being that it is a wonder that has been willed. The word is used both as an expression of admiration and a protection against the evil eye. An older version of the protection against the evil eye is the small blue bead or knots and tassels worked into children's clothing. The use of these charms was common; they are the 'nazarlık', the protection against the 'look'.

A rectangular cover using a single motif of two flowers and two leaves on a single stalk to fill both the ground and the broad border. Silk stem stitch and filled couch stitch on a green silk satin ground. *c.* 1860. 98 x 88 cm.

Inscriptions

The main use for calligraphy and the more standard writing on embroidery was for the inscriptions or as talismans.[1] Apart from the usual religious formulae, most of the inscriptions are either single words or short phrases which are statements as to who made them, or the occasions at which they were given. Sadly, they are very rarely dated. Most of the writing is in the older Arabic script; there are very few pieces made after 1923 using the Latin script.

The general tenor of the inscriptions is sentimental and often repeats popular phrases and folk sayings. There are a number of shirts with inscriptions running around the neck line, one of the most touching being that in which the embroideress says that she is working this for her brother who is going to join the army, and she hopes that he returns wearing it.

The most common phrases seen embroidered are the 'besmele' (In the Name of Allah), and the 'Kelime-i Tevhid', which is the Muslim Profession of Faith. The names of the Prophet and the first four Caliphs are also frequently used. Some large panels which were used in the Mosques or in the tents erected outside them for special festivals are embroidered with verses from various Suras written in different calligraphic scripts, making extremely decorative panels similar to those inside the Mosque.

p.207

Each end of this napkin is decorated with a view of a Mosque and its associated buildings. Domestic work with the design crudely drawn, using silks in colours developed early in the twentieth century, with metal strip which is virtually tinsel. The Arabic inscriptions read 'Ma Sha' allah' (What God wills) and 'Shuban Allah' (Praise be to God). c. 1920. 58 x 24 cm.

130

The tradition of talismanic shirts, 'tılsımlı gömlek', is very ancient, there are references to them in many stories that have their origin in Central Asia. These shirts are covered with a mixture of religious texts and magic symbols, and worked into the design is a complicated system by which every letter of every word has a numerical value which all add up in the most propitious way. The most magnificent of all these shirts, which are also called 'curing shirts', is that in Topkapi, which was most probably made for Sultan Suleiman; it is painted and drawn on cotton and is dated 1477-80. More common variations of these shirts to be used at home were embroidered with a few phrases and magic squares.

Writing was always held to be powerful and to have both magic and restorative properties. Ancient writing was even more powerful. There are examples of nonsense scripts being used on ceramics and metal ware, very much in the same way that the Kufic script was used in Spanish rugs of the fifteenth century. An example of nonsense writing is shown above, where a panel with a script like Nabataean or proto-Hebrew has been recycled to make a narrow veil to be hung at the head of a tomb or sarcophagus.

A strip that would have been used to cover the end of a tomb. It was very usual for clothing and textiles to be used in this way, when they attained great talismanic powers. This panel is made of sections cut from an earlier textile worked in metal thread, later mounted on satin. The script used is like Nabataean but it is nonsense. Originally before 1850. 200 x 52 cm.

NOTES

1. The word talisman is most probably a mishearing of the Arabic and Turkish word tılsımlı, entering all the European languages about the middle of the sixteenth century.

131

Composite fabrics

Textiles that were in constant daily use invariably tended to deteriorate and those that had embroidered areas on them suffered even more. Very often the weight of the embroidery, particularly when it included metal strip, could not be supported by the ground cloth and caused it to tear. The way in which the cloths were washed, very often being beaten by a stick against a rock, having been washed in a lye soap, also accelerated their destruction. The hand and bath towels that had large areas of heavy embroidery on them and which were washed frequently suffered more than most of the others. It was common practice for the panels of embroidery at both ends of these towels to be cut off and then sewn on to new lengths of towelling and used again. Skirt and sleeve borders were also resewn onto new garments, but this was less common as the dresses were made of stouter fabric and certainly not as frequently washed.

A much more common end for the surviving embroidered portions of domestic textiles was for them to be re-cycled by being incorporated into new objects. Not only was embroidery re-cycled but also portions of any garment that was made of an expensive or colourful fabric. The most common use for these pieces was to make them up into square covers, consisting of patches sewn together. Usually the patches were sewn alongside each other to make a solid fabric, but it was also common for the patches to be separated by lengths of braid or crocheted ribbon, giving a lighter fabric altogether. The pieces that were sewn together usually combined pieces recovered from many different types of textiles.

There was more to using pieces of old textiles than economy. It was believed that some virtue could be preserved from old objects, and using them enhanced the intrinsic value of the new article. This belief survived from shamanist ritual where the priests of the old religion always wore cloaks composed of pieces of textiles, even rags, given to them. In a very sophisticated way the Buddhist and Shintoist robes, the 'kesa', continue this tradition.

This qibleh cloth is intended to look like a panel of tiles from a Mosque. It is made of strips and fragments from eleven different garments from Rumeli and the Balkans, with the outermost border made from a commercially produced embroidered cloth. The strips are joined by ribbons of needle weaving. Many of these composites were made by dealers in Salonika, Kavala and Istanbul. Assembled about 1900 from much earlier pieces. 142 x 95 cm.

COMPOSITE FABRICS

In addition to the universal square cloth, the bohça, many other articles were also made — carpets, protective folders for books, counterpanes, cradle cloths, and in one instance in the sixteenth century a pair of underpants for a palace child was made out of a quilt facing.

The most spectacular of these re-cycled textiles are the wall hangings made in the traditional shape of the prayer rug, more particularly copying the embroidered rugs, the 'seccade', that were made in Bosnia and a number of centres in Turkey. The standard prayer rug, the 'namazlı', was usually a carpet woven in a knotted or a flat weave technique, although they could be woven straw or reed or even a plain length of cloth. The tradition is that every man possessed one and at the time of prayer he laid it on the ground with the head of the rug pointing towards the Holy Places in Mecca and then made his prayers without dirtying his washed hands or clothes.

p.148, 151

These prayer rugs were decorated in a very particular way. The main feature on them was an arch which represented the niche, the mihrab, that was constructed on the wall of the Mosque to indicate to the faithful the direction in which they were to pray. The direction itself is known as the qibleh, and that wall is known as the qibleh wall in the Mosque. The niche, in accordance with the verse in Sura 24 of the Koran, often had a lamp hanging in the centre and usually incorporated an oblong area at the base of the niche representing a pool of water, symbolizing both chastity and the font of life.[1] In various weaving traditions other symbols were also incorporated into the design of the prayer rug, the most frequent being ewers to contain water for washing and flowers. In some Caucasian versions the palms of two open hands were worked into the pattern outside the niche at the head of the rug, to indicate where the person praying was to place his hands during his prostrations.

It was rare for the heavy knotted rugs to be used by women, the reason being that women were expected to be within their houses at the times for prayer. The rug was meant to be used by men while about their business and unable to get into a Mosque or any other appropriate building to make their prayers. Women made their prayers within the house, usually in one of the inner rooms; it would have been inappropriate for a mihrab to be incorporated into a domestic building, so embroidered hangings were made that could act as qibleh cloths. Unlike the men's rugs which were knelt on, these domestic qibleh cloths were hung on the appropriate wall for the duration of the prayer and then taken down.

These cloths were made of the finest of all the embroidered pieces recovered from other textiles, often augmented with lengths of imported silks and damasks cut into long strips to act as ribbons, or with lengths of lace or crocheted ribbon. The edges were often decorated with lengths of tatting or oya work. Most of the domestic qibleh hangings were made totally of scraps, but there were more sophisticated versions.

A qibleh cloth made from an imported Bokhara door hanging with the central space filled with portions of two sashes and scraps from a Greek chemise. Assembled about 1870, the date of the imported embroidery, with pieces from about 1830. 153 x 94 cm.

135

A qibleh cloth with the mihrab section set between two mirror panels, all made from a single sash. This panel is set within five borders made from two scarfs, four towels and one turban cover, all joined by a needle-lace ribbon. Assembled about 1870. 152 x 100 cm.

136

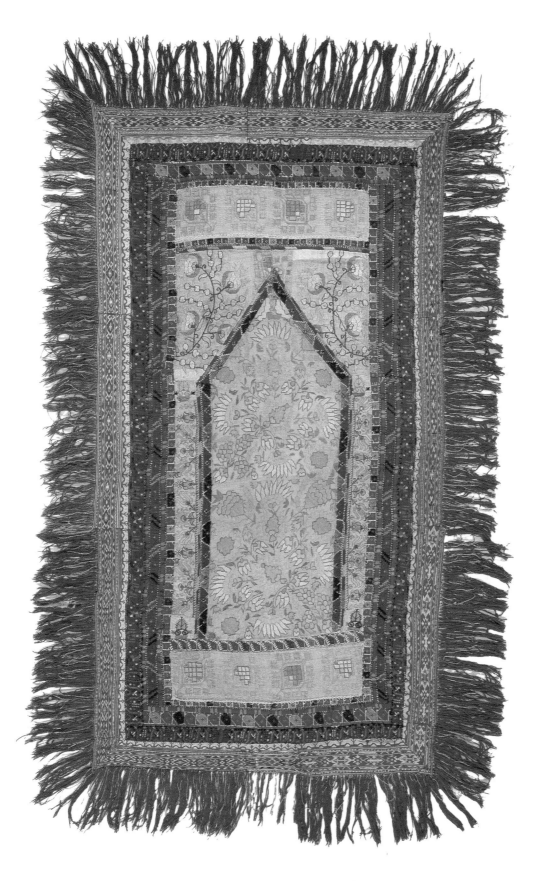

A qibleh cloth with the centre made of scraps from five sash and towel ends set within seven borders of Balkan costume edgings in a border of a woven and fringed Diyarbekir ribbon. Assembled *c.* 1870 of eighteenth and nineteenth century pieces. 138 x 84 cm including fringe.

It was possible to buy a prepared cloth which had the pattern of the mihrab printed on it, with floral patterns set about the columns of the niche. The intention was that the buyer would embroider over the printed patterns and then fill the area of the mihrab with selected embroideries. A further version was also available where the area around the mihrab had already been embroidered and the buyer had only to fill the mihrab with embroideries.

p.135

These wall mihrab cloths often contain some of the most ancient pieces of domestic embroidery that have survived: their second life as a religious article has ensured their survival beyond the life of the original article.

The forms of the wall mihrab hangings and the pieces from which they were made often identify the area where they were composed. The Istanbul pieces are very often professional work copying what had been a domestic tradition; other pieces are clearly dealers' pieces where many scraps have been cobbled together to make a larger piece that would be saleable. The hangings made in the Balkans are very distinctive in that they are invariably made of skirt ends and sleeves from festive dresses, usually in a dark red and very sombre. The pieces made in Rumeli are much lighter and usually incorporate the leg panels from embroidered trousers. Many of the Ottoman Greek versions are made from skirt borders set in parallel columns in the standard pattern. Some of these mihrab hangings from the Dodecanese are made in a linear pattern where the mihrab shape has been outlined with a cord embroidered over the top of the basic pattern.

p.42, 43, 44

The qibleh cloths are very sophisticated versions of recycling, but there are also very fine covers made from recycled embroideries. The mixture of colours and textures was very appealing, and the use of covers made up of patches had none of the implications that they would have had in other societies. The patchwork covers were very often over-embroidered to make a most handsome article. Many of the large covers would be assembled from large patches organized into very careful patterns before they were embroidered. The hangings generally known as Banya Luka work are made in this way.

p.140

NOTES

1. Sura 24, The Light: 'Allah is the light of heaven and earth, his light is as a niche in which there is a lamp, that lamp in a glass, the glass appearing as a shining star.'

A qibleh hanging composed of fragments from thirteen embroidered cloths joined by ribbons made from a French silk dress brocade. The largest piece is taken from an eighteenth century cover. Domestic work, assembled about 1870. 134 x 83 cm.

139

3 Large embroideries

In addition to the very large number of embroidered articles that were made for domestic use, including formal and informal costumes for men and women, there was also a considerable production of much larger pieces that were intended for use outside the home.

These large pieces were produced by professional embroiderers who worked in ateliers that were organized as small workshops, usually based on a family working together. It was essential that these pieces were made by professionals because they were often to be given as gifts and had to be recognizable as professional work. They were also likely to contain thread or strip made of precious metals that a domestic embroiderer could not have afforded and would have been less able to handle.

The embroiderers in these professional ateliers were members of the various guilds, the 'Cema'at', that existed throughout the Ottoman world; even the workers inside the Sultan's household would have been guild members. The guilds, and presumably the ateliers, had existed from the beginning of the Byzantine State and survived the Conquest intact.[1] In Istanbul they were centred at Tepebaşi and Galata or around the Palace at Topkapi. They also existed in other centres such as Bursa, Konya, Edirne and in many of the population centres in eastern Turkey. The main ones outside metropolitan Turkey were Salonika and Yanina in Epirus.

The records in the many population censuses taken from the fifteenth century onwards always mention weavers and embroiderers, and these figures must refer to the professional bodies.[2] The professional ateliers produced court uniforms for men and the heavily worked formal gowns for women. Some groups specialized in military uniforms and worked in ateliers which combined tailors, embroiderers and the makers of the metal-wrapped silk.[3] Other specialists produced the embroidered carpets, 'nihali', which not only incorporated precious metals but also, according to many references, were encrusted with pearls and precious stones. The embroidered covers for the 'Ka'aba',

A panel with a mihrab and lamp design that may have been used in a campaign tent as a qibleh cloth, The cartouches in the main border are filled with elegant flower sprays in a style reminiscent of Resht and Indian Mughal work. Many such panels were used in tents and they are all made of stouter materials than used in domestic pieces. Woollen appliquéd patterns are sewn onto a stout woollen ground with a little over-embroidery in silk and metal thread. These panels were made in Banya Luka, Bursa and Istanbul. Before 1800. 182 x 128 cm.

141

the 'Kiswah', which were part of the annual gift to Mecca, were also made by these ateliers, although the main pieces of the Mahmal AshSharif, as the convoy to Mecca was called, were made in Cairo.

There were special workshops that produced horse trappings, the embroidered saddle cloths and even the embroidered panels that were set into the saddles themselves. These same workshops also produced the embroidered panels that were made in the nineteenth century for lining carriages and the larger carts, the 'araba', that were used as passenger transport. The fame of these particular workers was so great that they produced the panels for many of the carriages that were made in Eastern Europe, and there are records of such panels being ordered from Hungary, Poland and Russia.

All the work that was done on leather, the small shields and the quiver cases was produced in a separate part of the capital, believed to have been the Yedi Kule area on the Sea of Marmora, near the tanneries. It is extremely unlikely that any domestic embroiderer would have attempted to work on leather; even the small embroidered slippers, the 'şipşip', would have been bought ready-made in local markets.

Above Detail from a large cover entirely covered with a date palm motif. Stem stitch with couched metal lines on white satin. *c.* 1875. 128 cm square.

A very simplified version of the curled branch pattern fills the ground of this cover, with sprinklings of a small yellow flower. The border is composed of a vine with leaves springing right and left from it. Good quality domestic work copying a much older textile. Couched silk work on satin. Before 1800. 104 x 101 cm.

142

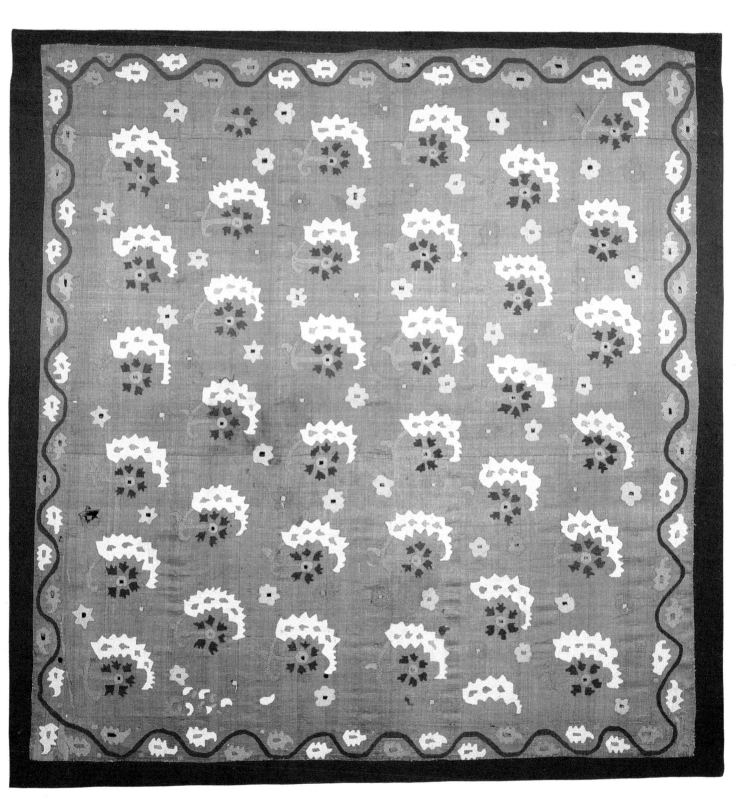

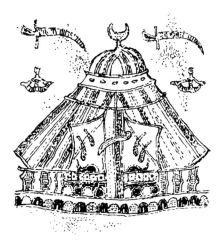

Tents

The most spectacular large pieces of embroidery produced were the tents, the 'çadır'. When the Ottoman army moved on its campaigns, which it did incessantly from the fourteenth century onwards, it always moved as a functioning city. It carried with it standard tents for the whole army, each of which, at most, would only have had a small decorated door panel. The commanding officers and their immediate entourage would be housed in grander tents, which would be part of elaborate complexes of tents placed within a wall of cloth panels so as to make a separate palace area. The moving city also had tents that could be used as assembly halls, portable mosques and even special tents for drinking coffee and resting. There were also tents for storing and for repairing equipment. In illustrations of the period one can see whole towns of tents surrounding the cities and castles under siege.

The Imperial campaign tents were so important that a special department, the 'Çadır Mehteri', was established in Topkapi to produce and maintain them. The department, at its height, had over 2000 people in it, the majority of whom were stitchers and embroiderers. Not only did the Tent Department provide for the army but it also supplied ceremonial tents to the many local rulers appointed by the Sultan to govern his provinces in the Balkans. There are many records of orders being placed for tents, with long discussions about how expensive they were.[4] The agent for George Rakoczi I, the Prince of Transylvania, wrote back to him in 1638:

> Here we have found another kalitka (made of Calicut cloth) tent with its courtyard, which had been ordered by the Çavuş Paşa of the Sultan (the Sergeant Paşa, who was the Head Door Keeper). Since the Sultan did not go abroad, the tent had been put up for sale. It is made of cotton both inside and out. The interior is decorated with flowers and it can be erected by only two men. The tent pleases your tent master a lot, but he does not dare buy it without Your Excellency's permission.

The interior of the campaign tent captured as booty from Francis I at the Battle of Pavia in 1525. The interior walls and the ceiling are covered in red thick cotton panels each set with a massive appliquéd and over-embroidered cartouche. The tent is a two-masted oval one, 8 m long x 3.5 m wide x 4.6 m at its greatest height. Istanbul Palace Tent Department, before 1525.

145

These tents were certain to have been pleasure or garden tents rather than those to be used on campaigns.

The tents made for the Commander of the Army, who could have been the Sultan himself or one of the Grand Viziers, were large, elaborate, and very often ornamented with appliqué embroidery. The tents were made in many shapes and usually supported by wooden masts. The standard tent was a round one based on a single central mast, but they were also made in rectangles with rounded ends and in square shapes which were supported by two or even three masts. The cladding was made of separate rectangular panels sewn together in lengths to make the walls, and triangular panels that formed the conical roof. The panels were made of linen or cotton or even of woollen broadcloth, usually of three thicknesses, and the outer face would be plain brown or red and the inside would be decorated.

The tents were not only decorated but were also furnished so as to remind the Sultan of the life he had left behind. After Jan Sobieski, the King of Poland, had captured the Grand Vizier's tent at the Siege of Vienna he wrote to his wife to say:

> It is impossible for me to convey to you the refinement and luxury which reigned in the Vizier's tents; they contained baths, small gardens, fountains, fish-ponds and even a parrot.

The decoration was carried out in appliqué work, with cloth patterns cut out in different solid colours and then sewn onto the ground fabric, often with one colour overlapping another. Small details of flowers and geometric ornaments would be embroidered over the appliqué work. The windows were made by cutting out squares in the wall panels and filling them in with rope lattice work to represent glazing bars, and blinds that could be rolled up were often added.

The appliqué technique is extremely ancient. Some of the oldest known fragments of embroidery employ it, and it was very common in Central Asia. The popularity of this work in Egypt under the Mamluks must have influenced the growth of the technique in Turkey after their conquest of Egypt. The industry survives today in Egypt, where one can see large tents being made on the roadside in Cairo, and in Morocco where the large wall panels called 'haiti' are still produced and used. The technique was used in Northern Persia, particularly in Resht on the Caspian, which gave its name to the pieces produced in that style. The hangings and prayer rugs made in the Balkans, which were commonly known as Banya Luka carpets, used the same technique of appliqué with over-embroidery until about 1915.

Some of the tents that have survived can be seen in various museums, but many of them are so large that they are not on display. They are usually described as military tents, although many of them must have been ceremonial or pleasure tents. Three tents that were part of the army equipment can be seen today in the Military Museum in Istanbul,

p.140

and others that were taken as booty by armies that opposed and defeated the Ottomans in battle can be seen in various museums in Europe. There are three at the Wawel (nos. 1211,1028 and 1210), and one at the Czartoryski Museum, both in Cracow. The Wawel tents were all captured between 1650 and 1699 and had previously belonged to the Wettin family in Dresden, but were donated to the Wawel by Szymon Schwarz who had bought them earlier. One of the oval tents is a three-master and the other a two-master; the circular tent has a single mast. There is also a garden tent in the Wawel but that is most probably Persian rather than Ottoman.

The tent of the Grand Vizier Damad Ali is held in the Heeregeschichtliches Museum in Vienna, and that belonging to the Grand Vizier Kara Mustapha taken at the Siege of Vienna in 1683 is at the Wagenburg Kunsthistorisches Museum in Vienna (No. S.220), together with about thirty velvet bolsters that were in it at the time. The other tent from the Siege is at the Zwinger in Dresden. It is the largest of them all, some 18 m long, but it is not on display. At the Bayerische Armee-Museum in Munich is the tent which is reputed to be Vizier Suleiman's which was captured at the Battle of Nagyharsány in 1678. The tent at the Hessian Military Museum in Schloss Friedrichstein is not on display.

A small tent captured at the Battle of Buda in 1686 is at the Hungarian National Museum in Budapest (Inv. 1927.54). The Esterhazy Tent from the Treasury at Frakno captured at Ersekújvár is also in Budapest and the two tents belonging to Odön Batthyány are at Körmend Castle, Szombathely. At the Sikorski Museum in London there is the Lanckorosenski Tent which was captured in 1621.

After the tents had been captured they were often used again by the victors as campaign tents. One of the Sobieski tents was used by Augustus the Strong, who was King of Poland and Elector of Saxony. It was captured from him by Charles XII of Sweden in 1702, who took it back to Stockholm, and it is now at Skoklosters Slott in Sweden. There are two other tents at Skoklosters. One belonged to Count Wrangel which he captured in Germany during the Thirty Years' War, and in which the peace agreement was signed in Munster in 1648. The other was captured at the storming of Ofen Fortress in Buda in 1686 by Count Niels Bjelke, who commanded the Imperial forces. A further tent dated 1633 is also there. This one is different from all the others in that it is made of a light white cloth which is unlined and decorated on the exterior with red cotton appliqué. The lightness of this tent would suggest that it is a garden tent and not a campaign tent.

Another tent with a strange history is the one at the Real Armería in Madrid. It was captured by Ernando Dávalos, Marques of Pescara from Francis I of France who lost it, together with his army, at the Battle of Pavia in 1525.[5] The tent was given by the Prince's descendant, Francisco Dávalos, to King Alfonso XII of Spain in 1881. Where

p.144

Francis I obtained the tent is unknown: it is very likely to have been a gift from Suleiman who had concluded a number of treaties with Francis, and there are many references to gifts being exchanged between them. If the Madrid tent is that from Pavia then it is the oldest tent extant. Unfortunately all the documents that would allow one to prove that this was the tent were destroyed by the army of Garibaldi, who raided the castle at Pescara in 1860.

The ceremonial tents which were used on special occasions as stands from which the Sultan and his entourage could witness the many celebrations with which the Ottoman year was filled were sometimes decorated on the outside as well and are very unlikely to have been taken on military campaigns. Other tents which were heavily decorated both inside and out were used in the Topkapi gardens as pavilions or as the lining for pathways and shelters during the Halvet fêtes, the occasions on which the Sultan's family retired from public life and spent a few days in seclusion. If they wished to go to the Mosque the tent walls were used to line even public streets to preserve the seclusion of the Imperial family.

p.16, 21

A carpet with a mihrab pattern used as a wall or couch cover. Fine gold and silver thread is worked in diagonal stem stitch on a woollen ground. This was part of the Imperial Esterházy Treasury, booty taken from the Turks before 1700. 155 x 111 cm.

Carpets and divan covers

There were special workshops within the Palace which produced the embroidered carpets used on the floor in the main Audience Chamber and in the Sultan's State rooms, and although they would not have been walked on with coarse shoes they deteriorated very fast and few have survived. Those that did survive, such as the twelve carpets with which the throne room was decorated for special occasions and which are referred to in the Palace Registry of 1680, were worked with so much gold that when the Court moved to the new Dolmabahçe Palace all the gold-embroidered textiles used in the old Palace, including these twelve carpets, were melted down for their gold and silver. According to the official account they produced nearly a ton of gold and 88 tons of silver.

Although none has survived it must be assumed that these floor coverings, 'nihali', were worked on a tightly woven linen or cotton, not dissimilar to the fabric used for lining the tents. The accompanying divan covers would have been worked on the same material, while the covers for the movable cushions would be of satin. They are always

p.186 described as being red or crimson, with the embroidery matching that on the sofas and the cushions. The smaller embroidered mats used for the trays on which food was served are also called nihali.

An inventory in Topkapi for the Gülsenabad Palace in 1717 states that it contained 414 cushion covers and 111 divan cloths, both plain and worked in metal tel work. Considering the hundreds of Palaces and Sarays throughout the Empire that must have been similarly supplied with carpets and cushions, one can understand the number of workshops and embroiderers that were involved in this industry.

The oldest surviving embroidered carpet is that still in Topkapi, most probably made in the seventeenth century. It is extremely large, 212 cm by 548 cm, made of a central large panel of red velvet with wide borders of green velvet. It is covered in embroidery in a couched stitch in a design that is reminiscent of both Tabriz rugs and those called Damascene or Cairene. It is not typically Ottoman work, the designs containing a large number of motifs derived from the Chinese repertory of pattern. No other carpets of a similar style or technique have been found, the nearest pieces being the suzeni of Islamic Central Asia.

Another version of these carpets was produced in the same appliqué technique as the tents, but different to that used for the nihali. These were the 'seccade', which is the conventional name for a carpet, used both on the floor and as wall hangings. These seccade were made on linen or wool, or even in a silk satin; they were heavily embroidered, and small pearls and beads were occasionally worked into them, usually as the centres of the flowers with which these rugs were covered. These smaller carpets were more popular in the Balkans than they were in Istanbul, and the main centres of manufacture were in Bosnia and Rumania, although many were made in Istanbul and Edirne. These are the carpets called Banya Luka carpets because the main centre for the trade in them was in that city.

p.140

The design of these rugs was usually a mihrab set within multiple borders, and they were most often covered with patterns consisting of large bunches of flowers or urns with bouquets of flowers in them. Views of houses and landscapes of rivers and kiosks were also very popular. The centre of the mihrab was often left without any decoration or with a very simple arrangement of trees or hanging lamps. It is unlikely that they actually functioned as the qibleh for prayer, but purely for decoration.

In addition to appliqué work these seccade were also decorated with all the other stitches found in Ottoman work and were very often heavily encrusted with gold wire and gold braid. They were also very often finished with fringes in silk or even gold thread.

A large bushy tree, which may be an oleander, set on a small mound, covers the ground of this carpet. This pattern was very popular in Iran and India. The border is filled with sprays of oleander tied with a very European bow. Running chain stitch in silk worked on a tambour frame on a fine woollen ground. c. 1860. 204 x 94 cm.

151

Horse and carriage cloths

The same techniques for making the larger cloths were also used for making the various horse trappings used on ceremonial occasions, such as horse caparisons — 'yapuk', saddle covers — 'çaprak' and saddles. The saddle covers were made in many sizes, from quite small ones barely larger than the saddle itself to those which covered the body of the horse completely, half lying under the saddle and the decorated end covering the horse's rump. Not surprisingly, only the rear half of most of these cloths has survived, and these parts are usually from 55 to 70 cm in width and from 110 to 160 cm long. One complete cover exists in the National Museum in Warsaw (Inv. No. 158259) and this is 110 cm by 142 cm and has all the various cuts in it that would allow it to fit on the saddle, but it would still make an uncomfortable seat. They are usually made of velvet or satin and over-embroidered in metal thread. Many saddle covers were made as presents to European royalty, together with the saddles themselves, which were covered in silver, often gilded and even encrusted with uncut rubies and pearls. The seats of the saddles would have had cloth panels set into them embroidered in the same style.

152

A fireplace or hearth panel. Such panels would have been used in campaign tents on the wall above and behind the portable stove. The central design contains the top of an arch which would have been above an open wall stove in the Palace, surmounted by repeats of a single spray which also fills the broad three-sided border. Istanbul Palace work. Before 1850. 116 x 70 cm.

A ceremonial panel to hang on the side of a horse. The central motif of a crescent and a large flame is an Ottoman regimental emblem. Very heavily stuffed dival work in gold and metal thread on a red woollen ground with a broad edging in macramé with long silk tassels. This piece is reputed to have been made in Syria or Cairo for the Viceroy of India's visit to Oman in 1901. 130 x 100 cm excluding fringe.

Large numbers of these saddles and saddle cloths were captured during the Ottoman campaigns in Europe and they can be seen in museums, together with the tents, in Poland and Germany. There were originally ten complete saddle covers in the Iparmüvészeti Museum in Budapest, but in many cases the undecorated and unlined portion that was under the saddle has deteriorated and been removed, leaving just the decorated half.

At the same time a number of other articles were also captured, among them the hearth cloths, 'ocak örtüsü'. These were used symbolically in the tents to reflect the place they would have had at home. The Europeans who captured them did not understand their use and although they were made of a woollen weave rather than of velvet or silk they were considered to be another form of horse cover. They were used as such and are still identified in some museums as saddle cloths.

The carriage cloths for use both inside and outside the carriages and carts were also made by the same ateliers, and were also given as gifts or even ordered by provincial governors.

Not only were these horse trappings made but the same workmen most probably also made the embroidered quivers, small shields and leggings that would have been part of the equipment.

153

Top The rump end of a horse cloth decorated with chrysanthemum heads in both the main field and the border. Silver-covered silk on a ground edged with a woven fringed ribbon. Booty from the Turkish campaigns before 1700. 129 x 63 cm.

Bottom The rump end of a horse cloth with three elaborate flower forms set between pairs of flowering branches within a three-sided border of a flowering vine. Silver thread on a velvet ground edged with a fine fringe. Turkish booty before 1700. 159 x 54 cm.

154

The rump ends of two horse cloths, each with a formal flower cartouche set between two large flowering sprays in a border containing the same elements but varying in scale. Gold and silver thread and silk on a velvet ground with a slit for attaching to the saddle. Turkish booty before 1700. *Top* 122 x 58 cm, *bottom* 162 x 60 cm.

Hangings

In the early years of the Empire the only decorations to be found on walls were ceramic tiles. These were both extremely decorative and rich in appearance and were also the most durable of all finishes. Walls were later decorated with paint or were hung with an embroidered or woven cloth, but it had never been a tradition for carpets to be hung on the wall — in fact a late twentieth-century custom. Other than the qibleh cloths the only other hangings that were used were the thick embroidered cloths hung on the outside of the mosque doors, called 'burqa', 'asmak' or 'asmaldık'.[6] They are made of a very heavy broad-cloth and usually lined and interlined, with the edges bordered with leather as a protection against the considerable wear they sustained. Some are also made entirely of leather but these are much rarer.

The patterns on these are always representative of some architectural feature — an arch or a gateway — in keeping with their position on a building. The door hangings are usually worked in metal thread which is couched onto the cloth, sometimes over cutouts of card which have been covered with strips of cloth or cotton wool. The stitches are usually large in scale and the hangings tend to look like armour. It is not uncommon for some formula from the Koran to be incorporated into the pattern.

NOTES

1. These guilds were called the 'public bodies' in Byzantium and had survived from the later Roman Empire. There were four main groups: the weavers, the clothiers and tailors, the dyers, and the embroiderers. The embroiderers were the 'Barbaricarii' and the 'Chrysoklavarii': foreigners working in Byzantium and the workers in gold, respectively.

2. The largest of the guilds were the weavers and tailors, followed by the dyers, who were divided into those who produce the more expensive purples and dark reds, and all the others. The embroiderers were divided into various guilds, some of which were the 'zerduzcu' (workers in gold) and the 'simkeş' (workers in silver). The 'sırmakescı' worked in metal wire; the 'divalci' produced dival work in metal strip. The cloths which had designs printed on them to be embroidered at home were made by another guild, the 'nakkaş', who were also the professional decorators and artists.

3. These other guilds were the 'terzi', the tailors for uniforms, and the 'kullabci' who made the metal-wrapped silk thread.

4. In 1626 the Hungarian Prince Bethlen asked his envoy to the Sublime Porte, Michael Tholdalagy, to hire professional tent-makers to work in Hungary. George Rakoczi, the Prince of Transylvania, ordered tents from Istanbul.

5. Francis I wrote to his mother after his defeat at Pavia, 'Of all that I had, only honour is left to me, and my life is saved.'

6. 'Burqa' is the word for a curtain or veil, 'Asmaldık' is the word that is used throughout Turkistan and the Islamic state of Central Asia for the square embroidered hanging with a triangular top that is used either inside the tent over the main door or, during the annual migrations, hangs on the side of the two main camels. Another name for the door hanging in these areas is 'engsi', usually a woven carpet with a main central field divided into four equal squares, a pattern called 'dört qatli' or 'hatçli'.

156

A corner from a large table or sofa cover with a design that expresses the ideal of civilized life. A large house in the country, a pond, trees and a tent in the garden. This motif fills the ground; more elaborate versions like cartouches are placed in each corner. The border is a continuous frieze of an arcaded house on a terrace with plants in pots on it, set in a garden full of trees and flowers with a large built-up pond. A small border composed of the same elements becomes a strip of vertical and horizontal geometric shapes. Silver-covered yellow silk and silk worked in small running chain stitch on a woollen twill ground. A portion of the original metal fringe still remains. c. 1700. The area shown is 80 x 70 cm, the whole cloth is 184 x 104 cm.

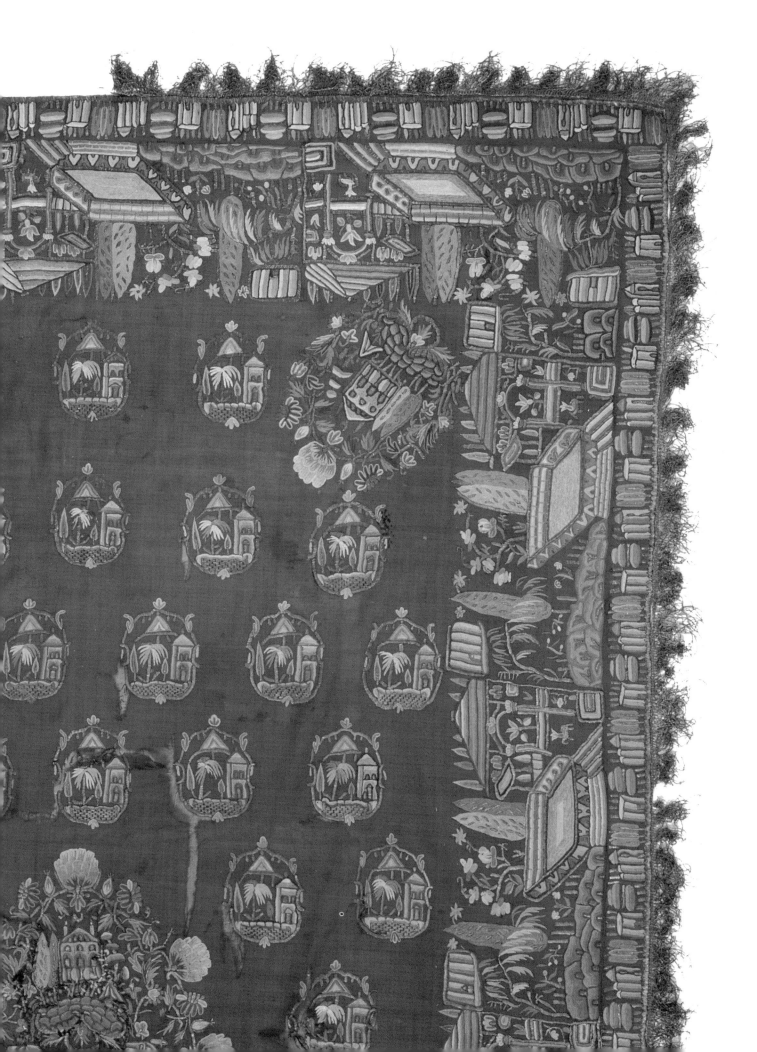

A quilt facing made in the
Ottoman style in Morocco, most
probably in Rabat. The pattern is
composed of a large and a small
rectangular bouquet set alternately and staggered to cover the
whole linen ground. At some
time the quilt was converted into
a tomb covering by being cut in
half and rejoined with a velvet
strip. The woven strip would
have been added at the same
time. Silk single brick stitch and
gözeme outlining in black.
Before 1750. 205 x 108 cm.

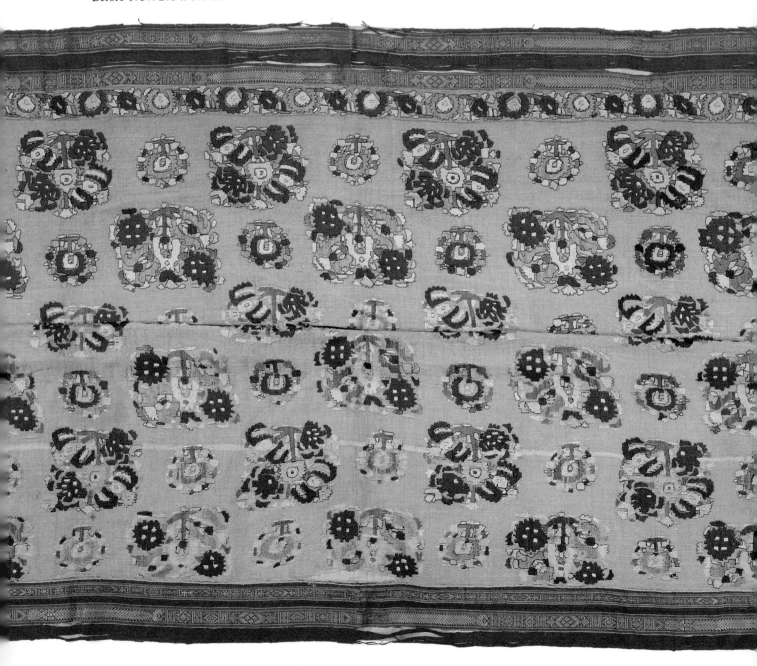

4 Influence of the Ottomans

It was inevitable that an Empire that spread from the Atlantic to the Caspian and that survived for eight hundred years should have had a strong influence on the culture of the peoples that it governed. The vast majority of the populations ruled by the Ottomans was Muslim, and Islam was the strongest influence on their lives; not only did it define the way that society worked but it also set out the framework within which the art of that society should develop.

Architecture was the principal form in which the general population was aware of art and it was the architecture of religion that they saw all around them, even in the smallest village. The Mosque and the many buildings associated with the religious complexes, the Medresseh, Library, Hospital, the Soup Kitchens for the poor and even the secular Hamam were the only permanent buildings and only they bore any decoration. The main use of art was considered to be the embellishment of the buildings, the books and the furniture of religion. Secular art was an unimportant side development of this function and was restricted to the decoration of domestic articles. It is unlikely that the ornamentation of the house or embroidery on clothes was ever considered as art at all. All these were seen as crafts rather than art, and weaving was established as the finest of the crafts.

The Court in Istanbul was the centre of all artistic innovation; it drew on native styles and forms but organized and developed them centrally, regulating them into various Orders that had to be applied according to strict rules. Art was used to glorify the Sultan, the Caliphate and all that was his, including his capital city. The two concepts of the Sultan as Caliph and Head of Religion and of the Sultan as Lord of the Lands and Ruler of the Temporal World were so fused that it is difficult to know if there was a line drawn between the art that celebrated each of these two different aspects or, if such a distinction did exist, where one would look for it.

Religion was the moving force in the development of artistic expression, exactly as it was in Christian Europe; the difference was that in

Europe there existed a middle class with power and money that enabled the members of that new sector of society both to promote and to buy art. In the Ottoman world there was the Sultan who owned everything, and the shallow layer of people that corresponded to the middle class in Europe were themselves slaves to the Sultan. On their death all their possessions reverted to the Sultan and not to their family, so the inclination to amass a great fortune and a collection of art was held in check. The great preferred to use their wealth during their lifetime to create mosques and libraries, or any religious foundation, which they saw as the only way for their names to survive.

Islam dictated what form of artistic expression was permitted and the restrictions that it imposed directly affected how art developed. The prohibition on portraying human beings, although not totally enforced in the Empire, was a critical fact in inhibiting the development of painting as exercised in Europe and China. This led to the channelling of artistic invention into the elaboration and over-elaboration of geometric shapes, into the creation of the many decorative scripts used for the written word, and to the creation of a rigid system where even the most natural forms of flowers and plants were stylized to the point of reducing them to geometric forms.

p.207

p.34

The miniatures found in books did often portray human and supernatural beings and this was allowed because the books were private and, in a physical sense, kept closed and unseen. Most of the population never opened any book other than the Koran and the exegeses of the Koran and these were never illustrated other than with a decorated frontispiece, an elaborate script and a gold dot used at the end of each verse. When Korans were printed even these embellishments disappeared.

Calligraphy was developed as an artistic exercise. It was an elaboration of the words themselves and of the shapes that they made on paper, never of the sense of the words. The written words which were decorated were invariably the words of the Koran or the formulae that had evolved in the practice of Islam. Calligraphy was not only used in books, it also decorated, as painted panels or as ceramic tiles, the inner walls of religious buildings and sepulchral monuments. It was the only decoration used on textiles for many centuries,[1] and it appeared in metal work and on glass as a part of the decorative scheme. In the wonderful, complex Islamic buildings of Central Asia the decorated words are set in coloured bricks on the outer walls in ever more elaborate versions of the Holy Names and the various ritual formulae, which are sometimes set out in complicated acrostic patterns.

These restrictions were enforced throughout the Empire and as the majority of the population was Muslim they were accepted without question. The vocabulary of ornament and design was virtually identical everywhere; it was a rigid system and even the way that the motifs were used was stipulated by an accepted code.

Right Two leg panels from a pair of women's trousers stitched together. The pattern on each is composed of two flower heads set in rows. Floss silk and silver strip on a silk core in double darning and stem stitch on a cotton tabby weave. Thrace or the northern Aegean Islands. *c.* 1800. 145 x 88 cm.

Far right A bolster cover in a European style. The size has changed and the field is filled with a pattern like a French printed cotton. The border is filled with repeats of a large spray arranged like cartouches. Silver thread and silk on a linen and silk tabby ground on one side only. Rumeli, before 1780. 90 x 58 cm maximum.

The repertory of design was used in two distinct traditions: the first, which covers the greatest geographic area, can be called the Islamic style that was prevalent throughout the House of Islam, the Dar al-Islam; the second can be called the Infidel style, which was common throughout the House of War, the Dar al-Harb, the world that would, through war, be converted to Islam. This second style was mainly developed in the Balkans and Central Europe and, to a certain extent, in the countries bordering the conquered lands. Certain features and motifs are common to the work in each area but the final products are not at all identical. The Ottoman Turkish style also influenced a far larger area of Western Europe when it was taken up as high fashion and influenced the arts, even appearing in the theatre and the opera house; it also appeared on the streets as adaptations of high fashion which became parody and caricature in popular culture.

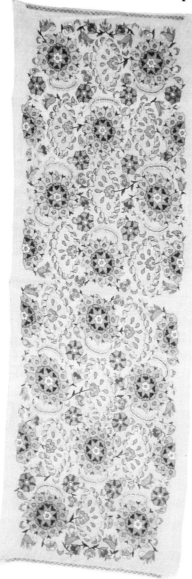

The Islamic Style

Above A strip of Zemmour work combining Italianate design and stitches with Byzantine imagery made during the Ottoman period in Morocco. A frieze of a water fountain with two small attendants between a pair of opposed 'fat' birds. Silk long-armed cross and four-sided stitch on a cotton ground. Before 1700. 98 x 25 cm.

The Islamic style already existed throughout the House of Islam and had developed there in many forms before the establishment of the Ottoman Empire. This dominant Islamic world of which the Ottomans were an integral part provided the basis for the greater part of their art, and on this firm basis the Ottomans elaborated and developed new forms, incorporating the various influences from their own heritage and from their non-Islamic territories.

The development of Ottoman art was principally influenced by the Court in Istanbul, and this Court art was copied in the provincial centres, from the Maghreb to Egypt after the fall of the Mamluks and throughout the Balkans. Even outside the Empire, in the lands stretching from the western shore of the Caspian Sea to the borders of China, the artistic influence of the Court was very strong. This influence was a consequence of political and commercial influence: the small Khanates and Sultanates in Turkestan were tied to the Ottomans by the various treaties made for their mutual defence against Persia, and although they controlled the land trade routes to China the main market for many of the products of these states was the Ottoman Empire and, in order to sell inside it, they had to enter into political alliances with the Porte and to make products that reflected the established taste.

A ceremonial cloth composed of a red square set within broad blue borders; the centre is filled with an eight-pointed motif decorated within and without with flowers and leaves in a very formal manner. The borders contain a looping vine with flowers and the corners are filled with an ogival four-lobed motif. Silk, metal on a silk core and silver wire on a silk ground. Professional work from Istanbul showing Persian influence. *c.* 1700. 110 cm square.

An Islamic Maghrebi style had been developed in Morocco, Algeria and Tunisia from the period of the great Arab conquests of the seventh and eighth centuries AD. It was an amalgam of pre-Mamluk and Mamluk Egypt, of the native Berber tradition and of the Moorish culture of southern Spain. The strongest form of it is to be found in architecture, but it also appears in the ceramics, in metal work and in textiles.

There are two main embroidery traditions in Morocco.[2] The first is that of Fez, Meknes and Zemmour, reflecting traditions prevalent before the arrival of the Ottomans. This early style is based on elaborate geometric patterns familiar from Mamluk work, which are also very similar to those found in the Greek Island of Naxos in the Cyclades and

163

in Palestinian costume. Zemmour work has particular distinguishing designs which can also be found in South Italian and Balkan work. The principal motifs are the fat bird, the opposed birds set on each side of a fountain, the skirted lady and heraldic beasts. This group of embroideries is worked in monochrome silk, with shades of red being the most common. Zemmour work also uses an outlining stitch in black. The stitch used is a small tight stem or seed stitch laid in two directions, making it appear like a small cross stitch. This stitch is sometimes worked very thickly to make a raised surface on the fabric.

The Moroccan embroideries that were most influenced by the Ottomans were of the second tradition, those of Rabat, Tetuan, Chechaouen and the Mediterranean coast. The most common articles found are cushion covers, long scarves and curtains; more rarely one finds quilt facings, square covers, the long strips used as mirror covers and the elaborate and ornate valances which were used as facings for couches and mattresses.

p.81

These groups of Moroccan textiles are all worked in the predominant Ottoman stitch, darning and double darning, which is usually set diagonally, with outlines worked in black stem stitch. Tetuan work is always floral and very similar to standard Ottoman designs. The range of colours used is different and it is this feature that allows one to distinguish these embroideries from very similar work from Algeria and Turkey. The main colours used are a slate blue and a soft pale blue, yellow, a range of greens, white and a coarse dark red. The silk used in Tetuan work was locally dyed and has tended to fade so the colours are now generally softer than they were originally, with the exception of the hard red which has survived in its original coarseness. It has been suggested that the Algerian tradition influenced the Moroccan one, but it is more likely that both were influenced at about the same time by the Ottomans as they had both been influenced earlier by the Mamluks.

A valance of Sale work again using an Italianate style that was common within the Ottoman Empire, appearing in Morocco, Crete, the Agean Islands and even in Ottoman velvets and brocades. Silk cross stitch and the back of cross stitch on cotton. *c.* 1720. 140 x 40 cm.

The valances made in Rabat and Salé are invariably worked in red silk and copy the baroque embroideries of central and southern Italy. They are usually based on wreath patterns and worked in darning stitch laid in two directions, which give the valances the appearance of woven brocades. Bolster and cushion covers are also worked in darning stitch, the area of embroidery being usually the two ends of both faces of the bolster, although some, the 'mhedda', are covered completely. The bolsters are worked with floss silk in a very long darning stitch, sometimes over five threads, so the embroidery tends to tear and disintegrate very quickly.

The dominant tradition of embroidery in Algeria and Tunisia is an Ottoman one.[3] The patterns are those found on either woven or embroidered Turkish textiles or on European brocades introduced during the period of Ottoman rule. Both types of pattern are invariably based on a central floral motif surrounded with leaf forms and with borders composed of isolated flowers or leaves. The embroideries are worked on single widths of a loose hand-woven linen or cotton. These strips, which are usually 40 cm wide, are sewn together in threes to make curtains, sometimes joined together with inserts of woven narrow silk ribbons in mixed colours. The embroidery is always contained within the width of each strip and does not necessarily fall into regular repeats. The two styles in Algerian work are both based on floral motifs. In the one, Ottoman designs are worked predominantly in red and blue silk with touches of green, white, yellow and mauve. In the other, the brocaded patterns, which are quite unique to Algiers, are worked predominantly in violet silk with very small highlights of green, red and gold. Sometimes a narrow panel of needle-weaving on a drawn thread base is incorporated towards the bottom of the panel; this must have been worked so that the additional weight made the curtain fall more gracefully.

Single widths of the muslin are often worked as long head-scarves, 'benika', very similar to the Turkish çevre used as a standard headscarf for outdoor wear. The benika often has a half-round pattern in the centre of the scarf, which would sit above the forehead. Another long single-width piece is the 'tenchifa', a towel used to wrap the hair after a bath. Cushion covers are also made in Algiers in the red and blue style and these are very similar to Turkish patterns. Bath towels were also embroidered like the peştemal, but they are called futa, which is a common word throughout North Africa and the Yemen for the wrap-around cloth worn by men.

The stitch used mainly in the red and blue work is running and double running, worked diagonally in sold blocks of colour called 'maalka' locally. This is a stitch that can be used for either one or double-faced work. The centre of the small floral motif is worked in brick stitch, stem stitch and long-armed cross stitch. The violet curtains are quite unusual in Ottoman embroidery in that the main stitch used

One of a pair of panels made to be hung on each side of an arch. Fourteen repeats of an Ottoman bouquet are set free-standing along the middle of the panel, with a conventional border and a base block of four bouquets drawn in a sixteenth-century Ottoman style. Silk darning on a local cotton lawn weave. Algiers before 1720. 268 x 48 cm.

is a small eyelet stitch worked in eight stitches and set out in diagonal lines.[4] The patterns of the violet embroideries are those found in brocaded Turkish textiles, which are, of course, similar to brocades made in Spain and Italy. These large blocks of pattern are filled entirely with the eyelet stitch worked in violet silk. The areas of the curtains not in violet are worked in red, blue and white in running or brick stitch.

A major use of embroidery in the Maghreb is for decorating leather, harnessing and saddles, and there are very wonderful pieces to be found of this work. The concentration of decoration on horse trappings expresses the important role that the horse played in that society. The other great area of embroidered decoration is in the ceremonial clothing for men and women. The embroidery on costume is very similar to Ottoman work and is carried out on velvet or thick brocade in both the dival technique and in couched metallic braid. This work is very similar to Albanian, Turkish and Northern Greek work and, incidentally, has very strongly influenced the embroidery traditions of the Muslim African states south of the Maghreb.

The Moroccans also used the appliqué technique very widely in the larger pieces of embroidery. These are the 'haiti', which are long wall panels, originally intended for tents, but which were universally used in houses. These haiti are worked on velvet and the only pattern used is a series of architectural arches, nine or eleven of them all identical with only the colour used for the background changing. More often than not the arches are left blank but on some of the pieces the arch is filled with a lamp or a bouquet of flowers, rather like the multiple prayer rugs from Central Anatolia.

Mamluk Egypt influenced Ottoman work very early in the twelfth century, when trade and political relations between the two powers were very strong. Mamluk Egypt was the stronger culture and by drawing on the traditions and textile skills of the Fatimids and the Ayyubids influenced the Ottomans at the beginning of their development. Although a Turki Mamluk aristocracy had ruled Egypt from 1250, when they usurped the last Ayyubid Sultan, the development of the plastic arts came mainly from existing internal traditions. The main outside influences came from various European countries with which the Egyptians had strong trading relations, rather than from neighbouring Arab traditions. Even after the Ottoman conquest in 1517 the evidence is that Ottoman art was more influenced by the Mamluks rather than that they changed the existing Mamluk style.

It was not until the Napoleonic invasions at the end of the eighteenth century that the later Ottoman style influenced Egypt. Mohammed Ali, a junior soldier from Kavala in Rumeli, went to Egypt in 1798 to fight with the Turkish Army against Napoleon. After the withdrawal of the French Mohammed Ali returned to Egypt to fight on behalf of the Turkish Sultan against the remnants of the Mamluks. He was appointed Governor General of Egypt in 1806 and organized the

p.208

A cover worked in white silk on white cotton in a style called 'Book Pattern' that was very popular in Cyprus and the Aegean Islands. Most of the work is needle weaving on drawn thread patches. Similar pieces were sold to be used as Koran wrappers. c. 1850. 83 x 58 cm.

last war against the Mamluks in 1811. He and his son Ibrahim Pasha extended the Ottoman Empire into Arabia and the Sudan, and in 1822 was made Pasha of Crete. It was under him until his death in 1849 that the Ottomans had the greatest effect on the arts of Egypt. It was the new Ottoman style that had been recently influenced by Europe that was most acceptable to Egypt, and more embroidery under Ottoman influence must have been made in Egypt after 1830, and before industrialization in 1880, than in the previous six hundred years. There is no particular form of this embroidery that deserves any special attention.

The Ottoman influence on Palestine and Syria was equally slight. The main contribution Istanbul made to the development of the textile arts in these countries was the providing of capital for setting up industrial production of velvets and brocades in Aleppo, Homs and Damascus, and later in Beirut. It was also under Ottoman influence that the small carpet industry of the Lebanon was revived. These factories were owned and run by Europeans and by French, Greek and Italian Stambouliote families.

Although the Ottoman Empire never extended into Central Asia (the area known as Transoxiana having been barred to them by the Safavids and later the Qajars of Persia) the influence of Istanbul was felt very strongly. The trade between China, the Khanates of Bokhara, Samarkand and Khiva and the markets of Europe, was still controlled by the merchants of Istanbul despite the fact that the routes had originally been opened by the Europeans themselves. Even after the Russian conquests and the creation of the Turkistan Government-General in 1867, and the final annexations of the Khanates to the Russian Empire in 1876, much trade with the area was still conducted through Istanbul and many of the textiles, particularly the silk embroideries, were made for the Turkish market. These were mainly the large covers called 'suzenis', which were made in professional ateliers in many cities throughout the area but marketed in Bokhara. Caucasian, Turcoman, Uzbek and Kirghiz embroideries all show many of the same features as Ottoman work, but it is difficult now to decide whether they are similar because they share a common tradition or whether one has influenced the other. They are very similar to work made in Turkey; the stitches, mainly darning and chain stitch, are the same, the colour ranges are similar and many of the motifs can be found in the work of both areas.

The Infidel Style

The influence of the Ottomans on the non-Islamic area can best be observed in Ottoman Greece and the Balkans. The Ottomans controlled parts of Greece even before the Fall of Constantinople (Istanbul), but after 1453 they held virtually all of Greece and by 1600 held all the Islands in the Aegean including Crete, except for a few years when the Venetians under Morosini temporarily recaptured them. The Ottoman influence can best be observed in the Turkish embroideries of Epirus, Skyros and Crete, where this type of embroidery was made alongside work in the native tradition. This local tradition had developed out of the Byzantine ecclesiastical style, which was overlaid with the European styles that the Franks introduced during their 300 year rule of Greece and the Islands.

In Epirus the embroidery was very similar to conventional Turkish work, using the same range of stitches and colours, but two distinct styles of design were developed, one for each of the two different ethnic populations. The first used the same repertory of patterns found in Istanbul — strictly floral and geometric — and the second a local style, presumably a Christian one, that portrayed humans, animals, angels and mythical beasts as well as all the floral motifs. This second style has more affinities to Caucasian or Persian iconography than Turkish. The same articles of clothing that would have been worn by both populations — the surcoat, waistcoat, blouse, sash and scarves — can be found decorated in either of the two styles, and the same is true for the decorations found on quilt and cushion covers. The quality of much of this work is so high that it could easily be mistaken for metropolitan work.

The domestic embroidery traditions of Albania, Yugoslavia, Bulgaria, Romania and Hungary share so many direct influences from Ottoman style it is often difficult to decide where some Balkan Ottoman work was made. The fashions of Istanbul, particularly of Phanar, from where many of the Governors of the Balkan provinces

p.82, 170

A bolster cover, probably part of a set of bed furnishings in the same pattern. A perfect example of the alternating pattern style, a long-petalled tulip and a fringed carnation are connected with a small leaf; both flowers are filled with a stylized circular filling flower at the base and with small flowers and stripes in the petals. The border is called the mountain border, deriving from a Chinese original. Floss silk couching on linen. Before 1700. 152 x 41 cm.

p.189

came, were introduced into the whole area as the dress of the aristocracy and the local court. Not only was the style introduced, but also the patterns and designs that were to be worked locally were received from Istanbul. The large embroideries, such as the military and pleasure tents, were actually ordered from Istanbul.

As early as the beginning of the seventeenth century there are records of embroideresses, weavers, workers in leather and makers of metal-covered silk and metal wire, 'skofion', being taken to Budapest to work there.[5] When Budapest was recaptured from the Ottomans in 1686 the Turkish workers in leather who had come from Edirne who were resident there were held as prisoners. The Ottoman influence can best be seen in the various cloths used as covers and the scarves, but even in the costume embroidery (which was more likely to preserve the native tradition) there can be seen the influence of the Ottomans. As would be expected, it is more evident in the Muslim populations of Albania, southern Yugoslavia and Bulgaria than among the Christian peoples.

The universal napkin was produced throughout the Balkans and Russia and retained the form of the Turkish napkin, with double-faced decoration at both ends. The patterns are invariably floral and geometric and in some napkins from South Russia one finds the fat bird pattern again.

The most interesting examples of Turkish influence in eastern Europe came from Poland. Not only were fashions and patterns brought from Turkey but the Polish aristocracy imported technicians to set up new industries on their estates. The Radziwill Princes organized a factory at Sluck with Armenian weavers from the Empire to make the silk sashes that became essential accessories to Polish noblemen in the first half of the eighteenth century. The weavers brought with them their own weaving frames and their special techniques; they even brought a metallic mangle that was used to burnish the silver and gold with which the sashes were woven. The patterns of the sashes were originally very Turkish in style, and were known as 'paşali', but they later copied Persian textiles, and eventually developed a Polish style that had little resemblance to the original sashes.

These Turkish textiles became so popular that factories were set up by the royal family at Grodno, by private individuals at Lipków, and eventually in many other cities where large brocades were woven that copied Turkish techniques but used baroque patterns. The best known of these was at Buczacz. Towards the end of the fashion sashes made in Cracow were sold and worn throughout Eastern Europe by the aristocracy and the military. By 1810 the industry had virtually died but the patterns and the techniques remained and have been a part of Polish textile art ever since.

The Ottoman or Turkish style had one unexpected influence on Europe, based not on conquest or trade but on aesthetic fashion.

A Yanina spread made in the Ottoman style. A broad border is composed of a multi-coloured tulip set between two hyacinths alternating with a tall thin-necked perfume flask, in turn surrounded by a thin outer border of a tendril sprouting leaves and flowers. The whole border is spattered with large green-bodied parrots and smaller red-bodied ones. A ewer with a bunch of red carnations and pink buds is set in each corner with each carnation surmounted by a blue cockerel. Before 1700. This cover was bought from the family of the last Khedive of Egypt and is reputed to have been brought to Egypt with Mohammed Ali. It had been used as a wedding sheet and is stained in the conventional way. The spread's pristine condition is accounted for by its having been kept in a drawer for two hundred years. 272 x 175 cm without fringe.

Although the Ottomans were the enemy and had been for some three hundred years, their defeat at Vienna and the gradual collapse of the Empire after that meant that Europe could treat them more lightly. The first sign of this was perhaps the baking of a bread roll in the shape of the Crescent which was eaten for breakfast, but it spread quickly until fashionable costume copied many features of Ottoman Court dress. Many operas and singspiels told the story of Christian slaves from the Seraglio and the harem, much music was written 'a la Turca' or 'a la Turcesca' and novels were written telling stories about the Ottoman East and depicting the life there. Even in popular art the figure of the Turk was very evident. It appeared both as demon and as the butt of political jokes. The figure and the costume were caricatured as the inept enemy and the villain that was always defeated.

It is not possible to detail all the influences that this aesthetic movement had on the embroidery of Europe but the evidence can clearly be seen once one is alerted to its existence. Many of the motifs are easily traced to their eastern origin and many of the new techniques copy these imported ones.

This napkin has a very straightforward version of the hunchbacked pattern, a carnation surrounded by a branch sprouting small flower buds. Stem stitch laid diagonally and very fine silver wrapped on a gold silk core on a light loose weave cotton ground. *c.* 1860. 54 x 13 cm embroidered portion.

A kerchief with a narrow vine set alternately with carnations, roses, lilies and daisies. Silk and fine gold thread in stem stitch with a drawn thread border in patterned needle weaving. Istanbul before 1720. 52 x 7 cm.

NOTES

1. Tiraz is the name given to the single line of script that was the only decoration that was woven into textiles for many centuries, in places as far apart as Baghdad, the Yemen, Egypt and Palermo. The line of script usually glorified the Ruler and mentioned the Master Weaver. This tradition lasted from the sixth to the thirteenth century.

2. The usual word for embroidery in Morocco is 'terz', derived from 'tiraz'. The various types of embroidery are called 'terz el-ghorza' (counted work), 'terz es-skalli' (Sicillian work, which is invariably work with gold), then each town calls its work 'terz Meknessi', or 'terz Rabati', etc.

3. The usual word for embroidery in Tunisia is 'triz', again from 'tiraz', and the main styles are 'triz akhla' (black work) and 'triz et-telli' (embroidery on a coarse net often in coloured wools).

4. The name of the stitch 'zeliledj' is derived from the Maghreb form of the Spanish word for a ceramic tile, 'azulejos', because when the eyelet stitches are worked in parallel diagonal lines they form small squares of the white ground fabric. This stitch is known locally as the Turkish stitch (this is the 'ciğer deldi' of Turkish work). It is not a common stitch and only used as a highlighting feature in some embroideries, never as a filling stitch. The outlines of the main motifs are worked in stem stitch or in diagonal stitch, called 'menezzel' locally. Other stitches used in the cushion covers are laid and couched stitch: 'meterrha' (which is the same as the Turkish 'atma').

5. The embroideresses are always referred to as 'bulya', a word that means, if anything specific, a Moslem woman, not particularly an embroideress.

173

5   Designs and patterns

The designs used to decorate Ottoman textiles are basically part of the general repertory of motifs used throughout the Near and Middle East. There is a very strong preference for designs derived from the natural world of flowers, leaves and trees, and the majority of decorated textiles use these designs exclusively. It is usually stated that this confinement to natural forms is a result of the restrictions in the Koran on representing the human figure in art, which is seen to be the same as the creating of idols.[1] However, the greater part of the art of the area before the birth of Mohammed, the Era of Ignorance, was also predominantly of natural forms, and Ottoman art continues this tradition, which was enforced but not instituted by the advent of Islam.

Originally these designs must have been direct representations of nature, but as they were copied and recopied the drawings became more and more stylized so that eventually many of them became merely tokens of the originals. It is possible that most of the representations of flowers and plants were first seen two-dimensionally, drawn in the various herbals and books on pharmacology, and in this form were easily translated into textile and embroidery designs.[2]

Before 1820 the designs are exclusively natural forms and geometric patterns. The repertory of designs in Ottoman art after that date also includes many representations of the scenery of daily life. The life portrayed is a tame, urban world, a world controlled by man; the garden he has created, not the natural untouched land; it is the life of the town-dweller with cultivated plants. The architecture portrayed is the Mosque, the tents and kiosks that ornament the gardens and occasionally the ancient columns and ruins of the past. When a landscape is shown it is an organized, idealized view of the countryside, particularly the Bosphorus; the garden scenes show kiosks, trees, pools and even wells. Common articles such as plates of fruit, cradles and pairs of slippers are also shown, along with the more extravagant sailing ships, trees, Palaces and Mosques.

Animals, birds and mythological figures appear in both woven and

On this sash a conventional flower spray is treated in a Baroque style derived from French brocades. Each branch is tied with a ribbon bow, flowers and leaves are drawn in a different style, and the rhythm of Ottoman art has given way to a design based on a mechanical loom. A sinuous vine with bizarre flowers and silver tassels is used in the broad border. Silk, silver thread, wire and strip on fine cotton. Istanbul *c.* 1830. 37 x 30 cm.

175

embroidered textiles. Birds are very popular: they are common creatures in the folktales and poetry and always carry a symbolic message. In the provinces that were less strict in the observance of Sunni doctrine even human figures appear; surprisingly, both men and women are portrayed together. Additionally, there are a large number of designs derived totally from abstract, geometric patterns and a small number of symbolic motifs, The patterns used on flat woven kilims and on knotted carpets, as well as those on the velvets and brocades, all form part of the same tradition and can be found repeated in embroidery.

A written script was occasionally incorporated into embroidery, but it was very seldom treated as a pattern in the way that the Kufic script was stylized to make a border in knotted carpets. When writing is used it is either in the form of a salutation or exhortation, or the repetition of the word 'Maşallah' or of the 'B'ism Allah' formula. Some pieces do have lines of poetry incorporated into the design, but that was more popular when the old Arabic script was used. After 1923, when the Arab script was abolished by law and Turkish was written in Latin characters, the use of writing as a decorative pattern became much less popular. The only written pattern that one does find is the 'tuğra', which is the stylized monogram of the Sultan; by tradition pieces that have a tuğra on them were made for Palace use, although it is clear that many of them were in circulation outside the Palace.

p.130

These common designs are used differently throughout the Empire and create in each separate country or province an homogeneous national style which is distinct from all the others. It is easy to distinguish one group from another: Ottoman work made in the Balkans is different from Istanbul work, Palestinian textiles are easily identifiable, as are Egyptian and Maghrebi textiles, although all of them use the same fairly limited group of motifs, similar materials and, virtually, the same range of techniques and stitches.

Inevitably embroidery patterns have been very strongly influenced by the general concept of decoration that exists in other arts. Not unexpectedly, embroidery designs have been most strongly influenced by designs found on other textiles, mainly grander weaves such as velvets and brocades or the knotted carpets, but even the humbler printed cottons and linens have influenced embroidery. The embroidered cloth very often aims at reproducing more expensive woven versions, or if not to copy, at least to produce a version that would sit comfortably alongside them.

The same designs are found painted inside religious buildings. They are used to decorate ceramic tiles, metal work, glass and even bead work, showing that there was a continuous interchange of patterns between the various crafts. The forms of these patterns and the way that they were used did change during the centuries to keep in touch with current fashion, but also to take advantage of new materials and techniques. The changes were never so dramatic as to allow one to be able to date embroideries into strict periods by the patterns alone; change was gradual and the introduction of new motifs did not automatically dislodge older ones, they merely expanded the total repertory available. Motifs from the earliest period were still being worked until the beginning of this century, and when the teaching of embroidery was introduced into schools after 1922 it was the oldest patterns that were used to form the basis of the new style.

frontispiece, p.10, 85, 92

Embroideries of the first period, the fifteenth and sixteenth centuries, are generally composed of one or two basic motifs that are worked with interconnecting elements to form a large, flowing balanced pattern that covers the whole surface area of the cloth, echoing the way that woven textiles are patterned. The most common motifs are the dianthus, tulip and hyacinth, the artichoke head and pomegranate, with the artichoke or acanthus leaf as the most common foliage. Both flower and leaf shapes are used either in profile or spread out. One flower form used is of no particular species but is a conventional flower shape, with petals arranged around a centre; this could be assumed to be a rose but it is not drawn in the same realistic way that the other flowers are and must be a stylized form rather than a true representation. In view of the Far Eastern origin of many of the floral patterns the shape could equally be a representation of a chrysanthemum, merged with the more common rose.

p.87

p.100, 101
p.126–7

During this early period the weavers created very elaborate versions of the floral patterns, based on large medallions and cartouches which are filled with many flower forms to make one large flower shape. Tulips are placed inside leaves, hyacinths are drawn within tulips and sometimes every petal of a dianthus is filled with a sprig of flower buds.

p.169

Medallions and flowers may be arranged as isolated repeats set in lines, with small motifs filling in the space between them, or two basic motifs used where the larger dominant motif is contrasted with a smaller one, but again set out in horizontal lines. A more elaborate version of this style is where the main dominant motif is set within the framework of a trellis. This trellis is usually a formal one spread equally balanced, vertically and horizontally, over the area, with the created spaces filled with a repeated design. Occasionally only one plane of the trellis is shown, with some part of the main design, a branch or a long leaf, extended to form an interconnecting line that twists between the main blocks. Sometimes the trellis shape is so broken up as to become a different pattern altogether, with the unifying shape destroyed and the separated units making little structural sense. Very rarely the medallions are set out on an over-all floral patterned ground or even a heraldic design of blue and white triangles. The woven patterns were then used by embroiderers.

p.13, 15, 117

p.109, 181

p.116

An analysis of the patterns of this period is given in the section on quilt facings in household textiles on pages 89–90.

Three symbolic patterns used even at this early date are the circular

177

spots arranged in threes, the two or three wavy lines set above one another, and the wheel composed of wavy spokes. All three are derived from the Ottomans' Far Eastern heritage. The three spots are the flaming pearls, the 'çintamani', of Buddhist iconography; this pattern was often called the 'sign of Tamerlane' by Arab writers trying to explain it without reference to its non-Islamic origin. Their story is that it represents the sign that Tamerlane made by dipping his thumb and two fingers in blood and pressing them onto the order authorizing the sacking of Baghdad in 1258. The two or three wavy lines are stylized versions of a Chinese water or cloud pattern which was used widely in knotted carpets; it is unlikely that they are the tiger stripes which is a favourite modern explanation. These two designs are often used together to make one motif, which was popular in the early sixteenth century and figures on a number of the Imperial kaftans. The wheel with wavy spokes is again derived from Buddhist paintings, a version of the 'chakra', the wheel of life. The Turkic version is called 'çarkı felek', and it represents the sphere of heaven or destiny. It remained a popular figure in central Asian embroidery, particularly in the shamanist pieces of the Uighur and Kirghiz and is commonly found in the suzani of Turkistan and Uzbekistan and even appears in Daghestani embroidery.

A fourth symbolic pattern used is the six-pointed star composed of two triangles placed pointing in opposite directions on top of each other. This is a common Judaic emblem and was used in one of the earliest of the great weaves, a mantle of Mehmed II of about 1470. The

This is the simplest version of the flower and two-leaf pattern, which still creates an extremely strong image. Stem stitch worked to look like couching with fine silver wire on a yellow silk core on a cotton ground with supplementary warps in silk. Central Anatolia c. 1880. 52 x 22 cm embroidered area.

It is very rare for the motif of Suleiman's Seal (common in woven textiles of the seventeenth century) to be found on an embroidery. It has here been adapted to a flower head and placed on a stalk with leaves. Stem stitch in silk and silver on a yellow silk core on a cotton ground, with some introduced supplementary wefts in silk and a fringe of a voided area with remnants of needle weaving in coloured silk. Edirne, before 1850. 43 x 23 cm embroidery and fringe.

pattern is called 'mührü Suleiman', the seal of Solomon. It is seldom used in embroidery but is very common in ceramic tiles and woven textiles.

The other designs common in Ottoman work fall into two groups. The first are those taken from the Byzantine or Western European tradition. These are the 'rumi' patterns, and include those which were to be seen in the borders of church and secular mosaics, usually a curvilinear leaf and tendril pattern which twists alternately from side to side. The second group are the 'hatayi' patterns, which are derived from Chinese, 'Cathay', originals. They would have been seen on Chinese ceramics and textiles which were extensively imported by the Ottomans. This group is best represented by a stylized lotus or chrysanthemum flower and its leaves, but also includes wavy cloud bands and stylized mountain shapes. Many of the rumi patterns were drawn by pen on the cloth before being worked and are often called reed pen, or 'saz', patterns, and in this form they become very elongated and curled, turning in on themselves.

During this time the embroideries are always contained within a border composed of repeats of a linear version of one of the motifs found in the main field. A common design is that of the small twig, the 'çubuk', used to join isolated flowers. The twig pattern is also used in the main field. The word means a pipe for smoking as well, and the carnation flower set on a twig is often called the çubuk pattern, particularly in Central Anatolian carpets. A number of other formal patterns which can be seen in the multiple borders of carpets are also used, the most common being that where the shape is reversed into itself, the patterns called 'medakhyl', the 'interlaced entrance'. These are always contained within two thin parallel lines.

The colour range is very limited: mainly red and blue with a little black and white. The embroideries are never monochrome but are conceived as blocks of solid colour without shading.

In the seventeenth and eighteenth centuries the general feel of the patterns gradually changes. They no longer have the wide sweep of woven textiles but become more concerned with smaller detail. The genius of this period is the sureness of execution and the ability to place the patterns artistically on the cloth. The larger floral patterns are standardized into contained blocks, the wide trellis bands become thin flower stalks, and attempts are made to make the flowers more realistic by using subtle variations in colour and tone to give a modelled effect. The standard pattern becomes an isolated, contained block of a curling stalk terminating in a single flower, with small subsidiary flowers and leaves branching off it. The stalk pattern was called at that time 'kambur', which is the word for a hunchback, a very good description of the curling-over of the branch. This pattern can be upright or horizontal and is ideal for a scheme where the same pattern is used in one direction and then reversed.

p.60, 72, 172

The tulip became a favourite design not only because of its easily recognizable shape but also because the name in Turkish, 'lale', when written in the Arabic script, is the same as the beginning of the Muslim protestation of faith, which starts with the words 'La Allah'. It combined a pleasing pattern with a reminder of the Faith, wittily catering to the Islamic preoccupation with religious symbols and the use of words and writing as pattern. Tulips became such a feature of court life that the whole period is known in Turkey as the Tulip Age, 'Lale Devri'.

p.92, 169

Two ends of a napkin joined together. The pattern is a repeat of crossed daggers in their sheaths and a carnation flower. This design symbolizes both honour and steadfastness. Gold thread and silk on a cotton ground. *c.* 1850. 80 x 41 cm.

p.26, 61, 63, 203

A wrapper with a very idiosyncratic design, the hunchbacked branch has become a blossom-filled band and fills the ground like a disintegrated trellis. Large leaf-like flowers fill the curve of each band. The border is composed of red and blue cartouches containing disintegrated lettering. Couched stitch in silk on a cotton ground, with many small decorations still left in ink outline and not completed. Before 1800. 122 cm square.

Where the standard small floral motif is not used a more elaborate version is developed, usually based on a container filled with flowers. This pattern does not specifically belong to the repertory of Islamic design but to that of a much larger area which includes Europe and the Far East. This vase and bouquet pattern was very popular throughout the Ottoman Empire and is a conventional motif throughout the Balkans, southern Russia, the Caucasus and Central Asia, as common in woven textiles as it is in embroidery. It was used most dramatically in the Polish sashes developed in the second half of the eighteenth century by the Turkish Armenian weavers working in Sluck and Lipków.

The decoration of the borders changes during these centuries: it becomes more common for a contrasting pattern to be used inside the border. Later, the flowing design within the broad border is abandoned altogether, replaced by a repeat geometric pattern worked in every colour used in the embroidery.

During these two centuries the uses for which embroidered textiles were made changed as living styles did, and the new designs were more suitable for decorating smaller articles, where the ornament is restricted to a part of the area and does not cover the whole surface as before. Because a single motif was repeated in lines it was necessary to introduce more colours to maintain the interest of the piece, and it is during

181

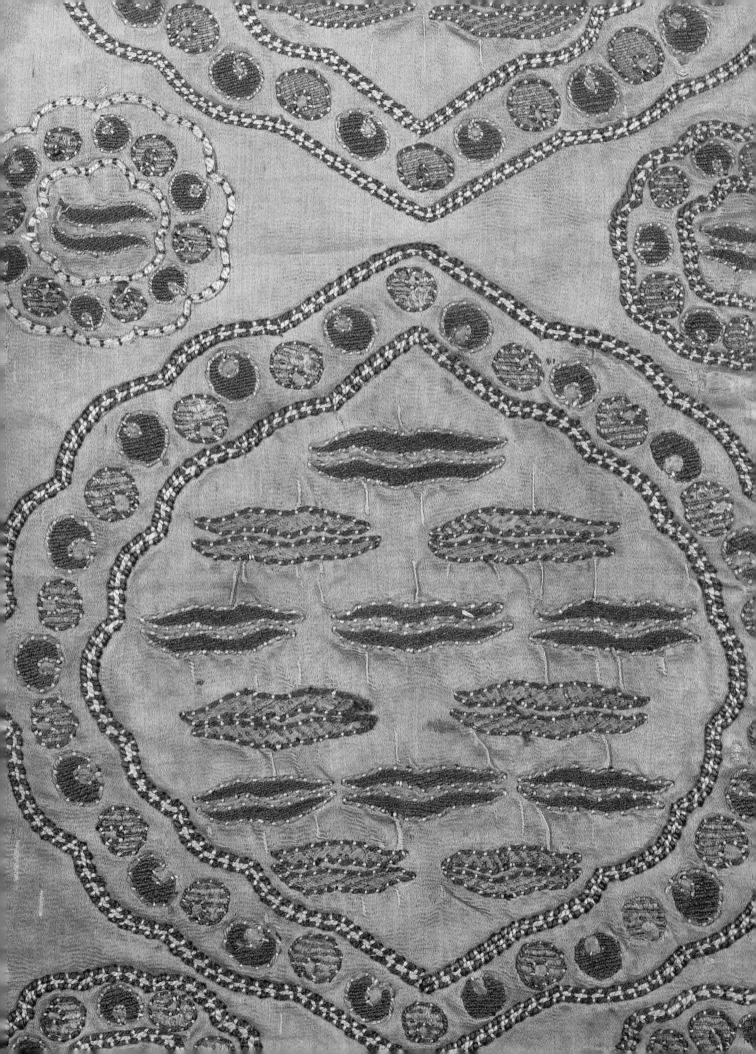

Above An arcaded trellis over an irregular border fills the border of this napkin like a frieze. The whole panel is filled with fruit and flowers and hints of columns and buildings. Silk and silver thread on a light cotton. Before 1740. 80 x 13 cm.

A detail from a large cover. A medallion with a broad cusped band filled with single çintamani pearls around a ground filled with pairs of Chinese cloud bands. The large medallion has a smaller round one placed at each corner. Silk couched work on a silk ground; unusually a white silk is used throughout for the over-couching which gives the whole embroidery a spotted appearance. Before 1720.

this period that many more colours of embroidery silks were introduced. It is not unusual for up to fifteen different colours and shades to be used on one piece.

In the nineteenth century patterns based on architecture and landscape were added to the earlier floral and bouquet designs. The favourite architectural motif is composed of a small building, a kiosk, set in a garden with a pool and a tall poplar tree. The three together form an ideal of civilization where all is ordered and calm. The kiosk pattern is often set in a small cartouche and is also included in a long landscape which must be derived from the views along the shores of the Bosphorus. Some patterns are also derived from the remains of Byzantium that were still standing in Istanbul and along the Aegean coast; stately Roman pillars, water fountains and even aqueducts. These last were considered to be very suitable to decorate the towels used in the hamams.

In earlier centuries the pomegranate was the only fruit in the repertory, derived from Spanish and Italian textiles where it had a symbolic meaning combining the Resurrection and Infinity. It is now joined by a number of other fruits: placed on a plate they become a popular motif. In 1705 Ahmed III had a room decorated in Topkapi where the upper wall panels are covered with piles of fruit placed on plates or dishes. It is known as the fruit room, Yemiş Odasi. Another version of the fruit pattern is a large fruit, usually a melon, with a knife stuck in it, representing generosity and hospitality.

The tents that were set up in the pleasure grounds erected during the annual holidays at the end of Ramadan are also shown on towels and covers. These are not the great campaign tents but the pavilions for eating and drinking, or those which, during the reigns of Ahmed III and Mahmud I, were used for viewing the new varieties and colours of tulips that were grown.

During the eighteenth century new European textile designs and patterns started to influence Ottoman embroidery. The strongest influence came from France, and established motifs started to be treated in a rococo manner, although it took a century or more for the patterns to be generally diffused. The main difference can be seen where formerly rigid and contained patterns now wander about the surface of the fabric and are no longer as conventionally symmetrical as before. More floral patterns are introduced and they are treated in the manner p.46, 50, 174 of Lyons woven silk brocades rather than Eastern fabrics. Even the Ottomans' innate skill with placing patterns on a surface was defeated by these florid and often aimless patterns which were used more to show the versatility of the new weaving techniques than to display the beauties of design.

The change in style also coincided with changes in the uses of fabrics and the decoration on them. The introduction of chairs meant that cushions changed shape and were mainly covered in woven fabrics rather than in embroidery; the introduction of tables required a new type of table cover, and the use of a fixed bed meant that quilt covers were no longer used. The general increase in the volume and variety of household furniture, free-standing cupboards, permanent beds, wall mirrors, dining tables and sideboards, meant that a whole range of new textile covers had to be made and decorated. Towards the end of this century many of these articles were produced by small manufacturing units, and the ateliers of the hand-workers gradually died out. The general standard of work deteriorated and a vast volume of second class, and even worse, products were placed on the market.

In the second half of the nineteenth century this trend was established, and although there are examples of very fine embroideries being most meticulously made, the majority of embroidery to be found was semi-industrially produced; it was coarse and very often quite rudimentary in execution. Silk was often replaced by mercerized cotton p.96 and to make up for the deficiencies in the material and the execution hundreds of new shades were introduced, which quite destroyed the original vigour and strength of earlier work. By 1870 practically no high-class embroidery was being made at all, and that which was produced was mostly tourist work executed with a chain-stitch hook, p.125 the patterns being those of an idealized Middle Eastern character which was more acceptable to the European market than to the local one.

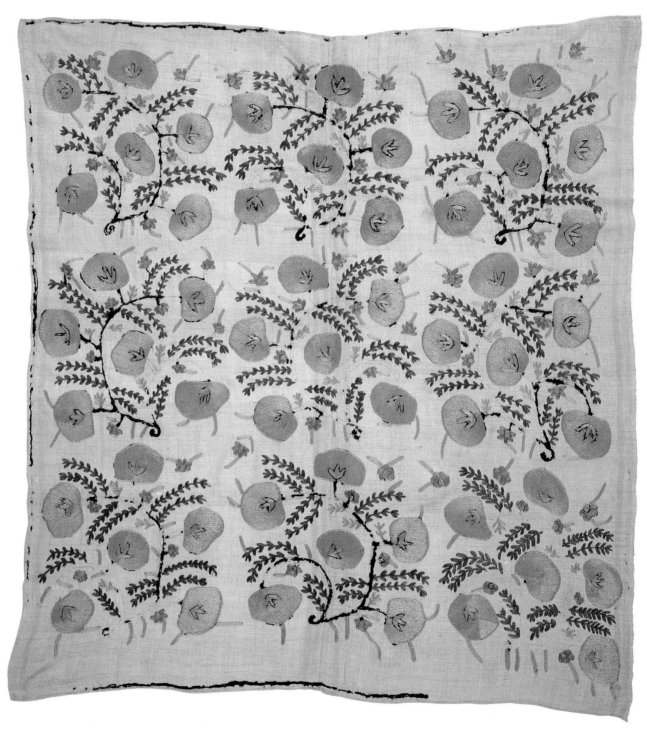

A bold design of six large gold poppy heads on a branch with blue leaves is repeated nine times to fill the ground of this wrapper. The black silk of the unifying stalks has deteriorated allowing the ink drawing to be seen. Silk chain stitch worked with a hook on a linen ground. *c.* 1870. 108 x 100 cm.

NOTES

1. The injunction does not occur in the Koran. Al Bukhari, a commentator on the Koran, writing between 840 and 870 AD, explains that the injunction against worshipping idols extends to the creating of them by drawing. This has become part of the Hadith Laws and is followed by the Sunni. Bukhari explains that the designers of idols are evil men setting themselves up as God, and they will be required, at the End, to breathe life into their creations and, if they cannot do so, will be made to suffer the torments of Hell for ever.

2. Many of the Greek herbals and pharmacopiae had been translated into Arabic with coloured line illustrations of the plants. In some cases only the Arabic translation of the original is known. Also by 1550 the new printed herbals were available with many line drawings in them. The same sources were used for European embroideries.

186

6 Materials

Cloth has been woven from the very earliest times — the loom was one of the first of man's inventions. There were ancient traditions of weaving both in the homelands of the Turki peoples in Central Asia and in the lands that they eventually conquered and ruled in western Asia and Europe. Initially cloth was woven domestically on simple strap looms and on small fixed looms, and was later produced commercially on larger looms. Most of the cloth woven was plain weave, although very elaborate decorative weaves were produced on the simplest of looms almost from the beginnings of the craft.

In many of the main urban centres of Turkey cloth was woven by as early as 1600 in premises that we would now consider to be factories. The industrial production of many types of cloth, including brocades, was introduced by the Genoese into the Aegean islands, particularly Chios, from the middle of the sixteenth century and they supplied the Ottoman Empire with much of its cloth needs, supplementing the production of Bursa and Istanbul. The mechanized system, based on equipment developed in Italy, was adopted by Turkish producers after the conquest of Chios by Suleiman the Great at the end of his reign in 1566.

Weaving was one of the primary industries of the Ottoman Empire and the manufacture of textiles, together with all the supporting industries, was the most important of all the international trades. A large proportion of the working population was involved in either the production of the primary materials or in their conversion into fabric and the subsequent processes of using the finished cloth. The language has a very large vocabulary for every type of fabric and for every article used in the manufacturing process. Also metaphors and similes drawn from weaving ornament and abound in both the spoken and literary language.

Ground fabrics

Cloth was woven of linen, wool, cotton and silk, usually of one type of yarn of a uniform gauge for each piece. Mixtures of cotton and linen,

A square Palace cover used for a table or even, from some accounts, as carpets. The pattern of elaborate flower sprays is executed in a late Renaissance style around a central geometric medallion. The silk velvet is covered with very high quality gold strip dival work and the card backing can be seen in some places. Some flowers are worked in gold wire and the centres of all the flowers are worked in pearls. *c.* 1840. 122 cm square.

187

or of cotton and silk, were introduced quite early, particularly when a special effect was desired, such as satin weave or a brocaded pattern. It was also quite common to use different gauges of the yarn to produce varied textures of the finished cloth.

Linen is considered to be the most ancient of the vegetable fibres used in this area for making cloth; the flax plant, *Linum humile*, was cultivated from the most ancient times and had most probably been introduced into Egypt from the Caucasus. Egypt produced vast quantities of linen and exported it both as yarn and as woven goods throughout the ancient world; linen cloth was one of the earliest trade goods, easily carried and of a high value. Because the growing of flax and the manufacturing process involved techniques requiring a level of organization which was difficult to reproduce elsewhere, the Egyptians had a virtual monopoly of the fabric for many centuries.

The use of *wool* must predate that of linen but it was not used in the Mediterranean as early as linen, mainly because of the climate but also because the dominant culture, that of Egypt, held the use of animal hair to be unclean. Sheep and goats had been domesticated in the Eastern Mediterranean, Babylonia and Central Asia from the earliest times and wool was the staple yarn used in that area. Although wool was considered unclean in Egypt it was a noble material elsewhere and was universally used in the colder climates. Its first use must have been to make felt, a textile technique predating the invention of the loom, being a method by which a fabric is created by compacting wet wool fibre. Felt was a standard fabric for the nomadic forefathers of the Turki

A large bath sheet, or peştemal, composed of three long panels, each embroidered at both ends and on both sides with a single motif. This very naive spray with ill-shaped rudimentary flowers, buds and leaves is worked in cotton and silk on a loosely woven cotton decorated with supplementary wefts in slubbed cotton. *c.* 1860. 182 x 149 cm.

188

tribes that eventually spread westwards. It is capable of being decorated and is resistant to hard wear. Felt is still being produced in Eastern Turkey and throughout Central Asia.[1]

Cotton, Gossypium arboreum, was grown and first used in India. A variety of cotton, *Gossypium herbaceum*, was introduced into the Mediterranean about 300 BC and despite its late arrival it eventually became the most commonly grown fibre in the area. It had two major advantages over linen: it was possible to spin more varied and finer yarns from it than from flax, and the processing required one operation less and used less water (it did not have to be retted, the process by which the flax plant is allowed to rot partially in water before the fibre is separated from the fleshy stalks).

Silk, the most perfect of textiles, was known long before it was imported into the area. Information about silk came from China, where it had been produced from before 1500 BC. The production processes had been kept secret and China held a total monopoly on the material. Silk is the fine thread covering the larva of the mulberry-leaf moth, *Bombyx mori*; the inner layer of the cocoon is loosened in hot water, which incidentally kills the larva, and then the fine thread is unravelled. Silk yarn is made of as many single strands of the natural thread as is necessary to achieve the required thickness. Imported silk cloth was so expensive and became such a drain on the economy of the Roman Empire that in AD 215 the Roman Emperor Heliogabalus declared that

A Bulgarian wedding handkerchief with a motif of a bird on its nest set above four gold borders. The very highest quality skofion thread in gold and silver has been used to make diaper and brick patterns, using coloured silk thread in the motif. The ground is silk weave with voided weft areas. Attributed to Plovdiv. *c.* 1850. 83 x 64 cm.

it was only to be worn by the Imperial family. In the fourth century AD the secret of silk was brought to Byzantium and its cultivation was first started there. Initially silk weaving was only allowed to be carried out in the Palace of the Byzantine Emperors in the area called the 'women's quarters', the 'Gynacaea', but the production and manufacture of silk very quickly spread to Alexandria, Antinoe and Damascus.

The Byzantines introduced the fabric into Europe as a luxury and there are many records of silk cloth and garments made from it being given as gifts to Emperors and Popes. The knowledge of how to produce and manufacture silk eventually spread into Sicily and then to Lucca, Genoa and Venice. Silk weaving became a great industry in Italy; it was the basis of many commercial and industrial fortunes and the Italians developed new technologies for working the material. They certainly invented a method for producing velvet even before the Chinese technique had been introduced into Europe.

Silk was used sparingly in the early Empire, either in embroidery or in the weaving of expensive fabrics such as multi-coloured damask or the various types of velvet. By the twelfth century silk was being produced extensively in Greece, in the Islands of the Aegean and in Anatolia, wherever the mulberry could be grown. It continued to be produced until the second half of the eighteenth century, when cheap silk became available from both Europe and China. This coincided with the spread of a disease that attacked the mulberries and virtually terminated the industry in many of the main European centres. The development of mercerized cotton and the artificial yarns that had many of the qualities of silk finally meant that it was no longer worth producing real silk. It is only in the twentieth century that the production of silk in Turkey has been started again.

Variety was introduced into the manufacture of plain fabrics by using crimped or slubbed yarns for the wefts or by changing the colours of the wefts in sections. There are examples of weaves where a different yarn is used for some portion of the warp threads, usually a narrow band of silk introduced into a cotton weave, which enhanced the appearance of the fabric and also strengthened it. All this decoration on the loom was invariably expensive and required capital investment in equipment. A much easier and far more varied form of decoration could be achieved by embroidery. This required no outlay in equipment other than a box of needles and a pair of scissors and some investment in the skills of embroidery.

Embroidery materials

Silk was the main thread used for the applied embroidery, cotton was only used in a few instances. The silk was always additional to the ground fabric and executed after the fabric had been moved off the loom, or already made up into the article. Silk was produced initially as floss, a thread in which many strands of silk are bunched together without being twisted, the separate strands being held together by the remnants of the natural gum from the cocoon. Floss silk gives a special sheen to embroidery worked with it: the flat threads reflect the light evenly and so stitches laid in different directions appear to be worked in different shades.

When the demand for silk thread expanded it was produced mechanically and the strands of the silk were twisted together very tightly to form an even thread. This thread could be made of any number of separate strands, depending on the thickness of the thread required. Twisted silk gives a very uniform appearance to the embroidery, and there is no difference in the way that light is reflected irrespective of the direction of the stitches.

Two domestic cushion covers. The velvet and brocaded cushions were extremely expensive and domestic copies like these were made using cotton or linen thread for the embroidery on a coarse cotton hand-weave. The patterns were taken from the grander versions, a single motif or a repeated motif for the ground and a small motif to finish the end arcades, always called houses. *c.* 1800. *Left* 65 x 43 cm, *right* 105 x 60 cm.

191

192

Metal was introduced very early into the manufacture of textiles. Gold, because it does not deteriorate and keeps its brilliance, was used to enrich woven fabrics. Silver and nickel were also used, even though they both tarnish. The producers of the various forms of metal for weaving and embroidery were classified very highly in the categories of the various guilds, and were always placed among the first groups in the parades of craftsmen which were held at the annual Bayram Festivals in Istanbul. Gold and, later, silver were used in many different forms, particularly in weaving brocades and velvets. So much silver was used in textiles that in 1725 Ahmed III had to place an injunction against its use.

Both metals were drawn out into a very thin filament, called 'sim', which was used exactly as if it were a silk thread. The producers of this metal filament were called 'simkes' and were centred in Istanbul. Another version of gold thread was produced during the eighteenth century by wrapping gold or silver around silk, usually yellow silk. This was called 'klaptan' and was made on a special spinning wheel called the 'kullâb'. Gold-wrapped silk was exported throughout the Empire and was known as 'skofium' in Western Europe — even the needle lace made from this material was sold as Skofion Lace.

An earlier version of gold thread was made by gilding very fine thin lengths of leather or, more likely, of animal membrane. This version is found on some early weavings but never in embroidery. Both gold and silver were made into wire of various gauges. These wires were called 'sırma' and were used either as straight lengths or twisted into coils called 'tel sırma'. Metal in this form was used as a surface decoration, the wire being twisted into the shapes required and then couched onto the fabric with small stitches worked from the back.

During the second half of the nineteenth century metal was worked by hand into embroidery as very thin strips of beaten metal. One end of the strip was made into a point and threaded through the fabric, and bent and made firm by pressure applied by the thumb. This technique is called 'tel kırma'. It is an extremely coarse way to use metal because it damages and tears the base fabric. This strip is most commonly silver which has been gilded, the gold content being less than 10% of the total. Other metal strips used are silver-plated nickel or even silver-plated copper, both of which give a coloured watered effect to the embroidery.

Pearls and precious stones were occasionally worked into embroideries or even over-embroidered onto woven or printed cloths. Small gold coins and later sequins were also used. Their use was rare but they were so impressive that travellers always mentioned them.

a Two varieties of silver wire are used in this border of drawn thread and needle weave. The ground is silk with warps in cotton, edged in needle lace. This work is usually attributed to the Maras area. *c.* 1850. 47 x 6 cm.

b Two large curved branch and leaf motifs worked in metal-wrapped yellow silk and touches in silk, on a silk background woven with thick supplementary silk warps. *c.* 1850. 41 x 17 cm.

c An Italianate frieze of two motifs worked in yellow silk partly wrapped in silver and outlined in brown gözeme stitch on cotton, Istanbul. *c.* 1850. 53 x 9 cm.

d Three curled branches are worked in four varieties of metal thread and strip and a little stem stitch in silk on a cotton weave. Istanbul *c.* 1850. 51 x 11 cm.

e Alternate leafy branches and small gold hillocks sprouting three-petalled flowers worked in gold thread and gilded silver strip on a cotton ground. *c.* 1850. 55 x 11 cm.

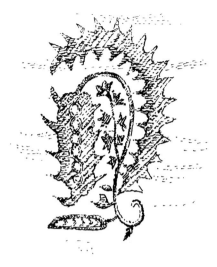

Decorative edgings

There were a number of techniques used to finish the ends of the cloth on which the embroidery was made. The most common was to remove the end weft threads, leaving the warps as a simple fringe. This fringe is sometimes twisted or plaited into separate strands making a more formal and distinctive fringe. In larger pieces the length of fringe can be up to 20 cm, and it is quite common for these fringes to be knotted in macramé work. More elaborate finishes were made by adding to the cloth a separate pre-made edge. These were commercially produced lace, fringes or braid made in silk or metal thread. Some finishes were worked by hand onto the natural edge in crochet work or tatting.

The best known of the hand-made edgings is the lace-like 'oya', which is also known as 'bebilla'. The technique is apparently very ancient and many of the minorities in the Ottoman world have laid claim to being its originators. There are references to cloths worked entirely in oya being given as gifts to Selim I in 1512. The most common usage of oya is to edge the headcloths worn by both men and women, the popular myth being that all the designs used had a meaning, and many unlikely examples are quoted. The main centres for the production of the more elaborate oyas were Smyrna and the eastern shore of the Bosphorus.

Oya is made without a pattern being drawn or held; only a needle and thread are used and endless series of knots are made 'in aria' to form a continuous strip of ribbon. The oya can be a repeated shape laid in sequence or, more imaginatively, a row of flowers or leaves; in some of the finest work landscapes are knotted which show trees, fruit, houses and even tiny animals. Oya is also used to make three-dimensional flowers and fruits which are incorporated into the edging for the headscarves. Oya is usually worked in a single colour in either silk or linen thread, although in some of the more elaborate flower knottings two or three colours are used.

A cheaper version of oya was produced with a crochet hook which was available in the bazaars throughout Turkey. It is not as fine as the more tightly knotted real bebilla, and is often starched to give it a more rigid handle.

Tatting is another method used to make an edging. Again this is a hand-held technique and produces a repeat pattern as a yardage.

A collection of plain and printed headscarves in silk and cotton to show some of the varieties of edgings in needle embroidery, 'oya'. The edging is worked in lengths on the hand and then sewn on to the scarf. It is traditional that each pattern has a meaning, usually romantic and sometimes subversive. Nineteenth and twentieth century.

NOTES

1. There were three qualities of felt produced throughout the area. Keçe was the standard quality used for making most rugs and clothing, kebe was the thickest quality used for making the walls of the round tent of the nomads and the thick carpets used in them, and arakiye was the very fine felt used for making caps and fine clothing.

7 Techniques

The simplest way to decorate cloth is when it is still on the loom in the process of being woven. The techniques of weaving allow the fabric to be woven as plain weave, twill or satin, and all these techniques alter the feel and texture of the cloth and even the appearance by creating internal patterns in the fabric.

If colour is required then the simplest method is by variously dyeing the yarns for the warp and weft before weaving and introducing them on the loom when required. Coloured yarns can be worked into the fabric as single blocks of one colour, or many different colours can be introduced selectively to produce very complicated patterns on the basis of colour alone. This method of creating patterns was extensively developed by the weavers and extremely elaborate textiles were created using weaving and tapestry techniques alone. Weaving, however, is an expensive undertaking, requiring special capital equipment and an educated work force. Even setting up the basic loom is a lengthy and very skilled process. Finally, most weaving is a static occupation and requires a dedicated space in which the operation can be carried out.

Embroidery, on the other hand, is the simplest way of decorating cloth once it has been taken off the loom, either in the piece or after it has been made up into a garment or some other article. The process is infinitely variable and involves much less expense and no initial capital outlay. When the cloth is held in the hand the only equipment necessary is a needle and thread; occasionally a frame can be used to hold the fabric taut while it is being worked. Furthermore, embroidery can be executed at every level of skill and ability and, finally, it is portable. The wide range of embroidery stitches that have been developed allow any effect required to be created, introducing variety into the surface decoration not possible on the loom.

Ottoman weaving predates the 1453 Conquest by at least two centuries. Bursa was the main centre and early records show how important the industry was to the town. Even when the Court moved to Istanbul and the Court weavers were established there, Bursa continued to supply large quantities of silk weaves to Istanbul.

Embroidery was produced throughout the Byzantine Empire. It was most probably introduced from Rome and developed and influenced by the traditions of Persia and China. Professional embroiderers were based in the City, as was all art, but in every main centre there must have been many different local traditions, with their own patterns and designs. Much of the professional work was dedicated to adorning garments and textiles associated with the Church and the Court. Embroidery was also a common domestic skill and was concerned with decorating the clothing and textiles used in the house.

The Seljuks and Ottomans had a native domestic embroidery which was part of the larger tradition embracing all of central Asia, western China and the northern States of India. The point at which the embroideries made after the formation of the Ottoman Empire can be called Turkish is an arbitrary decision. Very little embroidery remains from the Seljuks and the Ottoman Sultanates. The earliest surviving pieces that are indisputably Ottoman Turkish are from the fifteenth century, so perhaps one must consider that tradition to have started at the Conquest of Constantinople (Istanbul) in 1453.

The embroideries of the fifteenth and sixteenth centuries are worked in a very limited range of stitches, which are similar to a weaving process carried out off the loom. They are also those that satisfactorily cover the fabric with the required designs in the most economic way. The common stitch used is the 'pesent' — a darning and double stitch worked over three threads of the ground fabric and passing behind the fourth; virtually a twill weaving and not very different from a form of brocading that could have been carried out on the loom. However, with this stitch it is possible to work vertically and backwards on the fabric and to apply any number of colours in an area. The stitches are not technically demanding but have to be executed with great precision. Turkish embroidery was at this time more concerned with shapes created by blocks of colour, copying a woven fabric, rather than with producing the varied effects which were to be achieved later by using different stitches.

Embroidery had always been very highly valued and there are references by many of the classical Arab and Persian authors to the fact that embroidered textiles were sold at many times their weight in silver. Pierre Belon in 1588 describes Turkish embroidery:

> They make various works on white cloth in Turkey, the most common being, that they wish to embroider it, they first design the cloth by painting it, the which they outline with two threads, so that this work represents the painting. We have neither the same manner of working nor of embroidering.

Clearly Belon was not aware of embroidery techniques and that the method he describes had been current in Western Europe for at least 1500 years before his comment.[1] He also suggests that embroidery was a woman's occupation; in the same section of his book he writes:

> We find it hard to believe in our country that work on white cloth is held of such estime and value in Turkey, and that they make such a lot of it. The reason is that the women are normally kept shut indoors and that they have no housework to do, unless they are employed to do something. They do not have the habit of making lace, so they pass their time at embroidering white cloth.

However, Rycaut writing in *The Present State of the Ottoman Empire* in 1668, in the chapter dealing with the education of the young men serving in the Court, the İçoğlan, among a long list of what they had to do includes:

> To the former Lessons of School-learning and exercise abroad, are added some other accomplishments of a Trade, handy-craft or Mystery, in which a man may be useful to the service of the Grand Signior, as to sowe and embroider in Leather (in which the Turks exceed all other Nations) to make arrows and embroider quivers and saddles...

The work of the sixteenth and seventeenth centuries is always considered to be the highest point Turkish embroidery attained. This opinion is based on the aesthetic and dramatic value of the embroidery and the way in which it harmonizes with the weaving and the ceramic tile work of the same period. The grand embroideries of those centuries would have been seen side by side with these other decorated surfaces, and had to complement them.

During the eighteenth and nineteenth centuries Turkish art was more and more influenced by European production. The Europeans also introduced new industrial and semi-mechanized methods of production for both the ground fabrics and the threads with which to embroider. Sadly this was detrimental to the local weaving tradition which gradually deteriorated in terms of quality and lost its earlier genius. The technically more varied European embroidery tradition also changed the local style, mainly by introducing a wider repertory of stitches and a new way of looking at patterns, particularly a new pictorial school which depicted landscapes, architecture and even the human figure. These new designs, together with the increasing demand for two-faced embroideries which were identical on both sides, meant that new stitches were adopted from the general European repertory.

The embroideries of the late eighteenth and the nineteenth century are technically the most perfect of the Turkish embroideries. The new stitches were employed in a dazzling display of technical perfection and, together with the extended range of new colours that were available, produced elaborate and sustained works of art. These were strongly

influenced by the new fashions, particularly those coming from Paris. Turkish work was always shown at the various international exhibitions in Europe, and at the Great Exhibition in London in 1851 embroideries from Istanbul were awarded gold certificates, amongst which a number were given to specifically identified family ateliers.

After the beginning of the twentieth century the quality of embroidery deteriorated, as it did throughout Europe. Clearly there was little demand for it, as the industrialized centres of Europe were able to produce decorated textiles in an infinite variety and so cheaply that it no longer made economic sense to produce embroidery either professionally or even domestically in Turkey.

Stitches

The stitches used in Ottoman embroidery can be divided into two groups: the counted stitches and the stitches which are worked on a sketched pattern drawn on the ground cloth as a guide. The stitches can be further classified by whether they are worked on a solid ground fabric or one where some of either the warp or weft threads have been removed prior to being embroidered.

The surprising omission from Turkish embroidery is the cross stitch, probably because most of their work was two-faced and it is not possible to work cross stitch to be read both from the front and the back. It appears in most of the local native traditions of work in the Ottoman Empire, particularly in Greece and the Balkans, where it is almost the most common stitch. It is also found in Palestine, Syria and in North African embroidery. It appears in Turkish embroidery of the twentieth century, replacing many of the more complicated, time-consuming stitches.

Counted stitches

This group of stitches are worked by counting the warp and weft threads of the ground fabric before each insertion of the needle. A pattern is usually followed from a completed piece without any previous lines being drawn on the cloth.

Counted stitches, with the exception of the laid stitches and mürver, are those used when it is required to produce a two-faced embroidery.

Pesent – darning or running. The word is derived from the Persian word for 'that which pleases'. Pesent can be worked in any direction.

Ince – narrow or stem. Ince is worked over one thread at a time.

Sarma – satin, simple counted. This is worked in two forms: *düz iğne* — flat stitch, *verev iğne* — diagonal stitch. Sarma is the most common embroidery stitch and is also called 'Turk işi', Turkish work.

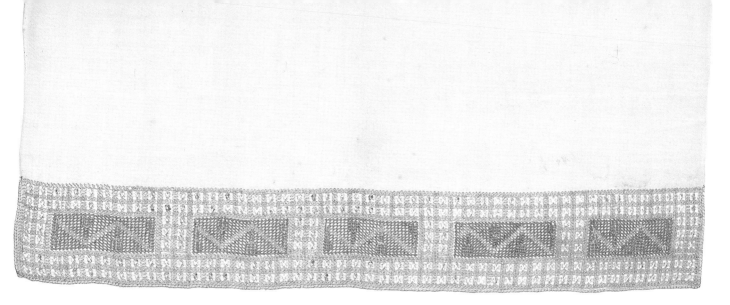

A napkin end which combines a number of techniques. The border is in pulled-thread work using silver strip on a yellow silk core with silver-plated copper strip used to make the metallic crosses inside each block of the pulled work. The five central panels are worked in muşabak in both silk and silver thread with the flowers worked in needle weaving. The edging of the cotton ground is blanket stitch in silver thread. *c.* 1870. 52 x 8 cm.

Tisto – split satin stitch. This stitch is rare, and is usually found worked in a very small size, when it can be mistaken for a small chain stitch.

Lokum susma – basket stitch. When the basket stitch is worked in triangles rather than in squares it is called 'üçgen susma', triangular susma.

Mürver – branch stitch. The word means the elder tree, and the square stitches when worked look like its branches. When each diagonal branch is worked in different colours a very complicated effect is obtained.

Muşabak – diagonal stepped stitch. The word is derived from the Arabic word for complicated, or to entangle, a very appropriate description. Muşabak work gives the effect of drawn thread work, because the diagonal stitch is wrapped around three threads in either direction and then pulled tight so as to make holes in the ground fabric.

Çivankaşi – florentine or hungarian stitch. This is a staggered version of susma.

Atma – couched stitch, Bokhara couched, or laid work. This couched stitch is worked by laying threads in one direction on the surface to be covered and then holding them in place by a row of stem stitch laid in the opposite direction, usually in another colour. Two types of laid work are found in Ottoman work. In the first each strand of the laid silk is held by the stem stitch worked from the back and placed regularly over the whole area. The second has another strand of the silk laid at right angles over the first layer at wider intervals and then the overlaid silk is held in place by small stem stitches placed regularly along its length. The differences are clearly visible on the finished work.

Atki – strap couched stitch. This version of couched stitch differs from the two above in that both the first laid thread and the second laid in the opposite direction on top of it are set with a space between them and then both threads are held in place by a cross stitch at their intersection. Atki is most commonly used to couch metal thread or tinsel strip.

201

STITCHES

Although the cross stitch is very rarely used in domestic Turkish embroidery there are occasional examples of it on floor carpets and large covers. In these cases the work has been carried out on a thick ground cloth where the warp and weft threads are not easily distinguished. A length of kanaviçe or etemin is sewn loosely onto the surface and used as a grid. Both of these are loose woven fabrics where the component warps and wefts are clearly seen, similar to embroidery canvas. Etemin has a larger space between threads than kanaviçe. The cross stitch is then worked over both the ground cloth and the top kanaviçe, and when completed the warp and weft threads of the kanaviçe are cut in many places and the threads are withdrawn. This laborious process is more frequently described than evident in any surviving pieces.

Sketched stitches

These stitches are worked over a pattern drawn or pounced on the ground cloth. The pattern can therefore be curvilinear and need not be a repeating one.

Kasnak, zincir – chain or tambour stitch. This chain stitch is worked with a needle with the fabric usually held in a tambour or frame. 'Kasnak' is the word for a tambour and 'gergef' the word for a frame. 'Zincir' is the common word for chain.

Suzani – hooked chain stitch. This version of chain stitch usually means that it has been worked with a crochet hook, a 'tığ'. 'Suzan' is the Persian word for needle and in Persia and Central Asia suzeni is the word both for needlework and the article embroidered.

Çin iğnesi – random filling stem stitch. Used to fill in an area in a random stitch, especially where the surface is to be shaded. This is called Chinese work.

Balık sırtı – fishbone or satin stitch. An irregular satin stitch used to fill an irregular shape. It can be worked in two directions but both stitches must be worked back to a central spine, but unlike feather stitch the two stitches must not cross. The stitch is also called 'kılıç balığı'.

Gözeme – outline stem stitch. This is an outlining stitch and is worked around large blocks of colour or within the blocks to separate areas worked in different stitches. The versions of gözeme are:

> *gidip gelme gözeme* – coming and going stitch: a double row outline worked in opposite directions.

> *diş diş gözeme* – toothed gözeme: a very closely worked outline stitch shaped like a saw edge.

> *çift gözeme* – paired gözeme: a very tight form of balık sırtı.

202

Ciğer deldi — eyelet stitch. This stitch is made like a buttonhole stitch but is worked in a circle and pulled tight to make a hole in the cloth. It is usually made of eight stitches. It is not common.

Drawn thread stitches

This group of stitches is only used where a block of warp or weft threads has been removed.

Kesme – needle weaving. 'Kesme' means cut and is the name of the needle weaving used in cut work. The weaving is usually done over three threads. The finished work looks very like the standard susma.

Antika – hem stitch or button hole. This stitch is used to secure the cut ends of the warp and weft threads that have been drawn out. It is invariably used around any area of kesme, although it is also used when the area of drawn thread is to be left unworked or where a large area is voided.

Antep – square outline stitch. This is used to make the outlines of squares on drawn thread work to produce an effect like muşabak on a solid ground.

Withdrawing threads from a length of material tends to weaken it, and even when the weaving is replaced with a filling there is a tendency for the fabric to tear.

Pulled thread work, çekme işi, however, tends to add strength to the fabric. This technique is worked by wrapping either warp or weft threads with the coloured silk and pulling them tight, making a solid bride and a hole at the same time.

This napkin is typical of the white-on-white drawn thread work popular in Cyprus and the Aegean Islands. Three pots of flowers are set within a three-sided border. Five versions of filling stitch, needle weaving and stem stitch in white and ecru silk on cotton. After 1870. 40 x 18 cm embroidered area.

Surface techniques

Zerduz – couched gold work. Zerduz is derived from the Persian word for gold, 'zar', and 'zarduz' is the standard Persian word for embroidery. Zerduz work in Turkey means that a gold or silver cord or braid is laid out in a pattern on the surface of the fabric and held in place by small stem stitches worked from behind and lost in the braid.

Dival – couched supported gold work. Dival work differs from zerduz in that the gold cord or braid has already been stitched onto cardboard or paper in the required design. The design is sometimes filled with cotton wool or with a thick thread to give it bulk. The supported gold pattern is then sewn onto the cloth by either buttonhole or stem stitch.

Anavata – couched cording. Anavata is the name of the technique when the cord to be couched is a twisted or plaited silk, or even multiply cotton.

All these drawn stitches are used for single-faced embroidery. These applied techniques are found on the usual fabrics but they are particularly appropriate for working on a less yielding ground material. Zerduz and dival are found worked on leather, felt, velvet and the coarser canvas used for making tents. The formal and ceremonial women's robes made of velvet are covered in dival work creating the large patterns called bindallı, the thousand branch pattern.

The embroidery on this quilt cover has deteriorated so that vestiges of the original ink drawing can be seen on each of the three strips of which it is composed. The ground is a trellis set around a motif of a large red leaf flanked by a pair of blue leaves. The border is a development of the tulip and artichoke leaf joined by a green leaf. The way that the Bokhara couching is worked can also be seen through the damaged embroidery. Bokhara couching and stem stitch on firm linen ground. *c.* 1840. 225 x 130 cm total size.

204

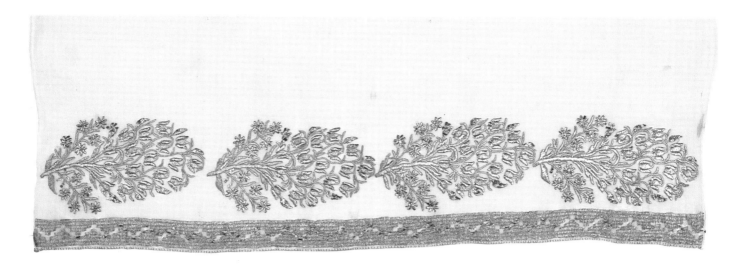

Metal work

A number of various forms of the noble metals are used in embroidery, usually to add value to the piece; when less noble ones are used it is only to add texture and sometimes weight. The standard method is for the metal to be applied to the top of the ground cloth in a pattern and then to be held down by an invisible stitch. The main versions are:

Sim – silver thread. This is very fine-drawn silver.

Klaptan – silk thread wrapped with metal. This is the commonest of all the methods for using metal in embroidery.

The special characteristic of sim and klaptan is that they are so fine that they can be threaded onto a needle and worked like any other yarn. The other metals are used without a needle, either laid on the surface or pushed through the fabric.

Tel sırma – wire embroidery or lace. This version of metal work uses a drawn wire of metal, usually gilded silver, which creates the required pattern before being placed on the fabric. This wire is also used coiled like a spring.

Tel kırma – metal strip work. When metal strip is used it is pushed through the fabric and then bent over in place by being pressed with the thumb nail. The strip can be as wide as 3 mm. This metal work often destroys the fabric it is worked on.

Tırtıl – spangles. Sometimes the wire is wound into tight springs before it is sewn onto the fabric. When used in this form it makes a thick layer of metal on the cloth.

Pul – sequins or small coins. Originally small coins were worked into embroidered work by having small holes drilled into them. They and the sequins that replaced them were often laid in rows rather like fish scales.

A napkin worked entirely in gold thread in two qualities and gilded copper strip on a fine cotton lawn. Four large sprays of fritillaries and daisies are set horizontally above a broad band of patterned and coloured needle weaving, edged in blanket stitch. Before 1850. 67 x 12 cm.

205

Applied embroidery

Applied embroidery, 'oturtma işi', is that technique where patches of coloured fabric are sewn onto the ground fabric to form the pattern. The tradition is very ancient, and the cloths found at Pasaryk are worked in this method and much Mamluk embroidery is based on applied work. Apart from its use in making the great campaign tents and some of the floor carpets, the technique was not common in Turkey, but it was very popular in parts of the Ottoman Empire, particularly Egypt and Morocco. The small rugs and hangings made in Yugoslavia at Banya Luka were based on this technique and are the Balkan equivalent of the work that is generally known as Resht work. The patches are sewn onto the basic cloth with a simple stem stitch or more rarely a form of blanket stitch. The patches can be layered over each other or even over-embroidered with any of the other stitches.

A sampler showing a range of isolated motifs, borders and edgings. They include gardens and landscapes, even a man smoking a pipe in his garden. The Armenian inscription is 'Ter im Ter' (Lord, my Lord). Formerly part of the F.H. Cook Collection, and illustrated in *Mediterranean and Near East Embroideries* (No. 71). *c.* 1750. 80 x 44 cm.

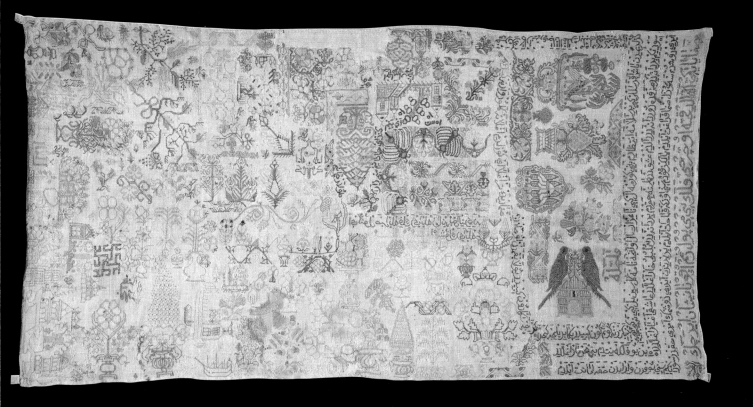

Samplers

Enough Ottoman samplers have survived to show that they were used but were clearly not very common. Rather than being exercises in the skill of embroidery, as they were in Northern Europe, they are repositories of the range of designs and motifs that were available. Surviving examples carry a number of motifs that are not to be found on any completed work, so perhaps the samplers were also used to develop or experiment with patterns and colour combinations.[2]

Samplers are not dated and very seldom signed: I know of one with an Armenian name on it, one with a name in Greek letters and a couple that have nonsense in the old Arabic script on them. Some of the early samplers have small panels of repeat patterns, very similar to the style of Mamluk and Spanish samplers, but the majority are covered with a large range of floral designs. A common way of showing a pattern is to reproduce a corner with two borders at an angle and the motif placed within the corner. All the countries within the Empire have produced samplers and they are all specific to their own areas; they come from the Aegean Islands, the Balkans, the Caucasus and from North Africa, during the periods when they were under Ottoman domination.

A sampler worked by two hands, the apparently older portion covered with isolated motifs and border patterns. The other part contains a number of much larger motifs contained within a large section of writing in two scripts of an unidentified passage in Turkish. *c.* 1750. 60 x 34 cm.

NOTES

1. Pierre Belon du Mans, *Les Observations de plusiers singularitéz et choses memorables.* Paris 1533, and 1588.

2. The word most commonly used for a sampler is 'nakiş çeşidli' or even just 'çeşit'.

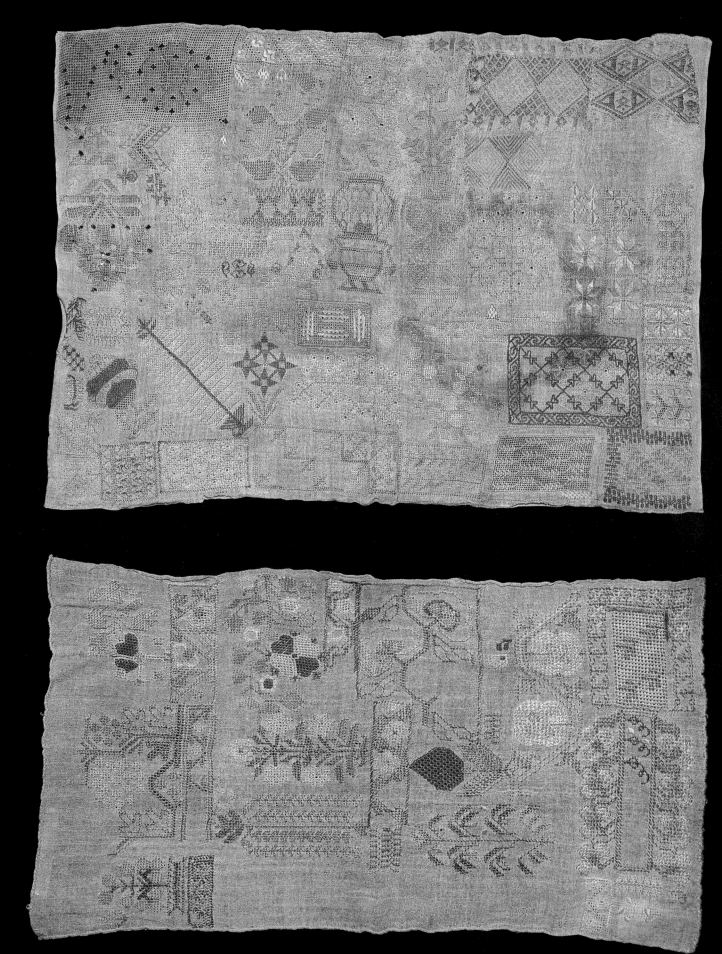

Dyes

Dyeing was one of the professional trades which was part of the important textile industry; dyers were formed into guilds and worked in designated areas of each town. The dyeing of yarn was a highly skilled craft in which Jews and Christians appear to have excelled: in Morocco it was exclusively a Jewish occupation. The dyers worked in all of the materials, undertaking to dye linen, cotton, silk and wool yarn and woven pieces in the length.

Until dyes were developed from chemical processes in the coal industry all dyes were natural, derived from animal, vegetable or mineral sources. Only two colours were obtained from animals, a particular purple — murex — was derived from sea mussels, and a number of shades of red from various insects. The oldest of the reds were kermiz red extracted from an insect, now reclassified as *Kermes vermilio*, found on a variety of oak in the eastern Mediterranean, and shellac red obtained from the lac beetle found on shrubs in India. At the beginning of the seventeenth century cochineal red was introduced from the New World, being extracted from a bug, *Dactylopius coccus*, found on a cactus. This red was the most intense available and as it was cheaper it eventually became the most popular red.

The sea purple proved too expensive to harvest and was replaced by the chemical 'mauvine' in 1856. The process of producing reds from insects also proved too costly and they were gradually replaced by reds from plants, and later by the chemical alzarine in 1867.

Many visitors to the Ottoman world included notes on dyeing in their descriptions of the bazaars and the trades that they found there. One of the most interesting was the study of dyeing techniques in Eastern Anatolia and the Aegean, commissioned by the French Government in 1794. This area supplied large quantities of dyed silk to the French market and they had hoped to develop local industries to supplant those imports. Guillaume Antoine Olivier undertook this study and published his findings in *Voyage dans L'Empire Othoman* in Paris 1801. In the second volume of that work he gives some details of dyeing processes and the following recipes for certain colours:

light green: boiled peach tree wood
green: boiled peach leaves
dark green: immature shells of the hazelnut
rose: boiled apple tree roots
light pink: boiled quince wood
yellow: boiled nettle roots
pale yellow: boiled broom flowers
orange: onion skin with alum
red: onion skins and crushed kermes

Not surprisingly this information did not help the French plan very much. Olivier could have added a number of other plants, such as larkspur, artichoke leaves, mallow flowers, mulberry, madder and thyme,

Top A sampler started in the sixteenth century with Mamluk border patterns and later filled with Ottoman motifs. There are examples of white silk work, muşabak, ciğer deldi and a little metal strip work. Mamluk and Ottoman from 1600 to 1800. 45 x 30 cm.

Bottom An Ottoman sampler of motifs and borders including a panel which shows the Arabic 'Huwa' repeated three times. This is the Dervish invocation 'Heh Heh', which means 'He, the Lord'. *c.* 1750. 40 x 20 cm.

209

which are mentioned by other writers. The British were also interested in discovering the secrets of the Ottoman dyes and Robert Walpole, in his edition of *Memoirs relating to European and Asiatic Turkey*, set out information which had been collected by John Sibthorp and others at the end of the eighteenth century.[1] Sibthorp gives these details:

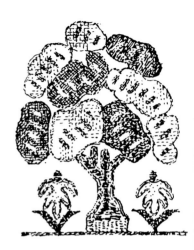

> *red:* Kermes from the gall on the holm oak, madder from the root of the madder, arbutus from *Arbutus unedo*, roots of the plane tree, *Platanus orientalis*.
> *blue:* Indigo, imported.
> *yellow:* Chestnut leaves, wood of the sumach, *Rhus cotinus*, various daphnes, mullein, leaves of St John's Wort, flowers of *Oxalis*.
> *green:* Fleabane, indigo mixed with chestnut leaves.
> *purple:* Myrtle berries, blackberry fruit.
> *brown:* Acorn cup of Valonia oak.
> *black:* First dyed with Valonia then over-dyed with vitriol or sulphate of copper.

There are innumerable other recipes to be found. Dyeing was a craft, and as it is possible to obtain dye from a very wide range of natural materials most dyers devised their own methods for obtaining the range of colours they required. Among the more exotic materials used are the lichens found on rocks at the sea shore: *Rocella tinctoris*, which produced a red, and *Rocella viridis*, producing a strong acid green. A dark red, which was known as 'bakkam', was obtained from boiling a wood, *Caesalpinia sappan*, also known as sappan or logwood, and black is made by reboiling a yarn already dyed in bakkam in a solution of iron sulphate. A dark purple is obtained from pomegranate juice.

Many shades can be obtained by dyeing the yarn in two different colours, and the colour can be intensified by soaking it for different lengths of time in either the colour or the mordant lake.

As important as the colouring stage is the method for fixing that colour. The process of using mordants is equally skilled and a large range is used. The most common and the oldest is alum, which the Ottomans exported into Europe. Other mordants used are yogurt, buttermilk, urine, watered yeast, the residue from cheese-making and the salts of tin, copper, iron, chromium and aluminium.

Once dyes were available from industrial chemical plants — first the anilines from the coal tar industry and later from the petro-chemical industries — the use of natural dyestuffs virtually ended. The earliest chemical dyes were imported into Turkey very soon after they were produced, the range of German blues from 1750 and the anilines from 1870. There is now some attempt being made to revive natural dyes but this is mainly for the wool yarn used for making carpets.

NOTES

1. John Sibthorp published his *Flora Greca* in ten volumes between 1806 and 1840. The edition included over 100 coloured engravings and was reputed to have cost £30,000, making it one of the most expensive publications of the time.

8 Collectors and Collections

Turkish embroidery was remarked upon by European visitors from as early as the twelfth century when pilgrims travelling from Germany and Italy to the Holy Land made landfalls along the Turkish Aegean coast and in the Aegean Islands. They noticed and mention the various types of textiles to be found and comment on the many embroidered articles that are traded on the streets.

The prelate Pietro Casola made a pilgrimage to Jerusalem in 1494 and he writes about what he saw in a market in a Turkish Aegean port during his journey:

> So many cloths of every make — tapestry, brocades and hangings of every design, carpets of every sort, camlets of every colour and texture, silks of every kind.

Pierre Belon in *Les Illustrations des Plusieurs Singularités*, written after his travels around Turkey and the Aegean and published in Paris in 1588, writes:

> Jewish women, who are free to move abroad without covering their faces, are common in the markets of Turkey, selling their needlework. They usually sell napkins [serviettes], handkerchiefs [mouchouers], sashes [ceintures blanches], cushion covers [souilles d'orilliers], and other such works of greater value, such as bed tents [pavillions de licts], in various fashions which the Jews buy to sell to strangers.

The implication here is not that it was only the Jews that made the embroideries, but that Jewish women who were allowed to move about unhindered could sell embroidery on the streets. It also indicates that not all embroidery was made at home but that there were professionals and semi-professionals who produced embroidery for sale. It is extremely unlikely that anything as valuable or as bulky as a bed tent could be sold casually on the street.

Pierre Belon also comments on how fine the work is and what large amounts the Turks are prepared to pay for fine embroidery:

> The Turks take pleasure in having white underclothing and so well worked that they do not complain at spending on it. One may see them buying two small handkerchiefs worked for 20 aspers, which we would not spend six sous on in France.

In 1589 five aspers were reckoned to be worth two pence, so the handkerchiefs were sold for four pence each, equivalent at that time to a day's wage for a craftsman, in comparison with a sou which would not buy a small bun.

There are many accounts of European travellers bringing back embroideries which were used and eventually perished. How much these early pieces influenced the development of patterns and techniques in Europe has still to be investigated; they certainly provoked great admiration. A piece of Ottoman work was brought back to Scotland and is now displayed as a flag made by fairies who gave it to the family that now owns it.

The main museum collections of textiles from Turkey of the great period are based on textiles sent as presents by the Porte to various European courts or on those captured in war. In about 1885 many of the museums in Europe acquired large collections of velvets and brocades of the great periods. Both Taksin Öz and Professor Wace have speculated that this was due to a decision at Court that all the old tomb coverings were to be replaced with modern cloth and new embroideries. It had been the tradition that the royal tombs were covered with the kaftans and other textiles of the dead and it was these that suddenly appeared on the market.

The various Sultans sent presents to their equals in Europe, usually valuable pieces of jewellery or porcelain from China, but there are many references to textiles as well, either made up into garments or as lengths of material. The non-textile gifts were, in the accepted tradition, wrapped in layers of cloth, as were the formal letters which were wrapped in folded envelopes of brocades and silks. The presents were accepted as magnificent but it was the textiles that were seen as marvels and went straight into the treasuries or were cut up and resewn into Church vestments or as decorations for Holy Relics.

Italy had the closest contact with Turkey for the longest period, and there are many examples of the influences that both national textile traditions have had on each other, particularly in the techniques and patterns evolved for making velvet. There are many examples of Eastern textiles in Italian museums, the most important of which are in the Vatican. Many of these are Coptic or Byzantine pieces that arrived as gifts or purchases by the Church from the great textile centres. The earliest examples that can be called Arab are the Fatimid and Mamluk textiles from Egypt. The velvets and brocades from Turkey and Persia

212

arrived very much later, about the beginning of the sixteenth century, and were again used principally for Church vestments or furnishings.

The movement of textiles and the diffusion of the techniques and patterns about the Mediterranean was so intense that it is now very difficult to be categorical about the provenance of these textiles; they could have come from a number of textile centres in Spain or the Near East or from the four main Italian centres. The few examples of embroidery in the collections were not considered as prestigious as the weavings, and that sadly is still the situation now. Even in the museums, churches and Palazzi in Venice amidst many woven textiles one finds virtually no Turkish or Ottoman embroideries, which is very surprising in view of the centuries of contact between the two cultures.

Italian, Flemish and Dutch paintings of the period up to 1750 very often show Oriental carpets spread on floors or tables, but I can recollect not one that shows the embroidery from the same area that produced the carpets. The textiles shown are invariably of European manufacture and are usually restricted to a few patterns, notably the pomegranate on the twisted ribbon and the wreaths of artichoke or acanthus leaves. These two were used as clichés for a combination of sumptuousness and holiness.

There were a number of ambassadorial visits made between Turkey and Persia to the Scandinavian Courts, and many of the presents exchanged at those meetings have been preserved in the Royal and National Collections, also a few very remarkable carpets from Turkey have been discovered in Swedish Churches. There are collections of Eastern textiles in Sweden which arrived either as gifts or as booty; the embroidered saddle given to Gustav Adolphus in 1626 is in the Royal Armoury in Stockholm, the letter envelopes are in the Swedish State Archive and there are Turkish embroideries and textiles in churches and castles throughout Sweden. In Denmark there are a number of very grand carpets from this period although the collection of textiles and embroideries from Turkey and Greece in the Museum of Fine Arts in Copenhagen was made at the beginning of this century.

The first English trade mission to Turkey was led by William Harborne in 1578, which resulted in English traders being given rights to trade in Turkey on the same basis as had been granted centuries before to the French and Italians. The Company of Merchants of the Levant was founded in 1581 by Queen Elizabeth under a treaty: 'because they had found out and opened a trade in Turkey, not known in the memory of any man now living to be frequented by our progenitors.' A generous but exaggerated comment. Harborne went out in 1582 as the first Ambassador from England to Turkey, and in 1586 the Levant Company was founded under a new charter allowing fifty-three English merchants to trade with Turkey. The Levant Company predated the East India Company by nearly twenty years and outlasted it, surviving until 1807.

There are records in the State Papers for Turkey that in 1593 the Sultana of Murad III sent a present to Queen Elizabeth consisting of:

First, two garments of cloth of silver. £68
One girdle of cloth of silver. £10
Two handkerchers, wrought with massy gold asps. £22
One shell of gold which covered the seal of her letter to her Majesty
    with 2 small diamonds and 2 small rubies. £20

The value of these two handkerchiefs or scarves at £22 is very different to the price of four pence a handkerchief of which Pierre Belon writes. I think that asp must refer to a coin or a tree and not to a snake; coins and trees are common subjects and I cannot recollect ever having seen a snake on an Islamic Ottoman embroidery.

At this early time the textiles that most impressed the Europeans were the carpets. English traders exported 'all sorts of cloth and kerseys, dyed and dressed to the best proof' to Turkey and brought back 'raw silk, cotton wool and yarn, grograms, chamblotte, carpets ... and divers other things'. There are many of these carpets still to be seen in collections and museums in Great Britain. Cardinal Wolsey had a large collection of carpets from Turkey bought by him via Venice, but there are no references to any embroideries.

Although Ottoman style was copied in costume and in theatrical entertainment from the beginning of the eighteenth century, there are no indications that embroidery was collected in either Turkey or Europe at any serious level. Even in Turkey the great collection of embroidery in Topkapi Sarayı is an accidental result of the conserving of the more highly appreciated and valued weavings and courtly costume that were wrapped in embroideries.

The first international exhibition at which Ottoman embroidery was shown was the Great Exhibition in London in 1851. The pieces shown had been made by families resident in Istanbul operating as professional ateliers making embroideries for sale. The majority of these pieces show a very marked European influence that followed the fashion made popular by Sultan Abdul Mecid. Some of the pieces at that Exhibition were bought by the South Kensington Museum, later to become the Victoria and Albert Museum, and these are the first recorded purchases of Turkish embroidery for a museum. The next important exhibition of Mohammedan art was held in Vienna in 1891 and while the textile section of this exhibition mainly covered carpets and woven fabrics, there were also examples of ceramics, silver, jewellery and miniatures.

In 1906 there was an important exhibition of Musulman art in Algiers organized by Georges Marçais under the auspices of the Government General of Algeria. In this exhibition for the first time the display of embroideries held their own with the carpets and other textiles.

The Burlington Fine Arts Club in London held an Exhibition of Old

Embroideries of the Greek Islands and Turkey in 1914. The Burlington had a long tradition of very fine art exhibitions and there for the first time embroidery was seen to be as worthy of collecting as the ceramics, ivories and paintings that they had usually shown, and the status of peasant art forms was elevated following the great revival of interest in national and regional costumes that was taking place in Central Europe and the Balkans. The Exhibition contained 192 pieces, of which about 40 were specifically described as Turkish or from Asia Minor. However, all the pieces, with the exception of those from the Ionian Islands, had been made in Greece and the Islands of the Aegean when they were both under Turkish rule, and it would perhaps have been more accurate to have described the Exhibition as one of Ottoman Embroideries. There was a short introduction on the Turkish pieces by Sir William Lawrence, who was a collector of Near Eastern Art, but his contribution was overshadowed by that of A.J.B. Wace, who was the prime mover of the whole venture.

The early collectors of Greek embroidery were mostly British diplomats and archaeologists working in Greece and Turkey between 1880 and 1914, and they collected very widely. They always considered that they were collecting Greek work but they were all very aware of the influence that both the Ottoman and Venetian Empires had on the work they were buying. The vast majority of their collections has been deposited with museums in Great Britain, and because of this the following museums have considerable holdings of Turkish embroideries: The Victoria and Albert in London, the Whitworth in Manchester, the Ashmolean in Oxford, the Fitzwilliam in Cambridge, the Royal Scottish in Edinburgh, the Laing Art Gallery in Newcastle-upon-Tyne and the Walker Art Gallery in Liverpool.

The largest exhibition held in the Near East which included Ottoman embroideries was that held in Alexandria in 1925. The prime mover of this exhibition was Mr Antony Benaki, who contributed most of the items to the exhibition. He later created the Benaki Museum in Athens, subsequently given to the Greek nation by his family.

One of the finest and earliest specialist books dedicated to illustrations of fine embroidery was *Mediterranean and Near Eastern Embroideries from the Collection of Mrs F.H. Cook*, edited by Wace and published by Halton and Company in 1935. The collection recorded in this volume was made by Frank Cook, who was the son of the founder of Thomas Cook's Tours. He was resident in Egypt for over twenty years and collected his textiles from 1880 onwards, and his wife Beatrice Lindell Cook continued to collect after him. She left her collection to the St Louis Art Museum during the 1950s, where most of them still are. This volume illustrates 120 pieces, of which only 14 pieces from the Caucasus, Persia, Central Asia and India and 8 from the Ionian islands could not equally have been classified as Ottoman; the title chosen by the editor carefully avoids any political implications.

Henrietta Brewer was an American archaeologist and anthropologist who also worked in the Near East. Her grandparents ran the American Independent Smyrna Mission in 1820, and she collected textiles and embroideries during her years there. Her collection was split between the Metropolitan Museum in New York, the Honolulu Academy of Arts and Mills College Art Gallery, Los Angeles. The last held an exhibition of her donated textiles in 1943, and although no collective name was given to the exhibition the pieces shown were all Ottoman textiles, having been made in areas ruled by the Ottoman Sultan before they were liberated. The 322 pieces of the Henrietta Brewer Collection are now in the Lowie Museum of Anthropology, part of the University of California, Berkeley; just over half of them come from areas within the Ottoman Empire, while many of her costume pieces are at the Metropolitan in New York.

Another American collector was Burton Yost Berry, a diplomat in Istanbul, who travelled extensively in Turkey and collected textiles as well as other Turkish art objects. He very clearly described his collection as Turkish, including the embroideries from Epirus and the Greek islands. He wrote entertainingly about his collecting mania and about his collections in a number of magazines of the period. His collection of 64 pieces was given to the Art Institute of Chicago to form the core of their holdings of these textiles.

The Museum of Fine Arts in Boston has a fine collection of Turkish and Ottoman textiles, and is particularly strong in brocades and velvets, donated by Denman Ross and Martin Brimmer. The Turkish embroideries and textiles were mainly collected by Elizabeth Day McCormick.

The Royal Ontario Museum has a large number of Ottoman pieces in its impressive textile collection. Many of the collections in Eastern Europe are based on textiles captured in battles against the Turks. The Turks campaigned all over Central Europe, and in the style of the day the army moved with a vast amount of equipment. In a contemporary document they are described as 'taking with them whole towns'. When the Grand Vizier Kara Mustapha Pasha was defeated after his Siege of Vienna in 1683 his camp was captured by the coalition of Europeans and a large number of tents, saddles and other textiles were distributed throughout Eastern Europe and Scandinavia. There are collections of these siege pieces in Cracow (Wawel and Czartoryski Museums), Dresden (Zwinger Museum), Budapest, Copenhagen, Vienna (Wagenburg Kunsthistorisches Museum), Stockholm and London. The National Museums of Munich (Bayerische Armee-Museum), Madrid, Rumania, Bulgaria, Albania and Yugoslavia all have large collections of Ottoman embroideries which are usually classified under the names of the various districts where they were made. It is in these museums that one can best see how the national styles were influenced by the Ottoman occupation.

Collections in Turkey

Although many textiles had already been lost by the policy of renewing the tomb covers, in 1914 the Evkaf Museum was founded to preserve what was left. It was this action that saved many of the great textiles, collecting them from the many religious foundations. This museum is now the Turkish and Islamic Art Museum in Istanbul. The Topkapı Sarayı was converted to a museum in 1925 after the founding of the Republic, and there are also important collections in the Archaeological Museum in Konya and the Ethnographic Museum in Ankara.

The Banks in Turkey were encouraged by the State to promote cultural activities, and apart from the magazines that many of them published dealing with national art they also made collections of art and crafts, which are very frequently put on exhibition. The main collections belong to the Yapı Kredi Bankası and the Ak Bank.

Additionally there are a number of private museums and collections that have now opened their extensive collections to the public.

TOPKAPI SARAYI MÜZESI, ISTANBUL This museum houses many treasures, including the Imperial costumes, that had always been stored in the Palace and which were discovered and put on exhibition after 1924. Among them is a very large quantity of embroideries which date from the sixteenth and seventeenth centuries. The collection also includes pieces that were used in the Old palace until the middle of the nineteenth century.

DOLMABAHÇE PALACE This Palace is still used for State occasions but it has also been left as a living museum. In it can be seen many textiles in the rooms in which they were used from 1853 until the 1930s.

GALATA KULEKAPISI MEVLEVI CONVENT, ISTANBUL This building of 1491 has been converted into a museum by the Ministry of Culture and now houses a number of different collections, amongst which is one of embroidered prayer rugs and hangings of the eighteenth and nineteenth century, mainly from Banya Luka and the Istanbul workshops.

SADBERK HANIM MÜZESI, ISTANBUL This is the collection of the Koç family. It was started by Sadberk Hanım Koç and was formed into a museum in 1980. It has been augmented by purchases made by the family, and a most valuable addition to the museum was the collection made by Hüseyn Kocabaş of Izmir, containing archaeological finds and some textiles.

Most provincial towns have small museums, and textiles and embroideries can be seen in most of them. They show how the traditions have survived and many recent pieces are displayed.

Glossary

Ağa honorific title for a social superior.

Anatolia the eastern Province of the Empire.

arakiye the finest quality of felt, used for caps.

asmaldık hanging for a door, usually a mosque.

atlas compound satin weave, often in silk.

ayna mirror.

Babüsaade main gate to Topkapi Palace, translated as the Sublime Porte.

banyaluka carpet or hanging made of appliqué embroidery, from Banya Luka in Bosnia.

bebilla greek word for 'oya'.

benika long head scarf in Morocco and Tunisia.

besmele the formula: 'In the name of God, the Merciful, the Compassionate'.

bez cloth of plain weave.

bezekci professional female decorator of brides and furnishings.

bindallı embroidery used on formal women's kaftans, ('bin' - thousand, 'dal' - branch).

bohça square textile cloth used for wrapping.

bostanci Regiment of Guards at Topkapi, literally gardeners.

çadır tent, large tents taken on campaigns.

Çadır Mehteri Department at Topkapi in charge of tents.

çaprak saddle cloth.

çarşaf bed sheet.

cema'at guild or association.

çeşit sampler, usually of pattern not stitch.

çevre square head scarf or shawl.

cicim weaving technique with supplementary wefts.

çintamani design of three circles, based on Buddhist motif of three flaming pearls.

çubuk a twig, also a pipe for smoking, a popular pattern.

Dar al-Harb House of War, the area to be converted to Islam by war.

Dar al-Islam House of Islam, the area already Muslim.

devşirme the annual collection of children from the non-Muslim provinces to be educated to join the Civil Service or the Army.

duvak wedding veil.

elvan multi-coloured, a Turkish form of the Arabic plural of laun, colour.

enderun inner section of the house. In Topkapi Palace it was the Head of the Civil Service.

enfiye snuff, from Arabic 'enfi', nose.

entari a long open gown.

ferace all-covering outdoor cloak.

futa universal cloth worn as a sarong.

gasmouli the children of a mixed marriage, Turkish and European.

haiti decorative panels used to line walls and tents in Morocco.

halvet private entertainments or rooms.

hamam bath, usually a public bath house.

harem area of the Palace where the Sultan's family lived, also where women lived in seclusion.

haraç tax paid by non-Muslims to exempt them from military service.

hatayi term for decorative patterns derived from Chinese art, usually a flower shape.

havlı towel with nap of terry weave.

hotoz the large formal head-dress of a patrician Turkish lady, originally made of horsehair.

içoğlan a page, student or servant at the Court.

janissary the army created from the young men gathered by the devşirme. ('yeni' - new, 'çeri' - recruit).

jeziya tax paid by non-Muslim.

kaftan universal robe, either open in front or closed.

kambur a hunchback, the pattern based on a curled-over tendril.

Kanuni Teshrifat Code of Regulations regarding dress and social precedence.

kapamaci retailer of ready-made clothing.

kaşbastı a head band, from 'kaş', eyebrow.

kavuk formal large turban; **kavukluk** turban stand.

kazzazci a worker in silk embroidery.

kebe thick felt used for carpets.

keçe standard-quality felt.

kemer belt, waist-band.

khilat the formal robes given as signs of honour.

klaptan thread bound with metal filament.

kullabci silk-spinner.

kuşak long sash.

Lale Devri Tulip Age, of the early eighteenth century, when tulips were in great vogue.

Maghreb the western countries of North Africa, from the Arabic 'maghreb', the West.

majlis a meeting room.

makrama plain-weave small hand towel.

makramaci the household servant with responsibility for all domestic textiles.

mangal portable coal-burning brazier.

maşallah literally, 'That which God has ordained', used as an expression of wonder or admiration, or as a charm.

maşlah a gown of heavy velvet, usually embroidered.

medakhyl a pattern in two colours where each is identical, a reciprocating, interlaced shape.

mendil a handkerchief or square scarf.

mhedda a large cushion, Moroccan.

mihrab arch positioned in a mosque to indicate the direction of Mecca.

minder hard stuffed cushion.

Muayede greetings or the response.

mücessem large rectangular body shawl.

musandıra cupboard for storage.

nakşe a pattern or design for a decoration.

namazli a carpet used for prayer, usually decorated with a mihrab.

Nevruz Persian New Year's Day, 22nd March.

nihali embroidered floor carpet.

nişan sign, order or award.

ölker nap on a fabric.

örme knitted or plaited.

örtü cover.

oya lace made with a needle, also called bebilla.

paşali like or worthy of a pasa, a quality of sash.

peçe veil, worn as a scarf.

peşkir napkin for wiping fingers, or small towel.

peştemal large unnapped towel, usually in three panels.

qibleh the direction of Mecca, towards which prayers must be said.

Rum, Rumi the name given to Byzantium; the common name for the Greeks and, by extension, westerners.

Rumeli the western Province of the Empire.

şalvar baggy trousers worn by both men and women.

sarık turban worn daily.

saz decorative style, elaborate patterns drawn with a reed pen, 'saz'.

sedir the raised portion of a room, with either a sofa or a bed on it.

selamlık the outer house, used by the men and visitors.

silecek large towel with nap of terry weave.

sim metal filament.

şipşip indoor women's slippers.

sırma metal thread made into lace or embroidery; sırmakesci is the craftsman who spins it.

sitil originally a padded, embroidered mat for holding a tray, now a large bucket or can.

skofion gilded parchment used as a textile yarn.

sofra place to eat, originally the leather mat on which to spread prepared food.

sünnet Moslem rituals, particularly circumcision.

suzani needlework for embroidery, from the Persian word for a needle.

tel metal wire used in embroidery.

tenchifa a narrow towel used for the hair, Morocco.

terzi tailor in Turkey, from the Persian word. In the Maghreb the word is used for embroidery.

tığ crochet hook for working chain stitch.

traş takım set of textiles used by the barber - apron, towels and hand cloths.

tuğra Sultan's formal signature, a complicated calligraphic form.

uçkur short sash.

yağlik a napkin to be used at meals.

yapuk large horse cloth.

yaşmak a veil for the lower part of the face.

yastık cushion or bolster.

yatak bed or a mattress for a bed.

yaz, yazılı writing, an inscription ('yazmak', to write).

yazma written or printed.

yemiş fruit.

yorgan quilt.

yüz örtüsü a face covering.

zerduz embroidery using gold wire or strip.

219

Bibliography

TEXTILE REFERENCES

Andrews, Mügül and Peter, *Türkmen Needlework*. Central Asian Research Centre. London 1976.

Arseven, Çelal E., *Les Arts Turcs Decoratifs*. Milli Egitim Basımevi, Istanbul.

— *L'Art Turc*. Devlet Basımevi, Istanbul 1939.

Atıl Esin, *The Age of Sultan Süleyman the Magnificent*. National Gallery of Art, Washington, New York 1987.

Barışta, Örcün, *Türk Halk Işlemeciliği Desen, Kültür ve Turizm Bakanlığı*. G.Ü. Basın, Yayın Yüksekokulu Basımevi. Ankara 1984.

Başbuğ, Semiha, *Türk Işlemeleri*. Olgunlaşma Enstitüsü, Istanbul 1964.

Bernès, J.P., *ABC Décor Collection, Maroc*. Vol 2. 'Costumes et Broderies'. Paris, December 1974.

Berker, Nurhayet, *Işlemeler*. Topkapi Museum Booklet No. 6. Yapı ve Kredi Bankası, Kültür ve Sanat Hizmetlerinden. Istanbul 1981.

— with Y. Durul, *Türk Işlemelerinden Örnekler*, Ak Yayınlar, Ak Bank, Istanbul 1971.

— *Türk Işlemeleri*. Yapı Kredi Bank. Istanbul 1991.

Berry, Burton Yost, 'Old Turkish Towels' in *Bulletin of the College Art Association, Chicago*. No. 1. Vol XIV (Dec. 1932). No. 2. Vol XX (Sept. 1938).

— 'Turkish Embroidery' in *Embroidery*. June 1936. Vol IV. 3.

Celal Lampé, Melek, *Türk Işlemeleri*. Istanbul 1939.

Denny, W. 'Textiles' in *Tulips, Arabesques and Turbans, Decorative Arts from the Ottoman Empire*. Alexandria Press. London 1982.

— 'Ottoman Turkish Textiles' in *Textile Museum Journal*. Washington, Vol. III. no. 3. 1972.

Dietrich, B. *Kleinasiatische Stickereien*. Plauen im Vogtland. Privately printed. 1911.

Esberk, Tevfik, *Türkiye'de Köylü El Sanatları*, Yüksek Ziraat Enstitüsü Calışmalarından, Sayı 44. Ankara 1939.

Fenerçioglu, Sevim, *Türk Işlemelerinden Motifler* (Turkish embroidery patterns). Ankara 1973.

Gentles, Margaret, *Turkish and Greek Island Embroideries from the Burton Yost Berry Collection*. The Art Institute of Chicago. 1964.

Gönül, Macide, 'Some Turkish Embroideries in the Collection of the Topkapi Saray Museum in Istanbul' in *Kunst des Orients*. Vol VI. 1969. Also published by Touring Club of Turkey.

Hopf, Carl, 'Anatolische Stickerien' in *Orientalisches Archiv*. Jahrgang III, Heft 4. Leipzig 1913.

Johnstone, P., *Turkish Embroidery*. Victoria and Albert Museum. London 1985.

— 'Some Unusual Turkish Embroideries of the Early Eighteenth Century' in *Textile Museum Journal*. Washington. Vol 24. 1985.

Krarup, Rigmor, *Graeske og Tyrkiske Broderier*. Det Danske Kunstindusrimuseum. Copenhagen 1964.

Mackie, L.W., *The Splendour of Turkish Weaving*. The Textile Museum. Washington 1973.

Marçais, G., *L'Exposition D'Art Musulman*. Catalogue. Algiers 1906.

— 'Les Broderies Turques d'Alger' in *Ars Islamica*. Vol. IV. London 1937.

Martin, F.R., *Stickereien aus der Orient*. Stockholm 1897.

Newberry, Essie, 'Turkish Towels and their Designs' in *Embroidery*, June, London 1936.

— 'The Embroideries of Morocco' in *Embroidery*, Summer, London 1939.

Onuk, Taciser, *Iğne Oyaları*, Türkiye Iş Bankası Kültür Yayınları, Istanbul 1980.

Öz, Taksin, *Turkish Textiles and Velvets*. Vol. 1. Ankara 1950.

— *Türk Kumaşı ve Kadifeleri*. Vol 2. Istanbul 1951.

— *Türk El Işlemeleri ve Resim dairesi*, Güzel Sanatlar 4. Istanbul 1950.

Özbel, Kenan, *El Sanatları*, Vol. IV. Eski El Işlemeleri, CHP Halkevleri Bürosu, Istanbul 1945.

von Palotay, G., 'Turkish Embroideries' in *Ciba Review*, Vol 102. Basle, Feb. 1954.

— *Török Hagyatek a Kalotaszegi Himzresben*. (Turkish Influence in Kalotaszeg Embroidery). A Neprajzi Muzeum Ertesitöje No. 29. Budapest 1937. Also published in *Europe*, September 1943.

— 'Les Influences Turques dans la broderie Hongroise.' in *Nouvelle Revue de Hongrie*. No. 30. Budapest. May 1927.

— *Törökös Himzesü Börtàskàk Erdélyben*. (Turkish embroidery on leather letter cases from Transylvania). Közlemények az Erdélyi Muzeum. Kolozsvar 1942.

Pesel, L.F., *Stitches from Eastern Embroidery*. Portfolio No. 2. Percy Lund, Humphries & Co. Ltd, London 1921.

— with E.W. Newberry, *A Book of Old Embroidery*. The Studio. London 1921.

Poidebard, R.P., 'Anciennes Embroideries Armeniennes' in *Revue des Etudes Armeniennes*. No. IX Paris 1929.

Rajab, Jehan, 'Some Towels and other Turkish Embroideries' in *Arts of Asia*. May-June 1984.

Ramazanoglu, G., *Turkish Embroidery*. Van Nostrand Reinhold Company. New York 1976.

Serjeant, R.B., *Islamic Textiles*. Librarie du Liban, Beirut 1972.

Sürür, Ayten, *Türk Işleme Sanatı*. Ak Bank. Istanbul 1976.

Taylor, R.R., *Işlemeler*. Catalogue for an Exhibition. David Black Oriental Carpets. London 1978.

220

— 'Quilt Facings and Mirror Covers' in *Hali*, June 1990, No. 51.

Tezcan, H. & S. Delibaş, *Costumes, Embroideries and other Textiles*. Edited by J.M. Rogers. Dentsu Inc. Tokyo 1980. Thames and Hudson 1986.

Wace, A.J.B., *Mediterranean and Near Eastern Embroideries from the Collection of Mrs F.H. Cook*. London 1935

— with C.E.C. Tattersall, *Brief Guide to Turkish Woven Fabrics*. HMSO, London 1950.

— *Catalogue of Algerian Embroideries*. London 1935.

Wearden, Jennifer, Turkish Velvet Cushion Covers. Textile Department Leaflet. No. 5. Victoria and Albert Museum. London 1988.

Exhibition Catalogues

David Black Oriental Carpets. *Embroidered Flowers from Thrace to Tartary*. London 1981.

Elio Cittone, *Tesori Ottomani del XVI e XVII Secolo*. Milan 1980.

Colnaghi, *Imperial Ottoman Textiles*. London 1981.

Louisiana Revy, *Kunst fra Islams Verden*. 8-18 °Arhundrede. Copenhagen 1987.

COSTUME ILLUSTRATIONS

Arif Pacha, *Anciens Costumes de l'Empire Ottoman*. Istanbul 1862.

Brindesi, Giovanni, *Souvenir de Constantinople*. Paris 1870(?)

Castellan, A., *Moeurs, Usages, Costumes des Othomans*. 6 volumes. Nepveu, Paris 1812. An English edition was published by R. Ackerman, London 1821.

Choiseul-Gouffier, Marc Gabriel, *Voyage Pittoresque de la Grèce*. Paris 1822. Illustrations by J.B. Hilaire and A.I. Melling. Most of the costume plates by Moreau le jeune.

de la Chapelle, George, *Recueil de Divers Portraits de Principales Dames de la Porte du Grand Turc*. Paris 1684.

Charton, Edouard, *Costumes Grecs et Turcs*. Paris 1768.

Fenerci, Mehmed, *Osmanli Kiyafetleri*. Istanbul 1811.

Ferrario, Giulio, *Vehbi Koç Vakfi*. Istanbul 1986.

— *Il Costume Antico e Moderno*, Milan 1827. 228 plates.

de Ferriol, M., *Recueil de Cent Estampes*. Paris 1714.

Labruzzi, L & Filippo Ferrari, *Costumes of the Ottoman Court*. Rome, 1828. 104 plates of costumes of the Nizam Jedid, the army which replaced the Janissaries.

Lachaise, *Costumes de L'Empire Turc*. Paris 1821. 61 lithographed plates.

Lejean, Guillaume, *Les Costumes Populaires de la Turquie*. Tour du Monde. Paris 1873.

Ligozzi, Jacopo, *21 paintings of Ottoman Costume*. Uffizi Gallery, Florence. 1576-1580. Catalogued N. 4369, 46-65. First Published in *FMR* March 1982 with a description of the Grand Seraglio by Tommaso Alberti.

Miller, William, *Turkish Costumes*. London 1804.

van Mour, Jean B., *Recueil de Cent Estampes representant differents Nations du Levant, Turcs sur les tableaux peints d'après Nature en 1708 et 1709*. Paris 1714.

Preziosi, Amadeo, *Stamboul, Souvenir d'Orient*, Paris 1865.

Racinet, Albert, *Le Costume Historique*. Paris 1888.

Rogier, Camille, *Galerie Royale Peints d'après Nature. Costumes de l'Empire Ottoman*. H. Gache, Paris 1845. 10 plates.

— *La Turquie*. Lemercier, Paris 1847. 44 lithographed plates.

Tatikian, B., *Costumes du Levant*. Smyrna 1850. 68 lithographed plates.

— *Album of Costume Plates*, Smyrna 1850. 50 lithographed plates.

da Zara, Bassano, *I Costumi ed I Modi Particolare de la Vita del Turchi* Rome 1545.

Anonymous:

Constantinopoli e di Turchi. Roma 1510.

Recueil des differents Costumes des Principaux Officiers et Magistrats de la Porte. Onfroy, Paris 1775. 96 Engraved plates.

Warsaw University, Cabinet of Prints, Collection of King Stanislas, 1780. 205 costume plates.

German Archaeological Institute, Istanbul. Kappus Pichelstein Collection. 1785. 208 designs of Istanbul and Turkish Costume.

There are many volumes of drawings of costumes of the Ottoman Empire in libraries and museums all over Europe. The main collections are in Topkapi, at the British Library and the British Museum, the Museo Civico in Venice, the Rijksmuseum, the Bodleian and in Vienna, Paris, Stockholm, Dresden, Florence and in Jerusalem.

Collections of watercolours

Many albums of costume drawings were made by visitors to the Levant, Turkey and Greece, very few of which have been published. The largest collection of them had been made by Henry M. Blackmer II, which were kept in his house in Athens. On his death his collection was sold at Sothebys, and the catalogue of the 11th, 12th and 13th October 1989 describes them in detail. Lots. 510-23.

Index

Acknowledgements

I wish to thank all those who have supported and contributed to this book, particularly Sevgi Gönül of the Sadberk Hanım Museum, Istanbul, Nurhayat Berker and Şennur Aydın of the Yapı Kredi Bank, Istanbul, Anne-Marie Benson of Phillips Auctions West Two, Michael Franses of the Textile Gallery, London, Clive Loveless, Joss Graham, Philippa Scott and Penny Oakley, who have kindly allowed me to use their textiles as illustrations. I would like to acknowledge a particular debt to Pauline Johnstone whose books on textiles were the first I saw after I had started to collect.

My best thanks and admiration go to Antony Maitland for his evocative and charming line drawings. I would also like to thank Angelo Hornak, who has made photographs of all the other embroideries which are from private collections

I also wish to thank the Curators and Keepers at these Museums who have been most generous with their time, showing me their collections and agreeing to allow me to use them in my book: Emese Pásztor of the Iparmüvészeti Museum in Budapest, Louise Mackie of the Royal Ontario Museum, Jennifer Harris at the Whitworth Art Gallery in Manchester, Robin Crighton and Carol Humphrey of the Fitzwilliam Museum in Cambridge and Pauline Rushton of the Liverpool Museum.

Photograph credits

I would like to thank and acknowledge all those who have kindly lent me photographs for this book:

Bernheimer Fine Arts, London: pages 82, 92, 104, 182
Fitzwilliam Museum, Cambridge: pages 18, 19, 22, 207
Joss Graham, London: pages 151, 181
Iparmüvészeti Museum, Budapest: pages 13, 15, 148, 154, 155
Clive Loveless, London: pages 85, 112, 117, 120
Phillips, London: pages 21, 37, 56, 66–7, 91, 109, 186
Real Armería, Madrid: page 144
Royal Ontario Museum, Canada: pages 161, 191L, 206
Sadberk Hanım Museum, Istanbul: pages 59, 110
Sotheby's, London: page 106
Spink & Son, London: page 108
Textile Gallery, London: pages 5, 6, 76, 80, 116, 126–7, 140, 143, 162
Walker Art Gallery, Liverpool: page 208
Whitworth Museum, Manchester: pages 24, 26, 75
Yapı Kredi Bank, Istanbul: pages 48, 60, 61, 68b, 111, 152, 180.

I would also like to thank *Hali* Magazine, London for their permission to reproduce the photographs on the frontispiece and pages 88, 100 and 101 taken by Peter Gates from my article in Issue 51.